Kingdom Come

Kingdom Come

Reflections in Honor of Jonathan R. Wilson

Edited by
Jason Byassee, Jeremy Kidwell,
Jonathan Wilson-Hartgrove, *and*
Leah Wilson-Hartgrove

CASCADE *Books* · Eugene, Oregon

KINGDOM COME
Reflections in Honor of Jonathan R. Wilson

Copyright © 2022 Wipf and Stock Publishers. All rights reserved. Except for brief quotations in critical publications or reviews, no part of this book may be reproduced in any manner without prior written permission from the publisher. Write: Permissions, Wipf and Stock Publishers, 199 W. 8th Ave., Suite 3, Eugene, OR 97401.

Cascade Books
An Imprint of Wipf and Stock Publishers
199 W. 8th Ave., Suite 3
Eugene, OR 97401

www.wipfandstock.com

PAPERBACK ISBN: 978-1-6667-3142-2
HARDCOVER ISBN: 978-1-6667-2390-8
EBOOK ISBN: 978-1-6667-2391-5

Cataloguing-in-Publication data:

Names: Byassee, Jason, editor. | Kidwell, Jeremy, 1980–, editor. | Wilson-Hartgrove, Jonathan, 1980–, editor. | Wilson-Hartgrove, Leah, editor.

Title: Kingdom come : reflections in honor of Jonathan R. Wilson / edited by Jason Byassee, Jeremy Kidwell, Jonathan Wilson-Hartgrove, and Leah Wilson-Hartgrove.

Description: Eugene, OR : Cascade Books, 2022 | Includes bibliographical references.

Identifiers: ISBN 978-1-6667-3142-2 (paperback) | ISBN 978-1-6667-2390-8 (hardcover) | ISBN 978-1-6667-2391-5 (ebook)

Subjects: LCSH: Wilson, Jonathan R.

Classification: BX4827.W49 K56 2022 (print) | BX4827.W49 K56 (ebook)

09/07/22

Permissions

Scripture quotations marked (NIV) are taken from the Holy Bible, New International Version®, NIV®. Copyright © 1973, 1978, 1984, 2011 by Biblica, Inc.™ Used by permission of Zondervan. All rights reserved worldwide. www.zondervan.com. The "NIV" and "New International Version" are trademarks registered in the United States Patent and Trademark Office by Biblica, Inc.™

Scripture quotations marked (NRSV) are from the New Revised Standard Version Bible, copyright © 1989 the Division of Christian Education of the National Council of the Churches of Christ in the United States of America. Used by permission. All rights reserved.

Scripture quotations marked (ESV®) are from The Holy Bible, English Standard Version®, copyright @ 2001 by Crossway Bibles, a publishing ministry of Good News Publishers. Used by permission. All rights reserved.

Scripture quotations marked (PME) are taken from the Phillips Modern English Bible, by J. B. Phillips, "The New Testament in Modern English", Copyright© 1962 edition, published by HarperCollins.

Contents

Introduction | xi
   Jonathan & Leah Wilson-Hartgrove

   The Making of a Theologian: Becoming Jonathan Wilson | 1
      Jason Byassee

   Artist Statement: On the Road and at the Table | 10
      Joy Banks

   Hot Cross Buns | 11
      Loren Wilkinson

Lament

   The World Rises While We Wait | 17
      Matthew W. Humphrey

   Groaning toward New Creation | 26
      Michael Swalm *and* H. Daniel Zacharias

   Jesus as a Moral Stranger | 36
      Reggie L. Williams

   New Monasticism in Our Secular Age | 44
      Tim Dickau

   Living Faithfully in a Neoliberal Age? | 58
      Andrew Shepherd

   Ads as Moral Cultural Liturgies in Post-Secular Context | 71
      Anna Robbins *and* Christopher Johnston

Reflection

Plain, Literal, Real Narrative | 81
A. K. M. Adam

"Listen! This Is Not What You're Expecting to Hear!" | 89
Anthony Brown

Reflections for an Irenic Spirit | 98
Axel Schoeber

Gospel Realism and the Epistle to Hebrews | 109
Craig A. Smith

A Christian Critique of Christian Britain | 119
John Berkman

Conversations with Jonathan | 131
Philip A. Rolnick

Toward a New Natural Theology | 141
Jeremy Kidwell

The Beatitudes | 149
Reinhard Hütter

Seeing the Kingdom | 154
Scott Kohler

"Trinitarian" | 162
W. Ross Hastings

The Fact of Jesus | 170
Stanley Hauerwas

Speaking Words against Whiteness | 175
Willie James Jennings

Invitation

Slowing, Silence, and Solitude | 185
Chris Hall

Pursuing Theology's Primary Mode | 202
Jeffrey P. Greenman

Earthing Heaven Now | 211
Jim Purves

Eating the Peaceable Kingdom | 219
  MARGARET B. ADAM

The Practice of Walking as Theological Knowing | 226
  MIKE PEARS

A Gospel of Fukushima | 237
  SOOHWAN PARK

An Intentionally Disciplined Way of Life and the Ministry of Spiritual Direction | 247
  SUSAN S. PHILLIPS

Embracing Partnership | 259
  TERRY SMITH

Rethinking "Church and University" | 267
  L. GREGORY JONES

Equipping the Saints | 276
  MARILYN MCENTYRE

Celebration

Dalit Christian Theology | 287
  CHANDRA MALLAMPALLI

For God So Loves the World | 296
  JENNIFER HARVEY

God's Work Is to Redeem Creation | 305
  JONAS KAMBALE MUSAMBA

A Note of Thanks for the Scholar's Gift | 312
  PETER HARRIS

The Church as Embodied Witness | 318
  PHILIP D. KENNESON

Learning to Be a Missional Church | 326
  ROB FILGATE

Join with All Nature in Manifold Witness | 332
  ROSS LOCKHART

Kingdom Realism | 343
  GATO MUNYAMASOKO

Church Matters | 349
    ISAAC VILLEGAS

Response to Kingdom Come | 355
    JONATHAN R. WILSON

Selected Bibliography of Jonathan R. Wilson's Writing | 360
List of Contributors | 365

Introduction

WHATEVER THEIR PARTICULAR BACK stories, the disciples who met Jesus on the road to Emmaus can be forgiven for being confused. They had, presumably, watched Jesus ride into Jerusalem as the leader of a popular movement that both exposed the corrupt authorities of his day and declared the reality of a different political order—God's kingdom—present and accessible to the poor and the outcast. Indeed, Jesus had said this kingdom belonged to the likes of them.

It was, no doubt, an exhilarating time for a couple of everyday people who'd been pushed around by the powerful—people who'd likely never "owned" anything. The kingdom of heaven was theirs, Jesus was their King, and his movement's power was so palpable that the religious and political authorities could do nothing to stop it. History had reached a tipping point, not unlike the Arab Spring or the nonviolent campaign in Montgomery, Alabama, that launched the civil rights movement. People who'd struggled to survive within horizons set by greedy men saw a dawn of new possibility. These two had sung their psalms of ascent on the walk up to Jerusalem, and the LORD, the maker of heaven and earth, had blessed them in Zion.

But how quickly it all fell apart. Jesus was dead, the movement was fragmented into a thousand pieces, and the associations that had so recently offered the promise of possibility now presented the potential for arrest and execution. You had to be careful who you talked to in the aftermath of a crucifixion. The authorities had reasserted their power, and no one knew who their next target might be.

We can understand why Cleopas and his traveling companion would be confused in such a situation. By most any account, Christianity in North America has been in a confusing transition over the course of our lives (four decades and counting). We are the children of baby boomers who grew up in an America where church membership skyrocketed after World War II and the cultural influence of evangelical Christianity led many in our lives to imagine doing great things for God. Yet we came of age with a generation that has questioned the church's intentions, exposed many of its abuses, and left the congregations many of us grew up in. We do not argue with those who observe that the "Christian century" wasn't all it was cracked up to be.

Yet we have remained in the church. The daughter and son of Baptists from both sides of the Canadian border, we are now members of the St. John's Missionary Baptist Church, raising our children on many of the same hymns we grew up singing, helping them learn the King James English that was long since outdated when we learned it. The kids are old enough now that they sometimes observe how few people our age are still part of the church (since grandparents still offer free babysitting, there are many more children than middle-aged adults in our particular congregation). Why do we still go to church? Like Cleopas and his companion, we have encountered the resurrected Jesus in the midst of our confusion and recognized him at our dinner table, in the breaking of the bread. We are Christians not because we're certain of anything but because we know what it feels like for our hearts to burn within us, and the best language we have to describe that experience is the story passed down to us in church.

This is a Festschrift to celebrate Jonathan R. Wilson, our father and father-in-law; Papa to our children. Jonathan has spent his life pastoring, preaching, teaching and writing for the church. When Leah was growing up, he had an office full of books on the campus of Westmont College where she would sometimes sit in the corner and read after school while he finished his work for the day. Impressed by the floor-to-ceiling shelves filled with tomes on theology and biblical studies, students who stopped in would often ask, "Wow, have you read all of these books?"

"Some of them more than once," was Jonathan's standard reply. When Leah was ten or so, she noted after a student left the office that Jonathan hadn't answered the question. "But how many of them have you never read?"

We aren't sure how many of Jonathan's books and articles we've never read, but we're glad to have read and learned from some of them more than once. Still, our primary impetus for organizing this volume wasn't the literature Jonathan has produced, but rather the steady stream of people who've sat at our dinner table over the years and shared how studying with Jonathan or reading his books helped them make sense of their own struggles with faith. We've always been struck by the incredible variety of these people and their vocations. They do not fit neatly into any denominational categories or schools of contemporary thought. Jonathan has not produced an army of "Wilsonians." He has, instead, spent his career helping a wide range of people listen to what was burning within them and become the unique gifts they were made to be.

This volume is a celebration of the conversations and vocations Jonathan has helped to cultivate through his commitment to the gospel of Jesus. Joy Banks, who knew Jonathan and his teaching well when they were both members of Grandview Calvary Baptist Church in Vancouver, contributed the linocut on the cover that tells the road to Emmaus story. Her interpretation captures four scenes that trace a journey from lament to delight that feels familiar. The confused couple on the road to Emmaus is in mourning. They have lost something they cannot get back. But with their new partner on the road, their lament turns toward reflection, which leads in turn to a practical invitation. They ask Jesus to dinner. And when they know him in the fellowship at the dinner table, they know themselves and their own deepest hopes anew, celebrating that the kingdom promised to them is in fact present, even if not in the ways they had expected it to be.

Lament. Reflection. Invitation. Celebration. We do not always come to these stations on the journey toward healing and wholeness in the same order, but they sketch a pattern we have known and one that so many of Jonathan's friends and former students have shared with us over the years. With the gift of Joy's art, it seemed that these four stages along the way could help to organize the wonderful and diverse contributions that so many shared to make this book possible.

Since we've already confessed that we didn't know Jonathan's scholarly work well enough to know where to begin this project, we must conclude by thanking Jonathan's former student Jeremy Kidwell and Jonathan's colleague Jason Byassee, both of whom enthusiastically embraced this project as editors and, in due course, helped us learn a great deal more than we knew about the theological conversations Jonathan has engaged over the course of his career. We have seen in another arena what we knew from dozens of conversations with the people whom Jonathan's life and ministry have touched over the decades. Because of his willingness to face the reality of a fragmented world, Jonathan knows how to lament. But his lament doesn't lead to despair. It inspires reflection. And within that reflection, always an invitation to practice. And in the practice of a way of life with Jesus, surprising celebrations.

For each person who has shared that journey with Jonathan—for each of the former students, colleagues, and mentors who've contributed to this volume, we are grateful. Gathering and editing their reflections has been an opportunity to see someone we've known and walked with for a long time in a new light. That in itself has been a delight.

    Jonathan & Leah Wilson-Hartgrove
    Rutba House, Ordinary Time, 2021

The Making of a Theologian
Becoming Jonathan Wilson

Jason Byassee

It was the early 1980s. A young pastor of a small but growing Baptist church in a Vancouver, BC, suburb stepped into a Christian bookstore in what we call East Van. He wasn't looking for anything in particular, but did he ever find something. A yellowish-brown book by an author named Stanley Hauerwas. That discovery of *Truthfulness and Tragedy* would change Jonathan Wilson's life. He would eventually attend Duke University to study with Hauerwas and write a dissertation with Stanley's senior colleague Tom Langford on the theologian Julian Hartt.

A great theological career was born.

Jonathan's wife Marti had recently made a life-changing announcement to him. Marti had a brash way about her. It would surprise none of the many friends who remember her with love to hear that she changed Jonathan's life one day while they drove home from Regent College, his alma mater. She could change a life, with just a word. She warned him first that she'd been praying about this, and she worried it might hurt him. He had applied for PhD programs before, in Old Testament, and been turned down. The wound was still fresh. Would this hurt more or heal? A more cautious person would have said nothing. Marti, whatever else she was, was not cautious. She was Jonathan's muse, who taught him to live with joy.

Her word to him that day: "You're a good pastor. I think you'd be an even better professor."

Jonathan Wilson is one of the leading post-liberal theological voices alive. And post-liberals know that the local matters. Story matters. The church matters. Friendship matters. Old books matter. The particular timbre of your beloved's voice matters (as does spelling words with British English if you're in Canada!). Where you were when your life changed matters, as does the color of the book cover. Where you go to church matters. Where you study matters. Medicine matters, both in how it can extend life despite ill health, as it did for Marti, and in how it can accidentally threaten life as well. Either way, it expresses our peculiar modern neuroses. Telling the truth matters. If you read much Hauerwas, you notice these themes recurring. He names names, mistrusting generalities, rendering specific faces, locations, difficulties and delights. All of it matters to God. It renders our particular and communal character, which presents anew the character of Jesus to others. That's what saints do.

One of the glaring weaknesses in Hauerwas's work has been inattention to the doctrine of creation. As a lover of Karl Barth, he emphasizes the christological so profoundly that creation can feel eclipsed. Jonathan's magnum opus (so far!) is *God's Good World*, on which he began work shortly after Marti's death in 2010. She is lovingly remembered in its introduction.[1] The book would not have existed without all the particulars listed above and many more known only to God. I've had the blessed fortune to live and work in and love many of the same places and institutions as Jonathan. Hence this volume. In this essay I want to tell you a bit more about a few of them, in addition to the ones Jonathan tells us about himself throughout his work.

I remember the first time I *saw* Jonathan for who he is. Yale's great Nicholas Wolterstorff had just lectured at Regent. Some of my friends from VST and I took the twenty-minute walk across the campus of the University of British Columbia to hear him. That's a long way to go, existentially. Jesus may have broken down the dividing wall between Jews and gentiles, as Eph 2 argues, but he seems to still be working on the dividing wall between Regent and VST. We are Regent's liberal frenemy. They began in our basement, soon outgrew those modest origins, bought their own property, and outgrew us. International students arrive at Regent and are surprised it's only one building—it seems bigger when you're farther away. One rare occasion that sees folks clamber over that dividing wall is a visit from a renowned figure from elsewhere.

---

1. Jonathan R. Wilson, *God's Good World: Reclaiming the Doctrine of Creation*. (Grand Rapids: Baker Academic, 2013), xviii.

At the pub after Wolterstorff's lecture, our group from VST asked for a table and looked around. And there was a table of Regent folks, seated with Wolterstorff. And who was right beside him, all up in his ear, but Jonathan Wilson, who was then teaching at neither place, but at Carey Theological College, a Baptist institution also on campus (we have too many seminaries for a place with so few churches!), successor to the chair previously held by the great Stanley Grenz, of blessed memory.

I knew Jonathan a little. We were both in the Duke doctoral student family tree. We'd met at the Ekklesia Project, a gathering of Hauerwas-influenced academics and activists in Chicago, where Jonathan had spoken and influenced me more than the great Hauerwas himself some years prior. This was the first moment I'd laid eyes on Jonathan in Vancouver, where I would later move and where we'd become friends. And where else would he be but sitting and listening to a great thinker, asking him questions, sifting answers, challenging his reading of Barth, connecting him with others? That man does not miss an opportunity to learn and grow. Jonathan invited me to join them, but we had our own table, where we repaired to grouse and gossip, on our side of the dividing wall. Jonathan is a better climber than most of us.

Jonathan is a theologian's theologian. He has read everything, and he knows everyone. He can introduce you to them. He'll tell you, charitably, of their gifts. He can also tell you what he sees as their flaws, but usually only if you ask (Stanley doesn't wait for you to ask!). Jonathan is a connector. He loves introducing people. And he *loves* theology. His eyes light up when the conversation turns to God, whereas honestly, many of us forget that first love. Whether the theologian is living, beside him, downing a well-earned pint at the pub, or long dead, but still giving life through their work, Jonathan has a willing ear, a happy eagerness to introduce them. I remember his face as he saw me that day, waving me over to meet Nick. He was radiant. "Hey, come over here, you two absolutely have to know one another." I hardly knew *him* yet. It didn't matter. We were both about the adventure of Christian theology, not just with Hauerwas's oft-imitated-never-bettered Texas twang, but in the Tennessee accents that mark both of our forebears. More modest. More churchly. Evangelical but recovering. Catholic but not Roman. Baptist but not Southern. Canadian but not originally. Biblical but not biblicist. Conversionist but not just once. Missional but wholistic and integral. In service to the whole church and the whole world.

Jonathan has something else that many of us lose along the way. He is still a curer of souls. He may no longer be a pastor, quite, though he loves the church, and is always serving on this or that board of deacons or missionaries or whatever. Though he has several stints as interim senior pastor and pastoral team leader on his nonexistent CV, he hasn't been a full-time working pastor since his days as an interim chaplain at Westmont College in Santa Barbara. The late-night calls from some Bible-study-initiated crisis got him out of bed too many times for him to continue that. "It made me realize I'm not a pastor anymore," he says now, still a little groggy. I didn't have the heart to tell him: at least at an *evangelical* college he wasn't dragged out of bed to hear about some sophomore's forlorn love life quite as much as some. Evangelical undergrads have the good sense to know that discussing, say, predestination is a worthy reason to call the chaplain in the middle of the night, while a hookup you accidentally started crushing on is not. Jonathan might no longer make a paycheck from pastoring, but he can't stop the habit. I have lost track of the number of friends who have found their way to his and his wife Soohwan's home in Nanaimo, overlooking the Salish Sea, for retreat and repair. It is a place of hospitality and grace, where Soohwan cooks and gardens and prays and works crossword puzzles and oversees A Rocha International as its board chair, responsible for creation care in twenty-two countries and growing. The guest rooms fill with those who are out of sorts, struggling, in need of something, they may not know what. And Jonathan listens. And asks questions. And heals. Not always religiously.

COVID-19 scratched the NCAA basketball tournament in 2020, akin to cancelling Easter in our local idolatries in North Carolina. My sons and I came into Jonathan's basement in Nanaimo and he hit play, without asking permission or giving warning, and up onto his screen flashed Duke's 1991 basketball victory over UNLV, the most important win in our mutual alma mater's storied sports history. We cheered like we didn't know the outcome, emerging triumphant, victorious, all over again.

In the Roman Catholic Church, St. John Vianney is the patron saint of parish pastors. He is remembered, simply, as the Curé d'Ars, the parish pastor of a tiny village in France, beloved worldwide for his worldwide impact as a confessor, healer, and compassionate friend. Jonathan, no longer a paid pastor, is, nonetheless, the Curé de Nanaimo. He is the repairer of souls of Vancouver Island. Just a word and he'll send you back ready to face life.

Or not even a word. Sometimes he just hits play, and Bobby Hurley slays the dragon all over again.

In Jonathan's introduction to *God's Good World*, he remembers a high school science teacher named Mr. Cox, at Glencliff High in Nashville, TN. "Prior to that class, I had been an indifferent student," he writes.[2] But the class, Jonathan says, in an echo of Immanuel Kant of all people, "woke me from my intellectual slumbers"—the key metaphor for the entire philosophical turn to modernity that was the Enlightenment. For Jonathan it was to flora, fauna, and the then-new field of ecology. "I was enchanted," Jonathan says, and anyone who has had a good teacher knows exactly what he means. His fundamentalist upbringing made studying science difficult, even had he been able to be a "big-game biologist." His parents' resistance wore him down and he went to the Free Will Baptist Bible college they preferred. It is remarkable to ponder what Mr. Cox would have thought of Jonathan's career, and of his gratitude to him in *God's Good World*.

In an interview with Jonathan I conducted for another project on mentoring, I asked him who his mentors had been. Who led him to faith, and then shaped his faith, to be the theologian he is? He began to tell me stories of powerful women, and being a good Baptist, they were fellow church members whom he called "sister," not just of his biological family. For example, Miss Laura Bell Barnard, a retired missionary from south India, who never married and never learned to drive. Jonathan became her driver, "and as I drove, she would talk. She was discipling me," he said. She taught him to play chess. To drink tea "the English way." And she told stories. One was of a young woman in India coming to faith in Christ due to Miss Barnard's ministry. The question was when to baptize her. Do it too soon, and they'll fall away and get discouraged; wait too long, and they won't feel accepted. "Being Baptists, we took that very seriously," Jonathan said. This was rather different from a southern evangelical culture that would baptize anyone who came to the front with a weepy conversion.

In another story, a new Christian was threatened by her fellow villagers who were unhappy with her conversion. Miss Barnard tried to protect her, but the woman was gone one day. The missionary went to a Hindu

---

2. Wilson, *God's Good World*, xv.

temple and found her there, grabbed her by the hand, and marched her out. Miss Barnard felt a very clear nudge from God, wheeled around, and saw a priest come at her with a drawn sword. She objected with just a word: "In the name of Jesus, I command you to stop!" and he froze. The two women left together. The story got the attention of a young Tennessean Free Will Baptist! It's more triumphalist than the sorts of stories we try to tell now about other faiths, with a danger of playing into Edward Said's orientalism (look it up. Or call up Jonathan). But ponder this angle of the story: women standing up against men's violence. A word being the only defence we have against a sword. And the name of Jesus is the only defense Christians should or need to call upon in the face of violence. Miss Barnard was hatching a pacifist, whether she meant to or not.

Another time Jonathan complained to Miss Barnard about the Pharisaical rules at the Bible college. She responded with one of those questions that changes your life: "Jonathan, which one of those rules is keeping you from following Jesus?" He was learning sensitivity to historical context, to local particulars, and to what matters amidst it all, what to fight and what not to. Aquinas called it practical wisdom. Baptists call it discipleship. He was becoming a theologian.

Another surprising mentor was a woman named Mrs. Cleo Purcell, an ordained FWB minister in the mid-twentieth century (really!). Her husband had been injured in a car accident and couldn't continue to work, and the congregation chose her to replace him and ordained her. She led ably, preaching and teaching, until the denomination realized that "liberals" were ordaining women and forbade it (though local congregations had actually chosen women pastors for many years—being Baptists, there was no authority to tell them otherwise). Mrs. Purcell surrendered her credentials, and then became director of the women's national auxiliary convention. After Jonathan mowed her lawn, Rev. Purcell invited Jonathan in and talked with him, fed him, served him tea. "She'd talk to me. She was mentoring me, though I didn't realize it till years later." He remembers her gravitas, the dignity with which she responded with grace to offense: "You just knew you were in the presence of someone who knew God," he said. Mrs. Purcell became part of the Wilson family: "Memories of her blur with memories around the family table." Like the Lord's Supper in the Bible.

Jonathan was not unwilling to be tutored by men! When Jonathan's first car, a 1952 MG TD, broke down, a member of his church towed the car to his home and spent many evenings and Saturdays teaching him how to repair the car. The Curé de Nanaimo is now again repairing an old car in his retirement (*plus ça change . . .*). The car was a pretext—to talk about the life of faith, and how to follow Jesus in a place that liked church on Sunday but not too much Jesus talk the rest of the week. For reasons unclear, men seem to need something *else* to talk around, to then slip in the important stuff indirectly. Cars, sports, exercise, cigars, lots of plausibly manly things will do. He wanted help, not cussing. But he also wanted help not thinking of women in sexually aggressive ways that his coworkers often did. Those of us in university or other liberal settings often mock piety. Then we create new ones. At least a piety based on the gospel has mercy baked into it. Who wouldn't give up cussing in a hot second if it could take a dent out of purity culture and its close twin, sexualized hostility toward women?

A Bible school professor named Dan Cronk, another retired missionary to India, was "intent on raising up new leaders for the FWB." Here Jonathan's eyes were opened to the cultural complexities of cross-cultural mission. Professor Cronk asked students if they were new to a village in India, a place far from any plumbing, and the newly hired villager prepares a sandwich and serves it to them with a brown greasy smudge on it, what do they do? He's their connection to the village. "He didn't answer it for us, he just got us thinking." Jonathan's work now in places as far flung as Amsterdam, Lebanon, India, and elsewhere had its origins in the missionary anthropology of Mr. Cronk's classroom. The youth group I traveled with said "eat whatever is put before you." But I think they got that from someone else.

And then there is Leroy Forlines, who washed Jonathan's feet (that's what Free Will Baptists do) when he was a teenager, taught theology for more than fifty years at the Bible college, and showed Jonathan that "theology is for life." In many ways, Jonathan's theology is an unfolding of that conviction in a larger arena.

It would surprise some on my side of the liberal/evangelical dividing wall to learn that Regent is not perceived as "conservative" everywhere. In communities like the FWBC in Tennessee, it's a dangerously liberal place. But one faculty member, Douglas Simpson, knew of Regent and directed Jonathan there. Jonathan was stepping out to risk coming here, and to find another vision of Baptist life, one more catholic and ecumenical, than he'd known possible. That was made possible partly by faculty welcoming him into their homes and lives. Dr. Jim Houston, founding president of Regent, responded to an impatient young Jonathan's frustration with arid, linear systematic theology this way: "'My dear boy, if you want to think differently, then I suggest you learn Hebrew'. He was right." And that led to a lifelong delight in the Old Testament, begun by Carl Armerding and brought to full flower by Bruce Waltke.

Another, a Canadian church historian, Ian Rennie, shook Jonathan's hand and exclaimed, "The first Free Will Baptist I've met in the flesh! I want to know all about FWBs!" The exotic gaze can run in multiple directions.

But, of course, mentoring is usually much more mundane than that. Pastor Roy Bell, late beloved leader of First Baptist Vancouver, would walk with Jonathan around the West End of Vancouver every other week, and talk to him about pastoring. He would push him through "rigorous analysis of, say, the business meeting: what was the emotional tone? What were the psychological dimensions? How could theology help us?" The Irishman was famous for his seventy-hour workweeks. He even wrote a book on the possible impact of *The Five-Minute Conversation*—he gave open-ended time to few. In fact, Jonathan now says, "I don't know who else he gave that kind of time to."

But the strongest mentoring voices in Jonathan's life have tended to be women. First his mother, Jean Wilson, who according to Jonathan is the clearest communicator and best teacher he's ever had. Then his wife, Marti, who "never had a guarded moment in her life. I've never had an unguarded moment in my life." The Nova Scotian helped Jonathan to see the spiritual danger in his family, his church, and in southern US culture writ large, a place that has birthed so much glory and beauty, and also slavery, Jim Crow, and one Donald J. Trump. A few years, after Marti's early death, Loren Wilkinson introduced Jonathan to Soohwan Park. To their surprise God called them to marriage. Soohwan's contemplative center is a powerful example to Jonathan, and her worldwide leadership as board chair of ARI is just the latest in a legendary career in international mission. And perhaps, above all, Leah Wilson-Hartgrove, who has been involved with this project to honor her father from the start. He describes Leah this way: she "takes seriously what Jesus says and she does it. She doesn't calculate." When Leah and her husband, Jonathan (same name, different person), moved to Walltown in Durham, NC, to start an intentional Christian community, they had their naysayers who said the idealistic kids would pull up stakes as soon as things got hard. I heard those questions, and asked a few myself. Leah's father would respond, "You got that exactly wrong." Jonathan knows well what his daughter is made of. Once, in the early nineties, Marti traveled to Ottawa for her parents' anniversary. Back in California, Jonathan had a medical emergency, and could have died. Marti flew home to be with her husband, and then got word that her father, whom she'd just left, had died. She sat in the kitchen of their house in a love seat next to the window, and eleven-year-old Leah crawled up into her lap and said, "Mom, everything is going to be OK, God is going to take care of us, whatever happens."

There are many more mentors who have made Jonathan the theologian he is. Many of these are his students, some writing in this volume. Others have been colleagues at Duke, Westmont, Acadia Divinity College, Carey, Regent, International Baptist Theological Seminary in Amsterdam, and elsewhere. Every great teacher, and Jonathan is certainly that, knows about "reverse mentoring," by which those whom we teach make us new. Many of his mentors have been friends, with whom he has approached life as a fellow conspirator. But the hardest teacher has been illness. Flannery O'Connor famously said of her struggle with lupus,

> In a sense, sickness is a place, more instructive than a long trip to Europe, and it's always a place where there's no company, where nobody can follow. Sickness before death is a very appropriate thing and I think those who don't have it miss one of God's mercies.

A severe mercy, that. Jonathan has faced down illness in the death of his beloved first wife. He faced it in his own brush with death in the early nineties. And he has faced it more recently in his prostate cancer, which for a time seemed to have metastasized and so about to endanger his own life. As a theological ethicist, Jonathan writes about death as one who has faced it too often, and also seen it defeated. Jonathan and Soohwan see his cancer as having been miraculously defeated—helped along by Soohwan's disciplined diet and caring for his condition, and more than a few answered prayers. To spend time with the Curé de Nanaimo is to be with a man who knows he might not have been here. But here he is. He knows life is a gift, not to be assumed. He is, as gamblers say, playing with house money. Or as Christians say, he is savoring life as altogether gift, none of it earned. It might not have been. But here it is. How can our life then not be altogether hallelujah?

Artist Statement

On the Road and at the Table

Joy Banks

EVERY EASTER AT MY church, where Jonathan worshiped for a season, we sing a song with the refrain, "You'll find Him on the road. You'll find Him at your table." The lines of the song, like the book cover art piece here, are inspired by the Emmaus resurrection story in Luke 24. Maybe it's because of that song or maybe it's because of the wisdom shared by other disciples, like Jonathan, that I have always thought of this story as an invitation to watch for the breaking in of Christ's resurrection reign in surprising places, through unexpected strangers. Where might I meet Jesus on the road this day? If I invited this stranger home for a meal, would I discover that I am the one being hosted and fed instead? This story is one that plays out over and over with possibilities for every generation and context, which is why I've depicted the scenes unfolding around a circle in a contemporary setting.

I discovered last year that there are some good arguments, with historic backing, for the possibility that the two disciples Jesus encountered on the road to Emmaus were a married couple, Cleopas and his wife, who could have been one of the Marys at the crucifixion. However, most artistic renditions of this story, not surprisingly, include only men around this resurrection table. I have found Jonathan to be someone who not only welcomes women to the table, but enthusiastically supports and equips women for leadership and ministry. I think he would be in favor of going with the Cleopas and Mary tradition for this piece.

Hot Cross Buns

Loren Wilkinson

12 months past
On the morning
Of Good Friday
Past daffodils
In rain-light,
Before the day's traffic woke the town,
Through Newnham Garden to Newnham Croft
I walked down aisles of bursting willow
And alleys by houses of weathered stone
To the fragrant, shuttered bakery shop:
To buy a dozen
Buns, hot (cut
With a cross &
Round as time)
For my family.

(This solstice
Again, violets
Push and splay
And deep trees
All luxuriate:
Their roots reach out in soil and time
Past Roman, Saxon, Norman bones placed
Past standing, horizontal under stone;
The rains pour down; the trees grow up
Round and round in the season's cycle.
The year turns
And it returns
Wet time; dry;
Cold time; hot
Bright, dark.)

The baker shop
In chilly dawn
Pulled people
Like a centre
From the town:
Old women, and men, like trees walking
And one who spread arms to his child,
In body's shape, the shape of a cross:
This upward axis, from earth to heaven,
This outward axis through which we act.
This hot bread
Holds the crux,
This centre in
The cycles where
All ways start.
(Cambridge, 1986;
Vancouver, 1987)

Hot Cross Buns
Easter, 2020

This time I bake
them by myself
masked & gloved
here in isolation
on Galiano island
and take them in the brightening spring, through the gate
up the stone steps, and the rocky path, past cedar & arbutus
to my friends where they sit, on their sun-blessed deck
6 feet apart on Easter morning around a bottle of red wine
each with their own cup, reading about the Resurrection,
waiting for bread
still oven-warm,
filled with ginger
lemon and orange,
glazed with honey.

(In the Duomo in
Its empty square
A blind tenor sings
Panis Angelicus
To empty chairs;
In the Vatican, Francis the vicar of Rome is prostrate and alone
before the altar in the crossing of that cross-shaped space, and
in Paris, the island at the city's heart is empty where weeping folk
once sang around the burning church, and Notre Dame waits
roofless and bare within its scaffolding to be built and filled again,
and in Vancouver,
London & Madrid,
Berlin, New York &
All around the world
The altars are empty.

Linked by gnostic nets
All people are islands
Within walls, who wait
Or walk and wonder
Six feet apart under
Skies made blue again on this planet's Holy Saturday, where
autobahns and cruise ships, planes & mines & power plants,
are stilled. And hospitals are filled, the morgues and crematoria,
and people walk, 6 feet apart (an arm's span, or a grave's depth),
And wonder: "Can these bones live? What is the Maker doing?":
The crown-shaped virus
Is a lovely thing, eager
To live and reproduce.
"Very good," God sees it,
Knowing all he makes:

Exploding stars,
colliding continents;
tornadoes, volcanoes;
Creation red with death
& we apes in His image,
Who, raised from stardust into consciousness and conscience,
crucify our Maker here at the center of all things, on our cross and His:
through which He gives His self to things, gives to things their selves:
crowned viruses, and weeds and people: who wait to be released:
We are treaded grapes and broken wheat waiting for their yeast.
These crossed buns say:
You are islanded no longer,
Lifted from the dead: by
Christ, the bread of life
God, the life of bread.

Lament

The World Rises While We Wait

Towards a Theology of Kingdom Patience

MATT HUMPHREY

"IF WHAT YOU HAVE written is the case, which we agree that it is, it begs the question—why hasn't the church embodied this kingdom ethic in its care for creation?" I was uncharacteristically moved to silence. I had come prepared to defend my key sources, my writing style, and to shore up the lines of argumentation that together built what I still hoped were a coherent case for a distinctly Christian ecological ethic. I sat staring out the window of Loren Wilkinson's office, while he and Jonathan Wilson sat quietly. In the window's reflection, I caught a broad smile slowly growing on Jonathan's face. This was the one question I had not come ready to respond to.

"That's probably not fair," Loren finally quipped as Jonathan's smile expanded into open laughter. "I've been pondering that for almost forty years and haven't answered it yet and neither has Jonathan." I breathed a deep sigh of relief. Like any graduate student, I had begun to quickly assemble a list of relevant sources to marshal to my defense: the problem lies within the social imaginaries of late modernity *à la Charles Taylor*; the cultural captivity of the church *à la Hauerwas*; the rampant individualism and the loss of teleology as a basis for ethical discernment *à la MacIntyre*. Fast forward to the years that followed, as I took up full-time work for A Rocha Canada, engaging a broad array of Christians and church traditions, and my list went on to include other pernicious factors—a church set on empire building rather than kingdom building;

a world where it is easy to live as though our relationship to creation (one of the four primary relationships entrusted to us in creation, as Jonathan would rightly insist!) doesn't matter or perhaps even exist; a church that had become inherently anthropocentric, focusing on an internal spiritual life and an external culture war while neglecting the very basis for this life we enjoy—the gift of a stable and superabundant creation.

There is an old proverb that when the student is ready, the teacher appears. Like many writers in this volume, Jonathan was a teacher who appeared at just the right time for me. I began graduate studies in September 2006, right around the time Jonathan was beginning to prepare his 2007 Grenz lectures, upon which our friendship began. Years later, as I began teaching myself, I discovered that the encouragement to ask hard questions is a teacher's greatest gift. Jonathan's question continues to haunt me—with the kind of holy haunting by which the Spirit is always beckoning us deeper into the very life of God given for the world. What follows is just part of an answer, developed over a decade, and with my deep gratitude to the teacher.

Jonathan writes, "We humans are made for four relationships: God, others, the rest of creation and ourselves."[1] Yet, we bear from experience how each of these are broken: we readily live as though God does not exist, as though we are not dependent upon or responsible to our neighbors, as though creation is simply a resource to be dominated or exploited, and by ever neglecting our inner life and health. On the contrary, Christian mission flows from God's work of healing and reconciliation in Christ for the sake of the world. Integral mission insists that all of these relationships be considered and healed. To faithfully bear witness to this reality of God's reconciling work in the world, the church must discern its role as work and witness in every time and place.

It is a temptation, considering the world's problems, to dream of large-scale top-down solutions. It is hard to pay much attention to the news of the world today and not see the high stakes of the growing environmental emergency that threatens our planet. I use the language of emergency advisedly, aware of how this can fuel a utilitarian drive towards quick and scalable solutions. Don't get me wrong—I'd love to see us solve climate change, reverse ecosystem degradation, species loss and extinction, as well as provide clean water, a livable wage, and the list goes on. But for those of us whose hearts are torn by the world's problems, an

---

1. Jonathan R. Wilson, "Bringing Good News," CBM, Jan. 10, 2019, para. 18, https://www.cbmin.org/bringing-good-news/.

acute problem persists: how to sustain a life of action for the sake of our neighbor and world when the scale of the problem so easily outsizes the scale of our solutions?

I remember a conversation with an intern fresh out of a master's degree in ecology and passionate about saving wetlands and the many creatures (primarily amphibians) who lived there. They begrudgingly spent hours engaging neighbors whose private lands bordered small ponds and wetlands, commenting to the effect of "I became a scientist because I love the world, but now I'm stuck dealing with difficult humans!" Indeed. God's work of healing and reconciliation begins with human image-bearers—the very same ones who have been formed within those four broken relationships in need of healing. Indeed, Christ our healer has entrusted this mission into broken human hands like yours and mine.

However, after spending time and energy working towards healing, we can become frustrated with the wicked problems of the world and lapse into cynicism, despair, or even withdrawal. We might amend our understanding of God's mission mandate to think it only ever really includes a few select people (like us) who really get it and either withdraw to live our lives or find ways to impose that upon other less enlightened ones. The core argument of this essay is that each of these options (and more) amounts to a form of theological impatience. Further, I suggest this is an acute danger for those of us who have been formed with what Jonathan calls the "Dialectic of the Kingdom." As Timothy Gorringe writes in the context of our climate emergency, "Theological ethics, that is to say, has a utopian dimension, helping us envisage the shape of the future. I am sure that this is right, but it is a long-term solution. Emergencies need much quicker responses."[2] I do not doubt the urgent needs of our world nor the Christian call to respond as part of God's mission. (There is such a thing as holy impatience.) But how might a robust theology of kingdom patience better equip us for doing this work over the long haul?

Gorringe suggests that in the face of the global emergency we now face, there are two scriptural models for action: the Jonah model and the Noah model. Jonah is called by God to go and preach against the people and the whole city repents. Gorringe quips, "I think as ethicists many of us want to be Jonah. We preach and we hope for repentance. But Jonah, as we know, is a romance."[3] We might read Jonah as a parody of the

---

2. Timothy J. Gorringe, "On Building an Ark: The Global Emergency and the Limits of Moral Exhortation," *Studies in Christian Ethics* 24 (2011): 23–33, esp. 27.

3. Gorringe, "On Building an Ark," 27.

Hebrew prophet: where other prophets respond to God's call, Jonah flees; where others are rejected or even killed for their message, in Jonah's case, Nineveh repents. Jonah turns the usual prophet's story on its head. And yet, Gorringe argues, many of us expect just this response. If we simply describe the problem, present a better version of our theology and ethics, we expect the world to repent.

But Gorringe also directs attention to what he calls "the Noah option." "Noah is warned by God, as the prophets are, and rather than being told to warn his contemporaries he is told to build an ark to rescue representatives of all creatures from the rising waters."[4] He amends what may be misheard as another kind of Garrett Hardin's "lifeboat ethic" by insisting that "the Noah story is set in the context of a covenant with the whole of Creation" and, reading this story in our own context (diverging from the biblical story), suggests we look "to multiple initiatives, all around the world, thinking not of one ark, but of many arks created for their local communities" as a means of facing the emergency before us.[5] Local communities demand messy engagement, cut through our impatience and idealism, and commit us to long-term investment. But how do we sustain it?

Gorringe notes several models for ark building, including the passage at the end of MacIntyre's *After Virtue* (which became the basis for Wilson's *Living Faithfully in a Fragmented World*). He notes the role of Benedictine monasteries as arks in the European Middle Ages and points to the Transition Town movement as a contemporary example of the same impulse. I might suggest that the Jonah model is a form of impatience, while the Noah model, as crazy as it sounds, is *patient* upon both God and the world. Its efficacy lies not so much in having a one-size-fits-all solution for the whole of creation—for it entrusts that job to the Creator, while being patiently faithful to the place it occupies.

In *The Stature of Waiting*, W. H. Vanstone develops an account of patience rooted in Jesus's sown act of giving himself over unto death. In an important chapter entitled "The Status of Patient," Vanstone, writing in 1982, offers an analogy. A person, in the prime of their life, has been in a terrible automobile accident and is now rendered helpless on the side of the road. What happens next? "Up to this point he was ordering and arranging his own affairs. . . . He was holding the reins of team projects

---

4. Gorringe, "On Building an Ark," 27.
5. Gorringe, "On Building an Ark," 28.

and purposes . . . he was creating his own immediate future and was in control of his own immediate destiny. But now, suddenly, he passes into the hands of others and becomes dependent on their decision and action. . . . The sick or injured person has now become a *patient*."[6]

Vanstone continues, identifying in this analogy something of our modern malaise—a broadening sense of disempowerment within a system that is indifferent to our personal and collective thriving. This is nothing new, of course. But in our modern world, the growing gap between the story we tell ourselves (of individual agency, freedom, and self-determination) and the ways that world constrains us leads to a sense of widespread resentment. "In ever widening areas of modern working life the individual operator finds that his own possibility of achievement, success or satisfaction depends almost entirely on the efficient functioning of a system over which he himself has no control. In this sense he tends to feel himself *the patient*, the object and even the victim of the complex system within which he works."[7] Indeed.

Vanstone contrasts this posture to that of Jesus, who was willingly "handed over" to suffering and even death. A theology of kingdom patience must take its cues from "the handing over of Jesus with His transition from action to passion, or His entry into passion."[8] The passion may be interpreted narrowly as the events surrounding Jesus's suffering and death, but Vanstone points out that it includes the whole of his life. What's more, while the word "suffer" has now taken on a thoroughly negative tone, its original meaning in English was simply "'to have something happen to one,' 'to be the one to whom something happens, or perhaps, 'to let something happen to one.'"[9] Read in this way, Jesus's suffering was a life willingly lived for the sake of another –in which he opened himself up to the agency of another and as such became *patient* to those around him, even to forces which may ultimately be hostile. Suffering and passion isn't about pain or misfortune as such, but rather opening towards "dependence, exposure, waiting" and "being no longer in control of one's own situation."[10] This is central to our life of discipleship.

---

6. W. H. Vanstone, *The Stature of Waiting* (Harrisburg, PA: Morehouse, 2006), 34.
7. Vanstone, *Stature of Waiting*, 40.
8. Vanstone, *Stature of Waiting*, 29.
9. Vanstone, *Stature of Waiting*, 29.
10. Vanstone, *Stature of Waiting*, 70.

The Christian is no longer the subject of his or her life but rather is subjected to all the gifts God has given. You might say the Christian is made *patient* not just to the violent whims of a broken world, though they will endure much, but also to the work of God by the Spirit set loose through all of creation. Our ark building and integral mission must therefore take their cues from this posture of being *patient* to the kingdom of God. What might this patience look like? Jesus gives us a key image in one of my favorite parables.

Robert Farrar Capon writes, "The Kingdom, Jesus tells his hearers, is like leaven, which a woman took and hid in three measures of flour, until the whole was leavened."[11] Consider this parable in light of the predicament we have been observing. There is precious little of the kingdom leaven hidden amidst a whole loaf of a world which, so far as we can observe, isn't welcoming towards it! And yet it is the whole world that God is set on raising up into new life. Capon continues, "When Jesus says that the *whole* is leavened, he's not kidding. The lump stands for the whole world. It's not some elite ball of brioche dough made out of fancy flour by special handling. And it's not some hyper-good-for-you chunk of spiritual fad bread full of soy flour, wheat germ, and pure thoughts. It's just plain, unbaked bread dough, and Jesus postulates enough of it to make it even handle like the plain old world it represents: that is, *not easily*. Indigestible in its present form, incapable of going anywhere, either to heaven or hell, except in a handbasket—and absolutely certain to wear out anybody, God included, who tries to deal with it."[12]

The kingdom of God is hidden in the world just as the yeast is "hidden" in the batch of dough. "And just as the yeast, once it is in the dough is so intimate a part of the lump as to be indistinguishable from it, undiscoverable in it, and irretrievable out of it, so is the kingdom in this world."[13] Kingdom patience is about learning to see differently and to bear witness to this mysterious work in our midst. We begin by recognizing, through the eyes of faith, that the leaven has been cast into this lump of a world—and we adjust our vision such that we can spot signs of this patient fermenting work and bear witness to others of all that we see.

Here Capon undercuts what Wilson has long had in his crosshairs—a two-kingdoms approach that is too cozy to worldly power at the expense

---

11. Robert Farrar Capon, *Kingdom, Grace, Judgment: Paradox, Outrage, and Vindication in the Parables of Jesus* (Grand Rapids: Eerdmans, 2002), 99.

12. Capon, *Kingdom, Grace, Judgment*, 100.

13. Capon, *Kingdom, Grace, Judgment*, 101.

of the gospel. There is not one set of rules for the leaven and another for the lump—rather, God is at work raising up the whole world. The question becomes how do we respond to this good news with our whole lives? On this Capon calls principally for patience. "What are the only responses you need to offer to yeast-in-dough? Well, patience, for one thing. And possibly discernment—to be able to recognize when it (not you, please note) has done the job. And maybe a little vigilance to make sure impatient types don't talk you into despairing of the lump before its time comes."[14] This is where this parable becomes a central image for a theology of kingdom patience.

God's work in this world is mysterious and sometimes hidden, like the leaven in the lump. This is work we participate in and bear witness to—but which, like a good sourdough, we can never quite anticipate. For those "impatient types" among us (this writer included), Capon suggests such an ethic can prevent us from despair.

> No matter what you do, the yeast works anyway. At your most, your responses advance your satisfaction, not its success. And even your negative responses—even your pointless resistances to the Kingdom—interfere only with your own convenience, not with its working. Indeed, by the imagery of bread making, they may even help the kingdom. Unless the dough is kneaded thoroughly—unless it resists and fights the baker enough to develop gluten and form effective barriers to the yeast's working—then the gases produced by the yeast will not be entrapped in cells that can lighten the lump into a loaf.[15]

Indeed: the world rises while we wait.

This chapter was written and finalized at the Feast of the Ascension. It is curious to observe that some of the final words the disciples hear from Jesus concern patience. In Acts 1, "he ordered them not to leave Jerusalem, but *to wait* there for the promise of the Father."[16] In Luke 24, "I am sending upon you what my Father promised; *so stay here* in the city until you have been clothed with power from on high." Jesus's final words to the disciples are "wait here." They await the promised Holy Spirit who will bring peace and guide them into all truth. But even with the Holy Spirit, they face persecution, danger, doubt, and all manner of confusion

---

14. Capon, *Kingdom, Grace, Judgment*, 102–3.

15. Capon, *Kingdom, Grace, Judgment*, 103.

16. This chapter uses the NRSV translation for Scripture references, unless otherwise indicated. Emphases were added.

over what the call of God was to be for them. Vanstone would say they are called to wait—to become *patient* to God's work in their midst, trusting that the leaven has indeed been lovingly cast and is at work raising up this whole lump of creation in the end.

Having learned from Jonathan to "construe the world according to the gospel" one might run full speed towards that end and give your all to advancing the kingdom in our midst. This essay should not be construed as arguing against this radical call to discipleship. Rather it suggests that you will, at some point, grow tired and weary. Kingdom patience calls us back, then, to trust God is at work, even when we cannot see it. We bear witness to the life of Christ, in both our success and our failure, in our faith and in our doubt. Above all, we find ourselves made *patient* by the divine physician who is healing us and all of creation, if only we can wait for it.

Jonathan says as much in the closing of *God's Good World*, noting the practices of presence and patience as two central acts by which the church embodies this ethic, no matter what may come. "If we locate our practice of presence in the redemption of creation, then we place ourselves in Christ and know that we are already participating in the conquest of evil and the victory of life over death."[17] Our belonging in Christ makes us patient for God to do God's work in God's time. "Patience is a primary mark of God's work in the world."[18] Having extolled these virtues of radical discipleship, Wilson immediately follows with two prayers that temper both: "How long?" and "Come, Lord Jesus."

These are prayers of kingdom patience, placing us in the same position as those first disciples—looking up to heaven and asking in prayer, "How long?" Perhaps looking out over the aching world in need of redemption and seeing our own inadequacy to transform it for the better, and pleading, "Come, Lord Jesus." A theology of kingdom patience doesn't absolve us of doing all the good we can but reorients that good to God's hidden presence already at work in our midst. It teaches us to acknowledge, even when we cannot see it, the God who holds the whole world and yet takes a risk on a little bit of leaven in confidence it will enliven and raise the whole lump.

"Why hasn't the church embodied this kingdom ethic in its care for creation?"

---

17. Jonathan R. Wilson, *God's Good World: Reclaiming the Doctrine of Creation* (Grand Rapids: Baker Academic, 2013), 220.

18. Wilson, *God's Good World*, 220.

We are impatient. Our impatience has led us to all manner of kingdom building which inevitably begin to look more like human empires than the great ecosystem of God. In a time when the church faces such urgent needs and concerns all over God's good world, we must continually readjust our vision to the patient work of God—learning the art of ark building instead of empire building. And perhaps, like Jonathan, a renewed imagination for the kingdom will teach us to become *patient* and so entrust ourselves once more to the God who is always already at work in us and in the world breathing new life and making all things new. Come, Lord Jesus.

Groaning toward New Creation

Michael Swalm and H. Daniel Zacharias

I consider that the sufferings of this present time are not worth comparing with the glory about to be revealed to us. For the creation waits with eager longing for the revealing of the children of God; for the creation was subjected to futility, not of its own will but by the will of the one who subjected it, in hope that the creation itself will be set free from its bondage to decay and will obtain the freedom of the glory of the children of God. We know that the whole creation has been groaning in labor pains until now; and not only the creation, but we ourselves, who have the first fruits of the Spirit, groan inwardly while we wait for adoption, the redemption of our bodies. For in hope we were saved. Now hope that is seen is not hope. For who hopes for what is seen? But if we hope for what we do not see, we wait for it with patience.

—ROM 8:18–25[1]

The apostle Paul's words in Rom 8:18–25 have been studied intensely, not only because the passage sits within the theological heart of Paul's

---

1. This chapter uses the NRSV translation for Scripture references, unless otherwise indicated.

theology (Rom 5–8), but because it is the "theological mantra" text for eco-theology.² This passage, along with other creation-centric texts, also holds an important place in Indigenous readings of Scripture,³ and will continue to speak to the church as we face the crisis of the anthropocene.⁴ The question we ask in this essay is what it can begin to look like for followers of Jesus to engage this text at the level of practice and how Paul's words invite this engagement. Jonathan Wilson rightly states in *God's Good World* that this passage was a pivotal one in helping us to "understand the church as the sign of God's redemption of creation and the telos of the new creation."⁵ Wilson's assertion that the church is a "sign" is an important one, as it neither absolves God's people of responsibility, nor insists that the responsibility is theirs alone. As Wilson later states, "God is redeeming creation and we are participants, everything that happens to us will be brought into alignment with that telos."⁶ Romans 8:18–25 provides good soil from which to sprout that alignment towards God's work of new creation.

The Groaning Creation

In a recent article John Gillman notes how scholars have read the passage variously with theocentric, anthropocentric, or ecocentric lenses, after which he argues convincingly for this passage being an interlocking story of God, believers, and the creation.⁷ Gillman, however, follows the common pattern of Western readings in talking about Paul's personification of creation. Indigenous theologians are not so quick to assume Paul's employment of literary devices, instead speaking of the land as the living

2. Cherryl Hunt et al., "An Environmental Mantra? Ecological Interest in Romans 8:19–23 and a Modest Proposal for Its Narrative Interpretation," *JTS* 59 (2008): 546–79.

3. See, for example, T. Christopher Hoklotubbe (Choctaw), "A Native American Interpretation of Romans 8:18–23," in *Oxford Encyclopedias of the Bible*, Oxford Biblical Studies, www.oxfordbiblicalstudies.com/article/opr/t998/e69.

4. The "anthropocene" is the label given to the current geological age due to the detrimental impact of human activity on the earth's natural systems. See Paul J. Crutzen, "The 'Anthropocene,'" in *Earth System Science in the Anthropocene*, ed. Eckart Ehlers and Thomas Krafft, 13–18 (Berlin: Springer, 2006).

5. Jonathan R. Wilson, *God's Good World: Reclaiming the Doctrine of Creation* (Grand Rapids: Baker Academic, 2013), 143.

6. Wilson, *God's Good World*, 145–46.

7. John Gillman, "The Story of Creation, Believing Humanity and God in Romans 8:18–25," *LS* 40 (2017): 36–57.

Mother Earth and signaling the relationality of peoples to the lands that sustain them.[8] The Hebrew Scriptures also speak of the land in relational terms, with the land obeying the command of Creator and working in the role of co-creator to create vegetation (Gen 1:11–12). This vegetation is later given by the Creator forever as sustenance for land animals, including humanity (Gen 1:29–30). This gift establishes the dependence of humanity on the gifts of the land. God then places humanity into a relationship of reciprocity for the good gifts of Mother Earth, as humanity is placed in the garden to serve and conform to her (Gen 2:15).[9] This intentionally cultivated relationship establishes an interdependence within the community of creation.[10]

In Gen 1 and 2, the earth is not something abstract or inanimate, but one to whom we relate and belong. Paul continues his discussion about the earth, stating that the whole creation has been groaning in labor pains (Rom 8:22). Paul does not make explicit the result of this labor, but as Beverly Roberts Gaventa has argued, the context helps the reader infer

---

8. The Indigenous worldview extends beyond Mother Earth to encompass our kinship with other fellow creatures. To quote Kidwell et al.: "Corn and all food stuffs are our relatives, just as much as those who live in adjacent lodges within our clan-cluster. Thus, eating is sacramental, to use a euro-theological word, because we are eating our relatives. Not only are we related to corn, beans, and squash, since these things emerge immediately out of the death of Corn Mother, but even those other relatives like Buffalo, Deer, Squirrel and Fish ultimately gain their strength and growth because they too eat of the plenty provided by the Mother—eating grasses, leaves, nuts, and algae that also grow out of the Mother's bosom. When we eat, we understand that we are benefiting from the lives that have gone before us, that all our human ancestors have also returned to the earth and have become part of what nourishes us today. Thus, one can never eat without remembering the gift of the Mother, of all our relatives in this world, and of all those who have gone before us." Clara Sue Kidwell et al., *A Native American Theology* (Maryknoll, NY: Orbis, 2001), 81.

9. See H. Daniel Zacharias, "The Land Takes Care of Us: Recovering Creator's Relational Design," in *The Land: Majority World and Minoritized Theologies of Land*, ed. K. K. Yeo and Gene L. Green (Eugene, OR: Cascade, 2020), 69–97, esp. 75–76, where I argue for the translation of "serve her and conform to her" for Gen 2:15. The choice of "conform" signals the choice to live in rhythm with the environment which one is a part of, rather than try to manipulate the environment to the individual.

10. The description "community of creation" is a preferred description for all of creation, as it not only highlights the relationality of creation, but also places humanity within creation instead of hierarchically above it. The designation is traced back to Jürgen Moltmann (*God In Creation: A New Theology of Creation and the Spirit of God*, The Gifford Lectures [San Francisco: Harper & Row, 1985]) and used more recently by Richard Bauckham (*Living with Other Creatures: Green Exegesis and Theology* [Waco, TX: Baylor, 2011]) and esp. Randy Woodley (*Shalom and the Community of Creation: An Indigenous Vision*, Prophetic Christianity [Grand Rapids: Eerdmans, 2012]).

the results of this labor, with "the glory of the children of God" (v. 21) mentioned immediately before the described labor pains, and our own groaning "while we wait for adoption" (v. 23).[11] Many Pauline scholars recognize the interconnectedness between humanity and creation. For instance, James Dunn states: "The point to be underlined here is the solidarity of humankind with the rest of creation, of adam with the adamah from which adam was made."[12] This interconnectedness is highlighted also in discussions of the futility to which the creation is subject (Rom 8:20), in part due to the failings of humanity in Gen 3. Equally important has been the discussion of our interrelated futures, as the creation's freedom from bondage to decay is intimately tied to humanity's redemption (v. 21). These areas of focus in scholarship are not untrue, but remain incomplete.

In our opinion, it is in part due to the anthropocentric reading of Scripture, which tends to obscure an additional component in the discussion of new creation. The choice to read this as "personification" of an otherwise abstract object removes the earth as an agent within this text. Mother Earth is an active character in this story, one with whom we sit in an ongoing symbiotic relationship of reciprocity. It is through the creation's agency that we are moving toward our redemption, and it is through our agency that creation moves towards redemption as well. The creation narrative indicates our dependence on Creator and the gifts of the earth for our life—the promise of eternal life continues to be bound to Creator and creation. In the introduction we quoted Wilson that the church is "the sign of God's redemption of creation and the telos of the new creation."[13] To this we can add that *the creation is the sign of God's redemption of the church and the telos of new creation as well.*

Having established the agency of creation, Paul moves to describe the act of mutual groaning. Paul describes the creation as groaning (συστενάζω) in labor pains right up until the present (8:21), after which he describes the groans (στενάζω) of the church as we "wait for adoption, the redemption of our bodies" (8:23). Paul will go on to talk about the groans (στεναγμός) of the Spirit on our behalf (8:26). The three agents in this cosmic drama, Creator, human creation, and nonhuman creation,

---

11. Beverly Roberts Gaventa, *Our Mother Saint Paul* (Louisville: Westminster John Knox, 2007), 53.

12. James D. G. Dunn, *The Theology of Paul the Apostle* (Grand Rapids: Eerdmans, 1998), 100–101.

13. Wilson, *God's Good World*, 143.

all groan towards new creation. As Susan Grove Eastman (summarizing Käsemann) has stated, "all human beings are embedded in and impinged upon by suprahuman realities . . . communion is the presupposition for a self that is capable of self-knowledge and action."[14] We can add to this Dale Martin's important study showing "the essential continuity of the human body with its surroundings."[15] We are interconnected and interrelated with the community of creation, with the agency of the earth and our agency playing upon one another, ultimately towards new creation. This belonging should cause us to be in rhythm with creation, and in the case of Rom 8, that rhythm of belonging and forward movement towards new creation comes by means of groaning. To *not join* in this ongoing action of groaning with Creator and creation is a profoundly arrogant move of dis-integration, dis-embodiment, and dis-memberment on the part of humanity.

In a masterful essay, Laurie Braaten traces the theme of creation mourning throughout the Hebrew Scriptures, and notes that "creation is an important member of God's family."[16] This means that creation's groaning, caused in large part by the ongoing effects of human sin, is properly responded to by joining in the act of groaning. Braaten highlights the act of mourning as a penitential rite,[17] though this participation need not only be restricted to that.

Participatory Groaning (Groaning in the Places We Are)

Two questions thus emerge from a close study of the relationship between humanity and nonhuman creation above: how are we called to "groan together," and what does this "groaning together" accomplish? Answering the latter question first will provide a foundation from which proposals may emerge for the former.

As stated above, a primary understanding of groaning is an expression of lament for the pain experienced, both in the case of humanity (present suffering) and creation ("childbirth"). It must be noted, however,

---

14. Susan Grove Eastman, *Paul and the Person: Reframing Paul's Anthropology* (Grand Rapids: Eerdmans, 2017), 104.

15. Dale B. Martin, *The Corinthian Body* (New Haven, CT: Yale University Press, 1995), 21.

16. Laurie J. Braaten, "All Creation Groans: Romans 8:22 in Light of the Biblical Sources," *Horizons in Bible Theology* 28 (2006): 131–59, esp. 157.

17. Braaten, "All Creation Groans," 157–58.

that each of these groanings (as well as the Spirit's groaning on behalf of an ignorant humanity in Rom 8:26) is not solely lamentation. Both also denote future benefit; they each have a telos toward which they are moving, and the groaning of each is indicative of that telos (though it may not be readily apparent within the groaning). As Powery puts it, "such groaning suggests the incompleteness of the salvation experience and of the fulfillment of God's righteousness in the present order."[18] The suffering of the church incites groaning, but suffering, according to Paul, has a purpose: the production of perseverance, character, and hope, mediated by the Holy Spirit (Rom 5:3-5). That is, the groaning born from suffering brings about the realization of the hope that is here identified as "adoption." Likewise, the groaning of creation as in childbirth is not simply a lament of the painfulness associated with birth as a result of the fall (Gen 3), and thus sorrow produced by human sinfulness, but is also an *expectant* groaning. The wail of a mother (Earth) during childbirth anticipates the wail of the infant soon to be born, and so the groan of creation awaits with eagerness the "revealing of the children of God."[19]

Yet there is a tertiary understanding of groaning that moves beyond both the immediate need for lament and the anticipation of a more joyful telos. Groaning bemoans what is, anticipates what will be, and is also a participatory act that works to accomplish the telos it awaits. Powery's assertion is true so far as it goes: "the Spirit's activity of groaning, particularly the act of 'groaning' and 'sighing' through the entire created order . . . is a catalyst for sociopolitical action and change."[20] We would add that this groaning expands the catalyzing beyond interhuman sociopolitical action to include action involved in the redemption of nonhuman creation as well. In the case of humanity, the groaning associated with suffering, particularly suffering for the sake of the gospel, is in itself a witness to that gospel: the reconciliation of *all things* to God's self (2 Cor 5:19). The groaning stands as a kind of speech-act that participates

18. Emerson B. Powery, "The Groans of 'Brother Saul': An Exploratory Reading of Romans 8 for 'Survival,'" *Word & World* 24 (2004): 315-22, esp. 320.

19. J. Richard Middleton, "A New Heaven and a New Earth: The Case for a Holistic Reading of the Biblical Story of Redemption," *Journal for Christian Theological Research* 11 (2006): 73-97. Middleton argues against a Platonic reading of redemption, insisting that "the biblical worldview leads to an affirmation of the goodness of creation, along with a desire to pray and work for the redemption of precisely this world (including human, sociocultural institutions) that earthly life might be restored to what it was meant to be."

20. Powery, "Groans of 'Brother Saul,'" 320-21.

in the very thing it hopes for. As Hunt et al. have it, ecological "Christian living in the present has an eschatological quality to it; it is a call to be 'already' what is 'not yet' fully realized, to walk in the Spirit and so be transformed according to the pattern of the age to come."[21] A church that groans in suffering is speaking words of witness that instantiate the very character to which it witnesses. When that church is unsure of how to bear witness well, the Spirit participates *with* the church, groaning when we are unable. Creation likewise accomplishes its telos through groaning. In childbirth, groaning denotes pain and anticipates joy, but it also brings about that joy; groaning is the vocalization of the work of child-bearing. This participatory groaning is a part of accomplishing the redemption of all of creation in that it bears witness to brokenness and, if humanity listens carefully to it, bears witness to the character of the emerging glory of the children of God it is birthing.

With these three interdependent meanings of "groaning," the above amended dictum begins to take theological shape: "the church is the sign of God's redemption of creation and the telos of the new creation,"[22] and *the creation is the sign of God's redemption of the church and the telos of new creation as well*. Said differently, the formation (birthing) of the church is the end result of the groaning of creation, and the renewal of creation is the end result of the groaning of the church. These mutual goals have as their unifying factor the groaning of the Spirit, who is at work in creation and in the church to bring about the renewal (revealing) of each. When the church is unable to truly understand or vocalize its groaning for the new creation, the Spirit takes up the cry and effects that renewal in ways the church has not anticipated or foreseen. The invitation of the Spirit to the church and to creation is to enter into this mutual groaning together to see the fullness of the kingdom come.

With this understanding of the teleological and participatory nature of groaning, we turn to the first question above: how do we (humanity and creation) groan together in this participatory way? In what follows, we offer some proposals that invite the church to a lived kingdom realism through its participation with creation in the Spirit.

---

21. Hunt et al., "Environmental Mantra," 575.
22. Wilson, *God's Good World*, 143.

Recognize Our Interrelatedness

The first step in learning to groan together is learning to recognize our togetherness. To be adequate, this recognition must move beyond a theological apprehension of the agency of Mother Earth and ultimately obtain practices that embody this acknowledgement. Acknowledgment of our interconnectedness is the first step in a journey that will lead away from dis-integration, dis-embodiment, and dis-memberment toward a deep integration, embodiment, and membership with the community of creation.

The church has written into its own sacraments the means by which we might more adequately understand and practice our integration with the rest of creation. Baptism (whether infant or believer's, immersion, sprinkling, or pouring) can be a deep practice of integration with the realization of our physiology—humans are 50–65 percent water—if we are willing to acknowledge that the water, far from being solely a cleansing medium, is integral to human makeup.[23] Baptism reminds us of our membership with one another as the church and with the creation to whom we belong. Another example is the funerary practice of intoning "dust to dust" as we inter a body, which is a moment of integration that vocally groans, awaiting resurrection (new creation) while at the same time declaring our deep interconnectedness (adam and adamah). Even the practice of Eucharist focuses on the gifts of the land to humanity (wheat and wine—obtained by human participation with creation), declaring them to be coterminous with the body and blood of God. The church then ingests the gift of the bread and the gift of Christ's body simultaneously, which stands as a clear example of "re-embodiment." This is probably the clearest example of a re-embodiment. Perhaps including thankfulness to the land our mother for these gifts during the practice of Eucharist would be an adequate first step toward recognizing how intertwined we truly are.

Listen for the Groaning of the Other

If the church and creation are deeply interconnected, it stands to reason that we should be able to hear the groaning of one another. It is an unfortunate reality of human nature that our own groaning typically drowns

---

23. It is interesting to note that the early church indicated its preference for baptism to be done in living bodies of water, with still water or sprinkling acceptable, but less than ideal, alternatives. See *Didache* 7.1.

out the sound of the groaning of the other. There are some practices, however, that could allow the church to hear the groaning of creation more clearly, and vice versa. This principle is most clearly evidenced with the Spirit interceding with groans on behalf of the church: the Spirit is able to intercede with these groans because the Spirit is God and because the Spirit indwells believers and indwells creation. Likewise, the church dwells within and as creation, and so should be able to hear and echo the groans it apprehends. To truly hear the groaning of creation, the church must be rooted in its place, and know its place well enough to be able to differentiate the groaning coming from others within the community of creation from the other noise that surrounds it.[24] This requires a church that is attuned to its locale and to the history and voices of that locale. In this regard, being led by the wisdom of the Indigenous peoples of that area can help us discern the groanings of the lands we dwell within. Other simple practices like regular observance during walks, involvement with local ecological organizations who do this discernment, and developing a knowledge of and respect for the history of our place would go far in attuning the ears of the church to the groanings of creation.[25] A prayer walk, though typically focused on human neighbors, could be repurposed to include nonhuman creation, opening the eyes of the church to creation's groaning. Further, the church could regularly practice spiritual listening, allowing the Spirit to fill in the groans we cannot hear through our ignorance and neglect. We can then listen to the groans of the Spirit and learn to groan in kind for creation. This listening, and especially the responding by believers, needs to go beyond personal piety and entrench

---

24. "Talk to the earth and it will teach you" (Job 12:8).

25. A practical example is discovering the at-risk species of one's province or state, and if one can get even more specific to one's watershed, it is even better. For example, in my (Danny's) context, several Nova Scotian species are considered endangered due to habitat loss, specifically old-growth forest (mainland moose, Canada lynx, American marten, Canada warbler, chimney swift, Bicknell's thrush, rusty blackbird). This has caused me to follow a number of groups that are monitoring logging and land use of old-growth forests, join the letter-writing campaigns, and increase awareness of the issues in my circles of influence.

While this may seem more challenging in urban environments, I (Mike) have witnessed many examples of human-generated trash becoming incorporated into places of natural beauty inadvertently. The incorporation of this garbage has caused natural flora (and fauna) to be forced to adapt to its presence, including flowers and trees growing around and through the trash. Careful work to remove the garbage without damaging flora and fauna is one simple yet powerful way of observing and involving myself in the process of renewal.

itself into our corporate liturgies and prayers, such that our weekly practices reflect and refract our Sunday mornings.

Allow Mutual Groaning to Inform Lived Kingdom Realism

Finally, when we are able to know how we are related to creation and how we are able to hear creation's groaning (and vice versa), we are invited into a participatory groaning that effects, even as it anticipates, new creation. This mutual groaning includes working *with* creation *in* the Spirit to bring about the birthing of new creation and the revelation of the children of God. This groaning can be advocacy on behalf of creation, but we believe that this advocacy still removes us a step from our interrelatedness with the rest of creation. In addition to advocacy, direct involvement with the groaning we heard above, reciprocal and echoing of that groaning, can take the form of gentle and/or radical moves toward the community of creation's flourishing. Church buildings or homes can go further, recognizing the need for deeper relationship with creation by implementing integrative and regenerative agricultural practices on the micro level in the neighborhood. Abandoned or vacant lots can be transformed into food forests. Church lawns (enormously wasteful and largely useless) can be slowly reoriented toward indigenous flora and fauna. Permaculture and regenerative farming principles can be adopted and maintained even in the most urban of settings. The flourishing of all creation, human and nonhuman, is the work of new creation ambassadors. These are simple ways that our reciprocal groaning can anticipate renewal and participate in the reconciliation of all things through the recognition of our mutual indwelling and mutual hope for the full redemption we await together.

Jesus as a Moral Stranger

REGGIE L. WILLIAMS

THE DIFFICULTY WE HAVE with race and religion in the United States is due to much more than our feelings about people who are different from us. It is also a Christian problem, stemming from our understanding of Jesus. Regardless of how we feel about "others," our interpretation of human difference is derived from ideas and faith claims that inform our understanding of the image of God, represented by the central animating figure of Christian devotion. In this brief essay I will offer a brief account of these claims, as one who was captivated by the study of theological ethics because I was a student of Jonathan Wilson.

I once thought biblical studies was the remedy for this problem of difference and division. But the problem is much more acute than our reading of Scripture. It is also a problem of the way we interpret, speak, and act out our understanding of relationship to God and God's ongoing activity in the world through the church. It is a problem of theological ethics, stemming from our interpretation of Jesus.

The difference between theological ethics and biblical studies was lost on me when I was an incoming student from a public junior college to a private Christian liberal arts college in the fall of 1992. As I understood it, to know the Bible was to live a faithful Christian life, and I had determined that I wanted to attend a college where I could learn the Bible in its original languages. To do so would give me greater access to the kind of knowledge that made for a faithfulness to Christ.

I wasn't aware of the gap between my understanding of "faithful" or even "Christian" and the version of reality those words invoked within the evangelical liberal arts college that I was entering. I was simply a zealous young adult Christian. I was quickly surprised to learn that few of my peers at my new college shared my zeal. But zeal was not the only thing that they didn't share with me. As a Black male student athlete at a white evangelical college, I was metaphorically a being from a different world than that of the members of the predominately white Christian community I was entering. My reading of the Bible was guided by a hermeneutic derived from a tradition of "God with us" that was formed within a Black community subject to the Christian world inhabited by my white peers and professors. We all read the same Bible in that Christian academic space, and we identified the God of our worship by the same names; but our hopes and our expectations for nearly everything related to God's work in the world through Christ were fundamentally different. What I knew about life in the kingdom of God was shaped by an interpretation of the way of Jesus that was derived within very different embodied experiences. It took years for me to arrive at that realization, and my road towards comprehension began with my undergraduate theology professor.

Jesus was the central animating figure of my Christian college community. He was the primary subject of devotion, and he was also a familiar political organizing principle. I chose to major in theology and church history in order to learn more about Jesus because of an introductory "Christian Doctrine" course I took with Jonathan Wilson. After that course, Dr. Wilson became my only theology professor for the duration of my undergraduate major and my seminary master's degree. In one particular undergraduate class with Dr. Wilson, we read *The Way of Jesus Christ: Christology in Messianic Dimensions*. It was a Christology text by the German theologian Jürgen Moltmann, in which Moltmann links together who Jesus is (Christology) with what Jesus does (Christopraxis). In so doing, he claims that Jesus is the "one that will be," which is to say, the one from the future. He argued that Jesus did not have the status of messiah; it was something that he suffered. The title of messiah described the opening of a new future—a new reality—initiated in the midst of the present history, which is a cumulative story of sin, suffering, and death since the fall. Jesus suffered in the hands of that present history, which, unlike him, will end. The cross and the resurrection reveal the form of belief in the messiah; the content is determined by the account of his life, which provoked authorities to kill him.

Moltmann's reference to form includes the transformation that believers must undergo to follow after the messiah into the inaugurated, new reality—a fundamental change of situation from member of the present history to citizen of the next. The content is the norm offered by Jesus's life, which illustrates the future life for all of creation. Jesus demonstrates the new future, and as messiah he inaugurates it, opening it to the world by his death and resurrection. In Jesus the messiah, fallen and sinful history proclaims its end by killing the one who has no end, violently demonstrating that they have no place in the future. The hope for the world lies in the interpretation of the meaning of his resurrection, and the content of new life in this world is to be found in Christ's life as the One revealed as the future of the world.

I remember peering through this window into an interpretation of Jesus that moves beyond theoretical Chalcedonian orthodoxy about two natures in Christ. It also places the end of all things (eschatology) inside of a Christ-centered frame, and views salvation in Christ as inclusive of all of creation, not just human beings. For our purposes, I want to highlight at least two other points from that early read of Moltmann. First, Moltmann moves beyond the doctrinal language of Jesus as fully human and fully divine to describe Jesus simply as the future human. Second, the future that Christ signifies is also space introduced for followers to inhabit now, as the body of Christ (church), existing within the yet undisclosed reality initiated by Jesus's death and resurrection. Hence, with Jesus we have both representation of the future human and the moral substance of its communal life together.

This is a glimpse of what has remained with me from one of the many undergraduate courses with Dr. Wilson. I should add that Moltmann was careful to ground his Christology in the Jewish hope for the messiah, which establishes Jesus as Jewish. But in our United States context (in slavery's wake, and in the wake of postimperial Europe) within the continuing Western-world racial/racist discourse about human difference, any Christian connection to the Jewish messianic hope is porous. Even the messianic lineage, when viewed uncritically from inside of the Western Christian tradition, becomes instrumental for the project of human difference that establishes "human" as white man. What I am saying is this: in the wake of the slave trade, the terms "human" and "citizen" historically refer to white people. Without direct attention to this problem, we inevitably face a moral crisis with Jesus. If we do not pay attention to the ongoing Western project of racial hierarchy, Jesus who represents the fully human man from the future and, at the same time, the moral life, is illustrative of something much more nefarious than it appears as innocent in Moltmann's book.

What I am describing here is a Jesus who is rendered familiar, and thus safe, to racism. One who can be understood in part by Moltmann's description of the cosmic Christ, and is yet a divine advocate of the interests and efforts of Western political ecosystems. As the "one from the future" and the harbinger of the kingdom, Jesus becomes religious biopolitical technology for building race-based systems and structures for whites only.

The Familiar Jesus as a Christological Problem

This Jesus is the central animating figure of Western cultural and religious life. Without him, race as a working ideology of human difference would be impossible as J. Kameron Carter explains:

> The modern racializing of bodies in social space is unintelligible apart from how Christian identity was reimagined during the Enlightenment and how both the content and the disposition animating Christian theology shifted. Christianity was severed from its Jewish roots, lopped off from the people of Israel to facilitate Western conquest. Thus it came to pass that Christianity became the cultural-religious reflex of Western existence.

What this means is this: embedded within Christology—even what Moltmann offers—is a race question. As it pertains to the historical body of Jesus, he was a Jew. But, as it pertains to the idea of Jesus as a figure of Western imperial conquest, religion, and culture, he is a conceptual organizing figure of the Occident and Western property. He is a white man. The dualism serves to fashion white supremacy as a modern christological problem. It is a contemporary Gnosticism. The Jewish body is subordinated to a divine ideal: white men. Jesus is now located within a hierarchy of racial valuing that is calibrated by an idealized, template human, which is simultaneously signified as a white fetish of cultural longing. Christ, the figure of sacred devotion, is simultaneously a white biopolitical tool and a despised racial other. The history of Christ as a political figure is the history of engagement with this problem.

The Fetish of Human Difference

Thus Jesus, the one from the future, is an apparatus for making sense of local conversations about the communities we should all desire. Put differently: longing for Mayberry becomes a Christian virtue. Jesus is the image of the persons in, and the population of the community of, Mayberry. Yet, identifying Jesus as moral stranger to this arrangement of ideal community is the remedy we need.

Minoritized communities of faith are unfamiliar with the privileges that are historically afforded to the idealized, white, "human" citizen. Jesus's strangeness to the world of white supremacy is precisely the faith remedy that is needed. Jesus the foreigner, or Black Jesus; someone completely outside of the realm of white supremacist logic, betrays the lie in the so-called divine privileging of violence against Black and Brown people. The familiar Jesus renders Black people as pathological by aesthetic labels placed on bodies within a regime of representation that distinguishes between the pathological (Black as intrinsically ugly, criminal, licentious, and unintelligent) and the citizen (ideal community member). The pathological are the embodiment of sin in a world structured by the all-too-familiar Christ. Jesus as a familiar being, the one through whom all that exists is known, is the one with whom and by whom we know one another, and by whom our vision of *imago Dei* is cast. This Jesus who is familiar has been identified by minoritized intellectuals as one to expose and to problematize.

Familiar Christ is an idol, representing human difference as racial categories, and those racial categories as the precondition for white supremacy. There is no recognizing the work of God in the world, in Christ, without direct reference to the ascendant status of white men, and the rightly ordered world in subjection to him. He is not the crucified savior; indeed, his crucifixion is but an unmentionable instance in the story of one who is risen with all power. He was preached to the enslaved in the antebellum United States to facilitate the transition from Protestant supremacy over so-called pagan Africans, to Christian slavery when the enslaved were counted among the Christians.

W. E. B. Du Bois and the Stranger

In 1919, W. E. B. Du Bois was one of the many Black scholars of the emerging Harlem Renaissance who engaged the problem of Christ as representative of white ascendancy. He examined the ethical irony of race by imagining an aesthetically rendered Jewish Jesus in the twentieth century southern United States with a story. "Jesus Christ in Texas" is situated at the heart of a collection of essays entitled *Darkwater: Voices from within the Veil*. He places a narrative of Jesus in the center of that collection, as if to say that one cannot understand the Western world without knowledge of the central motivating role of a white hermeneutic of Jesus. The story entertains a question of Christology in the United States based on Jesus's embodied history; how would the Jewish messiah be received if he were to visit the racist United States of America today? In a racist nation that claims to be Christian, Du Bois depicted Jesus as a moral stranger.

From the start, the reader is meant to identify the invocation of a recent historical lynching: "It was in Waco, Texas." Readers should connect those words with Jessie Washington's 1906 lynching in Waco, Texas, which is a clear indication that this narrative will not end well.

The story is steeped in irony throughout as an ongoing dialectic between misrecognitions and recognitions from the very first encounter with Jesus. Readers enter the story in the middle of a misrecognition between a prison guard and the stranger. The guard is startled and compelled to defend himself by emphasizing the racial malfeasance of the subject they are discussing—a black prisoner. Like all white power brokers in the story, the prison guard misidentifies the stranger with whom he is conversing (i.e., Jesus). This common set of misrecognitions happens in spaces where they can't see his features.

White people routinely misidentify Middle Eastern people as Black in Du Bois's narratives, linking Black and Jewish historical oppressions together under the weight of the color line that subjects minoritized people to white-only power structures. Insistence on Jesus as white is apologetic for white power over everything related to heaven and earth. At the end of the initial encounter between the stranger and the white power brokers who open the story, the stranger and the dehumanized Black prisoner make eye contact in the dark. The prisoner recognizes him, even in the dark, and the stranger, Jesus, becomes the prisoner's liberation.

Du Bois brings the narrative to a high point in the home of a white main character who goes by a military title, "the colonel." He knows substantial financial gain from exploiting Black prisoners, and invites the stranger to his home on the strength of an unfamiliar need to justify himself. It's a twist on the story of Zacchaeus the tax collector who practiced repentance after encountering Jesus (Luke 19:1–9). Yet, instead of vowing to give back to those whom he has exploited, the colonel hosts a party for his accomplices within the white community that is organized by foundational practices of exploitation. It is a microcosm of historical imperial domination with the material gain from exploitation funding lavish wealth in the colonel's house. At a key moment, the stranger and his wife are engaged in dialogue when the wife calls for tea and turns on the light:

> They had hardly seen him well in the glooming twilight. The woman started in amazement and the colonel half rose in anger. Why, the man was a mulatto, surely; even if he did not own the Negro blood, *their practised eyes knew it*. He was tall and straight and the coat looked like a Jewish gabardine. His hair hung in close curls far down the sides of his face and his face was olive, even yellow.[1]

The stranger is Middle Eastern. He is a Jewish man. But within their racial register he is Black. Their "practised eyes" located his brown body within a hierarchy in a white regime of aesthetic representation. But Jesus the stranger defies racial logic. He is off the grid, and thus an offense. He is rendered Black, but his blackness is being unregulated by the logics of the racial hierarchy. It is being as blackness, and blackness as not a racial possession but, "wholly other." As people indebted to a religio-racial order, the characters in the story are compelled by urgency to arrest this wayward racial moment. The story ends with the stranger Jesus joining in the experience of an innocent Black man who is lynched by a mob. They are the victims of a hegemonic humanity, acting as a hegemonic community. Outside of the exclusivity of divine, white being, this community fails to see and to value life.

Conclusion

The only remedy is to focus our attention on places we wouldn't imagine ourselves needing to see. Jesus as unrecognizable to the logic of white supremacy, as wholly and completely other to the way we understand being in a racial world, untethers him from the project of Western racial

---

1. W. E. B. Du Bois, "Jesus Christ in Texas," Wikisource, last edited July 9, 2021, §126, https://en.wikisource.org/wiki/Darkwater/Jesus_Christ_in_Texas.

hegemony, allowing us to view the image of God in bodies recognized as subordinate in a hierarchy of human worth and value. If our interpretation of the future of God with us is to include an end to the history of white supremacy, our interpretation of Jesus must be a stranger to the present history of racist discourse. He cannot be a white man. The role of a Christian ethic for our time is to make Jesus strange again. If it weren't for my theological studies with Jonathan Wilson, I don't think I would have come to recognize that truth.

New Monasticism in Our Secular Age[1]

Tim Dickau

The restoration of the church will surely come from a new kind of monasticism, which will have nothing in common with the old but a life of uncompromising adherence to the Sermon on the Mount in imitation of Christ. I believe the time has come to rally people together for this.

—DIETRICH BONHOEFFER[2]

THE TERM "NEW MONASTICISM" appeared in Jonathan Wilson's short book, *Living Faithfully in a Fragmented World*,[3] where Jonathan affirms both Bonhoeffer and Alisdair MacIntyre's call for a new form of monasticism. In that book written in 1998, Jonathan reflects on the insights of Alisdair MacIntyre to explore some of the weakening markers of Western culture. These markers include a fragmentation of our worldview, a lack

---

1. This essay is reprinted by permission and adapted from Tim Dickau, *Forming Christian Communities in a Secular Age: Recovering Humility and Hope* (Toronto: Tyndale Academic, 2021), 162–79.

2. Cited in Jonathan Wilson-Hartgrove, "The Beatitudes in the Desert," in *Sermon on the Mount: Christian Reflection*, ed. Robert Kruschwitz, Christian Reflection (Waco, TX: Baylor University, 2008), 60–67, esp. 60.

3. Jonathan L. Wilson, *Living Faithfully in a Fragmented World: Lessons for the Church from MacIntyre's "After Virtue"* (Harrisburg, PA: Trinity, 1997).

of both historical identity as well as a future telos or goal, a retreat to the therapeutic in our personal lives, and an overreliance on management in our leadership roles. In response to these distortions, Jonathan calls for a new monasticism that will resist these misshaping forces of Western culture by taking up practices that have usually been associated with monasticism. In so doing, he draws upon Bonhoeffer's quotation above. Noting the decline of local communities that can help sustain such a disciplined moral life, he also quotes MacIntyre, who ended his book *After Virtue* by voicing a longing for "another . . . St. Benedict," someone in the present age who could lead another renewal of morality and civility through community.[4]

At the date of publication of Jonathan's monograph, few people had heard of the names Shane Claiborne and Jonathan Wilson-Hartgrove, but their names—and the new monasticism movement with which they are associated—have now become common vocabulary among those seeking the renewal of the church amidst our secular age. In 2004, Jonathan Wilson-Hartgrove (Jonathan's son-in-law) pulled together an event that is often named as the "birthing" of new monasticism[5] by gathering several existing communities from across the United States—including the Bruderhof (established in 1920), Koinonia Farm (established in 1947) and Reba Place Fellowship (established in 1957)—in Durham, North Carolina, for a weekend.[6] The twelve marks of the new monasticism emerged from the dialogue over the weekend together: 1) relocating to the "abandoned places of empire" (the margins of society); 2) sharing economic resources with fellow community members as well as the needy in our neighborhoods; 3) extending hospitality to strangers; 4) lamenting racial divisions within the church and our communities while also actively pursuing just reconciliation; 5) humbly submitting to Christ's body, the church; 6) intentionally being formed in the way of Christ and the rule of the community along the lines of the old novitiate; 7) nurturing common life among members of an intentional community; 8) supporting celibate singles alongside monogamous married couples and their children; 9)

---

4. Wilson, *Living Faithfully*, 68–69. The original quote comes from Alasdair MacIntyre, *After Virtue* (Notre Dame, IN: University of Notre Dame Press, 1981), 263.

5. While this gathering brought many communities together, some form of "new monasticism" was clearly percolating long before Jonathan Wilson coined the term.

6. For the description of this event, see The Rutba House, ed., *School(s) for Conversion: 12 Marks of a New Monasticism*, New Monastic Library: Resources for Radical Discipleship (Eugene, OR: Cascade, 2002).

living in geographical proximity with community members who share a common rule of life; 10) caring for the plot of God's earth and supporting local economies; 11) engaging in peacemaking in the midst of violence and resolving conflict within communities along the lines of Matt 18; 12) committing to a disciplined contemplative life.[7]

While I was working on my doctoral degree, I discovered that all twelve of these marks had been pursued and practiced in some way or another within our community at Grandview Calvary Baptist Church, where I had pastored over the previous two decades. Though we did not set out to become a "new monastic" church, we (along with many other church practitioners in the West) analyzed the powers and malformations in our culture and sought to respond to those forces in ways that were shaped by a vision of God's shalom. To put this another way, we were searching for ways that we could faithfully be the church amidst the particularities of our secular age.

When Jonathan came to teach at the institution where I was studying, it was starkly obvious to me that I had found my doctoral supervisor! Having read Jonathan's book on MacIntyre, I had found a lens for viewing our own two-decade journey as the formation of a monastic type of community.[8] As those of us in leadership at Grandview became aware of the proliferation of new monastic communities across North America, we realized just how many other people were also trying to find pathways of fidelity to God's kingdom within our secular culture and amidst misshaping powers (including but not limited to autonomy, consumerism, inequality, racism, and creational degradation). We also recognized that many of the "attractional" church models that focused primarily on the Sunday morning service would not survive amidst the pressures of our secular age. The social isolation from COVID-19 restrictions further exposed the weaknesses of these attractional models, within which cracks have been appearing for a long time.

---

7. For a full description of these marks, see Rutba House, *School(s) for Conversion*.

8. In my doctoral thesis, I investigated our church's movement towards the kingdom of God expressed in and through the practices of radical hospitality, integrated multicultural living, seeking justice for the least, and pursuit of deeper participation in the life of God. Since these practices are both means and ends towards the kingdom, they can be described as four trajectories as follows: 1) from isolation to community to radical hospitality; 2) from homogeneity to diversity to integrated multicultural living; 3) from charity to advocacy to seeking justice for the least; 4) from confronting idolatries to repentance to deeper life in Christ. See Tim Dickau, *Plunging into the Kingdom Way* (Eugene, OR: Wipf & Stock, 2010).

The Monastic Vision

Our turn towards monastic practices in this period of transition for the church in Western culture was clearly not altogether "new." Monasticism has played a renewing and sustaining role within the church and society during numerous fragile periods of history. Numerous theological historians have also charted how monasticism has sustained the church through transitional and chaotic times by forming and fostering a stable culture of contrast. While popular notions often degenerate monasticism to groups of people who are uninvolved in the world, Walter Capps argues that monasticism is actually the West's most enduring form of a counterculture that can impact society.[9]

As Christianity moved from a persecuted minority to a position of power in the third century, Antony of Egypt left the city for a solitary life of prayer in the desert, where he rejected wealth and battled his inner demons. He was the first of many Christian monastics—such as Benedict, Francis, Claire, Bernard of Clairvaux, and Ignatius (to name just a few)—who were concerned about how the church had become captive to the surrounding culture. These monastics believed that through prayer and ascetic practices, a revitalized church could come into being, and so they went on to develop a common life that held together rhythms of work, prayer, and service. This communal type of monasticism (known as cenobitic monasticism, as compared to eremitic monasticism, which focuses on the solitary life) has significantly shaped and revitalized the life of the church and society throughout the history of Christianity.

For example, Benedictine communities became centers of evangelism and discipleship as they multiplied throughout Europe during the second half of the first millennium. And when a new monastery was established in the middle of a town, its presence often led to the development of schools, hospitals, agricultural projects, and commerce. Moreover, monastics not only produced much of the church's meaningful theology following the collapse of the Roman Empire but also preserved and copied numerous texts from a wide variety of Greek and Latin writers that we would otherwise not have today. The various rules of life from different monastic communities revitalized the surrounding society by fostering the habits and virtues of humility, discipline, hospitality, compassion, and prayer among monks and nuns as well as other Christians.

---

9. For this argument, see Walter Capps, *The Monastic Impulse* (New York: Crossroad, 1983), 7–11.

The rule of St. Benedict dignified manual labor and embodied a written constitution and rule of law that incorporated democratic notions within a nondemocratic society.[10] The rhythms of work and prayer in the Benedictine order also led to the introductions of clocks and modern scheduling. During periods of decline or decay, monasticism helped to shape a counter-community that formed people in the image of Christ, who then went on to shape the wider culture.

For the Grandview community, three features of monastic practices have been particularly compelling. First, monasticism recognizes that *we need community in order to integrate and reform our desires.* Because we live in a world that is saturated with advertising, movies, and images that are constantly trying to shape our desires through narratives that are at odds with the gospel, we need to encourage one another as we seek to be formed in Christ and shaped by the biblical narrative. Moreover, we cannot merely *think* our way towards right action, and so we need to take up practices that will reshape our desires, form Christlike habits in our daily lives and cultivate biblical virtues within us. Second, *we need others to commit to participate with us* if we are going to sustain these practices and habits. When we do not feel like praying, forgiving, seeking justice, or caring for the creation, it is immensely encouraging to have others support us, hold us to account, and walk this road alongside us. Third, *smaller, local communities tend to be more nimble and adaptable* because they are connected to their neighbors, and so they can be more responsive to their immediate needs and less inclined to have inhibiting bureaucratic procedures. The adaptability of smaller and more local communities became especially apparent during the ongoing season of COVID restrictions.

While some may look back to the age of Christendom with fondness, bemoaning the disintegration of a cultural foundation that supported the pursuit of Christian practices and habits, Christ followers will need to become more intentional about the practices of formation instead. Jonathan Wilson-Hartgrove told me that when he talked to Christians across America, both liberals and conservatives, nearly everyone expressed how difficult it would be to live the way that Jesus taught us to live, particularly in the Sermon on the Mount. His statement indicates that we clearly need the support of a committed community to take up a gospel-designed life.

---

10. For further insights about how monasticism impacted the church and society throughout the first century, see Robert Louis Wilkens, *The First Thousand Years: A Global History of Christianity* (New Haven, CT: Yale University Press, 2013).

Towards Common Practices

The renewing force of old and new monasticism is its potential through which the Spirit reshapes our desires, which are formed by both our practices and our beliefs. Amy Plantinga Pauw argues, "As the Augustinian tradition insists, the link between belief and practice is forged by human desire and attitude. Both our cognitive and practical efforts arise out of our loves. Right beliefs are by themselves insufficient in shaping good practice."[11] Or, as Charles Taylor puts it, "the relation between practices and the background understanding behind them is therefore not one sided. If the understanding makes the practice possible, it is also true that it is the practice which largely carries the understanding."[12]

Since our behavior and thinking work together to shape our desires, L. Gregory Jones suggests that church congregations should view themselves as training grounds for reshaping our loves. He argues that "congregations ought to be settings for catechesis in which desires are shaped by faithful instruction and inquiry, prayer and worship, and other corporate practices that are constitutive of the church's life."[13] Bernard of Clairvaux illustrates how discipleship can mold our desires, noting how the practices of confession and repentance can redirect our desires so that God can embolden our passion for good. He writes, "Thus, anger, when controlled, becomes the vehicle of good zeal; pride brought low can be pressed into service in defense of justice.... If a strong sexuality is brought under control and disciplined by the practices of works of mercy, the very quarter whence people are exposed to the darts of wickedness becomes itself an incitement to solicitude for others."[14] Relying upon the philosophy of Pierre Bourdieu, who suggests that bodily practices impact our thinking, James Smith argues that embodied corporate worship is crucial if our desires are going to be aimed towards God and the kingdom

---

11. Amy Plantinga Pauw, "Attending to the Gaps between Beliefs and Practices," in *Practicing Theology: Beliefs and Practices in Christian Life*, ed. Miroslav Volf and Dorothy C. Bass (Grand Rapids: Eerdmans, 2002), 33–50, esp. 45.

12. Charles Taylor, *A Secular Age* (London: Oxford University Press, 2007).

13. L. Gregory Jones, "Beliefs, Desires, Practices and the Ends of Theological Education," in *Practicing Theology: Beliefs and Practices in Christian Life*, ed. Miroslav Volf and Dorothy C. Bass (Grand Rapids: Eerdmans, 2002), 185–205, esp. 202.

14. Bernard of Clairvaux, cited in Jean LeClerq, *Monks and Love in Twelfth Century France* (Oxford, UK: Clarendon, 1979), 16.

of God, particularly in light of the power we give to other "cultural liturgies" such as the mall or the academy.[15]

At Grandview, our community had come to realize that one hour of corporate worship each week is insufficient to help us resist the onslaught of advertising and messaging that we encounter each day from all these compelling cultural liturgies. Though our shared rhythms of prayer and work will differ from the Benedictine Hours (given the diverse parenting and work schedules within any congregation), many folks in our community believe that we need to share daily or regular common rhythms with others in order to reform our loves according to the way of Christ.

To give an example from Grandview, the practice of forming mutual relationships with those who have less has transformed our collective view about how the world works—mainly, how it does not operate justly for those at the bottom. This transformed realization has motivated our efforts in working for justice and our commitment to mutual hospitality with those who have less. It has also shaped our desires, beliefs, and practices. If we do not have any contexts when we can come alongside the poor as friends, and if we encounter the poor only through television and media, our social imaginaries may follow the cultural view of the poor among us as problems, as failed consumers, or as a "drain on the system" rather than as neighbors of great value, whom we are called to love and by whom we are called to receive love.

Prayer is a central practice in this process of transformation and a staple in the common practice of monastics throughout history. At Grandview, listening prayer (or contemplative prayer) has been central to reshaping our desires, because it displaces the incessant urgings of the self and advertising and replaces them with the urgings of God (during the short period of time in which we are silent). Prayer that helps us move beyond ourselves has taken many forms, including contemplation, meditation, charismatic utterance, intercession, listening, and confession.

Along with prayer, humility is a necessary virtue for cultivating and persevering in the monastic life. Contemplation draws us away from the self and towards God, helping us to remember our place as creatures who are dependent upon our Creator and Redeemer. In the seventh chapter of his rule, Benedict lays out twelve steps of humility.[16] I have been par-

---

15. James K. A. Smith, *Desiring the Kingdom: Worship, Worldview, and Cultural Formation* (Ada, MI: Baker, 2009), 67.

16. See Benedict of Nursia, *The Rule of St. Benedict*, ed. Timothy Fey (Collegeville, MN: Vintage, 1981), 16–20.

ticularly cognizant of step 2 as an aid in countering what Taylor describes as expressive individualism: "The second step of humility is that a man loves not his own will nor takes pleasure in the satisfaction of his desires; rather he shall imitate the Lord by his actions."[17] Or consider Ignatius of Loyola's teaching on the three types and levels of humility in his *Spiritual Exercises*: "The first is to humble myself to total obedience to God; the second is to be ready for honor or dishonor, poverty or wealth, or anything else for God; and the third is to desire poverty, dishonor, and even be a fool for God, since Christ was himself."[18] When we embrace this form of suffering, we prune away our self-centered, consumerist inclinations. Or as Julian of Norwich reminds us, humility begins with a reordering and prioritizing of our love towards God: "Any time we look at our Maker with love, our importance in our own eyes diminishes, and we are filled with awe and humility and love for others."[19] For Augustine, humility was the base virtue because it situates us properly before God in order to develop the other virtues and reflects the character of God.[20]

The reshaping of our desires and the cultivation of humility through disciplined engagement with monastic practices will require both time and patience. Yet the notion that these practices can only contribute to our personal formation *over time* runs contrary to the cultural belief that we can quickly alter our character through our own manipulations and will. In writing about the wisdom of Benedictine practices, Joan Chittister reflects on how hard it is for us to believe that the practices of prayer, Scripture reading, stability, poverty, and obedience will shape our lives in good time, over a much longer period than a weekend seminar.[21]

---

17. Benedict, *Rule*, 18.

18. Saint Ignatius of Loyola, *Personal Writings* (London: Penguin Classics, 1996), 325.

19. Ellyn Sanna, *All Shall Be Well: A Modern-Language Version of the Revelation of Julian of Norwich* (New York: Anamchara, 2016), 38.

20. "If you should ask me what are the ways of God, I would tell you that the first is humility, second is humility, third is humility. That there are no other precepts to give, but if humility does not precede all that we do, our efforts are fruitless." Augustine, letter 118, cited in Joseph J. McInerney, *The Greatness of Humility: St. Augustine on Moral Excellence* (Eugene, OR: Pickwick, 2016).

21. Joan Chittister, *Wisdom Distilled from the Daily: Living the Rule of St. Benedict Today* (San Francisco: HarperOne, 1991). Chittister maintains this argument throughout the book, but discusses it explicitly in the introduction.

Embracing Common Practices with Grace and Humility

Humility is key to transformation in the monastic vision in part because common practices are not a magical mechanism that will automatically renew us. They require grace to be transformational. To put it otherwise, common practices are not immune from sin. As Lauren Winner writes in her excellent book *The Danger of Christian Practices*, practices are not "pristine," but can be deformed in ways that are often characteristic of the practice itself.[22] Winner focuses on three rather disturbing historical examples: first, how the Eucharist encouraged violence against Jews based on rumors of them desecrating hosts in the Middle Ages; second, how intercessory prayer was distorted by slave-owning women in their prayers and journals in the nineteenth century; and third, how baptism morphed from a practice of the church to private spiritual acts in nineteenth-century christening parties. These historical examples are unsettling for any community that has made common practices a shared goal.

Yet we do not have to look far into our corporate and personal lives to acknowledge how our own practices are often deformed in ways that are reflective of the practices themselves. At Grandview, I have observed how our common meals can bind us together in ways that exclude others. I have also noticed how a sacrificial commitment to seeking justice can lead to burnout. And I have witnessed how shared practices of prayer can reduce our personal need to struggle with God. Developing common practices is no guarantee that our community will flourish. Whether or not these practices will be transformational depends upon the mercy and grace of God—and whether we remain open to the Spirit's leading, conviction, and prompting. Participating in shared practices can be a way of trying to wrest control away from God, thereby denying God's freedom, avoiding dependence upon God's grace and eventually practicing a form of idolatry.

I want to state that we do not need to despair about the corruptibility of common practices. Winner does not dismiss practices but acknowledges that they are important for the formation of our personal and common life. However, it is vital that we remain alert to the ways that practices can be deformed. To review our common practices as a community, we invite other communities to assess our health, talk with our neighbors about their experience of our community (i.e., asking those who do not experience our community as hospitable to share why they

---

22. See Lauren Winner, *The Dangers of Christian Practice: On Wayward Gifts, Characteristic Damage, and Sin* (New Haven, CT: Yale University Press, 2018).

feel this way), and continue to grapple with the problems in our cities and world, which keeps us from fixating on our own formation. These checks and balances prevent us from writing our own narratives apart from the input of others and assess whether our practices are transforming us and the space around us.

Towards a Deeper Shared Life and a Wider Engagement with Place

In 2015, some people in the Grandview community, including Jonathan and myself, brought together over thirty people who were part of communities that associated themselves in some way with new monasticism, including Sojourners, the Bruderhof, Englewood, 24-7 Prayer, Reba Place, Northumbria, and other communities across North America and Australia. Interestingly, many of the people who came to this gathering had also been present almost ten years earlier at the gathering in Durham, North Carolina, and had helped to discern the "twelve marks of new monasticism."

We gathered for three days at the scenic Rivendell retreat center on top of beautiful Bowen Island off the coast of Vancouver. There we assessed the current state of new monasticism and explored how we might seek to expand and deepen its influence within the church. At the beginning of the consultation, we sought to understand the history of monasticism by learning about the origins of new monasticism and the connections between old and new monasticism from Jonathan Wilson and Charles Ringma.

Then David Janzen, who had been living into this vision as part of the Reba Place community in Chicago for many years, reflected on his experience of visiting and listening to numerous new monastic communities across North America over the previous years as part of the Nurturing Communities Project. He presented a graph with the shared life of a community on one side and its engagement with the neighborhood and city on another and then shared two observations. First, he said that many communities had a very minimal conception of common practices and, as a result, were unlikely to experience or contribute towards significant transformation in either their communities or neighborhoods. These communities fell in the lower quadrant of both axes. Second, he said that those who were higher in the shared life axis were often minimally engaged in seeking to transform their surrounding neighborhoods. Based on the maturing of his own community at Reba Place, Janzen proposed that we aim for the top corner of the graph, where we seek to develop *both* a deeper shared life *and* a wider engagement with our surroundings. Monastic practices should make us better neighbors—not more withdrawn. As many people at Grandview have sought to pursue a new monastic vision, which is held at the core of our church's mission, we have become more and more aware of the danger of being overly focused upon our own formation and so neglecting the great command in the process.

Forming Communities of Stability and Flexibility

While the twelve markers of new monasticism overlap with the traditional monastic vows of celibacy, poverty, and obedience among communities such as the Benedictines, Cistercians, and Franciscans, leadership in new monastic communities tends to be communal rather than hierarchical. A flatter leadership structure obviously has both strengths and weaknesses. Many new monastic communities are struggling to figure out how authority functions within their communities, and many also lack accountability to a larger governing body (a feature that was in place for older monastic communities). Our community has explored how we might develop a formal lay order, but we have not been able to turn the corner and begin this association of committed disciples. Some of the challenges that I have observed in trying to develop a lay order include developing an authority structure that reflects the order's relationship to the church and to the "scattered seeds" (those whom we have sent from our community to other contexts) along with how to respond to the differing degrees of commitment that people bring to the rule of life. Our community is not alone among new monastic communities who are trying to figure out authority structures and leadership roles. It is not surprising that two factors that raise questions about how new monastic communities will endure over the long haul include the lack of accountability along with confusion surrounding authority.[23]

In our story, the practice of stability has been essential to long-range community development and our pursuit of systemic change. One factor that has added durability to our community is how all the households

---

23. Jonathan Wilson-Hartgrove presents a convincing case for stability in *The Wisdom of Stability: Rooting Faith in a Mobile Culture* (Cape Cod, MA: Paraclete, 2010).

and groups of people who are living in geographic proximity have been held within the larger body of Grandview Church. This has allowed both some fluidity in the houses where individuals discern a call elsewhere while maintaining the stability for those remaining as others from the church are ready to move in. One example came from a house where three women moved out of the city for educational and vocational callings. Rather than disbanding with a sense of failure and guilt—which we have seen in other isolated community ventures in Vancouver—the women from the house felt free to pursue their callings while new people emerged to participate in a common vision for the house. Moreover, the church provides an overarching vision and set of practice that many households and neighbors have been able to participate in together so that each household does not have to make everything up from scratch.

The practice of stability raises further questions about the extent to which new monastic communities may eventually become institutionalized.[24] As older monastic traditions have become institutionalized, they have carried forward gains in ethics and justice for future generations. While each new generation needs to embrace their renewal in Christ personally, religious institutions have integrated and carried forward discipleship, worship liturgies, resources for healing and reconciliation, and approaches for prayer. While some creative communities may be inclined to "do everything new," they often fail to glean from the wisdom and traditions of institutions throughout history.

One advantage of older monastic communities is the way their institutional strength and longevity empowers them to envision long-term projects and plans. I witnessed this reality on two recent visits to monasteries. At St. John's Abbey in Minnesota, I learned about the Benedictines' massive plan to digitalize all the religious texts in the world, which has taken them into libraries, cathedrals, temples, homes, and caves around the globe. And at the Ignatius Jesuit Center outside of Guelph, Ontario, I saw how they were taking on a five-hundred-year plan to cultivate an old-growth forest to revitalize the land and forests on the five hundred acres surrounding their retreat center. It is difficult to imagine most new monastic communities—who often struggle to plan beyond a year or two—taking on projects with such a vast scope.

---

24. Hodgson defines institutions as "integrated systems of rules that structure social interaction." See Geoffrey Hodgson, "On Defining Institutions: Rules versus Equilibria," *Journal of Institutional Economics* 11 (2015): 497–505.

Towards Humility Rooted in Transcendent Hope

Towards the end of our new monastic consultation at Rivendell in 2015, we shifted our focus towards the future, curious about how we could retain the marks of new monasticism—especially the commitment to abandoned places of the empire—while also extending the practices of monasticism into the daily life of young families, those with demanding jobs and those who worked in different sectors of society, such as the marketplace and educational institutions. We asked how we might form distinct communities that also interacted deeply with our neighborhoods. We wondered together what sorts of new writing projects might resource a burgeoning number of new monastic communities in the North America. We deliberated on all these questions because we had one common hope: *that new monasticism would not fizzle out like so many other movements within the life of the church, but that it would have an abiding influence that would continue to renew Christian communities amidst our secular age.*

When it comes to the ecclesial structures required to implement this mission, I defer to Rowan Williams, who commended what he described as the "mixed economy of the church." Williams first used this term during a talk in South Wales around 2000,[25] referring to the way that both "fresh expressions" (a relational and dynamic initiative based on a theological vision) and inherited forms of the church could exist alongside each other and with mutual respect for one another within the same denomination. I think Williams's metaphor of the "mixed economy of the church" captures our need for renewed expressions of Christian community amidst our secular age. However, these experimental expressions of Christian community will need to be much more closely connected to the more institutional expressions of church in contrast to the marginal (and sometimes hostile) relationships that existed between ecclesial institutions and the "parachurch" organizations that proliferated during the modernist era, so that we can recover local expressions of creative initiatives while also reconnecting the church with the *missio Dei*.

---

25. See Rowan Williams, "Making the Mixed Economy Work," Rowan Williams (blog), May 6, 2011, http://rowanwilliams.archbishopofcanterbury.org/articles.php/2044/making-the-mixed-economy-work.html.

New Monasticism and the Flourishing of Democracy

Cultivating virtues is essential not only for our personal and community formation and flourishing but also for the formation and flourishing of our democratic society. This pursuit is not only about recovering the vocation of the church, but also about recovering our human vocation so that our entire world can flourish. In *Christ and the Common Life*, Luke Bretherton identifies two gifts that a church's pursuit of common monastic practices offers to society.[26] These churches can model covenantal rather than contractual relationships in communities. Bretherton identifies these covenantal forms—between people and people, corporations and people, people and the state—as integral to sustaining democracy. The effort to sustain covenantal church communities not only responds with gratitude to God, but also bears witness to political structures that God values.[27]

To give the last word to Jonathan, the covenantal community "is a new humanity created by God's power. This creation stands as a witness against the postmodern conviction that we are trapped in our communities and in the differences that mark us. Apart from God's grace, the human condition is marked ineradicably by difference and violence. By God's grace, we are made one new humanity by the peaceableness of hope."[28]

---

26. Luke Bretherton, *Christ and the Common Life* (Grand Rapids: Eerdmans, 2019), 333.

27. Bretherton, *Christ and Common Life*, 337.

28. Jonathan R. Wilson, *Gospel Virtues: Practicing Faith, Hope, and Love in Uncertain Times* (Downers Grove, IL: InterVarsity, 1998), 114.

Living Faithfully in a Neoliberal Age?

From Market Rationality to Neo-Monasticism

Andrew Shepherd

IN HIS INFLUENTIAL WORK *After Virtue*, Scottish-American moral philosopher Alasdair MacIntyre contends that the failure of the Enlightenment project to provide a secure, shared foundation for morality means that late-modernity is "fragmented" and characterized by a culture of "emotivism." In Western societies we now live in a culture in which three archetypal characters—the Rich Aesthete, the Therapist, and the Manager—provide people "with a cultural and moral ideal" that "morally legitimates a mode of social existence."[1] MacIntyre concludes the book by drawing a likeness between the collapse of the Roman Empire and the present day. In cryptic closing lines he intimates that the fundamental problem contemporary Western civilization faces is not that of Visigoths or Vandals waiting to sack cities, but rather an intellectual incoherence and thus moral barbarism that sow the seeds of civil and social disintegration. MacIntyre sees the development of the Benedictine monastic rule in the early sixth century as an attempt to construct "new forms of community within which the moral life could be sustained so that both morality and civility might survive the coming ages of barbarism and

---

1. Alasdair MacIntyre, *After Virtue* (London: Bloomsbury, 213), 40.

darkness."[2] To respond to the loss of a shared moral logic, MacIntyre looks expectantly for the emergence of a new St. Benedict-like character.

In *Living Faithfully in a Fragmented World: Lessons for the Church from MacIntyre's "After Virtue"* (1997), Jonathan R. Wilson offers a concise summary and sympathetic engagement with MacIntyre's work. In the second edition, with a new subtitle,[3] Wilson suggests that the contemporary emergence of the phenomenon of neo-monasticism[4] within the evangelical stream of the Western church can potentially be perceived as the St. Benedict-like characters MacIntyre hopes for. Wilson enthusiastically promotes the significance of this new ecclesiological phenomenon, stating categorically: "In the wake of the failure of the Enlightenment project and the rise of emotivist morality, the development of new monastic communities is essential to the faithfulness of the church."[5]

Like Wilson, I think there is significant explanatory power to MacIntyre's persuasive argument that Western civilization is morally fragmented and characterized by a culture of "emotivism."[6] I also share Wilson's proclivity to see neo-monastic communities as hopeful responses of "faithful living" with the potential to inspire and enable the church's witness within Western culture.[7] However, while sympathetic, in what

2. MacIntyre, *After Virtue*, 227.

3. Jonathan R. Wilson, *Living Faithfully in a Fragmented World: From "After Virtue" to a New Monasticism*, 2nd ed., New Monastic Library: Resources for Radical Discipleship (Eugene, OR: Cascade, 2010).

4. Whether monastic-like communities that arose during the twentieth century (the Bruderhof—1920s; Taizé and Iona—1940s; Northumbria—1970s) are understood as expressions of neo-monasticism depends on the scope of one's definition. Here, I understand neo-monasticism as a phenomenon that has emerged within Western Evangelicalism during the last quarter century. All movements require founding texts: in this case, The Rutba House, ed., *School(s) for Conversion: 12 Marks of a New Monasticism*, New Monastic Library: Resources for Radical Discipleship (Eugene, OR: Cascade, 2005).

5. Wilson, *Living Faithfully*, 27.

6. The loss of a shared moral rationality, civil fragmentation, and the triumph of a Nietzschean "will to power" morality are perhaps no more clearly illustrated than in the current state of politics and civil discourse in the United States.

7. Neo-monastic communities and movements can be identified in a range of countries, including the United States of America, Canada, the United Kingdom, Australia, and New Zealand. A number of these communities tell their stories in books published as part of the New Monastic Library series published by Cascade. A personal biographical note here is also appropriate. I have long association with neo-monastic-like communities, having spent five years living in an ecumenical Christian community—Kodesh—and more recently, at Ngatiawa River Monastery, the "spiritual

follows, I will critically interrogate this confidence in neo-monasticism. I will contend that while at a theoretical level MacIntyre's thesis of moral fragmentation holds, there is nonetheless a prevailing rationality and moral vision that exists within late-modern Western societies: that is, the rationality of the market and the moral vision of neoliberal capitalism. Further, I will argue that while the phenomenon of neo-monasticism may be interpreted as an example of "faithful witness," concurrently it can also be taken as a manifestation of this prevailing moral logic of neoliberalism.

Central to Wilson's argument in *Living Faithfully* is the contention that to live faithfully in a time of fragmentation it is necessary for the church to disentangle itself from the culture in which it finds itself. Wilson states emphatically: "If my critique of the life of the church in Western culture has validity, then the only way for the church to recover faithful living is for the church to disentangle its life from the culture."[8] Here, Wilson appears to both acknowledge that the church is embedded in and shaped by its historical and cultural location, and at the same time, to point to some sort of "ideal" church; a "pure" sociality that somehow exists separately and distinct from the cultural reality in which it emerges. For Wilson, neo-monasticism potentially carries this second characteristic. He writes: "To think of new monasticism as an ideology is to misconstrue new monasticism as a phenomenon generated by this age."[9] Wilson's assertion here seems to be based on an attempt to draw a direct lineage between ancient monasticism and the emergence of the recent phenomenon of neo-monasticism. But can such a straight line between ancient and contemporary neo-monasticism really be drawn? Can a "pure" church or pure "faith" really exist?[10] And, most significant for my argument, is it really credible to construe neo-monasticism as a movement with a historical lineage to the ancient monastic tradition but also to suggest that this phenomenon is somehow "pure" and not

---

home" of the self-designated neo-monastic movement Urban Vision.

8. Wilson, *Living Faithfully*, 59.

9. Wilson, *Living Faithfully*, 65.

10. To believe so runs counter to the Christian doctrine of the incarnation—that God, in Christ, enters the reality of the human cultural experience. Ultimately, I suspect that Wilson would agree with me that there is a concerning element of naïve ahistoricism to his claim that "new monasticism" is somehow not a "phenomenon generated by this age."

"generated" by the cultural milieu of early twenty-first-century neoliberal global capitalism in which it has arisen?

In what follows I will contend that neo-monasticism has not emerged out of "nowhere" but rather is a phenomenon that has emerged through the convergence of the cultural fields of neoliberalism and contemporary Western Evangelicalism.

Neoliberalism as Moral Vision

In *After Virtue* Alasdair MacIntyre suggests that the failure of the Enlightenment project to provide a secure shared foundation for morality means that late Western modernity is now characterized by moral fragmentation and a culture of emotivism. But is the contemporary world really as morally fragmented as MacIntyre and, following him, Wilson, believe?

In 1981, the year *After Virtue* was published, Western liberal democracies commenced a process that would transform their political economies and their societies. Influenced by the thinking of the Chicago school of economics, respective governments in the United States, the United Kingdom, and soon after, New Zealand, began to roll out neoliberal economic policies. "Reaganomics," "Thatchernomics," and "down-under" in Aotearoa/New Zealand, "Rogernomics" involved the corporatization of the public sector, the selling of state assets, and deregulation and privatization. These policies and practices brought massive changes to the economic, social, political, cultural, and, I would contend, also to the moral landscape.

Scholars have used a number of lenses—economic, political, social, cultural—in their attempt to give a substantive account of the power of "neoliberalism" and its transformation of the world during the last four decades. Increasingly, theorists are suggesting that the best way to understand "neoliberalism" is not primarily as a set of economic doctrines, practices, or policies, but rather as a metaphysical/religious moral vision. Arguably, while the Enlightenment project may have failed in its quest for a shared rationality for morality, *contra* MacIntyre, there does still exist a shared rationality or logic that shapes the moral imagination of Western culture—this is the moral vision that undergirds neoliberal capitalism.[11]

---

11. Recent substantive accounts that reflect on how neoliberalism functions as a moral vision include: Wendy Brown, *Undoing the Demos: Neoliberalism's Stealth Revolution* (New York: Zone, 2015), and Adam Kostko, *Neoliberalism's Demons: On the Political Theology of Late Capital* (Stanford, CA: Stanford University Press, 2018).

In an interview on her book *Undoing the Demos*, Wendy Brown succinctly describes the reigning moral logic of neoliberalism.

> I treat neoliberalism as a governing rationality through which everything is "economized" and in a very specific way: human beings become market actors and nothing but, every field of activity is seen as a market, and every entity (whether public or private, whether person, business, or state) is governed as a firm. Importantly, this is not simply a matter of extending commodification and monetization everywhere. . . . Neoliberalism construes even non-wealth generating spheres—such as learning, dating, or exercising in market terms, submits them to market metrics, and governs them with market techniques and practices.[12]

With neoliberal capitalism having conquered the globe, this economistic mode of envisioning the world is the "air that we breathe"; it is the *zeitgeist* of the early twenty-first century. It is my contention that this governing rationality of neoliberalism extends too to religious faith. That neo-monasticism can be understood as generated by this market logic becomes clearer as we reflect more deeply on the relationship between neo-monasticism and the broader cultural field of Evangelicalism in which it is situated.

Neo-Monasticism and Evangelicalism

In *New Monasticism and the Transformation of American Evangelicalism*, Wes Markofski, using the field-theory of Pierre Bourdieu, delineates how the identity of neo-monasticism, as with other phenomenon of the "evangelical left," is constructed by its relationship with other agents within the North American evangelical field. As with the phenomenon of the

---

A common argument offered by academic economists that the term "neoliberalism" operates merely as a political slur, a shibboleth employed by "left-wing" academics with no understanding of economics and is therefore devoid of any analytical power, has been undercut somewhat by the admission by three senior economists at the conservative and cautious institution of the International Monetary Fund (IMF) that a "neoliberal" agenda does exist. See Jonathan D. Ostry et al., "Neoliberalism: Oversold?," *Finance & Development* 53 (2016) n.p., https://www.imf.org/external/pubs/ft/fandd/2016/06/ostry.htm.

12. Timothy Shenk, "Booked #3: What Exactly Is Neoliberalism?," *Dissent*, Apr. 2, 2015, https://www.dissentmagazine.org/blog/booked-3-what-exactly-is-neoliberalism-wendy-brown-undoing-the-demos.

"emerging church," neo-monasticism "was born out of opposition"[13] to the dominant agents within North American Evangelicalism—the Christian right/conservative Evangelicalism and megachurch Evangelicalism. Markofski writes:

> The language of monasticism itself symbolizes reaction, negation, and opposition to the dominant religious, social, and political positions of the day. It is impossible to explain the neo-monastic point of view without reference to the social-historical field of American evangelicalism and the dominant positions against which its own religious and political standpoints are constructed.[14]

Markofski observes a relationship between the phenomenon of neo-monasticism and its emergence within a context shaped by the governing rationality of neoliberal capitalism. He writes:

> America's disestablishment of religion has promoted a culture of religious pluralism, voluntarism, and free-market competition in the religious field, where the competition between religious institutions for new adherents bears some resemblance to the competition between business institutions for new consumers. American evangelicalism in particular, is an exemplary case of the American religious model of religious pluralism, competition and choice.[15]

Contemporary Evangelicalism is characterized by ahistorical, "return to origins" tropes,[16] a pragmatism that is always innovating and employing new cultural methods for "communication of the gospel," and a theology-spirituality that emphasizes the voluntaristic choice of the individual. Such characteristics, embedded within a broader social-cultural field shaped by the moral vision of neoliberalism, provides fertile ground for the rise of "new" expressions of Christianity. "Seeker-friendly

---

13. Wes Markofski, *New Monasticism and the Transformation of American Evangelicalism* (Oxford, UK: Oxford University Press, 2015), 114. The work of Markofski and other substantive ethnographic research, including James S. Bielo, *Emerging Evangelicals: Faith, Modernity, and the Desire for Authenticity* (New York: New York University Press, 2011), should put to rest the pervasive mistaken notion of North American Evangelicalism as a monolithic entity.

14. Markofski, *New Monasticism*, 122.

15. Markofski, *New Monasticism*, 135.

16. Markofski, *New Monasticism*, 115, quoting from James S. Bielo, *Emerging Evangelicals*.

services" of evangelical megachurches and the "alternative worship" experiences of the "emerging church" can be understood as being rooted in the "aesthetic" and "therapeutic" impulse that typifies the prevailing moral culture of emotivism.[17] Even while identifying itself in "opposition" to these other expressions of contemporary Evangelicalism, the phenomenon of neo-monasticism can itself also be interpreted as a new form of religious *choice*.

There are interesting parallels here between "neo-monasticism" and "neoliberalism." The shared prefix of both terms is indicative of the way in which these phenomena seek to locate themselves as the inheritors of a tradition. Yet, as Wendy Brown notes, the relationship between neoliberalism and classic liberalism is less about continuity with an existing tradition but rather, following Foucault, she suggests neoliberalism is a "reprogramming of liberalism."[18] Likewise, while "neo-monasticism" may seek to cast itself as in continuity with historical monasticism, the extent to which this truly is the case is debatable. Markofski's observation, that those participating within the phenomenon of "emerging church" and "new-monasticism" are "overwhelmingly white, well-educated, 'solidly middle class' young adults under the age of 40," is significant.[19] The capacity for choice and the ability to self-direct one's own life are features that this demographic still possesses, even as these choices themselves are dictated by market forces. Is neo-monasticism simply a commodity, a lifestyle chosen by those who are disillusioned and/or disenfranchised by broader Evangelicalism, but who, at least at this stage, are unprepared to leave this tributary of Christianity completely?[20]

---

17. Wilson also sees these contemporary forms of Evangelicalism as generated by the aesthetic and therapeutic impulses of a culture of "emotivism." See ch. 3 of *Living Faithfully*.

18. Shenk, "Booked #3."

19. Markofski, *New Monasticism*, 107.

20. Those disillusioned and disenfranchised by contemporary Evangelicalism could join any number of already extant "third-order" movements endorsed by the Catholic, Anglican, and Lutheran churches. What prevents disenfranchised Evangelicals from embracing other traditions of Christianity is an important question, but one beyond the scope of this discussion.

Neo-Monasticism as *Technique*

The argument I am putting forward here, that neo-monasticism may have stronger genealogical affinities to the emotivist culture of limitless choices generated by the rationality of the market than to the tradition of historic monasticism, can be illustrated further by briefly reflecting upon two examples of the neo-monastic phenomenon: Urban Vision in Aotearoa/New Zealand and the internationalized Order of Mission, and the associated 3D Movements (3DM) programme, established by Mike Breen.[21] In what follows I will reflect upon the way in which Brown's understanding of "market terms," "market metrics," and "market techniques and practices" are evidenced in the structure, identity, and mode of being of these expressions of neo-monasticism.

While sharing traits similar to North American Evangelicalism, the evangelical church within Aotearoa/New Zealand also has notable differences. Expressions of contemporary Evangelicalism present in the North American context—conservative Evangelicalism; megachurch Evangelicalism; emergent church; neo-monasticism—all exist within New Zealand, but there is also much greater overlap and blurring of these movements. In the larger marketplace in North America, as Markofski observes, entrepreneurial evangelical Christian leaders seek to claim territory within this contested field and then often employ a strong "oppositional" identity as a way to create market differentiation. In the smaller field of New Zealand Christianity, the evangelical stream is characterized by strong relational connections, and contestation and territory claiming are less polarized. However, similar to elsewhere, Evangelicalism "down-under" is characterized by a high degree of pragmatism, innovation, and activism, and the associating corollaries of anti-intellectualism and a general lack of knowledge about, or entire disregarding of, the church's tradition.

The Urban Vision movement has its origins in the mid-1990s, when Justin and Jenny Duckworth, leaders in the interdenominational youth organization Youth for Christ, formed intentional households of young people living in "marginalized" neighborhoods.[22] Later, as the term "neo-

21. For Urban Vision and the Mission Order, see: https://urbanvisionaotearoa.org and https://www.missionorder.org.
 For the 3DM movements and 3DM resources, see: https://www.3dmovements.com and https://www.3dmpublishing.com.
22. See the autobiographical recounting of this story in Jenny and Justin Duckworth, *Against the Tide, Towards the Kingdom*, New Monastic Library: Resources for Radical Discipleship (Eugene, OR: Cascade, 2011).

monastic" came into currency, Urban Vision came to self-identify as a neo-monastic movement. The evolution of this movement reached a key moment in 2008 when Urban Vision chose to become a "missionary order" in covenant with Te Hāhi Mihinare, the Anglican Church in Aotearoa/New Zealand and Polynesia. The "participatory," "communitarian," "egalitarian" nature of neo-monasticism, observed by Markofski in North American neo-monasticism and common to the phenomenon elsewhere, has gradually given way to a more highly structured and controlled entity. Urban Vision as an "apostolic order" now has a clearly defined structure that distinguishes between "companions" who have undergone a three-year "formation" and signed up to a covenant; those undergoing this "formation" process; and the "last, the lost and the least" whom the movement prioritizes as their focus.

Urban Vision understands its structure as a contemporary manifestation of historic monasticism—in which experienced leaders—"abbots," as it were—lead novices through a process of formation to learn to adhere to a rule of life. While this structure seeks to imitate the structure of ancient monasticism there is also a striking resemblance to contemporary corporate structures. A senior management—composed of the original founders and senior leaders—sets vision and ethos and this is then outworked by middle-management—team-leaders—who oversee the "formation" of new members and ensure adherence to the ethos and an obedience in outworking of the vision. This is in contrast to the ancient monasticism of the Rule of Saint Benedict, where the Rule takes precedence and is safeguarded and applied by an abbot chosen by the monks. The abbot has authority but is directed by the Rule to take counsel with all the monks and to care for each one.[23]

Nor is this corporate-like character seen only in organizational structure. Fundamental to the movement is the importance given to a shared vocabulary. Many involved appear unaware of the extent to which the shared vocabulary draws heavily on contemporary "corporate-speak" and management theory.[24] This recent employment of management-

23. Benedict, *The Holy Rule of St. Benedict*, trans. Rev. Boniface Verheyen (Atchison, KS: Abbey Student Press, 1949), https://documentacatholicaomnia.eu/03d/04800547,_Benedictus_Nursinus,_Regola,_EN.pdf.

24. Within Urban Vision, the phrase "leaning in," used as an encouragement for greater commitment and effort, is drawn from the philosophy of life popularized by Facebook Chief Operating Officer Sheryl Sandberg's 2013 book, *Lean In: Women, Work, and the Will to Lead* (New York: Knopf, 2013). Sandberg's philosophy argues that, if they work hard enough, women can "have it all"—family, career, and happiness.

speak is in contrast to Markofski's observation of North America neo-monastic communities between 2006–2011, where "Urban Monastery participants and other neo-monastic and emerging evangelicals . . . strongly prefer relational, familial, and organic linguistic metaphors and strategies of action to business and marketing ones."[25]

Likewise, the nature and content of the "formation" process has strong corporate-like resonances. Formation utilizes a mixture of in-house teaching from the founders and senior companions of Urban Vision and also relies heavily on a "shared vocabulary" and tools drawn from the material of 3DM ministries.[26] The tools for "creating disciples" (that is, moral formation) consist of a series of geometric shapes. These "LifeShapes" are essentially basic self-organization and people-management concepts which, in a classic example of eisegesis, become principles extrapolated from biblical passages. Small "huddles" of people then utilize these "LifeShapes" as models for their intentional accountable relationships, with the aim of deepening personal faith, community life, and mission effectiveness. In contrast to the development of rich and creative liturgy and music, which feature in the shared life of prayer and worship of Urban Vision,[27] the prescribed "formation" process is strikingly shallow and formulaic. It is marked by uniformity and an absence of theological, biblical, and historical depth; and befitting Evangelicalism, it displays a strong attraction to *technique.*

The book received adulation and also trenchant critique. That the imperative/encouragement to "lean in" can intentionally be used to coerce or manipulate or unintentionally apply psychological and emotional pressure should be self-apparent. This is particularly the case within intentional communities with already high expectations on participant commitment.

Another key phrase widely used in Urban Vision is that of the principle of "the hedgehog"—understood as the need to focus on just one key thing—drawn from Jim Collins's *Good to Great: Why Some Companies Make the Leap. and Others Don't* (San Francisco: HarperCollins, 2001). Collins, as is often the case in business-corporate management books, "bastardizes" a philosophical concept, removing it from its context and tradition and utilizing it for purposes seemingly contrary to the original idea. In this case, the "hedgehog" principle is drawn from Isaiah Berlin's essay, *The Hedgehog and the Fox: An Essay on Tolstoy's View of History* (London: Weidenfeld & Nicolson, 1953).

25. Markofski, *New Monasticism*, 90.

26. See https://www.3dmpublishing.com.

27. The movement's liturgical worship draws on material and songs from *A New Zealand Prayer Book / He Karakia Mihinare o Aotearoa* and other neo-monastic movements such as Taizé, Iona, Northumbria, and also elements composed by Urban Vision members.

What do I mean by *technique*? Moral formation is intrinsically a complex activity involving contingency and uncertainty as a diversity of people with different backgrounds, personalities, giftings, passions, desires, and brokenness learn the practices and narratives of a tradition and over time are formed into a community faithful to this tradition. However, in the logic of market rationality, *efficiency* and *growth* are imperative. Accordingly, there arises the temptation for moral formation to be reduced to a bureaucratic uniform technique that seeks to ensure a guaranteed secure outcome and thus a return on one's investment of precious time and effort.[28] Shaped by the prevailing logic of neoliberalism, neo-monasticism thus becomes construed as a "technique" able to be utilized in multiple contexts, with the assumption being that application of this "technique" will lead to "success." Indeed, Urban Vision's choice to utilize the 3DM "tools" as formational material is itself a striking example of the interpretation of neo-monasticism I am advancing here. A brief genealogy of 3DMovements is revealing: the "rediscovery" and encouragement of "intentional missional communities" in St. Thomas' Church, Crookes, Sheffield, United Kingdom, an Anglican-Baptist local ecumenical partnership in the 1990s; the establishment of a monastic order by the senior rector, Mike Breen; and then the subsequent conversion of this mode of existence into a set of techniques and a model, franchisable and able to be replicated elsewhere around the world.[29]

The evolution from a fluid, organic movement to highly structured, more formulaic order is a transition common to earlier historical monastic movements and to human organizations in general. What is striking is the extent to which this structural transition within Urban Vision has involved a seemingly uncritical adoption of corporate management structures, theory and language, and the appeal of *technique*. Here, one is brought back to MacIntyre's prescience in *After Virtue* where MacIntyre offers a strident critique of the way in which "managerial effectiveness"—based on the so-called neutrality of social science—not only lends itself

---

28. This attempt to secure the future, to guarantee a successful outcome and a return on one's investment—symptomatic of market rationality—runs counter to the biblical understanding that the development and growth of the kingdom of God is a mystery outside of our control. See Mark 4:26–29.

29. To quote the 3DMovements website: "The leaders and people of St. Thomas' began learning how to live more like Jesus and connect with their unbelieving friends outside the walls of the church. *They developed tools and vehicles that allowed them to train others in this Jesus-shaped way of life, so they could in turn pass it on to others.*" https://www.3dmovements.com/where-we-came-from (emphasis added).

to the "dominance of the manipulative mode in our culture" but is itself based on the "moral fiction" that somehow the manager can control outcomes. Whether seeking to control individual or communal moral formation, derive a preferred social outcome, or employ a technique for successful church growth, MacIntyre reminds us that such "belief in managerial expertise is . . . one more illusion and a peculiarly modern one, the illusion of a power not ourselves that claims to make for righteousness."[30]

Conclusion

Confronting the reality of a fragmenting culture, Wilson optimistically suggests that the contemporary phenomenon of neo-monasticism may offer an embodied vision of faithfulness for the Western evangelical church. While sympathetic, I am less confident. I have argued that it is problematic to simply interpret and endorse neo-monasticism as a contemporary expression of ancient monasticism. Rather, it is more plausible to interpret neo-monasticism as a phenomenon that emerges when the entrepreneurial and innovative pragmatism of Evangelicalism converges with the logic of neoliberal market rationality. Whether neo-monasticism will continue to develop into the future and bring life to the stream of Western Evangelicalism or is simply another passing fad—such as "seeker-friendly services" or "alternative worship"—remains to be seen. However, a deeper understanding and analysis of the cultural soil within which neo-monasticism has germinated and grown should lead to a more humble and honest assessment of its potential future contribution and also make us more vigilant of its potential pitfalls.[31] At its

---

30. MacIntyre, *After Virtue*, 102. MacIntyre's argument that "the fetishism of commodities has been supplemented by another just as important fetishism, that of bureaucratic skills" (102) has been recently advocated too by David Graeber, who sees a correlative relationship between the emergence of neoliberalism and the rise of "bureaucratic techniques." David Graeber, *The Utopia of Rules: On Technology, Stupidity, and the Joys of Bureaucracy* (London: Melville, 2016), 142.

MacIntyre argues that because the bureaucratic skills of the manager are an "illusion" then what is necessary is a "skillful dramatic imitation of such control." MacIntyre asserts that: "It is histrionic success which gives power and authority in our culture. The most effective bureaucrat is the best actor" (102) correlates strongly with Evangelicalism's penchant for celebrities—the "charismatic leaders" of what Markofski's terms "a notoriously celebrity-driven subculture." Markofski, *New Monasticism*, 75.

31. In the afterword to *Living Faithfully* (65–70), Wilson poignantly notes the

best neo-monasticism may indeed offer the Western evangelical church a vision for faithful living in a world descending into fragmented and dark times. At worst, subsumed by market-logic, neo-monasticism may ultimately be construed as simply a new technique, offering an illusion that the embracing of this new model can lead to the growth and success of the church.[32] The fantastical nature of this second scenario and the extent to which this may be appealing are perhaps indicative of the fact that our imaginations have been shaped more by the governing rationality of neoliberalism than the moral vision presented in the historic Christian tradition of monasticism.

---

potential dangers that may beset neo-monasticism: *communal egotism, utopianism, romanticism, utilitarianism,* and *Pelagianism*. In an emotivist culture, Wilson's concern is that neo-monasticism could be construed in an individualistic utilitarianism mode as "a strategy for living well in a fragmented world," and to "make our lives better" (68). More dangerous, I have contended, is the utilitarianism in which neo-monasticism is seen as a technique to "save the church." This messianic-utopian fantasy inherently involves the other four dangers that Wilson highlights.

32. Here Graeber's assertion, while hyperbolic, merits attention: "Rational bureaucratic techniques are always in service to some fantastic end." Graeber, *Utopia of Rules*, 142.

Ads as Moral Cultural Liturgies in Post-Secular Context[1]

ANNA ROBBINS *and* CHRISTOPHER JOHNSTON

WHEN CHRISTENDOM DOMINATED WESTERN moral order, it was well documented that the practices of the church had a primary influence on the moral development of individuals, communities, and even nations. The origin of human rights, commitment to freedom and justice, and other values that underpin the morality of Western society also arguably have their grounding at least in part in Judeo-Christian beliefs.[2] Values were shaped by the teaching and practices of the church and the Christian life, whether through formal Bible study, preaching, fellowship, prayer, confession, Mass, worship, baptism, and so on, as they were reflected, and worked out, in wider culture. These religious practices were once considered public and therefore political acts, and for many people they still are. However, there is no question that their force to mark the course of the ethics of an individual, community, or nation is less significant in the Western world today than it has been for hundreds of years.

The decline of organized religion in the Western world manifests in at least two ways: one, there are fewer people of faith associating with

---

1. This paper was first presented at a politics conference at Acadia University, as a collaborative project between faculty members and students. Themes of culture, collaboration, post-Christendom, formation, and ethics all pay homage to Jonathan Wilson, whom it is a privilege to honor with this work.

2. See, for example, arguments about origins and directions for human rights in Nicholas Wolterstorff, *Justice: Rights and Wrongs* (Princeton, NJ: Princeton University Press, 2010).

organized religion; two, there is an unweaving of the church and Christian values from the political structures of Western liberal democracies. We see entrenched rights give way to assumed values in our own country, and around the world a new moral order is being shaped by media and technology. Despite the lingering values latent in some structures, people are seeking and expressing meaning for their lives outside of organized religion. This is the secular age.

Critiques of the secularization thesis notwithstanding, the Western world is undoubtedly increasingly secular, insofar as we define secular as distinct from sacred. This does not mean that all people in a pre-secular time were, in fact, religious, nor does it mean that there are no religious people in a secular age. The term "post-secular" recognizes the diversity of the present situation. The notion of "implicit religion," which indicates how people seek meaning for life outside of explicit or organized religion, and without any reference to transcendence, moves significantly to the fore.[3]

For McGill philosopher Charles Taylor, secularism is tied up with the "Great Disembedding," where the modern individual becomes extracted from premodern social imaginaries, and new social imaginaries emerge with the emancipated individual at the center. Social imagination in a secular context posits a covenant of free individuals who flourish without the embedding of church and world, such as exists in Axial religion.[4]

Driven largely by the influences of internal theological resources of the church, the very mode of operation of the process was itself "thoroughly disembedding," as it focused on "the disciplined remaking of behavior and social forms through objectification and an instrumental stance."[5] Taylor notes, "This final phase of the Great Disembedding was largely powered by Christianity. But it was also in a sense a 'corruption' of it."[6] The secular age is thus "an age of contested belief, where religious

---

3. Edward Bailey is a pioneer of studies in implicit religion. See Edward Bailey, ed., *The Secular Quest for Meaning in Life: Denton Papers in Implicit Religion* (Lewiston, NY: Lellen, 2002). This has influenced the study of theology from a perspective of lived practice rather than systematized approaches. See Martyn Percy, *Shaping the Church: The Promise of Implicit Theology* (Farnham, UK: Ashgate, 2013).

4. Charles Taylor, *A Secular Age* (Cambridge, MA: Harvard University Press, 2007).

5. Taylor, *Secular Age*, 155.

6. Taylor, *Secular Age*, 158.

belief is no longer axiomatic."[7] Layers of disembedding release the necessity of the transcendent from the social realm. Belief in God is no longer an integral part of social imagination. As we will see, the instrumentality of this view has parallels with capitalist interpretations of the human being and social order.

In order to grasp how such dramatic shifts in moral order take place, we must understand first the dynamics of social imaginaries. A social imaginary for Taylor is not merely a disengaged social "theory" about people: "I am thinking rather of the ways in which they imagine their social existence, how they fit together with others, how things go on between them and their fellows, the expectations which are normally met, and the deeper normative notions and images which underlie these expectations."[8] It is a "common understanding which makes possible common practices, and a widely shared sense of legitimacy."[9]

Social imaginaries are inherently dynamic. What is understood as human flourishing is always being revised, Taylor says. "The Great Disembedding occurs as a revolution in our understanding of moral order."[10] But how do these transitions in social imaginaries take place? Taylor suggests this happens as people take up, improvise, or are inducted into new practices. These are made sense of by the new outlook, the one first articulated in the theory; this outlook is the context that gives sense to the practices. And hence the new understanding comes to be accessible to the participants in a way it wasn't before. It begins to define the contours of their world, and can eventually come to count as the taken-for-granted shape of things, too obvious to mention.[11]

It could be thought, then, that dynamic change in the moral order happens primarily through intellectual shift. However, Taylor argues that it is instead a "long march" that is not one-sided. Changed practices can also lead to transformed ideas as practices are improvised amongst certain groups within a population. This is how our collective moral order is formed and shaped by, and into, new social imaginaries.

---

7. James K. A. Smith, *How (Not) to Be Secular: Reading Charles Taylor* (Grand Rapids: Eerdmans, 2014), 142.

8. Taylor, *Secular Age*, 171.

9. Taylor, *Secular Age*, 172.

10. Taylor, *Secular Age*, 157.

11. Taylor, *Secular Age*, 175–76.

One of the characterizations of life in a post-secular age is that many experience a cultural "malaise of immanence."[12] Having lost a sense of transcendence with the Great Disembedding, our social imaginaries become shaped by the material world alone, and what Taylor refers to as a need to experience a sense of "fullness" about life is missing. It conjures up Peggy Lee's song that asks, "Is that all there is?" and remains unsatisfied with an affirmative response. Whether understood as implicit religion, or as post-secular expressions of "fullness," we express more than a strictly material explanation for human life when we engage moral agency, ethics, and aesthetics.

Despite Taylor's suggestions about the fullness of life, in a capitalistic consumer culture, we find that our social imaginaries accessed through the practices of agency, ethics and aesthetics are, like most things, market driven. Max Weber understood the formative impact of capitalism on human beings. People come to possess a specific vision of what human flourishing should look like, and that becomes the goal—adequate savings, relative security, and an acceptable "standard of living."[13]

An example of disembedding is expressed in popular culture in ads. In a 2001 promotion for the Xbox, Microsoft released an ad in which a child is born, shoots through a window, aging quickly before crashing into a grave, followed by the tagline appearing on screen, "Life is short, play more!" This ad provides an example of a company providing a *momento mori* and exhorting us what to do with our all-too-brief time on earth.

The replacement of transcendent value with material value is inherent in popular advertising, as self-consciously demonstrated in the Christmas 2015 #MulberryMiracle ad which begins with a man giving a woman a bright red Mulberry handbag as a Christmas gift, in what appears to be their new home, as they sit on the floor surrounded by packing boxes and dimly lit by candlelight. As the woman stares at the bag in delight, the couple is interrupted by local shepherds and friends wearing party crowns who are bearing gifts. The scene quickly and cleverly evolves into a modern-day reenactment of the nativity scene, while the man nearly deconstructs the moment by stating "It's just a bag." The ad ends with laughter, the flash of a logo, and the tagline #MulberryMiracle.

---

12. See Taylor, *Secular Age*, 208–311.

13. James K. A. Smith, *Desiring the Kingdom: Worship, Worldview, and Cultural Formation* (Grand Rapids: Baker Academic, 2009), 52. Cf. Max Weber, *The Protestant Ethic and the Spirit of Capitalism*, ed. Talcott Parsons (New York: Scribner, 1958), 17.

James K. A. Smith, too, has a practical take on the malaise of immanence and lost transcendence experienced through the identification of human flourishing with market values. Smith posits a theology of culture where each person is an embodied actor rather than a merely thinking object. Building on Taylor's work, he prioritizes practices as the primary site of conformity and resistance to cultural norms. Further, he looks at cultural practices and institutions through the lens of liturgy—that is, through a desire to understand how ritualized practices can shape a people group.[14] The core claim is that liturgies, regardless of their origin, shape and undergird identities by forming the most fundamental desires and the most basic orientations to the surrounding world.[15] If Smith is right, and these liturgical practices have profound impacts on identity and beliefs, there must then be specific practices reinforcing the formation of those values in people and cultures, throughout the twentieth- and twenty-first-century Western world.

In a theological context, liturgy is the form of corporate worship that leads the faithful through the actions of approach, penitence, prayer and dedication to God. It has a formative power that is both repetitive and reflective. The rubric of liturgy as Smith describes it is broader than the form of a traditional worship service, but has the same formative impact on beliefs and behavior. Informed by postmodern philosophers, he presumes that what we desire shapes who we are.

Liturgy assumes responsible agency, that is, the ability to practice or refuse to practice, retaining the moral integrity of human beings and the shared polis. For Smith, liturgy involves re-narration, ritual, habituation, and reflection.[16] Unlike religious liturgies, which form a basis of resistance to cultural norms that lead to a perceived non-flourishing, secular liturgies are largely liturgies that manifest and extend the values of capitalism and consumerism. In this context, one value is primary: "Capitalism is identical with the pursuit of profit, by means of continuous, rational, capitalistic enterprise. For it must be so: in a wholly capitalistic order of society, an individual capitalistic enterprise which did not take advantage of its opportunities for profit-making would be doomed to extinction."[17] William Cavanaugh picks up on similar themes and sug-

---

14. Smith, *Desiring the Kingdom*, 36.
15. Smith, *Desiring the Kingdom*, 25.
16. Smith, *Desiring the Kingdom*, 36–40.
17. Weber, *Protestant Ethic*, 17.

gests that "for many people, consumerism is a type of spirituality, even if they do not recognize it as such. It is a way of pursuing meaning and identity, a way of connecting with other people."[18]

The development of consumer culture has gone through several manifestations. The accumulation and idolization of material goods were marks of early consumerism, yet in more recent years, what characterizes consumer culture is not attachment to things but detachment from them. Cavanagh encapsulates this by writing that "people do not hoard money; they spend it. People do not cling to things; they discard them and buy other things."[19] Consumerism is not so much about having more as it is about having something else.[20] This is the exaggerated language of consumption of which Jean Baudrillard wrote: "The symbolic values of creation and the symbolic relation of inwardness are absent from it [consumption]: it is all in externals."[21] Consumerism is an important subject for theology because it is a spiritual disposition—it is a way of looking at the world around us that is deeply formative.[22]

Smith considers marketing as an example of secular liturgies at work, leading to the shopping liturgy of consumer culture. Along with other postmodern theorists, he posits that it is the marketers who have honestly figured out the human heart—they understand that, at the core of the modern person, is an erotic creature—creatures that are formed and orientated most profoundly by love, passion, and desire.[23] Or, as Baudrillard states it, "advertising is prophetic, in so far as it promotes not understanding, but hope."[24] This is a hope of a purely immanent, and ultimately disappointing, kind. In contrast to our love for God, "desire should serve, not shape, our comprehensive view of reality."[25] Since the desire for more commonly manifests as a desire for more money and more possessions, "in marketing one finds the promise of a kind of

---

18. William T. Cavanaugh, *Being Consumed: Economics and Christian Desire* (Grand Rapids: Eerdmans, 2008), 36.

19. Cavanaugh, *Being Consumed*, 35.

20. See Cavanaugh, *Being Consumed*, 35.

21. Jean Baudrillard, *The Consumer Society* (London: SAGE, 1998), 115.

22. Cavanaugh, *Being Consumed*, 73.

23. Smith, *Desiring the Kingdom*, 76.

24. Baudrillard, *Consumer Society*, 127.

25. Oliver O'Donovan, *Finding and Seeking*, vol. 2 of *Ethics as Theology* (Grand Rapids: Eerdmans, 2014), 74–75.

transcendence that is linked to a certain bastardization of the erotic."[26] It is a masquerade of transcendence, cloaking the purely immanent frame, yet with a reach that is global in scope.

Michael Ignatieff agrees that our secular context is marked not only by individual moral formation, but by the emergence of moral globalization, with virtues shared and nurtured in a global moral order. He is optimistic about the shared values of capitalism, where the "cash nexus," to use Marx's term, "coexists happily enough with a post-imperial norm of equality," pursued by activists and advocates of justice. Most interesting is Ignatieff's observation that "the first of the new entrepreneurs of moral globalization are the executives of the multinational corporations."[27] If the executives of the multinational corporations are the vicars of global moral order, what are their secular liturgies?

In many ways, we might consider ads as secular moral liturgies for a global moral order. Increasingly they are becoming self-consciously so, overtly encouraging specific moral values alongside the marketing of products. In these ads, we are invited to re-narrate our own experiences of life, as we watch them in repeated ritual, and share them over social media. They exhort habituation, overtly in terms of the virtues promoted, and also subtly in the identification of virtues with products. Websites provide venues for reflective discussions that lead to fresh narrations of our moral agency and order.

A 2013 television ad by Thai cellphone provider Truemove-H begins with a young boy caught stealing medicine for his sick mother and rescued by a nearby vendor who pays for the pills and has his young daughter give the boy a bag of soup to feed his family. The ad then skips forward several decades and shows the same vendor collapsing at work and his daughter forced to sell their home and business to pay the medical bill. After seeing the daughter weep at the sight of the enormous bill, the emotionally charged music begins to swell and the final scene shows her waking up to find that the bill has been paid in full. She reads the accompanying letter to learn that "all expenses paid thirty years ago, with three packs of painkillers and a bag of veggie soup." As the viewer comes to understand that the young boy had grown to become a successful doctor, the screen goes dark and reads, "Giving is the best communication."

---

26. Smith, *Desiring the Kingdom*, 76.

27. Michael Ignatieff, *The Ordinary Virtues: Moral Order in a Divided World* (Cambridge, MA: Harvard University Press, 2017), 14–15.

These liturgies, of course, have individual impact on agents, but more significantly they reinforce secular moral order around promoted values of the marketplace, as citizens of the polis narrate their collective identity through the ads produced by entrepreneurs of "moral globalization." The requirement for a moral formation to sustain a stable pattern of consumption undermines the potential for a disruptive ethic to flourish. The immanent serves the immanent in a circular malaise.

In the absence of real transcendence, our values are reflected and shaped in popular culture by corporate interests, as evidenced in ads as secular moral liturgies. In an era dominated by consumerism and secularity, the ideas presented here raise the question as to whether there is yet a role for religion and its liturgies. In public gestures to the transcendent, we find at least the potential for a formational liturgy that is not shaped entirely by capitalistic ideas of human flourishing. This formative vision of human flourishing produced what Martin Goodridge describes as "secular practitioners," who are future oriented and time aware, "certain that they can control the outcome of their actions," and "in the growing conviction that they are capable of controlling their relationship with their environment."[28] There are resonances here with Weber's concepts of rationalization and rational action. But rather than large, organizing concepts, these are understood as much more localized and practical. Goodridge contrasts "secular practice" with "Charismatic action" to denote the difference in practice between those driven by modern processes, and those who yet engage practices of grace and Spirit that transcend the rational.

Because religious liturgies retain a notion of the transcendent there is potential that they do not by necessity reflect capitalist cultural values, and in them may be found seeds of critique, resistance, and adjustment. At least they present in intent an alternative to the consumerist values shaping popular culture and shared moral order. Though their formative power appears limited in the face of globalized secular moral liturgies, greater exploration of their counter-formative impact is required—if they haven't already been so compromised as to be unrecognizable.

---

28. Martin Goodridge, "The Secular Practice as Implicit Religion," in *The Secular Quest for Meaning in Life: Denton Papers in Implicit Religion*, ed. Edward Bailey (Lewiston, NY: Lellen, 2002), 4–21, esp. 16.

Reflection

Plain, Literal, Real Narrative
Continuing a Conversation about Language and Reality

A. K. M. Adam

JUST A YEAR OR two ago (so it seems), Jonathan and I were in graduate seminars together, reading Macintyre and Milbank and arguing over all manner of arcane topics in the grad lounge. In those days our theological interests and thinking were closely bound by shared reading lists and curriculum; we were at the cutting edge of more-than-modern theology. In retrospect, those were glorious days of deep drinking at unfathomable wells of wisdom, and Jonathan has gone on from there to share even greater draughts of his distinctively gentle, unsettling, yet encouraging insight with generations of students, colleagues, congregations, and communities. In the paragraphs that follow, I'll adopt a conversational and retrospective tone, noting mostly just sources from our shared world of reference of those days, and not putting on a formal academic voice or peppering my points with airtight, up-to-date references; my argument will thus, to some extent, hark back to our discussions in the Rathskeller, just one floor down from the Gothic Bookshop, where we found many of the books that challenged and inspired us. Jonathan will, as he so often did, keep a thoughtful silence while I talk—though I expect that eventually, someday, he will remind me of false steps I've taken, wiser pathways I should take.

Those were years in which we wrestled with a second linguistic turn in theology. During the first turn, critics devoted scrutiny to the words of Jesus, and to some extent to the language of theology, with particular attention to what language does to its users. Our discussions had moved beyond that romanticized version of language; we had read Wittgenstein[1] and Foucault and Derrida, and were trying to work out a more sophisticated account of the relation of theology to *Les mots et les choses*,[2] of power and knowledge, of meaning and usage. We sensed the need to account carefully for language, since we were exploring the necessities and possibilities of narrative theology — and without using language, our potential for "narrative" diminishes significantly. Our language, our narratives, intertwine somehow with the undeniable conditions of everyday experience, and both of these are entangled with narratives about times past; but how shall we account for those intertwined entanglements?

Two of the key sources for our deliberations in those days were Hans Frei's essay "The 'Literal Reading' of Biblical Narrative in the Christian Tradition: Does It Stretch or Will It Break?"[3] and Kathryn Tanner's chapter "Theology and the Plain Sense."[4] These were pivotal texts, hot off the presses, that helped set the agenda for our reading group's conversations.[5] Frei's essay set out his case for thinking of the object of reading in a way that evades some of the historic complications of thinking about a "literal sense" without giving up its usefulness as a uniquely authoritative point of reference. Frei has in view the way that biblical criticism modulated its

---

1. Fergus Kerr's *Theology after Wittgenstein* (Oxford, UK: Blackwell, 1986) had recently been published.

2. The original French title of Foucault's book, translated under the title *The Order of Things*, trans. Alan Sheridan (New York: Vintage, 1973).

3. In *The Bible and the Narrative Tradition*, ed. Frank McConnell (New York: Oxford University Press, 1986), 36-77; now more easily consulted in Frei, *Theology and Narrative: Selected Essays*, ed. George Hunsinger and William C. Placher (Oxford, UK: Oxford University Press, 1993), 117-52.

4. In *Scriptural Authority and Narrative Interpretation*, ed. Garrett Green (Philadelphia: Fortress, 1987), 59-78.

5. Further in the background lay Brevard Childs's "The *Sensus Literalis* of Scripture: an Ancient and Modern Problem," in *Beiträge zum alttestamentlichen Theologie*, ed. H. Donner et al. (Göttingen, Germ.: Vandenhoeck and Ruprecht, 1977), 80-93; and Raphael Loewe, "The 'Plain' Meaning of Scripture in Early Jewish Exegesis," in *Papers of the Institute of Jewish Studies in London* (N.p.: Jerusalem, 1964), 1:140-85. Since the late eighties, the topic of the literal sense, the plain sense, and the ordinary sense has generated a bibliography that would by itself overfill the space of this essay — without even taking consideration of the copious literature on "the theological interpretation of Scripture." While estimable minds have set themselves the task of resolving the problem of "the literal," none has settled the matter to my satisfaction.

sense of "literality" from the semantics of the words themselves (taking for granted the veracity of their expression and the actuality of their referents) to the critically determined original sense of the text in its historical context. Whatever the benefits or detriments of such a change, the alteration at one point in theological discourse effects changes at all points further along, and Frei advocates construing the "literal sense" intratextually, with a view to taking the matters narrated in the Christian Bible (focusing on the narrative depiction of Jesus as the Christ) as paradigmatic for understanding everything outside the biblical narrative.

Frei refers to this primary function of the literal sense as the "plain sense," an identification that Kathy Tanner develops further in "Theology and the Plain Sense," her contribution to the Festschrift in Frei's honor. She takes up Frei's descriptive definition and enriches its theoretical backing, taking pains to avoid ascribing "the plain sense" to any features intrinsic to the text. Rather, she hews to the descriptive account that resonates with Frei's own characterization: the plain sense "is the obvious or direct sense of the text according to a *usus loquendi* established by the community in question" (that is, the community that uses these specific texts "to shape, nurture, and reform" its identity).[6]

The literal sense, and its more nuanced "plain" attendant claim center stage on the basis that "the tradition of the *sensus literalis* is the closest one can come to a consensus reading of the Bible as the sacred text in the Christian church."[7] That consensus makes a great difference, since it gives force to claims that "the Bible says x" or "y is contrary to biblical teaching." The difficulty, of course, is that Frei's "the closest one can come to a consensus" falls far short of any actual consensus, as a cursory examination of the relevant literature will reveal.[8] Moreover, the reservation "in the Christian church" risks restricting interpretive legitimacy to Christians—and since the history of Christianity displays no consensus about what counts as truly "Christian," the problem of the literal sense's authoritative status intensifies. While Frei and Tanner painstakingly restrict their treatment of the literal-plain sense to description, many of their supporters ascribe to the literal-plain regulative authority. It would be an overstatement to say that this gesture turns the literal sense from

---

6. Kathryn E. Tanner, "Theology and the Plain Sense," in *Scriptural Authority and Narrative Interpretation*, ed. Garrett Green (Philadelphia: Fortress, 1987), 59-78.

7. Frei, *Theology and Narrative*, 37.

8. Critical readers who wish to push back at this point should make very sure to include (at least) Orthodox and Roman Catholic constituencies in their consensuses.

a careful description of how communities relate to canonical texts into what my sort of Christians (and any other readers, so long as they agree with us) agree that this text means—but that overstatement comes awkwardly close to capturing both the appeal and the problem that arises from traditions' ascribing authority to the literal sense.

What is wanted, what some people argue is needed, is a textual degree zero:[9] an ascetical, austere, unornamented, nonideological semantic reference point by which all the various interpretive gestures can be assessed. Merely stating such a premise evokes the impossibility of its achievement. Where is the nonideological reader who can pin down the neutral reference value of a particular utterance? Should such an interpreter be male (as most of those who lay claim to impartiality turn out to be), they fall immediately under suspicion of their judgment being corrupted by the privilege and power that men have wielded over the past thousands of years of public interpretive deliberation from the Middle East to Europe and the Americas. One can repeat that suspicious gesture indefinitely, across all manner of advantages and oppressions.[10] Moreover, the importance of this degree zero literal sense may be particularly acute for those who hold authority; for those who hold no sway in the first place, defining and protecting the primacy of a literal sense may matter a good deal less than it does to those who could lose power if their own definition of the literal sense dissolves.[11]

---

9. Adopting the terminology from Roland Barthes's *Writing Degree Zero*, trans. Annette Lavers and Colin Smith (London: Jonathan Cape, 1967).

10. Another work that figured prominently in our reading in the late eighties was Richard Bernstein's *Beyond Objectivism and Relativism: Science, Hermeneutics, and Praxis* (Philadelphia: University of Pennsylvania Press, 1983), in which Bernstein coined the term "Cartesian anxiety" to describe the felt urgency (relevant to this essay's topic) of securing a fixed point of reference from which all other inferences can be justified. Richard Eldridge contributes a lapidary summary of Bernstein's view of interpretive discernment in his "Review of *Beyond Objectivism and Relativism: Science, Hermeneutics, and Praxis*, by Richard Bernstein," *Philosophy and Literature* 8 (1984): 292–93, esp. 292: "The task of an inquirer, in seeking to justify a theory at a historical moment, is to discern which parts of his tradition—perhaps its art, its physics, its epistemology, or its sociology—are most plausible and worth preserving and to modify either his theories or criteria of theory choice in light of a judgment about what in his tradition is sound."

11. It is not surprising, for example, when vibrant interpretive traditions from cultural groups who have been kept at arm's length from political and academic power (colonized peoples, women, racial minorities, members of lower social classes) show greater openness to interpretations that relativize the importance of the allegedly real, necessary, critical, historical, literal sense of biblical texts.

The literal sense further attracts the authority of reality. When various interpretations of an expression can be categorized as "figurative" or, worse still, "allegorical," they bear the invalidating stamp of fantasy, of unfettered imagination. By contrast, then, the literal sense must engage with the real. This association of figurative interpretation with unreality moves to the foreground with the Reformation. The alternative constructed concord between the literal and the real is then reinforced when "literal" and "real" are made to interlock with "historical" such that they seem to form a sturdily rigid foundation for claims about correct or legitimate interpretation.

The connection between "literal" and "real" depends more on intuition (and, paradoxically, colloquial figures of speech) than on any demonstrable lines of implication. One can say that a particular expression really means x, which locution gives the impression that there is some extrinsic reality with which y (the real meaning) shares the quality of realness. Closer examination finds holes all through that associative inference. There is no property of meaning that adheres to linguistic expressions in the first place, such that one could isolate a real meaning from one particular expression. This holds all the more truly the more one finds all linguistic expression (and thus all linguistic uptake) to partake of figuration, and the more one observes the constant change in semantic and syntactical conventions. Even if there existed some esoteric one-to-one relation between expressions and a definitive true meaning for them, no expression nor any meaning can bind itself to the events of history. The whole compound of literal, real, and historical in this context rests on assumptions and intuitions that require some sort of putative metaphysical filaments to hold literal uses of language, and facts, and retrospective analysis of the past in a fixed relationship. No one has shown the existence of such filaments, though; and the confident expectation that they must so exist obscures the ways that linguistic expression works and the ways that language can serve the purpose of narrating historical events.[12]

On one hand, this elision of reality, literality, and historicality provides a welcome staging area for theologies that assert a strong positive relation between things that the Bible seems to claim about reality, and

---

12. The same patterns of linguistic expression serve to narrate fictional events and historical events; the language itself has no traction on "the real." In those days past, our colleagues were reading Hayden White on narrativity, language, history, and truth (mostly in essays that followed his magisterial *Metahistory: The Historical Imagination in 19th-Century Europe* [Baltimore: Johns Hopkins University Press, 1973]).

reality itself, and our retrospective descriptions of reality—which, to be fair, include many historic and contemporary Christian theologies. At the same time, an observer who doesn't share Christian premises about these matters (or who holds to a theology that treats differently the three-way interplay of Bible, literariness, and reality) may find this account of interpretation problematic. It seems to rule out the possibility of understanding the operations of language or reality apart from Christian doctrine in a way that differs from the possibility of simple harmonic motion, or baking, or football, or most phenomena apart from the Bible, language, history, and reality. One might feel uneasy about the claim that a chemist cannot truly understand acid-base titration apart from confessing faith in the eternal triune God of Christian faith; it ought to be possible to suppose that nonbelievers could understand linguistics or human history without signing a statement of Christian faith. To assert the contrary builds the interpretive philosophy around the goal to which it is intended to lead; it bakes the supposedly correct answer into the method by which the answer is derived.

There is a possible characterization of the literal sense that might work for all participants in interpretive discourse: women and men, Black, white, and every shade of human race, for all expressions of human sexuality or none, proletariat, bourgeoisie, capitalists. It is a definition of "literal sense" with some presence in Christian tradition, though often as not it has been pushed away, stretched, or contorted to fit a more agreeable purpose. It will satisfy no one, though, because it serves no party's interests, advances no cause, and resolves no doctrinal or disciplinary conundrums. It would contribute to making sense of our interpretive labors, though, and would help more precisely to identify the textures of disagreement that set readers of the Bible (and any other text) at odds.

The desired literal degree zero takes its cue from a traditional characterization of "literal" among early scholars of hermeneutics: that is, very often interpreters have referred to the literal sense as "the literal, grammatical sense." Taking Irenaeus's famous metaphor of the mosaic of a prince rearranged to look like a dog,[13] we may construe the appearance of the prince in question as the literal sense; the representation as a dog would fail the test if we were to compare it to the living prince's visage and could not perceive there any hint of the prince. Similarly, the literal sense of a linguistic expression (let us say, "This is a mosaic of the prince")

---

13. Irenaeus, *Against All Heresies* 1.8.1.

would fail the test of comparison if the image in question depicted a dog.[14] This version of the literal sense serves its function acceptably so long as participants in the conversation agree that the prince could not be mistaken for a dog (a safe reservation under almost all conceivable circumstances).

One prominent problem with this version of the literal sense is that conflicts about interpretation rarely, if ever, arise when all the participants to the conversation agree about the sense of the relevant terms in a disputed proposition. There are numerous princes of England just now, but none of them looks so much like a dog that the literal reference of a royal portrait could mix the royal personage and the corgi. In other words, *we can agree on the literal sense of a linguistic expression precisely to the extent that it is not implicated in our disagreements*. Once we disagree about the semantics of a word (or longer expression), however, we can no longer recur to the literal sense, since from this point on, our disagreements already include divergent assessments of the literal sense itself.

These things—the literal (and figurative) uses of words, history, and reality—hold together not by virtue of metaphysical threads, but by the interlocking of shared lives for which language and behavioral conventions, expectations and assumptions, operate together to sustain us. If we encounter a word we don't know, we often just watch how it works in its contexts and derive a working hypothesis of its sense from the ways the word is used and received. If we are uncertain about reality (as happens only relatively rarely, compared to the proportion of the time that we go forward as though we know perfectly well what is real), we can ask friends, or again observe others' relation to what seems real, to learn about the actual way of the world from the shape of their lives. If we are in doubt concerning our apprehension of past events and people, we can read more, listen more, observe the course of other events and people whom our focal question will have affected. All these are corrigible; all these are relational; all these suffice to maintain the everyday business of communicating accurately, ascertaining what's what, and reasoning about what probably was what in days gone by.

If all of the above hangs together, then we needn't—indeed, we can't—rely on qualities inherent in language to do the heavy lifting of

---

14. This example begs the question by stipulating what a prince looks like, what a dog looks like, and how manifest a resemblance we can expect between members of the sets that they represent (and omits altogether the question of dogs named Prince); such are the limitations of short essays.

establishing the reality, the actuality of theological truth of any topic about which we care. Instead, we have to trust reality to take care of itself (or trust God to take care of reality) and strive as carefully and thoughtfully as we can to make God known through our own words and actions. Many observers might dismiss this as an unrealistic, or flimsy, or unacceptable basis for faith. But speaking strictly for myself, I know that having witnessed the presence and grace manifest in such conversation partners as Jonathan Wilson has constituted a much more convincing ground for faith than anything I've learned about philosophy of language, or metaphysics, or doctrines about their relationships.

"Listen! This Is Not What You're Expecting to Hear!"

A Sermon on Mark 4:1–34

Anthony Brown

Listen! A farmer went out to sow his seed. As he was scattering the seed, some fell along the path, and the birds came and ate it up. Some fell on rocky places, where it did not have much soil. It sprang up quickly, because the soil was shallow. But when the sun came up, the plants were scorched, and they withered because they had no root. Other seed fell among thorns, which grew up and choked the plants, so that they did not bear grain. Still other seed fell on good soil. It came up, grew and produced a crop, some multiplying thirty, some sixty, some a hundred times. Whoever has ears to hear, let them hear.

—MARK 4:3–9[1]

LISTEN! THIS IS NOT what you're expecting to hear!

---

1. This chapter uses the NRSV translation for Scripture references, unless otherwise indicated.

Jesus introduces the parable Mark records at the beginning of the fourth chapter of his Gospel with this word, "Listen!" And he ends it with "Whoever has ears to hear, let them hear!"

"Listen!" and "let them hear!" are the same Greek word, a command echoing the beginning of the great prayer of the Jews, the Shema.

> Hear, O Israel [Listen, O Israel]:
> the Lord is our God
> the Lord alone.
> You shall love the Lord your God
> with all your heart,
> and with all your soul,
> and with all your might.
> (Deut 6:4–5)

This is the level of authority Jesus is using as he sits down in the boat and begins to teach in parables. "Listen!" "Hear, O Israel!" It is not a request for people to pay attention. It is a command from God to hear and obey.

In his Gospel, Mark begins his account of Jesus's ministry with him teaching in a synagogue. Next, Jesus is teaching in a house that is bursting with people. Following that, Mark tells us about a large crowd gathered at the lake. Then another crowd gathers at the lake, this time so large that Jesus asks the disciples to have a small boat ready for him in case of the crush. And finally by chapter 4, the crowd is so big that even before Jesus begins speaking, he gets into the boat and pushes off a little way from the shore so that people can hear him.

Why are they all coming? Why is the crowd swelling and swelling? They are coming because they have heard that Jesus is proclaiming that the kingdom of God is at hand. For the Galilean masses nothing could have been more exciting. The prophets of the Hebrew Scriptures had predicted that God would intervene on Israel's behalf, bringing this present evil world to its knees and decisively defeating the enemies of his people. They were expecting a messiah, a supernatural deliverer—David, Moses, and Elijah rolled into one—a messiah who would usher in the kingdom of God. So it is not difficult to imagine the excitement in Galilee when the news began to spread that someone was proclaiming that the kingdom of God was at hand; someone who was casting out demons, healing the sick, and teaching with such charisma that some even said he was Elijah raised from the dead.

The crowd was now so huge that if he was to announce the revolution they expected, there would have been little the authorities, Jewish or Roman, could have done to prevent a significant insurrection. People flock to Jesus from all over the Galilean countryside in a rising tide of anticipation and messianic fervor, and . . . he tells them a story! A story, which, if they understood it, would reverse all their expectations about how the kingdom of God was going to come.

> Listen! A farmer went out to sow his seed. As he was scattering the seed, some fell along the path, and the birds came and ate it up. Some fell on rocky places, where it did not have much soil. It sprang up quickly, because the soil was shallow. But when the sun came up, the plants were scorched, and they withered because they had no root. Other seed fell among thorns, which grew up and choked the plants, so that they did not bear grain. Still other seed fell on good soil. It came up, grew and produced a crop, some multiplying thirty, some sixty, some a hundred times. Whoever has ears to hear, let them hear. (Mark 4:3-9)

Mark has already told us something that the crowds weren't expecting—that Jesus is a teacher—but so far in his Gospel he has not given us much of Jesus's teaching. The series of parables that Jesus gives here make up the first significant block of his teaching that Mark records. Mark has told us back in chapter 1 that Jesus's purpose is to proclaim the kingdom of God, but this is the first time we are going to have that fleshed out for us.

For Mark, as for Matthew, this parable is first in importance. It is their prime example of a parable. And this is the first and only parable that Mark records in his Gospel that has a subsequent explanation from Jesus himself.

For the crowd, some things about this story are familiar. For example, the form of Jesus's story. Parables of all kinds were common not only among Jewish teachers but throughout the Roman world. Likewise, the style of the parable with its repetition of threes—two sets of three seeds, three adverse conditions, three degrees of productivity—was a familiar rhetorical device. The choice of a sower as the subject would not be particularly surprising either. A sower was frequently used as a metaphor for a teacher in the ancient world, and even the least educated members of the crowd would have heard stories of this kind before.

The subject matter of the story itself would have been very familiar to this gathering of countryfolk. Today, when we are used to modern agriculture with its pesticides and mechanical efficiency, we may find the idea of a peasant farmer apparently wasting precious seed by casting it all over unplowed ground rather odd. However, in first-century Galilee, the common means of planting was to spread the seed and only subsequently to plow it in. Inevitably, some of this seed would be eaten by birds, some would fall in soil too shallow to support it, and some would be prevented from growing by weeds and briars.

Agricultural historians tell us that the normal yield of a first-century Israelite harvest would have been about seven and a half times what was sown, with a good crop being perhaps tenfold. Yet, although Jesus's parable is obviously about abundance, it is not beyond the realm of possibility to have a harvest of thirty, sixty, or even a hundredfold. Even though Jesus's hearers would be impressed by these yields, they would not be put off the story by his use of an overexaggerated figure.[2]

Nor would the crowd have had difficulty recognizing that this story had a deeper meaning that related to their hope that God was once again at work among them. As Tom Wright puts it, "A sower sowing seed is not just a familiar picture from everyday family life. It's a picture of God sowing Israel again in her own land after the long years of exile; of God restoring the fortunes of his people, making the family farm fruitful again after the thorns and thistles have had it their own way for too long."[3]

Yet, while there was a lot about this parable that was familiar to the crowd, there was also a great deal which must have come as quite a surprise. For example, the crowd must have been puzzled that Jesus adopted as his image of God's activity in the world a story in which so much of the sowing apparently goes to waste, producing no fruit, like seed thrown carelessly into places where it cannot grow. No one expected God's action to be so apparently haphazard, inefficient, and lacking in calculation.

Nor would they have expected that God's activity could be devoured, or parched, or choked; or that the Messiah would appear, at last, only to tell them that God's work was fragile. They anticipated that God's kingdom would come by the sword, through the military conquest of their enemies, but Jesus's explanation of the parable casts the realizing of the kingdom in a very different light. The kingdom is coming as nothing more than a message! What is approaching is not an army, but a word! More than that, it is not even the kind of irresistible message that will

---

2. Commentators offer differing viewpoints on the numbers recorded by Mark. For judicious assessments of this and many other debates in Mark, see R. T. France, *The Gospel of Mark*, NIGTC (Grand Rapids: Eerdmans, 2002).

3. Nicholas T. Wright, *Mark for Everyone* (London: SPCK, 2002), 43.

overwhelm everyone who hears it. Far from it! It is a message that can all too easily be rejected, or wasted, or crowded out.

The parable reveals that God's activity is not one great act of deliverance and judgment. Rather, God's operations in history result in some cases in opposition and failure. Jesus signals that how God works to produce abundance—and he certainly promises abundance—is not at all how people are expecting him to do so.

> Don't you understand this parable? How then will you understand any parable? The farmer sows the word. Some people are like seed along the path, where the word is sown. As soon as they hear it, Satan comes and takes away the word that was sown in them. Others, like seed sown on rocky places, hear the word and at once receive it with joy. But since they have no root, they last only a short time. When trouble or persecution comes because of the word, they quickly fall away. Still others, like seed sown among thorns, hear the word; but the worries of this life, the deceitfulness of wealth and the desires for other things come in and choke the word, making it unfruitful. Others, like seed sown on good soil, hear the word, accept it, and produce a crop—some thirty, some sixty, some a hundred times what was sown. (Mark 4:13-20)

A little later, when Jesus's disciples are alone, Jesus starts to answer their question about the meaning of the parable by saying that this parable shows them a mystery. What is "the mystery of the kingdom"? Perhaps most simply it is that the kingdom is already present, but in a form unrecognized by most. The reign of God has already arrived, as limited and veiled as it may so far appear. Jesus's healings, exorcisms, and authoritative teaching have demonstrated this, and now it is being revealed in the parables. The problem with this is that Jesus's description of the unveiling of the kingdom was neither what people were expecting, nor what they desired. The Galilean crowds were anticipating the rescue of all Israel, the vindication of their leaders, the kingdom of God arising all at once in a blaze of glory. Instead, Jesus says it is like a farmer scattering seed, apparently all over the place, a goodly amount of which will come to nothing. Using the parables is Jesus's way of indicating that, while the kingdom is surely coming in all its abundance, its revealing is not going to accord with most people's expectations.

But if those who listened to Jesus beside the Sea of Galilee weren't bargaining on Jesus's message, it is no less expected among us today. And one element in particular.

When he was alone, the Twelve and the others around him asked him about the parables. He told them, "The secret of the kingdom of God has been given to you. But to those on the outside everything is said in parables so that

> they may be ever seeing but never perceiving,
> and ever hearing but never understanding;
> otherwise they might turn and be forgiven!:
> (Mark 4:10–12)

This is not what we expect to hear from Jesus. What does he mean by this? That the parables *prevent* people from receiving forgiveness?

In the narratives leading up to this one we are told that the scribes from Jerusalem and even Jesus's own family members were those who had "seen but not perceived, heard but not understood." And yet if these are the ones Jesus says are "those on the outside," why does he keep addressing them? And, on the other hand, those who are on the inside—those who have received the mystery of the kingdom of God—don't seem to understand the parables any better than anyone else. Hence Jesus says to the disciples in verse 13, "Don't you understand this parable? How then will you understand any parable?" Even those ostensibly on the inside can fail to perceive what is being revealed to them. And Jesus seems genuinely unhappy with them, because they don't understand.

We don't expect to have to work to understand what Jesus is saying. We expect it to be clear who is inside and who is outside, and we don't expect Jesus's message to involve the kind of condemnation implied by his phrase "otherwise they might turn and be forgiven."

In order to understand what's going on here, we need to realize that Jesus's teaching is always in response to something. This parable follows the first occasion when Israel's chief religious authorities announce their verdict on Jesus: He is possessed by the chief demon, Beelzebul. This is followed by the account of Jesus's family coming to find him, in which he states "Whoever does God's will is my brother and sister and mother," again emphasizing the growing distinction in the responses people are making to his ministry and message. It is into this context of different responses to himself that Jesus introduces the story of the sower and the responses of the different types of soil to the seed. Whatever else it may concern, we must not miss that this parable is about the receptivity of all people to Jesus's message. The parable carries a message for those who are openhearted and open minded, but also for those who are hard hearted and closed minded.

With these latter in mind, Jesus quotes from Isa 6, in which God commands the prophet

> Go and tell the people: "Be ever hearing, but never understanding; be ever seeing, but never perceiving." Make the heart of this people calloused; make their ears dull and close their eyes. Otherwise they might see with their eyes, hear with their ears, understand with their hearts, and turn and be healed. (Isa 6:9–10)

These words, of course, are from the point in the call of Isaiah when the prophet is instructed to preach to people whose hearts are hard and who will not respond. As unfamiliar an idea as it may be to us, it is Isaiah's conviction that by sending a prophetic message that would go unheard, the people's hearts would be hardened further. In the very next chapter, Isa 7, this is illustrated when the prophet encounters the leader of the nation, Ahaz, and we are told, "Again the LORD spoke to Ahaz, 'Ask the LORD your God for a sign, whether in the deepest depths or in the highest heights.' But Ahaz said, 'I will not ask; I will not put the LORD to the test'" (Isa 7:10–12). Ahaz piously rejects God's word and in doing so shows us how a hard heart is hardened further when it's exposed to God's word.

This seventh chapter of Isaiah is also one which is often quoted at Christmastime, because it introduces the idea of Immanuel—God with us. Verse 14 says, "Therefore the Lord himself will give you a sign: The virgin will conceive and give birth to a son, and will call him Immanuel." Isaiah goes on to make clear that it is the hearer's response that alone determines whether having God-with-us is a blessing or a curse.

If this word of Jesus in Mark chapter 4 is apparently too harsh a word of judgment in our ears, we need to remember that it's directed at men who are so hard hearted that they are plotting to kill Jesus, God-with-us, in the name of God! They have put themselves outside of the realm of God's forgiveness. So for them, God-with-us is a message only of judgment.

But what about the crowd? First, we need to see that there's a distinction between "the great crowd" and "those outside." The great crowd are the ones told to "Listen!" So their ultimate response to Jesus is nowhere presumed. By telling the parable, Jesus is beginning to clarify for the crowd that there is a decision to be made. In the face of increasing criticism, increasing expectations, and now open rejection of Jesus, the moment of decision is at hand. So, the parable says that the unexpected word is being proclaimed, and hearers must be careful how they respond. The parable of the sower describes the ways in which Jesus's announcement of the kingdom is received, or rejected. And it is not what the crowd were expecting.

But Jesus's warning is not done!

> Consider carefully what you hear. With the measure you use, it will be measured to you—and even more. Whoever has will be given more; whoever does not have, even what they have will be taken from them. (Mark 4: 24–25)

Those who embrace Jesus's message of the kingdom—who have received the secret of the kingdom and are willing to follow Jesus on Jesus's own terms—will receive all that the kingdom truly is, but those who have not embraced this secret will lose even what they have—the message of Jesus that they have been offered. There are those who flatly reject Jesus, the scribes and Pharisees who are already plotting to kill him, but there are many more in the crowds who hear Jesus gladly but are not prepared to accept the way of discipleship.

The three other parables that follow—the lamp on the stand, the seed growing in secret, and the mustard seed—all emphasize the ultimate establishment of the kingdom. Nothing and no one can prevent God's reign from being established in all its fullness and abundance. Jesus's ministry, which is suffering so much opposition at this point and not seeming to win many truly devoted disciples, is not what it seems. Lots of seed seems to be bearing no fruit, like that on the path, or in the thorns, or the shallow soil. Jesus's message may seem hidden, like the lamp under a bowl. Where the growth of the kingdom will come from may not be apparent, like the seed growing in secret in the soil. That the kingdom can ever be realized from such small beginnings seems doubtful, like the potential of the mustard seed. But each of these parables is Jesus's way of declaring that, as strange as it may seem, and despite the outward appearances of his ministry, the kingdom is present in all its fullness—in all its abundance—albeit embryonically in these humble beginnings.

Jesus's calming of the storm, which is as much a parable as any of the stories that he tells in the passages preceding it, will illustrate again the conflict being experienced in Jesus's ministry at this point. It will end in Jesus's victory because of who Jesus is: Immanuel, God-with-us. And those who are "with him," the term Mark uses to describe disciples, will receive the kingdom.

While today most of us may not experience the same daily reminders of Jesus's words, the sowing of crops or the lighting of lamps, the challenges to respond to him and to be fruitful remain just the same. Likewise, the reasons for failing to follow Jesus remain just the same. And Jesus's warning remains just the same: "Listen! The harvest is certain. The hidden will be revealed. The smallest seed will become the greatest plant.

"Whoever has ears to hear, let them hear!"

Reflections for an Irenic Spirit

Axel Schoeber

Dear Jonathan,

You and I have been friends for a long time, over forty years. We were often separated by many miles. Consequently, we were both delighted to work together on the same faculty for eight years. We share multiple memories; some are edifying. In retrospect I am struck by your ability to cultivate friends and to keep those friendships in good repair. Distance is not a barrier for you. I am also struck by the irenic spirit you consistently display. Your interactions manifest the reality that the kingdom of God has come among us. You treat people with persistent kindness, gentleness, and respect.

I am delighted to contribute to this Festschrift. You will receive insightful essays and show them the honor they deserve. I choose a different format. Our mutual friend, James Houston, has demonstrated letter writing has a revered history as Christians have taught, admonished, encouraged, and loved one another through paper and ink. I will write you a letter to tell a story. You have encountered the tale before. Yet a good story is worth reading again. It is about an irenic spirit who is too little known. He reminds me, in several ways, of you. I hope you enjoy. Of course, like any good storyteller, I begin with the end.

Gérard Roussel mounted the elevated pulpit to preach. He had come to Mauléon as bishop of Oloron, now in southwestern France. He proposed a reduction in saints' days to observe. The people could engage in more productive pursuits. Suddenly, a man rushed forward with an axe to shatter the supports for the pulpit, and Roussel came crashing down. He was picked up "half-dead"[1] and carried back to Oloron for treatment. The physicians prescribed a treatment of "taking the waters," but he never made it to his destination. Arriving at Clairac, the monastery he had been appointed abbot of in 1530, Roussel died nearby from injuries suffered in the fall. The year was 1555. His attacker—Arnauld de Maytie, a country gentleman—was tried before the *parlement* in Bordeaux and acquitted on account of his "pious and beautiful action."[2] A Catholic bishop is murdered by a devoted Catholic layman, who is acquitted by a largely Catholic court because they find his action "pious and beautiful."

Let me add another intriguing element before I begin the story. John Calvin was for a time a *Geraldini*. As his faith in Jesus was becoming deeply personal, he saw in Gérard Roussel both a friend and a model to learn from and follow.

This high regard did not last.

Gérard Roussel was famous in his day. A leader in church reform over three decades, he was widely known in France and beyond. He had friendships with many reformers, including Jacques Lefèvre d'Étaples, Guillaume Briçonnet, Martin Bucer, William Farel, John Calvin, and Philip Melanchthon. Born about 1480 near Amiens in Picardy, by 1501 he was collaborating with the humanist "master" Lefèvre d'Étaples, assisting his translations of classic texts, and adding his own scholarly comments and publications. He did not obtain a doctorate, but a master of arts. Still, his academic abilities were widely recognized. At some point, he was appointed priest in the Ardennes village of Buzancy.[3]

Roussel was invited to participate in 1521 in the renewing work of the Circle of Meaux, just east of Paris, where Guillaume Briçonnet was bishop. There he wrote a commentary on *De arithmetica* by Boethius, and, with Josse Clichtove, published a translation with notes of Aristotle's *Magna moralia*.[4] Roussel was appointed priest at the church of Saint-

---

1. This account is found in Charles Schmidt, *Gérard Roussel, Prédicateur de la Reine Marguerite de Navarre: Mémoire, servant à l'histoire des premières tentatives faites pour introduire la reformation en France* (Geneva: Slatkine Reprints, 1970; orig. pub. Strasbourg: n.p., 1845), 163–64.

2. Schmidt, *Gérard Roussel*, 164.

3. Michel Veissière, *L'évêque Guillaume Briçonnet (1470–1534)* (Provins, Fr.: Société d'histoire et d'archéologie, 1986), 202.

4. Josse Clichtove, *Opus magnorum moralium Aristotelis . . . elaborata et breviusculis annotationibus explicata*, trans. Gérard Roussel (Paris: Simon de Colines, 1522), 32a.

Saintin in Meaux. He assisted Lefèvre in the translation of the New Testament into French, which appeared in 1523.[5] Roussel had a prominent place among the preachers in Meaux. In the summer of 1524 (the time when an evangelical preaching manual was being produced in Meaux under the direction of Lefèvre d'Étaples),[6] he became a daily lecturer for common folk on the Letters of Paul and provided learned lectures on the Psalms. He wrote an unpublished commentary on Romans. Yet, of fifty-three epistle lessons selected for the preaching manual, forty-one come from the Pauline corpus, making it likely that many of the sermons attached to these lessons were originally preached by Roussel. His preaching was so effective, Briçonnet increased the number of lecturers to four to visit the larger towns in the diocese. Roussel defined the approach of the preachers at Meaux for his former colleague Farel, who urged them to be more direct in challenging church abuses: "The time has not yet come. It would be a pointless battle against the gates of hell until the gospel is known."[7] In the final legal proceedings against the Circle of Meaux by traditionalists, Roussel was condemned on February 5, 1526, for encouraging the following: iconoclasm; disparaging the pope; distributing the Gospels, Psalms, and Letters of Paul in the vernacular; refusing to recite the *Ave Maria* in the liturgy; and replacing it with the Lord's Prayer until "his bishop should correct him."[8] Roussel had already fled for Strasbourg by early October.[9] The academic battle between scholastics in the Faculty of Theology and the *parlement* of Paris, and humanists in many places was threatening to turn deadly.[10] King Francis I had protected humanists, but could no longer shield them after he was taken hostage by his archrival, Emperor Charles V, at the battle of Pavia on February 24. Scholastics had the upper hand until the king's sister, Marguerite, secured his return from captivity in March 1526.

---

5. Veissière, *L'évêque Guillaume Briçonnet*, 233.

6. Jacques Lefèvre d'Étaples et ses disciples, *Épistres et Évangiles pour les cinquante et deux sepmaines de l'an* (facsimile of the first edition pub. Simon du Bois; Geneva: Droz, 1964).

7. Roussel to Farel, Aug. 24, 1524, in A.-L. Herminjard, ed., *Correspondance des Réformateurs dans les pays de langue française*, 9 vols. (Reprint, Nieuwkoop: De Graaf, 1965), 1:no. 117, pp. 270–73.

8. C. Schmidt, "Gérard Roussel, inculpé d'hérésie à Meaux, 1525," *Bulletin de la Société de l'histoire du protestantisme français* 10 (1861): 219–21.

9. Veissière, *L'évêque Guillaume Briçonnet*, 371.

10. Jacques Pauvant of the Circle of Meaux was executed for heresy in Aug. 1526.

In Strasbourg Roussel was warmly lodged in the home of one of the leading pastors, Wolfgang Capito. He chose a pen name for added personal security, *Tolninus*.[11] The Reformation in Strasbourg impressed Roussel. He already taught *un évangile pacifique*, and the irenic Evangelicalism promoted by Bucer and his colleagues attracted him.[12] He rejoiced in the frequent preaching—pursued with piety and humanistic scholarly rigor—the chanting of the psalms in the vernacular, and more. He marveled that they celebrated "communion as in the time of Christ"[13]—probably offering bread and the cup to all.

Roussel was recalled by Francis I "with honour"[14] in April 1526 to lead the *évangélique* movement in France. He joined the court of Marguerite d'Angoulême, accepting the role of Marguerite's court preacher. He writes to Farel, however: "We must often practice dissimulation."[15] He felt his life was still in danger. Yet this stance was also principled, choosing not to cause offense over "lesser" concerns to concentrate on the gospel. Once the gospel prevails, the time arrives for greater boldness.

After the marriage on January 24, 1527, of Francis I's sister, Marguerite, to Henry, king of Navarre (in the southwest of France today), Roussel was appointed confessor to the royal couple. Marguerite—first d'Angoulême, then de Navarre—was the heart and protector of the *évangélique* movement,[16] but *ecclesiastical* leadership often now fell to Roussel.

---

11. Schmidt, *Gérard Rous*sel, 50–52, 59, 61.

12. "While it is natural to afflict those who are not sufficiently advanced in the doctrine of the Spirit, to empower them to rise above the exterior world, yet—while allowing them to be carried away to invisible regions by faith—they [the preachers] believe that they ought not to scandalize the neighbour and ought to accommodate themselves to the neighbour's 'measure.'" *Quædam porro sunt, quæ plerosque offendere possent non eousque provectos in doctrina Spiritus, ut cuncta externa contemnere queant, sola interim nixi fide quæ sic in invisibilia tota rapitur, ut proximum non negligat, sed per charitatem ad mensuram illius se summittat atque attemperet.* Schmidt, *Gérard Roussel*, 188–91 (in Latin original), 55–58 (in French translation). English translation is mine.

13. *Communio proxime ad Christi tempora.*

14. Erasmus, writing to John à Lasco, May 17, 1527, in Erasmus, *Epistolæ* (Basel: n.p., 1536), 386, cited in Schmidt, *Gérard Roussel*, 65.

15. *Dissimulanda nobis sunt plurima.* Roussel to Farel, Aug. 27, 1526, in Schmidt, *Gérard Roussel*, 69, 197–98.

16. A point conclusively and thoroughly made in Jonathan A. Reid, *King's Sister— Queen of Dissent: Marguerite of Navarre (1492–1549) and Her Evangelical Network*, 2 vols. (Leiden: Brill, 2009).

His friends in Strasbourg supported his efforts. Capito called Roussel "as solid in his judgment as [he is] ardent in his zeal for the glory of God."[17]

The *évangéliques*, however, did not have the same influence with local judicatories as traditionalists. The latter engaged in legal harassments, beginning in 1528,[18] associating them with the dreaded "Lutherans." French *évangéliques* appreciated the Lutheran gospel focus but needed to avoid being caught in this legal trap.[19] However, there were signs the evangelical network might yet prevail. Francis, consistent with his humanist sympathies, in 1529 imposed several new chairs in ancient languages on the Faculty of Theology in Paris over the objections of traditionalists. At the University of Bourges humanistic learning and evangelical preaching were openly permitted, particularly in 1532-1533. John Calvin and Théodore de Bèze participated in this environment. Roussel continued as chaplain to the king and queen of Navarre and was appointed as abbot of both Clairac, southeast of Bordeaux, and Userche, northeast of Bordeaux.[20]

In this mixed atmosphere, emotions ran high and were on prominent display in 1533. Roussel was in the middle of the action. Marguerite de Navarre arranged for her court preacher to become the Lenten preacher in Paris in 1533.[21] His success was astounding, particularly when we remember Paris began the Saint Bartholomew's Day massacres in 1572 and "forced" Henry IV to revert to Catholicism in 1593, if he wanted to unite France politically and end the Wars of Religion. So, five thousand (or more) people flocking to the Louvre Palace to hear the preaching of an *évangélique* stirs our astonishment. Much historiography has portrayed the clash between Catholics and Huguenots as inevitable. Roussel's popularity demonstrates there was a "third option" in France in the early 1530s: traditionalists, Protestants (at this stage, both Lutherans

---

17. *Aussi solide dans son jugement qu'ardent dans son zèle pour la gloire de Dieu.* Tr. by Schmidt, *Gérard Roussel*, 75, from the Latin: *Homo ut acri judicio, ita zelo gloriæ Dei vehementi præditus.* Capito to Marguerite, May 22, 1528, in Capito, *Commentarii in Hoseam* (Strasbourg: n.p., 1528), 8.

18. See Schmidt, *Gérard Roussel*, 76-77.

19. See Reid, *Queen of Dissent*.

20. Schmidt, *Gérard Roussel*, 78-82; Eugene F. Rice, ed., *The Prefatory Epistles of Jacques Lefèvre d'Etaples and Related Texts* (New York: Columbia University Press, 1972), 246-47.

21. Details are given in a long letter from Pierre Siderander to Jacques Bédrot, May 28, 1533, in Schmidt, *Gérard Roussel*, 201-11.

and Reformed), and the non-schismatic *évangéliques*.[22] In hindsight, however, 1533 was the apex of evangelical success.

How did events unfold? After the pre-Lenten Carnival in 1533, Francis I left the capital, while Henry and Marguerite de Navarre remained. The queen arranged for Roussel to preach at the Louvre daily, and such large crowds came that a larger venue was needed. His followers were given a nickname, *Geraldini*. Schmidt attributes the eagerness of Parisians to the contrast between Roussel's message and the subtleties and obscurities of scholastic preaching.[23] Florence Volusene explains the points in Roussel's message that the Faculty of Theology disputed in a letter to Henry VIII's chief minister, Thomas Cromwell.[24] Roussel spoke against compulsory fasting in Lent because works should come from a heart purified by faith, and the church should require nothing beyond what is in Scripture. A German student in Bourges writes home that Roussel was attacked for declaring justification comes solely through the merits of Jesus Christ.[25] The Faculty, displaying its normal antagonism to Evangelicalism, sent delegations to Francis, his chancellor Duprat, the Bishop of Paris Du Bellay (who was sympathetic to the *évangéliques*), and the president of the Paris *parlement* (who shared the antagonism of the theologians, but sensed the political tide). None would act against Roussel. The Faculty then sent out rival preachers who denounced Henry, Marguerite, Roussel, Du Bellay, and Francis I as complicit with heresy. Noel Beda led the way. These rival camps produced increasing agitation in Paris. Roussel was physically attacked and nearly injured.[26] The Sorbonne condemned several declara-

22. Axel Schoeber, "John Calvin and the "Still-Born" Third Option in the French Reformation," in *Calvin@500: Theology, History, and Practice*, ed. Richard R. Topping and John A. Vissers (Eugene, OR: Pickwick, 2011), 86–97. Denis Crouzet, *La genèse de la Réforme français, 1520–560* (Paris: Sèdes, 1996), 239, 344, also argues for three movements at this time. Reid, *Queen of Dissent*, 2:570, 2:642, argues for three strains of religious literature in France during this period: Catholic, Protestant, and *évangélique*, and that opponents, both Catholic and Protestant, saw the *évangéliques* as a distinct group.

23. Schmidt, *Gérard Roussel*, 85–86.

24. Apr. 25 [1533] in James Gairdner, ed., *1531–1532*, vol. 5 of *Letters and Papers, Foreign and Domestic, Henry VIII* (London: Institute of Historical Research, 1880), no. 212, pp. 99–100.

25. Basilius Mourner to Georg Sturz, June 13, 1533, in Otto Clemen, "Zwei Briefe von Baslius Mourner," *Mitteilungen der Vereinigung für Gothaische Geschichte und Altertumsforschung* 12 (1912): 109–11, esp. 110.

26. Urbanus Rhegius to Philip Melanchthon, July 8, 1533, in Heinz Scheible, ed., *Melanchthons Briefwechsel: Kritische und kommentierte Gesamtausgabe: Texte* (Stuttgart: Fromman-Holzboog, 2003), 5:no. 1344, p. 459.

tions by Roussel, concluding "that they appear to be favorable to the errors of Luther."[27] Eventually Beda and two other preachers were banished until the king chose to reverse the order.

At this point, it is hard even to imagine the eventual outcome. The *évangéliques* had emerged unscathed. A young John Calvin returned from his studies at Bourges and became a friend and admirer of Roussel—a Geraldini.[28] Many Evangelicals were rejoicing that gospel renewal was imminent in their beloved France. Yet the story did not finish here. It was Nicolas Cop, the new rector of the University of Paris, who overreached by declaiming at length to the whole university on justification by faith. Francis had generally supported humanists, including Evangelicals, but also generally stood against clearly identified Protestants. He took seriously his sacred calling as the Most Christian King. Cop fled to Basel, and Calvin also left Paris—giving the impression he helped produce the infamous address.

At this time Roussel received a letter from Pope Clement VII praising his evangelistic preaching and giving him permission to read Luther without interference.[29] The pope was confident Roussel was both orthodox and not schismatic.[30] However, Cop's university address had shifted momentum to the traditionalists. Beda returned to Paris and urged that Roussel be burned as a heretic. Though he was released, Marguerite had to intercede for her chaplain: "The king will find that he [Roussel] is worthy of better than fire, and that he has never held an opinion to merit it, nor felt anything heretical."[31] Roussel would not preach in Paris again. For his part, Francis sought outside help to reunify traditionalists and

---

27. Cited in Schmidt, *Gérard Roussel*, 87: "qu'elles paraissaient être favorables aux erreurs de Luther."

28. See Jean Dupèbe, "Un document sur les persécutions de l'hiver 1533-1534 à Paris," *Bibliothèque d'Humanisme et Renaissance* 48 (1986): 405-17; Reid, *Queen of Dissent*, 2:431.

29. See Henry Heller, "An Unknown Letter from Clement VII to Gerard Roussel," *Bibliothèque d'Humanisme et Renaissance* 38 (1976): 489-92. Heller plausibly argues this undated letter was written at this time.

30. Jean de Salignac, one of the theologians of the Sorbonne, reported in 1533 that nothing Roussel was preaching was heretical; cited in Francis Higman, "De l'affaire des placards aux nicodémites," in *Lire et Découvrir: La circulation des idées au temps de la Réforme* (Geneva: Droz, 1998), 618-29, esp. 622-23.

31. *Le Roy trouvera qu'il est digne de mieulx que du feu, et qu'il n'a jamais tenu opinion pour le mériter, ny quy sente nulle chose hérétique.* Marguerite to Montmorency, date uncertain, but Roussel is in Paris. Cited in Schmidt, *Gérard Roussel*, 106n3.

évangéliques, by approaching Bucer and Melanchthon to draw up a proposal to unite on essential points and offer liberty regarding secondary matters. Then, on October 19, 1534, the infamous *placards* of Antoine Marcourt were posted in various places in northern France. Their condemnation of the Mass as blasphemy once again turned Francis against Protestants and the *évangéliques*. Roussel was on the "most wanted list" of the *parlement* in Paris.[32]

Roussel retreated to Navarre, where Marguerite could clearly protect. He attempted again the strategy deployed in Meaux to develop a renewed diocese that could impact the *réforme* of the nation. In 1536 Roussel was appointed bishop of Oloron, below the northern slopes of the Pyrenees—a popular choice with many. Poets wrote verse to celebrate his shining example.[33] Yet, there was much opposition from corrupt priests and traditionally minded local *seigneurs* and royal counselors.[34] In 1545 Henry issued an ordinance against disorders in the churches, particularly in Oloron.[35] Henry shielded his wife's favorite, even after her death, but Roussel functioned under pressure throughout his bishopric. His death fit this pattern.

In addition, long-time friends were upset with Roussel's elevation to the episcopate. Calvin excoriated his old friend[36] in a published letter. He resorted to false accusations: Roussel did not excommunicate Protestants[37] or commit "multiple homicides."[38] He rejected Roussel's character:

---

32. Reid, *Queen of Dissent*, 2:432.

33. See examples of such poems by Nicolas Bourbon in Schmidt, *Gérard Roussel*, 243–44.

34. Gustav Cadier, *Gérard Roussel (1480–1555): Sa vie, son influence sur la Réforme française* (master's thesis, University of Geneva, 1947), 71.

35. Cadier, *Gérard Roussel*, 78.

36. *A un ancien ami, de présent évesque*. *Ancien ami* could mean "old friend" or "former friend"—the latter in this case. It was published in *Epistolæ duæ, de rebus hoc sæculo cognitu apprime necessariis* (Basel: Balthasarem Lasium & Thomam Platterum, 1537) and translated into French in *Traité des Bénéfices, où il y a plusieurs matières et questions bénéficiales, décidées selon la simple et pure verité de la Parole de Dieu* (Geneva: N.p., 1554). Excerpts quoted in Schmidt, *Gérard Roussel*, 114–17.

37. *Toi qui blâmais jadis les abus du clergé de Rome, tu acceptes maintenant une dignité qui t'oblige . . . à prononcer peut-être des excommunications dont pourtant tu reconnais l'injustice.*

38. *Malheureux, tu dois rendre compte de la mort de tant de gens devant le Seigneur! tant de fois es-tu homicide! tant de fois coulpable de sang, duquel il n'y aura pas une goutte que le Seigneur ne redemande de ta main.*

> There remains [this point] that we in no way wish to reject from our company those that the Lord recognizes and avows as his servants. But in you, is there any [such] semblance? In whom life has no appearance of Christian vocation and even is totally distanced from the way of the Lord?[39]

Calvin's opinion differs wildly from those who eagerly welcomed Roussel to Oloron. Calvin had had a different perspective in 1533: "Long ago I myself admired [you], whose example had been of immense profit for me."[40] Why the change? The choice to accept a Catholic bishopric was unforgiveable. Calvin closes with rhetorical overkill: "I will never hold you for a Christian or a man of good. Goodbye."[41] His hostility remained implacable.[42]

Charles Schmidt, a Protestant, in 1845 depicted Roussel as a diligent leader, committed to doing good. Often, while touring his diocese with a translator, he preached two or three times a day, ensuring his gospel sermons were understood by his Basque-speaking parishioners. He celebrated Mass, dispensing bread and the cup. He expounded the "mystery of the sacrament,"[43] apparently comfortable with various explanations of the Eucharist, including different Protestant understandings and a simplified transubstantiation. He focused on instruction of the young, including children. He created schools and taught in them, modeling love of knowledge and "purer religious conviction."[44] He created study circles for youth.[45] He eschewed episcopal splendor, preaching in lay dress and using his revenues for schools and works of charity. At Clairac as abbot,

---

39. *Il y a cela seulement que nous ne voulons point rejeter de nostre compagnie ceux que le Seigneur reconnaist et advoue pour ses serviteurs. Mais en toy y a-t-il rien de semblable? duquel la vie n'a aucune apparence de vocation chrestienne et mesmes est totalement eslongnée de la voye du Seigneur?*

40. *Jadis j'ai moi-même admirée et dont l'exemple a été pour moi d'un profit immense.*

41. *Je ne te tiendrai jamais ni pour chrestien ni pour homme de bien. Adieu.*

42. Farel to Calvin, Apr. 16, 1540, in Herminjard, *Correspondance*, 6:no. 860, pp. 209–10, asks Calvin to encourage Roussel because the former has heard good reports about Roussel's efforts in Oloron. Calvin to Farel, about May 13, 1540 (in Herminjard, *Correspondance*, 6:no. 863, p. 223), refuses.

43. Henri de Sponde, *Continuatio Annalium Baronii* (Leiden: Sumptibus Fratrum Anissoniorum, & Ioan Pos, 1678), *t* II, 523. A partisan Catholic writer, Sponde, still describes Roussel's teaching on the Mass as "*une remonstrance sur le mystère du sacrement.*"

44. Sponde, *Continuatio*, t II, 523.

45. Cadier, *Gérard Roussel*, 74.

Roussel granted the town "a liberal constitution of self-rule."⁴⁶ Roussel fit in regular time at Marguerite's court, continuing as her confessor. He typically had dinner with her, discussing things learned and spiritual.⁴⁷ He also wrote, though censorship prevented publication. His important works were *La Familière exposition*—a catechetical manual to instruct priests in training—and *Forme de visite*—instruction for visitations to parishes. The Sorbonne condemned *La Familière exposition* in 1550. Roussel traveled to the opening session of the Council of Trent in 1545, disappointed when Trent quickly defined doctrine in a traditionalist direction and denounced Protestants as heretical.⁴⁸ Still, he sought to make Oloron a model of renewal *within the Catholic Church*. Apparently Roussel was considered for appointment as a cardinal in 1553.⁴⁹ Roussel still had national stature and considerable respect. The Jesuits spoke strongly against that possibility, and it never happened.

We can now consider Roussel's death again. Mauléon, the site of the attack on Roussel, is in a Basque region, known for strong religious traditionalism.⁵⁰ He sent his vicar general to address some resistance; Arnauld de Maytie led those who angrily chased him away. Roussel asserted his authority, convening a synod and preaching people should honor the saints by imitation, not adoration. De Maytie smuggled in the axe he used on Roussel's pulpit. With irony we note De Maytie's son became the next bishop of Oloron. The archives of the town of Clairac preserve the record that Roussel "institutes the poor as his heirs general and universal. July 8, 1555."⁵¹ On the way to some springs for treatment, he died at the village of Louvie on August 15, 1555. Buried at Nérac, there is no sign of his tomb today.⁵²

---

46. Reid, *Queen of Dissent*, 1:68.

47. Henry Heller, "Marguerite of Navarre and the Reformers of Meaux," *Bibliothèque d'Humanisme et Renaissance* 33 (1971): 271–310, esp. 285.

48. See Alain Tallon, *La France et le concile de Trente (1518-1563)* (Rome: École française de Rome, 1997), 63–172, 754–70.

49. Larissa Taylor, *Heresy and Orthodoxy in Sixteenth Century Paris: François Le Picart and the Beginnings of the Catholic Reformation* (Boston: Brill, 1999), 124.

50. Cadier, *Gérard Roussel*, 83–84.

51. *Il institue les pauvres ses héritiers généraux et universels. Du 8 juillet 1555.* A. L., "Recherche d'un document important relative à Gérard Roussel," *Bulletin de la Société de l'histoire du protestantisme français* 10 (1861): 342.

52. The details above are found in Cadier, *Gérard Roussel*, 85.

Let me summarize Roussel's approach. As the choice was increasingly forced on people between the word and the Mass, Roussel refused to choose, affirming both biblical preaching and the Eucharist as renewing factors. He was a committed bridge-builder who appreciated many fellow leaders, while also avoiding fitting neatly into any of the theological camps hardening around him. Roussel was a Catholic Evangelical, diligent in pursuing gospel-based reform in an irenic manner.

So, Jonathan, why do I tell this story in a Festschrift in your honor? Gérard Roussel reminds me of you. You have had setbacks in your career, though not as severe as Roussel. You have been a diligent bridge-builder—across theological identities, among various theological schools and different denominations, impacting leaders in many parts of the world. Roussel's legacy was diffuse enough that his memory was largely forgotten. I cannot predict how widely your teaching and writing will be remembered. I do know your investment in so many people in so many parts of the globe will constitute a powerful legacy, reflecting your irenic spirit and approach. Thanks for caring so deeply for the Lord Jesus Christ, his church, and so many colleagues in ministry and academia, including me.

Faithfully yours,
Axel

Gospel Realism and the Epistle to Hebrews

CRAIG A. SMITH

I HAD THE JOY of being Jonathan's colleague and kindred spirit at Carey Theological College for seven years. A highlight for me during this time period were the times we met together. There was never a set agenda. We would share the highs and lows of our daily life. Sometimes we prayed. We covered an array of topics broader than Jim Carrey's smile. There was only one topic where we stood diametrically opposed, entrenched in our immutable stances. College basketball. He was a Duke Blue Devils (this name alone should make a Christian wary of handing over their allegiance) die-hard and I was a Kansas Jayhawks devotee. In this safe space we bounced ideas off one another, challenging and refining our thinking. The thing that we most agreed upon and were terribly passionate about was the gospel of Jesus Christ. His story never ceased to capture our hearts and minds. As Jonathan so aptly notes, the gospel is "the story of truth" that "teaches us what the real world is and how to live in that real world."[1] It is the story of God's love for which there is no substitute.[2]

---

1. Jonathan R. Wilson, *God So Loved the World: A Christology for Disciples* (Grand Rapids: Baker Academic, 2001), 20.
2. Wilson, *God So Loved*, 21.

Story of the Kingdom

God's story is the story of Jesus Christ. It is also the story about his kingdom. This kingdom is about the reality that God loves the world and demonstrated this through his son. According to Wilson, believers learn to live as God's people by embracing four characteristics of the kingdom: reality, perfection, value, and openness.[3] The purpose of this short paper is to use the first and third characteristics as lenses to examine and elucidate the situation that the Hebrews were facing, and which the author was addressing in the Epistle to the Hebrews.

The Reality of the Kingdom

The author of Hebrews states that his readers were "enlightened," which is a colorful metaphor meaning that they became believers (10:32), probably sometime before the Edict of Claudius (AD 49). They were most likely Jewish Christians,[4] or at least, predominately so. These believers heard and received the message of Christ's gospel through individuals who heard and saw Jesus (2:3). They experienced the grace of God who testified to this salvation which they received through signs, wonders, various miracles and gifts of the Holy Spirit distributed according to his will (2:4). In 6:4, the author uses the same Greek word for enlightened (φωτίζω) as he did in 10:32, suggesting that the following description in 6:4–5 is a depiction of the readers. They tasted the heavenly gift, shared in the Holy Spirit, tasted the good word and the powers of the coming age (6:4–5). They were immersed in the story of Jesus and the reality of the kingdom.[5] For them, the gospel was not an unattainable ideal or an ideology to fulfill their inner being or an impossible promise waiting to be realized.[6] By faith, the Hebrews accepted the kingdom of God as a present experience inaugurated by Christ through his teaching (Matt 5:1–10),

---

3. Wilson, *God So Loved*, 25.

4. Moffatt proposes the dissenting view that the Hebrews are gentile Christians. James Moffatt, *A Critical and Exegetical Commentary on the Epistle to the Hebrews*, International Critical Commentary (Edinburgh: T&T Clark, 1924), xxv. See Lane's discussion, which argues convincingly for Jewish Christians whose roots are in the Hellenistic synagogue. William L. Lane, *Hebrews 1–8*, Word Bible Commentary 47a (Dallas: Word, 1991), liii–lx.

5. A fuller discussion of the reality of the kingdom of God can be found in Wilson, *God So Loved*, 25–28.

6. Wilson, *God So Loved*, 26.

parables (Matt 13:24–52), and deeds of healing (Matt 20:29–34) and of exorcism (Matt 15:21–28). One can probably also say, they participated in the kingdom of God in the same way Jesus did as he shared in the more mundane and normal aspects of being human (e.g., eating dinner with friends, sauntering through the *agoras*, attending synagogue worship), thereby showing that the "kingdom is present... in every human place."[7] The readers partook in the "actuality," "reality," and "concreteness" of the kingdom so that "the ideal [of the kingdom] was [being] made real, the promise [was being] fulfilled, [and] the potential [was being] realized"[8] in them by being in Christ.

This reality of the kingdom was subsequently tested through a significant trial. The author reflects on this experience in Heb 10:32–34:

> Remember those earlier days after you had received the light, when you endured in a great conflict full of suffering. Sometimes you were publicly exposed to insult and persecution; at other times you stood side by side with those who were so treated. You suffered along with those in prison and joyfully accepted the confiscation of your property, because you knew that you yourselves had better and lasting possessions.[9]

Some scholars suggest this might refer to the persecution of the church of Jerusalem after Stephen's martyrdom (AD 33), while others suggest a period of suffering under Emperor Nero or Domitian.[10] However, most scholars are in agreement that the author of Hebrews is describing the experience of many Jews and Jewish Christians living in Rome after the enactment of the Edict of Claudius (AD 49). The primary source about this event is the account of the Roman historian Suetonius (AD 69–122?), in *Lives of Caesar*, who wrote, "Claudius expelled from Rome the Jews constantly making disturbances at the instigation of Chrestus."[11] At this point in time, Rome did not distinguish between Jews and Christians, who lived in communities within Rome. Tensions

---

7. Wilson, *God So Loved*, 27.

8. Wilson, *God So Loved*, 27.

9. This chapter uses the NRSV translation for Scripture references, unless otherwise indicated.

10. F. F. Bruce, *The Epistle to the Hebrews*, New International Commentary on the New Testament (Grand Rapids: Eerdmans, 1990), 267.

11. Likely, Suetonius, who is writing in Latin, has misspelled the Greek name *Christos*, possibly intentionally, since *Chrestus* was a common name of a slave at that time.

and conflicts increased in these communities as Jews came to faith in Christ. Claudius likely grew tired of the conflicts and eventually expelled many Jewish Christians from Rome (n.b. Priscilla and Aquila were two Jewish believers who fled Rome and relocated in Corinth; Acts 18:2–3). It is not clear whether their personal losses were due to fines or taxes levied on them by magistrates or whether their property was looted after they were imprisoned and/or expelled from the city, though the latter is more likely.[12] The ensuing crisis and persecution from the Edict of Claudius appears to have been without bloodshed. Through this period of time, those who were able to remain continued to believe and practice the reality of the kingdom.

The author of Hebrews writes about a subsequent persecution. Most scholars agree that this is the Neronian persecution directed at Christians in Rome after the Great Fire of AD 64. Fifteen years had passed since the Edict of Claudius, and many of the exiled Jewish Christians had returned and many new converts had been made. Emperor Nero was sixteen when he took the throne (AD 54). In the early years of his reign under the tutelage of Seneca and Burrus, things remained stable.[13] However, with their deaths, Nero came under the influence of Tigellinus, the head of the praetorian guard, who was anti-semitic and anti-Christian. Tacitus, the Roman historian (AD 55–120), attributes blame to Nero as the one who started the fire in Rome since he had the desire to rebuild certain areas of the city. The fire burned out of control, destroying two-thirds of the city (n.b. only four of the fourteen precincts not destroyed belonged to Nero and Tigellinus). Nero could not blame the Jews for fear of reprisal since, at the time, many Jews lived in Rome. He had to look elsewhere. Tacitus records that Nero "fastened the guilt and inflicted the most exquisite tortures on a class hated for their abominations [n.b. this probably refers to the Lord's supper of eating the body and blood of Christ], called Christians by the populace."[14]

---

12. Eusebius logs how Emperor Domitian confiscated property from his adversaries: "Domitian, having shown great cruelty toward many, and having unjustly put to death no small number of well-born and notable men at Rome, and having without cause exiled and confiscated the property of a great many other illustrious men, finally became a successor of Nero in his hatred and enmity toward God." Eusebius, *Church History* 3.17.

13. Everett Ferguson, *Backgrounds of Early Christianity* (Grand Rapids: Eerdmans, 2003), 32–33.

14. Tacitus, *Annals* 15.44.

The level of intensity of the Neronian persecution was significantly greater than the persecution, fifteen years earlier, under Claudius (AD 49). Tacitus describes the persecution of these Christians as "hatred of mankind [and that] mockery of every sort was added to their deaths; covered with the skins of beasts, they were torn by dogs and perished, or were nailed to crosses, or were doomed to the flames and burnt, to serve as a nightly illumination, when daylight had expired."[15]

The Hebrews were familiar with these events and most likely knew some of those who had been persecuted and killed in this crisis. They were affected in different ways by this crisis. First, some individuals and possibly house churches (n.b. the Hebrews were likely made up of several house churches) began to separate themselves from their house group or from other house groups. Some may have stopped meeting together entirely (10:25). As a result, there appears to have been some tension between leaders and certain individuals and house groups (13:17, 24).

Second, some may have been drifting away from the Christian faith and possibly moving back or considering moving back to Judaism since the Jews were not being persecuted by Rome. For this reason, the author warns them in the first of five warnings in the epistle that the punishment for turning away from salvation found in Christ is greater than the punishments under the Mosaic covenant (2:2–3). Furthermore, the author devotes two-thirds of the letter to show how Jesus is superior to the Mosaic covenant. Using the comparative adjective (*kreittōn*; κρείττων) as a literary device to achieve this, he shows how Jesus, his ministry, covenant and benefits to his followers are superior to the Mosaic covenant, so that they might remain as Christians:

Jesus is the superior revelation and revealer (1:1–4)

Jesus is the superior mediator (1:5—7:28)

Believers receive: a superior salvation (6:9)

a superior hope (7:19)

a superior covenant (7:22)

Jesus is the mediator of the superior covenant (8:1–13)

Believers receive: a superior covenant based on superior promises (8:6)

Jesus is the superior sacrifice (9:1—10:39)

---

15. Tacitus, *Annals* 15.44.

| Believers receive: | a superior purification (9:23) |
| | a superior lasting possession (10:34) |

Jesus is the provider of a superior future (11:1–40)

| Believers receive: | a superior heavenly home (11:16) |
| | a superior future (11:40) |

Third, understandably, there was a growing fear of death among them (2:15) but, as a result, some were becoming "sluggish" or "lax" in appropriating the truths of the gospel. The effect of this was that the faith of some was faltering so that they were struggling to persevere, and some were even considering leaving the faith (6:4–6). For this reason, the author delivers some of his strongest and harshest warnings against ignoring God's word (3:7–19; 12:25–31), rejecting Christ's redemptive sacrifice and benefits (10:26–31), and falling into spiritual immaturity (5:11—6:12).

Applying Jonathan Wilson's insight into the reality of the kingdom makes clear that the Hebrews were living the story of the kingdom, partaking in its reality. Wilson also enumerates two difficulties of abiding in the reality of the kingdom that are helpful for understanding the attitude and mindset of the Hebrews before and after the Great Fire of Rome. First, when people's desires and expectations of what the kingdom of God should look like are at variance with the kingdom of God that Jesus established and proclaimed, people struggle to believe and practice the kingdom of God.[16] When the Hebrews initially believed and even during the persecution under Claudius, they had "confidence/conviction" (παρρησία) in Christ and the kingdom of God (10:35). However, during the persecution under Nero, this confidence and conviction began to waiver. For this reason, the author offers several exhortations: "hold firmly to the end [your] original conviction" (3:14), "show the same diligence to the end" (6:11), "hold unswervingly to the hope [you] profess" (10:23), "persevere" (10:36), and "run with perseverance the race marked out for [you]" (12:1). In addition to encouragement, the author also reminds them that the kingdom of God is still present and real, even if it seems hidden and unseen. Just as Jesus founded and lived the kingdom of God in the context of suffering and evil, the author reminds them that the kingdom of God is also present in the conditions of suffering and evil that they are experiencing. In fact, he shows that those who have

---

16. Wilson, *God So Loved*, 28–29.

faith in God have always worked out their salvation amidst struggles and trials. For this reason, he encourages the Hebrews to see their trials as opportunities for God's discipline, though painful, to produce a harvest of righteousness and peace (12:11). They are to follow Jesus, the *archēgos*, ἀρχηγός (2:10). As *archēgos*, Jesus 1) founded the Hebrews' salvation, 2) has been exalted as the "champion" of the faith, overcoming death and the devil (2:9, 14–15), and 3) has set a path as the "trailblazer/forerunner" for his brothers and sisters to follow (2:16; 6:19–20). Their race,[17] which includes suffering, is the same as Jesus's, except without the requirement of providing a sacrifice of atonement (12:1).

According to Wilson, the second reason why believers have difficulty living the reality of the kingdom is their lack of trained eyes to see the reality the kingdom and their failure to submit themselves to the necessary discipline in order to see how the kingdom is present and active in their midst.[18] The author of Hebrews would concur. In Heb 5:11–14, he uses the language of maturity/immaturity and solid food/milk, combined with the image of an athlete in training, to make this point. From the Hebrews' perspective, they think they need more "milk," which refers to "the elementary truths of God's word" (5:12).[19] However, if they ingest a diet of milk, they will remain immature and possibly regress. From the author's perspective, they need the word of righteousness, which refers to the teaching and life of righteousness expressed by Christ. They need to enter into Christ's story, into his kingdom's story. This is the path of maturity during their time of hardship. To do this, they will need "trained senses," which develop through constant practice as followers of Jesus. These "senses" are an inner faculty of the believer. The cognate noun is found in Phil 1:9 where this "sense" refers to the "insight needed to know

---

17. This word, ἀγών (agōn), used here is found six times in the NT. Typically, it has the meaning of "fight" or metaphorically "struggle" (cf. Phil 1:30; Col 2:1; 1 Thess 2:2; 1 Tim 6:12; 2 Tim 4:7). The author uses it here in the sense of a "race" but retaining the sense of struggle. This is the kind of race God has marked out for his children (12:1). For more explanation on *archēgos*, see: Alfred Ernest Garvie, "The Pioneer of Faith and of Salvation: A Study of the Personal Experience of Jesus as Presented in the Epistle to the Hebrews," *ExT* 26 (1915): 502–4; George Johnston, "Christ as Archegos," *NTS* 27 (1981): 381–85.

18. Wilson, *God So Loved*, 29.

19. Des Cotes observes rightly that "we will never reach maturity by merely sharpening our belief system. We must grow beyond our doctrines—the elementary teachings of our faith—towards the concrete knowledge of faith that these beliefs invite us to." Rob Des Cotes, Imago Dei Christian Community, letter to supporters from Sept. 10, 2015.

how to love." In Heb 5:14, it refers to the inner faculty for discerning good from evil. They need this inner sense in order to discern and see the reality of God's kingdom in the midst of suffering, and to choose to follow the way of Christ, which includes suffering, and not revert to Judaism or turn away from the faith.

The Value and Costliness of the Kingdom

According to Jonathan Wilson, the kingdom of God is of great value because it announces the good news. Jesus proclaimed "it as a reality, as something present, actual, and everlasting."[20] The good news is also of great value because it announces that the promises of God have been fulfilled. The flip side of the value of the kingdom of God is its costliness. While traveling around Caesarea Philippi with his disciples, Jesus summarized this costliness:

> Whoever wants to be my disciple must deny themselves and take up their cross and follow me. For whoever wants to save their life will lose it, but whoever loses their life for me and for the gospel will save it. What good is it for someone to gain the whole world, yet forfeit their soul? Or what can anyone give in exchange for their soul? (Mark 8:34–37)

The kingdom of God costs a person their entire self and all that he or she has.[21] As Wilson astutely observes, this expectation can only make sense if "there is another kingdom, against the kingdom of God, into which [humankind] is born and in which [it] lives."[22] This is the kingdom of sin (John 1:29; 3:19) and death (Rom 5:12), which is under the control of Satan (John 14:30). Because these kingdoms are diametrically opposed, believers must choose the kingdom to which they will commit

---

20. Wilson, *God So Loved*, 33.

21. C. S. Lewis captures the essence of this total commitment and single focused commitment, "If its picture [of what salvation entails] was true then no sort of 'treaty with reality' could ever be possible. There was no region even in the innermost depth of one's soul (nay, there least of all) which one could surround with a barbed wire fence and guard with a notice *No Admittance*. And that was what I wanted; some area, however small, of which I could say to all other beings, 'This is my business and mine only.'" C. S. Lewis, *Surprised by Joy: The Shape of My Early Life* (New York: Harcourt Brace, 1984), 171–72.

22. Wilson, *God So Loved*, 35.

themselves and live.²³ Both Jesus and Paul aver, believers can have only one Lord (Eph 4:4–5; Phil 2:10; Matt 6:24). Daily renouncing the kingdom of sin and death and submitting to the rule of God through Christ is the way believers live in the reality of the kingdom.²⁴

Wilson's observations about the costliness of the kingdom provide another helpful lens for looking at the situation of the Hebrews. The Hebrews are being faced with the costliness of the kingdom of God and the challenge to live the way of the kingdom (as Jesus did), during the period of Nero's tyranny against Christians. For this reason, the author of Hebrews exhorts them to fix their eyes on Jesus, the author and perfecter of their faith (12:2). Because of the particular situation the Hebrews are facing, the author emphasizes certain aspects of the way Jesus lived in order to help them during this arduous time. According to the author, this life entails enduring opposition possibly to the point of death (12:3–4), submitting in obedience to the Father (5:7–8), holding on steadfastly (3:14; 10:23), maintaining the sabbath celebration rest of God²⁵ (4:9), and living in faith (10:36—11:40), in holiness, in peace and love with others (12:14; 13:1–3).

The Hebrews are being confronted head-on by the kingdom of the world, the kingdom of sin and death. They are being tempted to collude with the world and save their lives but forfeit their souls. The author warns that to do so would be to crucify Christ again and subject him to public disgrace (6:6). G. K. Chesterton wrote, "Christianity has not been tried and found wanting; it has been found difficult and not tried."²⁶ The Hebrews' Christian faith was being tried and tested in much the same way the exodus generation was tested. The author of Hebrews declares that the exodus generation did not enter because they had sinful, unbelieving hearts that turned away from God (3:12). They were not able to enter the promised land and God's rest even though they heard the message. Unfortunately, they did not combine God's message to enter

---

23. Thomas More sums up this thought well: "If you have not chosen the Kingdom of God, it will make in the end no difference what you have chosen instead," quoted in Christopher W. Mitchell, "C. S. Lewis on Authentic Discipleship," *Knowing and Doing* (Spring 2011): 4.

24. Wilson, *God So Loved*, 35.

25. For further discussion on the phrase "sabbath celebration of God," see Craig A. Smith, "Jesus, the Founder of Sabbatismos," in *The Earliest Perceptions of Jesus in Context*, Library of New Testament Studies 566 (London: Bloomsbury, 2018), 236–52.

26. G. K. Chesterton, *What's Wrong with the World*, vol. 4 of *Collected Works* (San Francisco: Ignatius, 1987), 61.

the land with faith and action (4:2). Instead, they fixed their minds on the negative reports of the other ten spies (Num 13:26–29, 31–33) and refused to enter, desiring to return to Egypt (Num 14:1–4, 10). These Israelites feared the kingdom of the world more than they trusted God to act on their behalf (Num 14:11–12). They were not prepared to count the cost to enter God's rest and to live the risky life of faith. The author of Hebrews uses this as an example to exhort the Hebrews to count the cost to remain in the rest that Christ had founded for them. They were not to turn back to Judaism or fall away to unbelief. Instead, they were being called forward into a life of faith to an unseen future, just as the heroes of faith did and were commended for it (11:13).

Conclusion

Applying Jonathan Wilson's insight into the reality of the kingdom to the Epistle to the Hebrews shows that the readers were living in the story of Jesus and in the reality of the kingdom. When the Neronian persecution came, they began to waiver as they saw and experienced the kingdom of the world, sin and death, before their eyes. Although the kingdom of God seemed invisible to them, the author is confident that they are mature, having eyes to see the kingdom, and will remain steady, continuing to follow the way of Jesus diligently to the end.

The costliness and value of the kingdom of God, as Wilson describes it, sheds light on what the author of Hebrews was expecting of his readers. Nero's pogrom of persecution against Christians in Rome brought the kingdom of the world in stark relief with the kingdom of God and the personal cost of following the way of Jesus. This lens of the costliness of the kingdom of God goes a good distance in explaining the method of exhortation the author of Hebrews uses in his letter or, as he calls it, his "word of exhortation" (13:23).

A Christian Critique of Christian Britain[1]

How a Solitary Public Witness Transformed Christian Ethics

JOHN BERKMAN

IN THE FALL OF 1987, Jonathan and I enrolled in Hauerwas's graduate seminar "Practical Reason and Personal Identity." The first week we studied Elizabeth Anscombe, reading *Intention* and, I think, "Modern Moral Philosophy." Universally agreed to be Anscombe's most influential work, they provided some of the key conceptual moves that made possible later work, including Alasdair MacIntyre's *After Virtue*. Anscombe was a mysterious figure, combining intellectual brilliance with eccentricity: the classic caricature of an Oxbridge academic.

At the same time, Jonathan and I were learning about the importance of apprenticeship in the moral life, or in more adequately Christian terms, the witness of the saints. While we knew we could learn from Anscombe's intellectual brilliance (if we could understand her), we knew nothing of Anscombe as Christian witness. Although Anscombe never advertised it, *Intention* and "Modern Moral Philosophy" were contingent intellectual by-products of a public Christian witness. If she had not made her solitary public witness to a fundamental moral principle, Anscombe would not likely have written either *Intention* or "Modern

---

1. The title of the essay is a reference to Jonathan's muse Julian Hartt, namely his book *A Christian Critique of Christian America*.

Moral Philosophy." This essay in honor of Jonathan tells the heretofore unknown story of Anscombe's witness, and how it transformed the future of Christian ethics.

To Be a Catholic Is to Be a Witness

Anscombe's passion, from her Oxford undergraduate days (1937–41) onwards, is to give Christian witness to her society. In the summer of 1938, two months after being received into the Catholic Church, Anscombe contributes an article to Britain's leading Catholic newsweekly. Articles were being solicited from "under twenty-fives" to express their Catholic views and the life each intends to live. While others write of becoming journalists, farmers, nurses, etc., Anscombe has a greater "ambition." She "chiefly wants all who are outside the Church to become Catholic, and all Catholics, saints." However, since her generation is inoculated against Christian preaching and doctrine, a "full Catholic life in the world," for Anscombe will be to embody "the Catholic social scheme." "We must be the first to . . . to deal justly, suppress usury, underselling, unjust prices and wages, to respect and increase the human dignity of the poor by restoring to them greater control over their own lives." It is only the failure of regular Catholics to witness, to live their faith in the marketplace, that prevents England's wholesale conversion to Catholicism.

Witnessing against Unjust War

By the spring of 1939, having completed her mods examinations, Anscombe's concern for social justice turns to the impending war. Her fiancé Peter Geach has to make a decision about participation in any forthcoming war. Anscombe co-authors *The Justice of the Present War Examined*, a pamphlet that argues two points.

First, according to Catholic just war principles, Britain is waging an unjust war. Undoubtedly, there is just cause for warring against Germany, but that is not why Britain's rulers have taken Britain to war. Britain's stated goals are to avoid further national embarrassment, protect the status quo with regard to her power and colonies, and to utterly destroy Germany.

Second, having argued that Britain's stated purposes, ends, and especially its intended means for warring are unjust, each and every British Catholic must conscientiously consider the arguments, for the war *is* unjust, and then the Catholic sins in participating in it.² A state demanding that its citizens sin on its behalf is a government asking to be worshiped, and Catholics must defy it.³

Anscombe's view is that each Catholic in conscience must make their own individual judgment; it is morally impermissible for a Catholic to unequivocally trust the state (and, e.g., blame it afterwards for prosecuting an unjust war).⁴ Here Anscombe diverges from the English Catholic hierarchy's interpretation of just war doctrine. Anscombe is echoing what Victor White, OP, eloquently states shortly before the outbreak of WWII.

> The scandal of "the failure of the Churches" during the world-war of 1914–1918 ... [is] too evident for us to ignore. ... The "recruiting parsons" may have helped to fill the trenches during the war; they certainly succeeded in emptying the pews afterwards. The shallow casuistry with which they sought to evade the Sermon on the Mount disqualified them in the eyes of thousands from being taken seriously as authentic representatives of Christ. ... The "God our help in ages past" so constantly invoked was the petty British tribal god of the Recessional. ... [The Churches] excelled all others in the propagation of self-righteous cant, ... elevating the Kaiser to the dignity of Anti-Christ. ... When the war was over and seen as the sordid and futile waste it really was, it was widely felt that "Christianity had failed." Failed, not the world only, but its own message. The war to end war, the war which was to establish the reign of righteousness and justice, left the world worse off and with more injustice than before. Christians had succumbed to propaganda instead of bearing witness to the truth.⁵

---

2. Elizabeth Anscombe and Norman Daniel, *The Justice of the Present War Examined: A Criticism Based on Traditional Catholic Principles and on Natural Reason* (henceforth JPWE; Glasgow: Burns, 1940), 34. In 1981, Anscombe republished only the first half. Since the second half of the pamphlet has never been republished, citations will be to the original pamphlet.

3. JPWE, 31. They appeal to the Fribourg *conventus*, which instructs Catholics to reject the modern doctrine of state sovereignty, as it is in harmony neither with reason nor the doctrine of the Church.

4. JPWE, 30.

5. Victor White, "Wars and Rumours of War," *Blackfriars* (June 1939): 404-6.

Apprenticing to Wittgenstein

From the early 1940s to the late 1950s, Anscombe devotes her time and energy to learning philosophy from Ludwig Wittgenstein, and then, as his literary executor, translating, editing, and publishing his work. If Anscombe's witness to her faith had been limited to her early undergraduate publications, some might interpret them as a youthful enthusiasm following her reception into the Catholic faith. However, while learning from Wittgenstein in the 1940s, Anscombe is familiarizing herself with the attitudes and methods of Oxbridge philosophers. Anscombe faithfully attends meetings of, and reads numerous papers to, the Cambridge Moral Sciences Club, the Oxford Jowett and Philosophical Societies, and the Socratic Club, and attends lecture courses offered by colleagues. Unlike her mentor Wittgenstein, Anscombe is constantly engaged in conversation with philosophers with whom she profoundly disagrees. As she writes in 1938, Catholic witness in her station involves "arguing with our non-Catholic acquaintances, and frequenting non-Catholic meetings and trying—not always cautiously—to maintain the Catholic view." The goal? "That every man and woman in England should be conscious of the one significant choice: to be, or not to be, A Catholic."

By the late 1940s, still under thirty and unpublished, Anscombe already has a formidable philosophical reputation. When asked in 1948 by Somerville's principal to evaluate Anscombe, Oxford's Waynflete Professor of Philosophy Gilbert Ryle has the following to say:

> Dear Principal, I am on little more than nodding terms with Miss Anscombe. I have heard Miss Anscombe take part in philosophical discussions [and] have no doubt that Miss Anscombe has real philosophical power. . . . She is a real philosophical scholar & has, I gather, gone very deeply into Medieval philosophy . . . I think the whole sub-Faculty is in some awe of her. She is a forceful, even severe character & when she speaks her mind, there is no doubt what her mind is. . . . She has not, so far as I know, yet published anything. . . . From the point of view of the advance of the subject I have myself no serious doubts. Miss Anscombe is very likely to be a force. Yours sincerely, Gilbert Ryle

Despite this high praise from the most influential Oxford philosopher of the postwar era, Anscombe is developing a deep antipathy to the way her colleagues do philosophy. They are not serious, delighting in what she calls argumentative trickery, gleefully debunking the efforts of anyone trying to do serious work. "What a clever boy I am," is Anscombe's summary caricature.⁶ While the "clever boys" claim that one's practical morals are independent of one's theorizing about ethics, Anscombe can see behind the curtain, that metaethical claims do entail practical moral commitments. When the leading Oxford moral philosophers challenge her, she will draw back their curtain.

In Solitary Witness against Mass Murder

Anscombe's focus on Wittgenstein is momentously interrupted in March 1956, when Oxford University's eighteen-member Hebdomadal Council propose awarding an honorary degree to former US President Harry Truman.⁷ Anscombe and her husband Peter Geach are appalled. How can Oxford honor a person who is not merely a mass murderer, but arguably the world's most notorious and unrepentant mass murderer?

However, Oxford University's arcane procedure for awarding honorary degrees gives Geach an idea. At Oxford, even after an honorary degree is publicly announced, the decision has to be ratified by Congregation, the University's parliament. Moreover, Congregation votes on whether to ratify Truman's honorary degree on May 1, a mere seven weeks before Encaenia, when Truman is scheduled to receive the degree. Geach urges Anscombe to attend the May 1 Congregation, speak against awarding the degree to Truman, and solicit Congregation to vote "*non placet*" ("it does not please us"), thereby denying the degree for Truman.⁸

Pragmatically speaking, Geach's proposal to Anscombe is dubious. Anscombe is without a permanent (i.e., tenured) position at Somerville College. While Somerville has arranged a series of short-term appointments since 1946, Anscombe would not be granted a permanent appointment until 1964. Moreover, Janet Vaughan, Somerville's principal who has worked assiduously to arrange temporary appointments for Anscombe, is currently a member of Hebdomadal Council. Nevertheless, Anscombe fearlessly gives her solitary witness at Congregation, highlighted by an impassioned speech, in which she asks "If you do give

---

6. I am most grateful to Professor Ronald Hustwit for sharing these notes with me.

7. The Hebdomadal Council was Oxford's chief executive body from 1854 to 2000.

8. According to Mary Geach, it was Peter Geach who first suggested that Anscombe protest the degree.

this honor, what Nero, what Genghis Khan, what Hitler, or what Stalin will not be honored in the future?"

Prior to the meeting of Congregation, Anscombe had graciously given the council notice of her intent, so when Anscombe finishes her speech, the vice-chancellor asks Alan Bullock, a prominent historian of the Second World War, recruited in advance to respond to Anscombe, to "say a few words." Bullock's long speech includes a key line that greatly exercises Anscombe:

> A great many people were involved in the responsibility of the manufacture and delivery of the bomb, and we can't select one man as being solely responsible even if his was the signature at the bottom of the order for the bomb to be dropped.[9]

When Bullock finishes and the proposal put to a vote, "there was an overwhelming chorus of 'Placet,' and as far as could be heard, no voice against."[10] In fact, three others voted "*non placet*" with Anscombe, two of whom were Anscombe's colleague Philippa Foot and her husband. At Congregation, Anscombe's protest had failed spectacularly.

While roundly voted down, Anscombe's protest had side effects of an unimaginable magnitude. The image of a youthful female Oxford don making a solitary protest before the Ancient House of Congregation captured the imagination of the press worldwide, who brought the world's attention to Anscombe's protest against Truman's murderous injustice. Portions of her speech were picked up in an untold number of newspapers around the world, large and small, with Anscombe's line likening Truman to Nero, Hitler, and Stalin almost universally repeated by the press. Anscombe's speech at Congregation made her world famous, more so than ever again.

Continuing Her Campaign

Her defeat at Congregation on May 1 does not end Anscombe's witness. Immediately afterwards, Anscombe writes up her experience, reiterates her objections to Truman, and calls on her colleagues to boycott Encaenia. Anscombe publishes this in booklet form by the end of May, entitled *Mr. Truman's Degree*. She distributes it to colleagues planning to attend

---

9. *Oxford Mail*, May 1, 1956.
10. *Oxford Mail*, May 1, 1956.

Encaenia, and retails it for one shilling out of her home in St. John's Street and at W. H. Smith's in Oxford.

At the end of *Mr. Truman's Degree*, Anscombe wonders why her Oxford colleagues are so willing to honor Truman. Might it be related to the fact that the two dominant Oxford moral philosophies over the previous forty years both repudiate "the idea that any class of actions, such as murder, may be morally excluded"?[11] This constitutes Anscombe's first characterization of Oxford moral philosophy. While brief, it piques the interest of a senior producer at the BBC.

In the summer of 1956, Anscombe makes two fateful decisions. First, befuddled by Alan Bullock's ludicrous and yet applauded defense of Truman, Anscombe wants to think more deeply about ascribing intentions to individuals, and what such intentions entail. So Anscombe proposes to lecture on "Intention" during Hilary term (January–March) 1957. Although Anscombe had lectured at Oxford for nine years, these would be her first lectures not focusing on either Plato or Wittgenstein. Second, Anscombe accepted an invitation from the BBC Talks Department to "develop the theme of the relevance of Oxford philosophy to situations such as the one which inspired your pamphlet."[12]

Satirizing Oxford Moral Philosophy: Why Justifying Murder Does Not Corrupt the Youth

Seven months later, on January 27, 1957, at the BBC Studios in London, Anscombe records her broadcast talk "Oxford Moral Philosophy: Does it Corrupt the Youth?" Given a second opportunity to characterize Oxford moral philosophy, Anscombe intuits that it might be best not to directly accuse her colleagues of justifying murder. So Anscombe makes the highly unusual choice to *satirize* Oxford moral philosophy.

To determine whether Oxford moral philosophy corrupts the youth, Anscombe first proposes a criterion: Oxford moral philosophy can be corrupting the youth only if it teaches them something other than the "highest and best ideals of society at large." If the Oxford moralists do not

11. G. E. M. Anscombe, *Mr. Truman's Degree* (Oxford, UK: Oxonian, 1956), esp. 71.

12. See Benjamin Lipscomb, "The Women Are up to Something," *Royal Institute of Philosophy Supplement* 87 (2020): 7–30, esp. 22n40. Lipscomb references BBC Written Archives Centre, RCONT3—G. E. M. Anscombe, A. E. Harvey to G. E. M. Anscombe, July 18, 1956.

influence the youth away from the ideals of British society, but say, merely mimic them, they can in no way be accused of corrupting the youth.

This is exactly what Anscombe pompously argues in defense of the Oxford moralists. Bereft of binding principles, the Oxford moralists are incapable of guiding the youth towards anything but conventional morality, "the spirit of the age."[13] The vitriol in Anscombe's "defense" of her Oxford colleagues strikes home when her colleagues realize that by "ideals of British society," Anscombe has in mind the British government's high-minded justification of mass murder.

In her BBC talk, Anscombe answers her question *and* proffers a comprehensive critique of Oxford moral philosophy in thirteen paragraphs, a mere 2200 words.

The bulk of the broadcast is devoted to the two-step method by which her colleagues justify murder. First, they reject the otherwise almost universally held view that morality is something inherent in human actions and character, setting aside the language and practices of justice traditionally conceived. Second, they instrumentalize ethics, transforming it into a form of public policy, in which the "rightness" of a human action depends on its "managerial" prowess.[14] The Oxford moralists' managerial morality combines appeals to "responsibility" and "decreasing suffering" with banal or fantastic examples and mad calculations regarding the future's "total situation." Their tacit assumption of prophetic infallibility allows them to justify mass murder as the "right" thing to do in certain cases.

Anscombe's BBC broadcast does not go unnoticed. The responses that please Anscombe the most are penned by Oxford's two most widely read moralists: R. M. Hare and Patrick Nowell-Smith. Their letters to the *Listener* chide Anscombe like weary schoolmasters, convinced that Anscombe is an ignoramus with regard to ethical theory. At Oxford, Anscombe neither lectures nor publishes in ethics, apart from her privately printed polemic pillorying Truman.

---

13. G. E. M. Anscombe, "Does Oxford Moral Philosophy Corrupt the Youth?" (henceforth OMPCY), *Listener*, Feb. 14, 1957, 267.

14. "You can learn at Oxford [that justice] . . . is a term like 'well-arranged.' . . . Injustice may be nobody's fault, and . . . what is required is good arrangement. . . . With this goes preference for policy—which is an effort to calculate and promote the general good over archaic and metaphysical conceptions of justice." Anscombe, OMPCY, 267. Anscombe will imply that rhetoric about "the best interests of all" is used by those with power to justify injustices against the poor, widows, parents, and criminals.

In responses dripping with condescension, Nowell-Smith highlights Anscombe's ignorance, while Hare highlights her inconsistency.

Nowell-Smith:

> Miss Anscombe seems to be (though I can scarce believe that she is) ignorant of the difficulties involved in drawing a distinction between an act and its consequences. For example, was Mr. Truman's "act"
>
> a. the signing of an order,
>
> b. the killing of a number of Japanese, or
>
> c. the saving of a number of Japanese and other lives?
>
> If it was the first only, Miss Anscombe has, on her own principles, as little right to condemn it as Mr. Truman's supporters have to defend it, since both judgements turn on its consequences. But if the killing is to be included in the nature and quality of Mr. Truman's act, why not the saving of lives? . . . It is with the elucidation of just such difficulties that moral philosophy is concerned.[15]

Hare:

> She thinks it wrong to judge acts by the foreseen consequences of committing them; for example . . . that the person who ordered the atom bomb to be dropped on Hiroshima had no duty to consider whether anybody would be killed by the explosion. Yet in a recent pamphlet Anscombe accused Mr. Truman of being a murderer.[16]

In her initial response, Anscombe ignores their challenges. Instead, she first provokes them further, accusing Hare of questioning her sexual morals, and mocking Nowell-Smith's "colossal difficulty" making sense of an action that is at once

a. sending chocolates through the mail,

b. poisoning your aunt, and

c. collecting an inheritance.

---

15. Patrick Nowell-Smith, "Oxford Moral Philosophy," *Listener*, Feb. 21, 1957. The author has added the letter designations *a*, *b*, and *c* to the quote.

16. Richard M. Hare, "Oxford Moral Philosophy," *Listener*, Feb. 21, 1957.

Second, Anscombe invents a neologism to characterize their moral theory.

> Mr. Hare is openly a consequentialist. It should be stated clearly that this means, and he has implicitly stated, that there is no sort of action whatever of which it is correct to say "One doesn't have to consider whether to do this or not, in any circumstances; it is simply excluded."[17]

As for Nowell-Smith, Anscombe finds his denial that he's a consequentialist unpersuasive, and cites page numbers from his best-selling book as evidence.[18]

Anscombe concludes her initial response by bemoaning their moral blindness. The problem is *not that they claim* that committing fraud, evicting widows, or killing the innocent is good; the problem is that *their theories indirectly justify such acts*, because their theories exclude any basis for condemning such acts as inherently bad.[19]

Having been put on the defensive, in their second letters to the *Listener* Hare and Nowell-Smith give earnest replies. Hare does not deny that Truman, as a means to his ends, deliberately chose to instantly obliterate some eighty thousand innocent civilians, but argues that Truman's action was morally right. Hare avoids calling this "murder," but if pressed, Hare will defend murder "in some instances."[20] Hare then asks: "What else could possibly be the right answer . . . ? Seek to produce the worst consequences?" If Anscombe wants to pin the label "consequentialist" on him, she should explain what it means. "If it is the opinion that we are morally responsible for what we willingly and wittingly bring about, is it so damnable a heresy?"[21] Similarly, an enraged Nowell-Smith accuses

17. G. E. M. Anscombe, "Oxford Moral Philosophy," *Listener*, Feb. 28, 1957.

18. Nowell-Smith's and Hare's moral philosophies justify intrinsically wrong actions in slightly different ways. Nowell's Smith's *Ethics* ([Hammondsworth, UK: Penguin, 1954] 308) has one "frame a moral principle under which [one] 'manages'" to bring the action, whereas Hare's *The Language of Morals* (Oxford, UK: Oxford University Press, 1952) instructs one to formulate "a new 'decision of principle,'" which constitutes an "advance in [one's] moral thinking." Anscombe, "Modern Moral Philosophy" (henceforth MMP), *Philosophy* 33 (1958): 1–19, esp. 42.

19. Anscombe, "Oxford Moral Philosophy," *Listener*, Feb. 28, 1957.

20. In *Language of Morals*, Hare avoids almost completely the terms "murder" and "kill." In later works he will write of situations in which murder is the right act (e.g., Richard M. Hare, *Moral Thinking: Its Levels, Method, and Point* [Oxford, UK: Oxford University Press, 1982], 135.)

21. Richard M. Hare, "Oxford Moral Philosophy," *Listener*, Mar. 28, 1957. Contrary

Anscombe of injustice. It is a travesty for Anscombe to substitute a simple case of poisoning by chocolates for his difficult example of the bombing of Hiroshima, and then claim that he has "colossal difficulty" with the simple example.[22]

Having elicited actual moral viewpoints from Hare and Nowell-Smith, Anscombe's tactics change, and she replies seriously and earnestly, focusing on Nowell-Smith, since Hare has already made clear his position. Her chocolates example, far from a "travesty," perfectly parallels Nowell-Smith's Hiroshima example.[23]

a. signing of an order	a. sending chocolates through the mail
b. killing of a number of Japanese	b. poisoning your aunt
c. saving of a number of Japanese and other lives	c. collecting an inheritance

In both examples, *b* is an act of murder, as a means to the end of *c*. How can the chocolates example be obvious, yet the Hiroshima example difficult? Nowell-Smith is a "child of his times" in not being able to see the parallel, and "how his philosophy helps him not to!" What infuriates Anscombe is how Oxford moralists obfuscate the obvious:

> The suggestion that no one can treat "Do no murder" as an intelligible commandment in a broadcast without a preliminary exposé of the philosophical problems of defining an action seems to me in a high degree comic.[24]

It is indeed comic, but also tragic, for Nowell-Smith to claim that despite Truman's order, attributing to him the killing of innocent Japanese "was not altogether obvious." For Truman proudly and repeatedly proclaimed his full responsibility, most recently to the British press when collecting his Oxford degree.

By the end of the exchange of letters in the *Listener*, Anscombe considers her characterization of the Oxford moralists in "Does Oxford

---

to the common claim that Anscombe first used the term "consequentialist" in "Modern Moral Philosophy," Anscombe's letter of Feb. 28, 1957, in the *Listener*—published almost a year prior to MMP—is her first use of "consequentialist."

22. Patrick Nowell-Smith, "Oxford Moral Philosophy," *Listener*, Mar. 14, 1957.

23. According to Anscombe, the problem with Nowell-Smith's example is that his "saving of a number of Japanese and other lives" was not factual. It was well known that the Japanese wanted to surrender.

24. G. E. M. Anscombe, "Oxford Moral Philosophy," *Listener*, Mar. 21, 1957.

Moral Philosophy Corrupt the Youth?," in particular the "consequentialism" of Hare and Nowell-Smith, to be definitively confirmed.

After Anscombe had recorded her original talk, she was so pleased with it that she immediately prepared a second, on the so-called principles of the Oxford moralists, and submitted it to the BBC as a potential follow-up broadcast, even before responses to Anscombe's first talk were published in the *Listener*. However, as she ruefully noted in one of her letters to the *Listener*, the Oxford moralists had "'scared off' the BBC" from letting her do a follow-up lecture on the wireless. Instead, Anscombe had to content herself with giving a revised and extended version of it to the Voltaire Society. In preparing it, while focused on Hare's defense of "consequentialism" and Nowell's-Smith "colossal" difficulty with action-descriptions and intention, Anscombe's central focus was on those persons, whether political leaders or Oxford philosophers, who went about trying to legitimate mass murder. When she published the paper in January 1958 under the title "Modern Moral Philosophy," her views on the Oxford moralists became available to the wider philosophical world, and quickly created a remarkable sensation. For in this paper, Anscombe not only characterized the Oxford moralists, but genealogized them, showed the historical origin of their views.

For Anscombe, the root failure of the modern moral philosophers was their having misunderstood and inflated their role. The Oxford moralists had abandoned their appropriate role of analyzing morality, and had instead fancied themselves as seers, who through infallible divining of the "total situation" of the future, were now abrogating to themselves the role of deciding who should live and who should die, justifying mass murder of the innocent according to their prophetic insight.

Anscombe was not a believer in these new beings with divine powers currently residing in Oxford. She would stick with the wisdom of great philosophical traditions, and of the legitimate representatives of God, which prohibited the killing of the innocent as both a requirement of natural justice and the divine law. This absolute prohibition of directly killing the innocent was not up for grabs, as per the Oxford moralists, but was rather a necessary presupposition of any and all legitimate theorizing about morality. It was Anscombe's great witness throughout her life to this fundamental moral truth, and in so doing reoriented moral philosophy towards the absolute protection of innocent human life, and towards the flourishing of all human being.

Conversations with Jonathan
The Dialectic of Creation and Redemption

Philip A. Rolnick

In the action-packed biblical accounts of Saul and David, there is war with the Philistines, palace intrigue, and a complex, uneasy relationship between these first two kings of Israel. But in the context of this political drama, and in spite of their conflicting interests, a beautiful friendship arises between Saul's son Jonathan and David.

Knowing that his father Saul is determined to kill David, Jonathan arranges a secret tryst with David. In a hiding place known to both of them, Jonathan cleverly sets up a signal—safe or unsafe—by the location of three arrows that he will shoot upon his arrival (1 Sam 20:18–22). Given the threats they variously face, the meeting that takes place is bittersweet. As they part, Jonathan famously says, "Go in peace, since both of us have sworn in the name of the Lord saying, 'The Lord shall be between me and you'" (1 Sam 20:42).[1] Against his father's interests—and his own—Jonathan promises David that their friendship will take precedence. Through the following centuries, Jonathan's words have offered an invaluable dictum for personal relations: in all that we say, and in all that we do, let God "be between me and you."

Most of us will never have to worry about life-and-death competition in acceding to high political office. But all of Jesus's followers can benefit from taking Jonathan's words to heart. In every human relationship, we

---

1. This chapter uses the NRSV translation for Scripture references, unless otherwise indicated.

can pray that the Holy Spirit will be between us, that our relationship will have an additional power and quality—the betweenness of the Holy Spirit.

From our first meeting thirty-five years ago to the current moment, my friendship with Jonathan Wilson has been blessed by this betweenness. Together, we have often sought to understand more of the God who is between us. In what follows, I want to converse with our contemporary Jonathan about his views on creation and redemption.

Interrelated Gifts: Creation and Redemption

The Gift of Creation

In the divine act of *creatio ex nihilo*, our relationship with God, with Father, Son, and Spirit, is initiated by God even before we are present. The first gift is a preparatory grace, the majestic formation of an expansive universe home. Into the divinely imbued fecundity of this home, all that has ever lived comes into being. This movement from nonbeing to being is astonishing; no greater change than this can be conceived. Creating something out of nothing reveals a power that is uniquely God's. Creation is non-accidental, intentional, and purposive. The God who is inherently relational—who is love, who is Father, Son, and Spirit—forms a universe that will provide for new life, new relationship, and new love: "For thus says the Lord, who created the heavens . . . who formed the earth and made it . . . he did not create a chaos, he formed it to be inhabited!" (Isa 45:18).

Jonathan has thought long and deeply about creation, sharing his insights through several publications, but especially through *God's Good World*. The title already reveals Jonathan's love of creation, and his subtitle reveals a need of our time: *Reclaiming the Doctrine of Creation*.[2] Jonathan wants us to rethink creation to deepen our understanding of the Creator God, the cosmos, and our place and purpose within it.

From the outset, Jonathan delves into the meaning of creation as gift. God has absolutely no need to create. Jonathan's view of creation is nothing like a neo-Platonic emanation; creation does not simply flow out of the divine nature by necessity. Instead, creation is God's intelligent choice, God's plan, God's gift. Reflecting on God's action, Jonathan adds that the "corollary of creation as gift of God is creation received by

---

2. Jonathan R. Wilson, *God's Good World: Reclaiming the Doctrine of Creation* (Grand Rapids: Baker Academic, 2013).

humans."³ Every gift has a gift-giver and a gift-receiver; every authentic gift is doubly affirmed—in the giving as well as in the receiving. From the initiation to the reception, there is freedom. God initiates (creates) in freedom; we receive, refuse, or ignore in freedom. Coercion has no role in the economy of grace.

The freedom of the gift closely resembles the freedom of love. Within the Trinity, the mutual gift of the Persons, the perichoretic movement from Father to Son to Spirit is biblically summarized as, "God is love" (1 John 4:8, 16). In eternity and in space-time, the Trinitarian movement away from self and toward the other sets the directional pattern of love. Creation displays this same pattern of love—the divine movement toward human sons and daughters of God. As Jonathan puts it, "Creation as the work of God is a gift because that work gives to the cosmos the overflowing joy of being alive and in relationship with the Father, the Son, and the Spirit, whose own life together is one of eternal, overflowing, ecstatic love. No greater gift can be given."⁴ The movement of love—away from self and toward the other—was captured in a medieval dictum: the good shares itself (*bonum est diffusivum sui*).⁵ Creation is a divine sharing, a movement toward those who are not God, but who are called into divine love.

Creation is not merely a repetition of some or even many aspects of God's being. It is fresh, novel, original. It is God's venturing beyond the divine perfection of Father, Son, and Spirit. Jesus's exhortation, "Be perfect, therefore, as your heavenly Father is perfect" (Matt 5:48), invites us to venture into the ultimate meaning, value, and purpose of the life we have been given.

Awakened to the generosity of our universe home, though we may still err in a thousand ways, at least we know ourselves as recipients of a wondrous gift from the God of love. Once awakened, we become the people who, at the deepest part of our being, learn to say "thank you." We are rightly amazed by divine generosity.

Creation makes what is infinitely good, true, and beautiful in God's being progressively accessible to humanity. As a result, Jonathan is

---

3. Wilson, *God's Good World*, 99.

4. Wilson, *God's Good World*, 99.

5. The dictum apparently originated with Pseudo-Dionysius, *The Divine Names*, in *Pseudo-Dionysius: The Complete Works*, trans. Colm Luibheid and Paul Rorem (New York: Paulist, 1987), ch. 4. Aquinas alludes to it (*ST* I.28.5 *obj.* 2) and comments on it in *In librum beati Dionysii De divinis nominibus expositio* (Rome: Marietti, 1950).

profoundly world-affirming: "All that is good, true, and beautiful has a place in God's creation."⁶ Being so pro-creation, Jonathan warns against escapism in Christian teaching, the false and unnecessary notion that we should just hold on and bear the pain because this world will not last.⁷ A better response to creation's challenges is the cheerful acceptance of responsibility. There is work to be done on the world and on ourselves. Thus Jonathan cites Julian Hartt: "In Jesus Christ . . . we might become, in the whole circuit of our life, and in the vital center, what we are in the creative seeing of God. 'Be transformed' is the imperative of the righteous God communicated in Jesus Christ."⁸ Holding back or holding on, burying the one talent like the third servant in Jesus's parable of the talents (Matt 25:14–30), is simply irresponsible, as well as ungrateful. Evidently, human endeavor, struggle, and development are part of the plan of creation. But human transformation must be in response to the Creator. As Hartt puts it, "Victory in this struggle is impossible without the power of God."⁹ Our endeavors are not to be autonomous; they are rather submissions to and cooperating with God's plans. When combined, submission and cooperation constitute the conformity that is the secret of human creativity. One of the many wonders of creation is that it is set up for human creativity.

The Gift of Redemption

Jonathan creatively conceives redemption in terms of telos. This telos (goal, purpose, or final cause) is first given in creation and then reiterated and recalibrated in the cross and resurrection of Christ. Jonathan shifts our attention from an original sin to the original telos, its loss, and its eventual restoration by Christ: "If we think about the fall as teleological rather than original, then redemption and restoration also have a teleological orientation. In this case, redemption reclaims the world as

---

6. Wilson, *God's Good World*, 107.
7. Wilson, *God's Good World*, 106.
8. Julian Norris Hartt, *A Christian Critique of American Culture: An Essay in Practical Theology* (New York: Harper & Row, 1967), 87, as cited by Wilson, *God's Good World*, 120n26.
9. Hartt, *Christian Critique*, 87, as cited by Wilson, *God's Good World*, 120n26.

creation and realigns it with its journey toward the realization of its telos in the new creation."[10]

Because of the teleological deviation of the fall, the *homo viator*, the wayfarer, is not only thrown off course, but is ruinously confused—deprived of any sense of the authentic destination. Intended to be on a journey toward God, the wayfarer has become a wanderer. The fundamental orientation of how to live one's life in creation has been disrupted, a disruption so thoroughgoing that some do not even know that they are living in a creation.

That millions of our contemporaries do not know, do not care, or do not believe in either God or creation is a serious problem addressed by Jonathan's work as minister, professor, and author. The belief that nature alone is real—naturalism—is on the rise. This dreary vision of an unknowing, unfeeling, and utterly accidental universe dulls and deadens its adherents. The naturalist vision is the dark antithesis of Jonathan's intertwined conception of creation and redemption. The naturalist world is without a purpose; and because the overall context is purposeless, all who adopt this worldview live and die without a given purpose. They are of course free to devise one of their own, but such efforts typically devolve to personal preference. And since all human beings die, any self-created purpose has a well-marked expiration date.

Confronting this ideational darkness and the behavior it tends to foster, Jonathan counters, "We see death and life clearly only when our eyes are opened by the apocalyptic intervention that is the incarnation, crucifixion, and resurrection of Jesus Christ."[11] For Jonathan, *apocalyptic* means "the shocking, world-shattering revelation of Jesus Christ to a world that assumes the rule of death and the undeniable 'reality' of the way the world is, always has been, and always will be."[12] Jonathan wholeheartedly rejects the skepticism of such "realism"; in fact, he considers such "realism" to be a false counsel, an advocate of unreality. Having tasted the substantive reality of the gospel—of creation redeemed and reoriented by Jesus Christ—Jonathan writes with a confident sense of what actually is real.

Consequently, in the starkest possible contrast to naturalism, Jonathan focuses on the dual, interrelated gifts of creation and redemption,

10. Wilson, *God's Good World*, 119.
11 Wilson, *God's Good World*, 109.
12 Wilson, *God's Good World*, 109n9.

in which redemption restores, redirects, and renews creation. Looking to the redemption of Christ, Jonathan is clear eyed about what is and is not accomplished: "Redemption does not return the world to an original state. Rather, redemption returns the world to its telos."[13]

Jonathan argues that "the telos of creation is grounded and guaranteed not in this world but in the blessed life of God."[14] Moving our attention from the world to our relationship with God helps us cease "our frantic pursuit of control."[15] Paradoxically, we gain more control when we stop seeking it by ourselves and for ourselves, and instead, seek divine guidance. In the difficult world we live in, our best shot at "control" comes from cooperation with an infinite Superior. Nonetheless, the illusions of the self-in-control are difficult to dispel. Against such illusion, Jonathan counsels "that we should remove from our vocabulary the language of 'lifestyle' or 'lifestyle options' and be very careful when we talk about '*ways* of life.'"[16] He so strongly opposes this sort of autonomous self-direction because such popular talk seems to imply that the telos for our lives has not already been established in Jesus Christ, "who is the redemption of creation."[17] Popular expressions like "lifestyle" mask a serious problem: the forgetfulness, ignorance of, or rejection of the gifts of creation and Christ.

Human commitments are informed by experience as well as by instruction. Experience has a way of deepening, broadening, and sometimes correcting our previous concepts of things. So while we can be confident that the Father, Son, and Spirit always loved humankind, we should also ponder the meaning of the adventure into which the Son was sent. Being born into a particular family, in a particular country, in a particular historical context, this eternal Son became a human son, one who fully experienced the raw unfairness of kangaroo courts, scourging, public mockery, and crucifixion. He patiently bore them—and overcame them all.

Sent by the Father, the Son's incarnate experience was earth's greatest adventure story. Looking at Jesus's adventure, Jonathan adds a creative twist: "Knowing the goal of history revealed in the resurrection of Jesus

---

13. Wilson, *God's Good World*, 120.
14. Wilson, *God's Good World*, 105.
15. Wilson, *God's Good World*, 105.
16. Wilson, *God's Good World*, 111.
17. Wilson, *God's Good World*, 111.

Christ calls us to an adventure."[18] In this adventure, by continually keeping before our minds the gift that Christ and the Spirit never cease giving, we may become agents of grace, participants in the ongoing adventure that the incarnate Son began. There is no greater privilege. Having received the gift of redemption, we are reoriented toward the divinely given telos—the divinely prepared destiny that begins in time and will continue in eternity, as we take up our part in what Saint Thomas calls the "fellowship of eternal happiness."[19]

The Dialectic of the Kingdom: Seeing Creation and Redemption Together

In "The Dialectic of the Kingdom,"[20] Jonathan treats creation and redemption as interwoven realities, as two basic components of the kingdom. He uses "kingdom" as a summary term for "the many dimensions of the good news," and as "the reality of God's redemption of creation."[21] He uses "dialectic" as a looking back and forth that yields perspective. Just as two eyes are required for seeing perspective, Jonathan wants us to gain perspective on both creation and redemption by seeing the two together. He thus defines dialectic as "holding in relationship two works of God that cannot be properly and faithfully thought and lived apart from each other."[22] He uses creation to inform redemption and redemption to inform creation: "One of the gravest errors we can make in our witness to the good news of Jesus Christ is to separate creation and redemption from each other."[23]

Consistently developing the back and forth between creation and redemption, Jonathan tries to head off a theological problem: "If we present the gospel as redemption apart from creation, as a spiritual rescue operation that merely directs our discipleship to an inner disposition or an entirely future state of affairs, then we leave a vacuum in our lives that other

---

18. Jonathan R. Wilson, *A Primer for Christian Doctrine* (Grand Rapids: Eerdmans, 2005), 53.
19. Thomas Aquinas, *Summa Theologica*, trans. Fathers of the English Dominican Province (New York: Benziger, 1947), II–II.24.2.
20. Wilson, *Primer for Christian Doctrine*, 49–70.
21. Wilson, *Primer for Christian Doctrine*, 51.
22. Wilson, *Primer for Christian Doctrine*, 51.
23. Wilson, *Primer for Christian Doctrine*, 49.

ideologies rush in to fulfill."[24] Without the complementarity of creation and redemption, something beautiful is left behind: "When the doctrine of creation is mostly absent from our theology and account of the gospel, the *joyful* reality of God's redemptive work is muted."[25] There is joy rather than asceticism in Jonathan's vision: what we have received in creation and in Christ is splendidly beautiful and should be enjoyed. Jonathan wants us not only to receive the gifts of Father, Son, and Spirit, but to experience the everlasting happiness that they bestow.

Having received prodigious gifts in creation and in the incarnation, teachings, death, and resurrection of Christ, we are given the noble opportunity, not really a birthright but more like a "re-birthright," of responding with our own efforts. And our disoriented world sorely needs assistance. Human efforts to promote the good, the true, and beautiful in creation can themselves be continuously guided by the presence of the Holy Spirit—the Teacher, Guide, and Living Gift to those awakened to the realm of grace. The Holy Spirit perpetually reminds us of Jesus Christ, whom Jonathan refers to as "the one criterion" of "all that is good and true and beautiful."[26]

However, apart from the Spirit, our own efforts to be helpful are likely to be inadequate or even harmful. Efforts at social improvement need the tempering factor of humility. Having been righted by God, we need to remember how easy it is to be wrong. In Jonathan's words, "We must guard the gift-reception dynamic . . . in the continual cultivation of the spirit and practice of receptivity."[27] Being recipients of grace, Jonathan reminds us "that we are dependent but not that we are passive."[28] Briefly commenting on Gen 1–3, he infers that we are "blessed by being given work."[29] Creation is not solely about God; it is also about us and our efforts—in relation to God and to each other. Citing the apostle Paul, Jonathan lifts up the newness of creation's redeemed life: "Therefore, if anyone is in Christ, the new creation has come" (2 Cor 5:17). And as

---

24. Wilson, *Primer for Christian Doctrine*, 104.
25. Wilson, *Primer for Christian Doctrine*, 125; emphasis added.
26. Wilson, *Primer for Christian Doctrine*, 115.
27. Wilson, *Primer for Christian Doctrine*, 101.
28. Wilson, *Primer for Christian Doctrine*, 102.
29. Wilson, *Primer for Christian Doctrine*, 102.

Jonathan comments, "And so begins the lifelong journey of learning to see everything new."[30]

Recipients of Grace

Having received the gifts of a created universe and of the incarnation of the Son, we may first pause and take stock of our situation, then develop a sense of thanksgiving, and then perhaps consider our own smallness and imperfection before God. But actually, we are at our best when we are not thinking of ourselves at all, but rather thinking of God and others. Being made in the image of God, we think most clearly, most completely, and most accurately when we see ourselves in relation to God; and our actions and relationships most fully flourish when, conscious of the source of our being, we seek partnership with that divine source.

One of the great problems of our age is that there is too much talk, thought, and concern about the isolated self. When the self thinks about the self, the result always tends to be too much or too little, and to boomerang back to self-centeredness. William Temple, former archbishop of Canterbury, observed that the self "contemplates its own state of deliverance from self-centeredness and finds in that a self-centered satisfaction. It is not merely pride in being good; it is pride in being delivered from pride; it is pride in being humble."[31] Our situation is difficult, but it is not impossible. We have, should we think to ask, the assistance of the most powerful, most wise, and most loving Father, Son, and Holy Spirit. Jonathan's thoughts on creation and redemption attempt to re-turn us toward God, who really does have the power to re-deem, re-center, and re-direct us toward the eternal telos. In this re-turning toward God, we are blessed with peace, even in the midst of the greatest difficulties.

Some Personal Reflections

Jonathan's multifaceted publications have a winsome combination of seriousness and joy. Even in his early work, he was guided by a sense of telos: "The purpose of Christian doctrine is not merely to make us more knowledgeable but to make us more mature as followers of Jesus Christ,

---

30. Wilson, *Primer for Christian Doctrine*, 111.
31. William Temple, *Nature, Man and God* (London: Macmillan, 1934), 390.

to make us more like him."[32] Everything of Jonathan's that I have read is loyal to this stated purpose.

Publishing is a strange and difficult task because it requires communicating with people who are not present, almost all of whom will not know and will never see the author. But when Jonathan publishes his thoughts, they are not qualitatively different from those he shares in personal conversations. Those of us who have experienced his private conversations sense that the conversation, always enjoyable in its own right, inevitably includes a transcendent third. As Jonathan, the son of Saul put it, "The Lord shall be between me and you" (1 Sam 20:42); as Jesus, the incarnate Son of God put it: "For where two or three are gathered in my name, I am there among them" (Matt 18:20).

Whether we know Jonathan as family member, friend, minister, or author, his words, actions, and relationships point us toward the Trinitarian Author of our being, the Author and Redeemer of creation. But Jonathan also points us toward the joy of our own adventures in the redeemed creation, and, ultimately, to the eternal fellowship of light and love—with God and with all others.

---

32. Wilson, *Primer for Christian Doctrine*, 12.

Toward a New Natural Theology

Jeremy Kidwell

ONE OF THE FEATURES of Jonathan's legacy that has always struck me has been his tendency towards holism, which resulted in a certain tenacity in trying to connect all the dots in our claims about God's being and our life together as God's people. I know for him this knowledge was anchored in his engagement with the work of Julian Hartt—particularly the notion he took from Hartt and developed further in his own theological reflection that God's work in creation and redemption are intertwined. Jonathan draws special attention to the consequences of our failure to reckon with this intertwining particularly in *God's Good World*. As Jonathan suggests, "One of the greatest tragedies of theology's neglect of creation has been the church's complicity in the destruction of the natural world and thus also of conditions that contribute to the flourishing of life."[1] He also drew attention, far earlier, to this same intertwining in terms of epistemology in talking about the doctrine of "humankind" in *A Primer For Christian Doctrine*.[2] Here Jonathan observed the tendency by theologians in the twentieth century to orient around either natural theology or biblical theology at the expense of the other. He goes on to observe, sagely, how all the things that humans experience, including God's creation and Scripture, are mediated through a process of interpretation, commending humility in theological reflection as we bear in mind the limitations and

---

1. Jonathan R. Wilson, *God's Good World: Reclaiming the Doctrine of Creation* (Grand Rapids: Baker Academic, 2013), 9.

2. Jonathan R. Wilson, *A Primer for Christian Doctrine* (Grand Rapids: Eerdmans, 2005), 78–83.

contingency of every human person and culture. I'm struck by the ways that Jonathan brings together holism and humility in the exhortations that ring out across that book: "We must instead bear witness to God's redemption of creation in word and deed—by caring for all creation, the whole person and the whole world."[3]

In reviewing the work that Jonathan has produced over a lifetime as I worked on this volume, I was struck by the massive shift in the issues that preoccupied Christian theology across the decades he has worked as a public theologian. In his early work, looking back upon the twentieth century and grappling—alongside other theologians like Stanley Hauerwas—with the legacies of the liberal theological project, he contended with the Christian flight from churches, cultural pluralism, biblical authority, pacifism, gender roles, and leadership. While it's not quite clear to me whether the church has gained much ground on these issues, a panoply of new ones has also come along to preoccupy contemporary theologians, including Jonathan in his most recent work: climate change, theological reflections on embodiment, Christian responses to anti-Black racism, and reflections on intersex conditions and gender identity.

I've always found Jonathan's scholarship to be a balm as I struggled (as a theologian trained in what was once called without irony an "evangelical" tradition) with the persistent anxiety, veering towards hostility, expressed by church leaders and theologians, towards the views of a so-called "secular world" and its attempts to revise our understanding of "nature" and what might be baptized as "natural" in terms of gender, sexual orientation, climate, and earth-system stability—and, in more implicit ways, racial superiority and privilege. Just over the past few years I've had Christians try to convince me that grassroots social movements protesting anti-Black racism (that is, Black Lives Matter) and climate change represent terrorist plots to overthrow government and social order. These movements, in spite of strong Christian presence among them, were seen by individuals as threatening a status quo or perceived norm, which in turn was perceived to be essential to social, economic, or political stability. As we look towards the increasingly sharp and sometimes violent rhetoric of contemporary Christians against critical race theory, climate change science and policy, and accommodations of non-cis-gendered people, I want to suggest that there is some linkage across these shared concerns. So much of the wariness that one can find

---

3. Wilson, *God's Good World*, 9–10.

Christians expressing today relates to this concern: should we adopt this revised view of what is "natural" or the consequences that cascade from that revision? As I will go on to suggest, at the heart of all these kinds of concerns lies a certain kind of assumption about the stability of our views of what is "normal" and, by extension, how much we should allow the world around us to challenge our established convictions. And it is also important to emphasize that I think concern is formulated in this way most often by those who are not on the margins—that is, chiefly by White, male, cis-gendered, Euro-American scholars like me.

What I'd like to explore in this essay, taking up Jonathan's pattern of humility and holism, is the ways that we might think about what we find in the natural world—those things that God has made, which includes our human bodies. I mean to offer only a tentative proposal here, drawing on the work of some contemporary theologians I know both Jonathan and I have been reading and engaging with, towards what we might think of as a new natural theology. Not the sort, as Jonathan observed so many years ago in his primer, which is set up as a polemic against biblical theology, but a different kind, which can help us to appreciate the ways that biblical theology is already doing this same sort of work, presenting us with a dialectic of the kingdom. As Jonathan observes, "we do not have 'an environment'; we are a part of creation," and all of the authors of the Bible and the incarnate one are also part of creation in the same way.[4]

Having set some of the basic parameters of the discussion, I want to offer a brief survey of two recent attempts to find a "new" natural theology and natural law (neither of which are terribly new) and then finish with an equally brief commentary on where I think we might want to be eventually in terms of how we think about the world around us and its relation to thinking theologically.

The Protestant Revival of Natural Law

One of the most sustained and noteworthy efforts in natural theology has, somewhat unexpectedly, come from the Reformed theologian Alister McGrath. Starting at the turn of the millennium, McGrath undertook a substantial project in what he called "Scientific Theology." The project produced a series of books, three academic volumes,[5] a follow-up

---

4. Wilson, *God's Good World*, 23–24.
5. Alister E. McGrath, *Nature*, vol. 1 of *A Scientific Theology* (Grand Rapids:

collection of essays,[6] and a shorter volume for lay readers.[7] I remember discussing the series with Jonathan as we were setting up a workshop for scientists and theologians to have a roundtable discussion at UBC and Carey in 2008, as we both wondered what might come of the project, and Jonathan has published charitable but constructively critical reviews of each of McGrath's three volumes. There are many resonances between these two theologians. Both reject forms of naïve realism (the assumption that our personal knowledge is a straightforward representation of the world outside our minds) but are also cautious of the individualism inherent in wholesale rejections of realism, and both work in response to a kind of cautious appreciation of the legacy of Karl Barth, Charlotte von Kirschbaum, and by extension their student T. F. Torrance in reshaping the modern project of natural theology.

As a historical theologian McGrath offers several helpful correctives to the contemporary reception of natural theology. In contrast to some contemporary detractors, he is quick to point out that natural theology is a relatively mainstream part of Christian theology, arising frequently in the Bible (particularly in the Old Testament), and as part of reflection across the centuries of Christian tradition.[8] In McGrath's view, more liberal pantheist approaches that sought to pursue natural theology as a substitute for the doctrine of God, or those that sought to displace Christian Scripture, represent a minority account.[9] He ultimately situates natural theology as a kind of theology of the everyday: "the systematic exploration of a proposed link between the everyday world of our experience and another asserted transcendent reality."[10]

Building on this characterization, and drawing on Rom 12:2, McGrath suggests that *Christian* natural theology draws on Christian discernment, "seeing nature in a specific manner, which enables the truth, beauty and goodness of God to be discerned, and which acknowledges

---

Eerdmans, 2001); *Reality*, vol. 2 of *A Scientific Theology* (Grand Rapids: Eerdmans, 2002); *Theory*, vol. 3 of *A Scientific Theology* (Grand Rapids: Eerdmans, 2003).

6. Alister E. McGrath, *The Order of Things: Explorations in Scientific Theology* (Malden, MA: Blackwell, 2006).

7. Alister E. McGrath, *The Open Secret: A New Vision for Natural Theology* (Malden, MA: Blackwell, 2008).

8. See Alister E. McGrath, *The Science of God* (Grand Rapids: Eerdmans, 2004), 47.

9. McGrath, *Open Secret*, 2–3.

10. McGrath, *Open Secret*, 2.

nature as a legitimate, authorized, and limited pointer to the divine."[11] The key takeaway here for my concern in this chapter is that McGrath poses natural theology as a relatively orthodox and uncontroversial way of giving (and trusting the results of) theological attention to the natural world.

I'd like to occupy this discerning space of theologically interested deference to the "everyday world of our experience" for the remainder of this essay and explore a bit further what it might mean for Christian ethics. There have been a number of attempts to advance an "everyday theology" in recent decades, so a reader might be justified in asking why we need to bother with natural theology to attempt this move. My answer here is to highlight the implicit holism that is represented in this account of natural theology. Here, natural theology includes the phenomena which might be called "nature" and those elements of everyday embodied human experience which might be ascribed to "culture." At least in the way that I want to describe natural theology, we find ourselves attending, by the guidance of the Holy Spirit, to our perception, sensation, other beings, and so much more. And highlighted in this way, I wonder if the process of engaging in natural theology might do some of the work of repair that Jonathan calls for so urgently (and rightly) in *God's Good World*.

However, it is also important to emphasize that this expansiveness can be deceptive. So much has turned on the way that "our" is defined in looking towards the everyday. In considering how observations of the tangible and sensible world around us can flow into a Christian ethic, we might be pressed to ask, how do we actually decide what things might be considered "natural" in natural theological reflection? And moreover, how or can we move from a sense of "normal" to generalizations about human nature and conduct?

In my view, there are two ways to go about doing this: one is the way of homogenization, and the other is the way of pluralism. In the former, we might strive to find a maximally universal account, and likely by extension a maximally generic account. There are traces of this kind of thinking in utilitarianism and some forms of natural law reasoning (as I will note below). In the latter approach, the opposite is the case—as much as possible is drawn in and reckoned with and natural theological statements made in this mode may be as much about recognizing, preserving, and finding solidarity in difference as they are about finding continuities

---

11. McGrath, *Open Secret*, 5.

across our various experiences. Here we might locate some of the recent attempts to account for the agency and cognition of other-than-human-animals in Christian theology, or the even broader attempts in eco-theology to attend to the multiplicity of agencies swirling all around us.

From Natural Theology to Natural Law

In many ways, as I have already hinted above, natural *law* thinking represents the ethical side of a natural theology coin. Though in practice they can often be quite sharply contrasting, this is both ironic and strange. Just like natural theology, as McGrath describes it, modern natural law traditions are wide ranging and diverse, though theologians do not always appreciate this fact. Vincent Lloyd emphasizes this range of possible approaches in his recent book, *Black Natural Law*, drawing attention to the well-developed but often ignored tradition of Black natural law.[12] Like McGrath he also notes the plurality of modern approaches to natural law, but while McGrath works hard to demonstrate that natural theology can be *Christian* and straight-forwardly orthodox, Lloyd has different emphases. Part of the reason for this is because, in contrast to natural theology, natural law has often been used in the service of positivistic theological programs with quite narrow conceptions of "human nature." Lloyd's opening case study is the conservative US Supreme Court justice Clarence Thomas, but other examples abound. As I have already hinted above, and as Lloyd argues, thinking around what is "natural," outside a default White and privileged theological posture, tends to produce different kinds of methodological reflexes. Many of the same commitments remain—in particular, the notion that natural law opens up an epistemological space for considering the relation of everyday observation and embodied perception to a theological understanding of the world. However, Lloyd argues that, in some contrast to (default White) Euro-American natural law traditions, the Black natural law tradition offers a more complex account of human nature: "It includes the capacity to reason, but also the capacities to feel and imagine."[13] Further, Lloyd argues that the overall approach in Black natural law is more apophatic: "Just as God exceeds all worldly descriptions, the image of God in humanity exceeds

---

12. Vincent W. Lloyd, *Black Natural Law* (New York: Oxford University Press, 2016).

13. Lloyd, *Black Natural Law*, xi.

all worldly descriptions."[14] These two—the apophatic and embodied dimensions of Black natural law—work together. In Lloyd's description, "the Black natural law tradition claims that reasoning, feeling, and imagining are characteristically human capacities, but these are descriptions that evoke rather than denote, human nature that is unrepresentable."[15] In Lloyd's final point of contrast, Black natural law is not primarily about providing support for ethical propositions, but can be seen as process oriented. It is not about a kind of "do this, don't do that" dynamic, but is much more complex and rich. And this process of considering human nature in a more complex, embodied, and apophatic way is itself generative: "This process when engaged in collectively, catalyses social movements and offers a critique of the wisdom of the world."[16]

Can it be that the prevalence of broken relationships and families, sexual abuse, self-harm, and indifference to suffering that we find among Christians and Christian communities is somehow a consequence of a certain kind of theology? This is a diagnosis that Jonathan has laid down across a number of volumes, and one which I have also found hard to ignore. I find Lloyds's analysis, and the case studies he provides drawing on the life and work of Frederick Douglass, Anna Julia Cooper, W. E. B. Du Bois, and Martin Luther King Jr. to be compelling. If we are to pursue forms of theological thinking and Christian ethics that are both holistic—connecting up themes like ecclesiology and worship with bodies, meals, environments, and art—and humble, there is something to be recaptured in the natural theology traditions, particularly the ways that Lloyd emphasizes apophaticism, shared action, and felt imagination.

As a Christian theologian whose own life includes a journey through anxiety and depression, I've spent quite a lot of time reflecting on this question of what it means to be human. So much of our collective thinking around mental health relies upon a pathologized notion of mental "ill health," where to be anxious is to be broken and in need of fixing. In this way of thinking, an anxious person is taught to mistrust their body as it veers away from a "norm" and find ways to hide or medicate what could otherwise be characterized as a special sort of sensitivity. This posture can be found in relation to quite a wide range of what are sometimes called disabilities, and also to many other physical conditions. To have

14. Lloyd, *Black Natural Law*, xi.
15. Lloyd, *Black Natural Law*, xi.
16. Lloyd, *Black Natural Law*, viii.

a condition such as these is to dwell uneasily, in some cases more than others, outside the space of "normal." This sense of pathology extends to the ways that we conceive of and provide treatment for much of what fits under the umbrella of neurodiversity, including ADHD and autism. As we learn more about how the human mind and brain are interwoven, and as we understand more about neurological and biochemical conditions which produce these conditions, it has become increasingly clear that these are not just problems that can or should be corrected but also bodies that are different in noteworthy ways. Thus neurodiversity might be seen as different from some other medical conditions that unambiguously lead one to seek some sort of correction.

I raise this because, depending on how a Christian chooses to deploy natural theology, we can end up with quite sharply different views on how we should be oriented towards our own bodies when they do not do what we expect or desire, or do not look like what is classified as "normal." If one takes the kind of approach that I have tentatively offered here, I wonder whether we may end up being more charitable towards ourselves, and in that small minority of cases where someone finds themself persistently in the "normal" category, I wonder whether there might be an opportunity to offer more grace—not just on an interpersonal level, but in the very mode of our theological reflection—to one's fellow creatures.

The Beatitudes

The Very Locality of Kingdom Realism

Homily to the Lutheran and Episcopalian Students
on the Fourth Sunday after the Epiphany

REINHARD HÜTTER

Now when Jesus saw the crowds, he went up on a mountainside and sat down. His disciples came to him, and he began to teach them. He said: "Blessed are the poor in spirit, for theirs is the kingdom of heaven. Blessed are those who mourn, for they will be comforted. Blessed are the meek, for they will inherit the earth. Blessed are those who hunger and thirst for righteousness, for they will be filled. Blessed are the merciful, for they will be shown mercy. Blessed are the pure in heart, for they will see God. Blessed are the peacemakers, for they will be called children of God. Blessed are those who are persecuted because of righteousness, for theirs is the kingdom of heaven. Blessed are you when people insult you, persecute you and falsely say all kinds of evil against you because of me. Rejoice and be glad, because great is your reward in heaven, for in the same way they persecuted the prophets who were before you."

—MATT 5:1–12[1]

---

1. This chapter uses the NIV translation for Scripture references, unless otherwise indicated.

Dear Brothers and Sisters!

This is the end of the sermon. Jesus himself has spoken. It is, after all, his famous Sermon on the Mount. What else is there to say? Let us not forget: it was on top of a mountain where Moses received the Ten Commandments, the very way of life for Israel as God's chosen example of righteousness and holiness for all the other nations and people in the world. It is now also on a mountain where Jesus, Israel's Messiah, offers his own authoritative interpretation of this way of life by going right to the very heart of God's intention, of God's point in and with this way of life. This teaching of Jesus is not for anyone who happens to drop by and listen in on Jesus talking. Rather, this teaching is for Jesus's disciples, the *ekklesia*, the final gathering of Israel, the renewed Israel at the end of time, and that means it is also for you and me.

By the time Jesus appears on the scene, the Decalogue had been taught for centuries upon centuries in Israel, and not the least by prophets like Micah, whom you heard just a few moments ago (Mic 6:1–8). And Jesus makes quite clear a bit further down in his sermon: "Do not think I have come to abolish the law or the prophets; I have come not to abolish but to fulfill." But what would the genuine fulfillment of God's law look like? What would it look like if the Decalogue were fulfilled in its very spirit, to the very core of what God intended? In the Sermon on the Mount Jesus offers his authoritative answer to this question. And what an answer, indeed! A surprising, if not to say shocking, picture opens before our eyes. It looks like the world has been turned upside down. A counterintuitive, if not outright alarming, set of affirmations smacks into the face of our established hierarchies of values and our entrenched desires for well-being, acceptance, security, and success. "Good for those who mourn," "Good for those who are meek," "Good for those who are persecuted for righteousness' sake"?! Well, we surely are attracted to the second half of each of these paradoxical affirmations, these strange announcements, or better, unlikely promises of blessing. Who of us would not like to be comforted, inherit the earth, receive mercy, be called "child of God," own the kingdom of heaven, and see God? But what about the first half of each of these Beatitudes? What is the deal here between the first and the second half? How do they hang together? How does the transition from the first part to the second come about? First the work, then the reward? First the suffering, then the joy? Wrong! No hidden works-righteousness here! That would allow us the easy out of turning away from the challenge by denouncing it as proto-Catholic, as a way of works. But, boy, this transition is a challenge indeed! If it is not a matter of an "if-then," a reward for our heroic ethics, what is it then? Indeed, how can we find ourselves in the first half, and then, as a matter of fact, also in the second half of any of these Beatitudes? Is it at all humanly possible to occupy that space that Christ intends in the Beatitudes, and for this matter, in the whole Sermon on the Mount?

It is indeed not easy to occupy the spaces God calls us to occupy. This was already very hard for Israel, if not close to impossible. At least it sounds that way when we listen in upon a prophet like Micah calling Israel to task, or to be more precise, God calling Israel to task. The God of Israel has a controversy with his people. God is *contending* with Israel. God has raised Israel from Egypt, has brought it by this very raising into being as God's people, has protected and sustained it, has gifted it with a way of life, a way of righteousness, goodness, and justice—and Israel does not really know what to do in response, how to live in thankfulness. In his exasperation, the prophet becomes facetious: "Should we shower the Lord with ten thousand rivers of oil? Should we offer our first-born child to God?" Why is it so difficult for Israel to understand? Why is it so difficult to occupy the space God wants us to occupy? The prophet Micah circumscribes this space in utter clarity and simplicity: "He has told you, O mortal, what is good; and what does the Lord require of you but to do justice, and to love kindness, and to walk humbly with your God?"[2]

Now, this seems to be much more straightforward than the Beatitudes: doing justice, loving kindness, walking humbly with our God. This space seems to be relatively easy to occupy. Or is it really? Let us put ourselves into Israel's shoes for a moment. Do we really and genuinely want to occupy this space with our whole heart, all the time? Or do we just comfort ourselves with the thought that we indeed could occupy this space if we really wanted to? Are the doing of justice, loving kindness, and humbly walking with our God our true priorities, guiding everything else we do? Do we lose sleep over them at night, do we fret over them during the day? Do we even ever get as far as the apostle Paul who says these profoundly honest words about the space he cannot occupy on his own, because he finds himself bound to another space: "So I find this law at work: although I want to do good, evil is right there with me. For in my inner being I delight in God's law; but I see another law at work in me,

---

2 See Mic 6:7–8.

waging war against the law of my mind and making me a prisoner of the law of sin at work within me" (Rom 7:21–23).

God's intention is wonderful. We wholeheartedly agree with it! The Beatitudes are a great idea, indeed, a most sublime ideal; only—too bad, we are not there; we don't occupy their space. And what does it help to be told what is good if we are not good, what does it help to be told to do justice if we are not righteous? Yet precisely in light of this dilemma, Paul exclaims, "Thanks be to God, who delivers me through Jesus Christ our Lord!" (Rom 7:25). God has seen Israel's misery; God has seen our misery.

The only One who is good steps in for us and makes us good, the only One who is just steps in and justifies us, the only One who is love steps in and makes us lovable. The Son of God humbles himself by becoming a human being in order to walk humbly with us and take upon himself the most humbling fates of all: an unjust and despised death on the cross. And so this cross becomes the very seal and guarantee of God's goodness, God's love, and God's humility for us. For this very reason, the cross makes Micah's injunction as well as Jesus's Sermon on the Mount, and especially the Beatitudes, "good news." God has made you good through giving away for you his goodness on the cross, God has justified you by giving away for you his righteousness on the cross, and God loves you with an undying love, because you are part of Christ poured out for you, ever since your baptism. This is the wisdom of the cross, the hidden logic of the world, a foolishness wiser than human wisdom, and a weakness stronger than human strength. On the cross, God has occupied our space of sin, death, God-forsakenness, despair, rebellion, and weakness. So that now, indeed, in Christ our space has become God's space and God's space our space! Dare we open our eyes and recognize this stunning exchange? Dare we say with Mary, the first Christian: "Here I am, the servant of the Lord; let it be with me according to your word"? What might happen when we say yes like Mary did, and another Mary later on did too? What might happen when we let ourselves be transformed by the goodness, love, and humility of the One who already occupies our space? What might happen when we let the wisdom of the cross transform the conventional wisdom of our lives? What might happen when we let God meet us in our space and let God take charge of our life through Christ's goodness, love, and humility? I don't know for sure, but Jesus seems to be quite sure, because he sees clearly where I only see through a mirror dimly:

> Blessed are the poor in spirit, for theirs is the kingdom of heaven.
> Blessed are those who mourn, for they will be comforted.
> Blessed are the meek, for they will inherit the earth.
> Blessed are those who hunger and thirst for righteousness, for they will be filled.
> Blessed are the merciful, for they will be shown mercy.
> Blessed are the pure in heart, for they will see God.
> Blessed are the peacemakers, for they will be called children of God.
> Blessed are those who are persecuted because of righteousness, for theirs is the kingdom of heaven.
> Blessed are you when people insult you, persecute you and falsely say all kinds of evil against you because of me. Rejoice and be glad, because great is your reward in heaven, for in the same way they persecuted the prophets who were before you. (Matt 5:3–12)

We might, indeed, come to see, we might indeed believe that the space of the Beatitudes is our space, because God already has occupied it for us—and holds it for us. Here, in the Beatitudes, God's will is fulfilled, because God is here already. Here, God's reign already is breaking into this passing world; here, the wisdom of the cross already shines forth brightly into the world like a city on a hill.

So let us long for the space that God holds for us in the Beatitudes, let us seek the life according to the Beatitudes, because they indeed are our place of habitation in this passing world as we wait for our heavenly dwelling in Christ, the very heart of God's goodness, love, and humility.

And now let us step together into this space. Come, taste and see, how friendly the Lord is.

Seeing the Kingdom

Scott Kohler

The kingdom is present and actual in our world, but we have difficulty seeing it. We need to have our eyes trained . . .[1]

JONATHAN WILSON'S THEOLOGY STUDENTS have never had to wait very long to hear about the kingdom of God. Kingdom-talk arises easily and often in his teaching because the Bible talks about the kingdom. Jonathan, it's worth saying, is the kind of theologian you'd be glad to bring home to meet your church: his theology is closely responsive to the biblical text and biblical images. If the kingdom is prominent in the Bible, it ought to figure significantly in our accounts of theology.

In a 2007 essay, Jonathan set out a proposal for configuring a whole theology around the theme of the kingdom.[2] The task has scarcely begun to be pursued outside of the guild of biblical studies. Maybe the reason it's still more of a wish than a reality is that it's easier said than done. For academics, kingdom-talk can call to mind oppressive systems and powers, or can be set aside as the mistaken prophetic hope of a diminished

---

1. Jonathan R. Wilson, *God So Loved the World: A Christology for Disciples* (Grand Rapids: Baker Academic, 2001), 29.

2. "Theology and the Kingdom," in *From Biblical Criticism to Biblical Faith: Essays in Honor of Lee Martin McDonald*, ed. William H. Brackney and Craig A. Evans (Macon, GA: Mercer University Press, 2007), 282–93. The theme of vision and the importance of seeing the kingdom is highlighted in this essay as well.

"historical Jesus." For the church, the problem runs perhaps at a more basic level: kingdom-talk is demanding, and calls for a response to a reality. More of a challenge than that, and what I'm concerned with here, is the simple trouble of seeing the kingdom of which Jesus spoke.

Vision Problems

In John 3:3, while carrying on a conversation with an inquirer named Nicodemus, Jesus introduces the idea of "seeing" the kingdom, and right away it is accompanied by a word about the difficulty of the task: "Very truly I tell you, no one can see the kingdom of God unless they are born again."[3] Seeing the kingdom—even being able to recognize its reality, a necessity for any who would enter into a kingdom-centred life—requires such a transformed imagination that it can be likened to a new birth. Any who are not reborn in this way are unable to see it.

This isn't the only time Jesus mentions vision problems. In Mark 8, when his disciples display some of their characteristic confusion about his words and actions, Jesus asks them, "Do you still not see or understand? . . . Do you have eyes but fail to see . . . ?" The next story Mark tells his readers is of Jesus healing the blind man at Bethsaida, a healing that is only moderately successful at first. The man sees people, but "they look like trees walking around" (8:24). We get Mark's point: the work of curing the disciples' blindness isn't going to be immediate or easy.

The church—today's disciple community—has the task of proclaiming the same kingdom Jesus proclaimed. We've been called to show it to the world, but find that we can't easily see it ourselves. We're a bit like Israel, knowing that God plans to "lead the blind," but discovering to our own disappointment that even though we are God's servant for the task, we ourselves have a spectacular case of blindness:

> Who is blind but my servant,
>   and deaf like the messenger I send?
> Who is blind like the one in covenant with me,
>   blind like the servant of the LORD? (Isa 42:19)

So we find ourselves in a difficult position. We serve Jesus, who began his ministry with the announcement that "the kingdom of God is at hand," went on to tell dozens of stories about the kingdom, ultimately suggested

---

3. This chapter uses the NIV translation for Scripture references, unless otherwise indicated.

that his pathway toward death on the cross was wrapped up with this kingdom reality, and called his followers to be his "witnesses." Yet we don't even know how to see the very thing that was his central concern.

For the rest of this essay I'd like to consider the obstacles and opportunities around seeing the kingdom as they arise in two arenas, the church and the world. I will begin with a brief definition and description of the kingdom, with some help from James William McClendon Jr., and then move on to a consideration of how the kingdom can be seen—or obscured—in both church and world. As I consider these two arenas, I will also engage with the thought of Julian Hartt, who has been a significant dialogue partner for Jonathan.[4]

Kingdom as God's Rule

A lot of ink was spilled in the twentieth century over the question of the kingdom of God. Should we understand it on the analogy of a geographic territory over which an earthly monarch rules? Or should we understand it as that rule or reign itself, the dynamic of commanding control and ultimate decision? After we sort that out, what about the time of the kingdom? Is it a future reality for which we wait, or a present—or at least in-breaking—reality of our lives? The majority of interpreters have opted for saying that the kingdom is more about God's reign than his territory, and that although the fulfillment of God's kingdom remains future, the kingdom has been inaugurated already.

James William McClendon Jr., the rare instance of a theologian who gives the kingdom a fairly prominent position in his work, begins his *Doctrine* with a long section titled "The Rule of God." This way of referring to the kingdom is particularly appropriate given McClendon's "Baptist" perspective, since it points to the present activity of God in the world and especially the church as the Scriptures convey God's word to the community. For McClendon, the distinctive feature of Baptist communities is their tendency to read Scripture in an immediate way: *this* life we are living together is *that* which the Scriptures have told us about, and the realities belonging to a future *then* are experienced and active in the community's life *now*. These two features, that the kingdom is a *reality*

---

4. A revision of Jonathan's Duke dissertation on Hartt was published as *Theology as Cultural Critique: The Achievement of Julian Hartt* (Macon, GA: Mercer University Press, 1996).

and that it is experienced in some form *now*, are axiomatic for Jonathan's theology. In his words,

> the kingdom is not an ideal for which we are to strive; it is not an ideology by which we are to live; nor is it a promise for which we are to hope. Rather, in Jesus' words and deeds the kingdom of God is a reality in which we are to live.[5]

Jonathan's insistence on the reality of the kingdom, together with the active nature of God's rule in McClendon's formulation, can help us understand how we might begin to watch for God's kingdom, despite the obstacles to seeing well.

The Kingdom in the Church

And there are obstacles. Jesus once told a memorable story about a speck and a log lodged in a pair of siblings' eyes. This saying is not a bad place to begin considering the presence of the kingdom in the church, because the church itself has often become the blinding log in any eye intent on seeing the kingdom. The reasons for this are many, ranging from supposed rampant hypocrisy among individual Christians to that deadly error of Christendom, conflating the church and the kingdom of God. The church has a relation to the kingdom of God (that of witness to it and participant in it) but, in the words of Julian Hartt, "the church is not the kingdom of God. The church is the servant of that Kingdom, and it is often timid and proud." Yet Hartt goes on to wonder at the truth that though the church's "vainglorious clamor the gospel gets itself proclaimed! For which thanks be to God alone."[6]

So the first place I want to suggest that we need to look for the kingdom is within the church. Despite the church's historic and persistent shortcomings, God is active in the church, using the church for his purposes, and sometimes making the church miserable in the process, as he shakes it around to clear off the dust and grime of its own sin. The church may be a mess, but it is God's mess, and it is a useful mess as far as God sees it. With his book *Why Church Matters*, Jonathan has borne witness to a persistent belief in the importance of the church, despite its failures. "The church is the witness to and servant of (the) kingdom." But the

---

5. Wilson, *God So Loved*, 25–26.

6. Julian N. Hartt, *Toward a Theology of Evangelism*, Julian N. Hartt Library (1955; reprint, Eugene, OR: Wipf & Stock, 2006), 71.

church is distinct from the kingdom, and "when the church loses sight of its distance from the kingdom, bad things happen."[7] This duality of affirmation and warning made its way into the preface of the book, with a charming dedication to his wife Marti, "whose impatience with the church and patient practice of prayer contribute far more to the church's faithfulness than anything I may write."[8] These two attitudes—patient prayer to God for the church and impatient attention to the church in its failure to respond faithfully to God—belong together.

We are, then, right to approach the church with proper reverence as the community called in Scripture the bride of Christ. The church has a special place in God's plans. Yet we are also right to look at the church with honest recognition that in its reality as a human institution, it is still sinful and in need of redemption itself. This God-intended community is flawed by its own stubbornness and blindness. In our attempts to see the kingdom in the church, we might be looking for something that the church itself doesn't yet see. Our search is for the activity of God, and it sometimes seems that nothing is more prone to being overlooked or misinterpreted than the activity of God.

But there will be signs of the kingdom. Evidence of hope and life exist in even the most unimpressive church settings. Among those declining and aging churches that seem to be long past the point of the "effective ministry" of which the practitioner-experts like to speak, we continue to discover the proverbial prayer warriors whose housebound work points to real hope founded on the resurrection of Jesus and the presence of the Spirit. From time to time, among the pews full of glazed-over eyes, the preached word breaks through and snaps someone out of their somnambulant state, summoning them to true discipleship. This is the active rule (kingdom) of the living God. And, of course, there remain also those churches that do stand out as lively and winsome embodiments of the gospel, in which truthful speech, forgiveness, hospitality, and the recognition of the reflected glory of Christ in one another flourish together.

If we find ourselves, like Marti Wilson, impatient with the church, that isn't necessarily a bad thing if it's accompanied by patient prayer. This prayer will expect to see the kingdom of God even in the most shadowy corners of this community and will persistently ask the Lord of the

---

7. Jonathan R. Wilson, *Why Church Matters: Worship, Ministry, and Mission in Practice* (Grand Rapids: Brazos, 2006), 80.

8. Wilson, *Why Church Matters*, 6.

church to help us take up the faithfulness that he has already embodied in his life among us.

The Kingdom in the World

I grew up among conservative Baptists who were still enamored with and tethered to a mid-century vision of church life that included antagonistic ideas about the relationship between the church and the world. The "world" was what we were supposed to avoid. Jesus was right when he said we weren't supposed to be *of* the world, but many in the church thought he might have reconsidered that part about being *in* the world. The world was maybe even the enemy we were called to fight. While I was learning to walk and talk in the late 1970s, our church was encouraging congregants to burn their rock-and-roll records. School dances, movie theaters—and for an earlier generation even the bowling alley—were seedbeds of dangerous influence and not to be trusted. They epitomized the world.

The line between avoiding supposed worldliness and avoiding the actual people in the world, however, was never clear. We were supposed to fight the influence of the world; did that mean we were also supposed to fight the *people* in the world? Jesus and the Gospels seemed clear on a few things that suggested otherwise. Whatever the world was, God created it, and now God loved it too. God's work in Jesus was aimed at the reclamation of nothing less than the whole world. There was no limit to how far Jesus would go to do that work of reclaiming the world. He crossed boundaries that the holiness watchdogs of his day had carefully constructed. And he suggested to his followers that he would show up in surprising places and people, even places and people that were "out there" in the world.

The dialectic is a tricky one to sustain. As Jonathan points out in *God's Good World*, there is a danger in some contemporary circles of overreacting against worries about the world. The old "world" construed by mid-century Evangelicals and fundamentalists as the danger we guard against easily becomes, to another generation, the "culture" we are eager to engage and sometimes more than happy to embrace. Along with a proper insistence on the world as God's good creation, we also need to see the disaster of the world's rebellion. "Without an account of the world in rebellion against God, the way things are today becomes 'natural.'"[9] In

---

9. Jonathan R. Wilson, *God's Good World: Reclaiming the Doctrine of Creation*

the words of Hartt, the world is under the sway of "lies and illusions" that obscure its vision of life and the purposes of God.[10] We need an account of the world and "worldliness" that recognizes this. Jonathan defines worldliness as "living as if the claims of the world and the rule of death have not been publicly humiliated and defeated by Christ."[11]

Yet precisely because the world can and must also be construed in terms of its createdness, as "God's good world," we know that God is at work in it. His work, however, is a struggle—a fight for the world's good. The world "is made to be creation as God sustains and provides for it. God's providence is, in this respect, God's work of claiming even this rebellious world as creation."[12]

This work of God can appropriately be called his kingdom. Hartt sees the kingdom as an all-embracing reality that everyone in some way already participates in.[13] He suggests that the kingdom is in the world already to be seen. The demand of the kingdom is the summons to "creative transformation." If we understand that participation in the kingdom means being touched by the activity of God, this is not much different than what Jonathan says. The apostle Paul's way of putting it in 2 Cor 5:19 is memorable and concise: "God was reconciling the world to himself in Christ."

So where do we see the kingdom of God in the world? We see it both in those situations in which the world's rebellious ways visibly lead to frustration and death and in those wonderful moments when the world tells and lives stories of new possibility. Whenever the world sees that self-preservation, greed, and self-aggrandizement lead to brokenness, we are seeing the kingdom of God as God exposes the illusions and lies that would suggest they lead to success. And whenever the world sees that the way of humility and honesty—which we believe take their ultimate form at the foot of the cross—can lead to genuine transformation we are again bearing witness to that same kingdom. In both our critique of cultural illusions and our applause for inklings of transformation, the church finds space to retell the story of Jesus and pray that it will be received as true.

(Grand Rapids: Baker Academic, 2013), 205.

10. This phrase comes up again and again throughout Wilson, *Theology as Cultural Critique*. See esp. 119–21.

11. Wilson, *God's Good World*, 203.

12. Wilson, *God's Good World*, 64.

13. Wilson, *Toward Theology of Evangelism*, 75.

On Talking about Seeing

In the task of seeing the kingdom, we need training and teaching, and Scripture is our best teacher in this regard.[14] In Jonathan Wilson's Scripture-imagined theology, we find a number of pointers to help us know where and how to look for the kingdom. In this essay, I've tried to gesture toward how we might see the kingdom in both the church and the world. But an essay remains an exercise in language, and words are never a substitute for sight itself. As disciples we need to pray for keener eyes, which are a gift from the same Spirit to whom Jesus pointed in his conversation with Nicodemus. This prayer is always sustained by participation in the worship of the church, because "worship is a practice that corrects our vision and thus enables us to see and desire the destiny of the world that has been revealed in the gospel."[15] This gospel of the kingdom is at work in the church and the world to bring the world to its proper destiny. Jonathan's work has consistently pointed his readers and students and friends to the kingdom's reality. That is a gift to be received with deep gratitude.

---

14. Wilson, *God So Loved*, 29.

15. Jonathan R. Wilson, *Gospel Virtues: Practicing Faith, Hope, and Love in Uncertain Times* (Downers Grove, IL: InterVarsity, 1998), 14.

"Trinitarian"

The Transcendent/Immanent Ground for Ethics[1]

W. Ross Hastings

JONATHAN AND I PASTORED *within a mile of each other in East Burnaby, BC, Canada, in the late eighties and early nineties, but unfortunately did not meet. Jonathan has been a mentor to me, especially in the area of Christian ethics. He ran an informal workshop for Regent students for a few years when he was a professor at Carey Theological College, one that was very influential. A number of students from that group went on to do PhD work in ethics and became professors. I, as a rookie professor teaching ethics, simply tagged along in those workshops when I could, and learnt a tremendous amount about the crucial nodes of discussion in theological ethics. Jonathan has lately given me very helpful feedback on my writing of the book* Theological Ethics, *which he did with great restraint and grace, knowing that I was more of the Reformed than the Anabaptist persuasion. Jonathan was a regular guest also in my missional church course at Regent, in which he lectured on new monastic communities. I have discovered in recent years that Jonathan loves to refurbish old cars and I have gained further respect for him as an all-round, grounded, and creative person. I have witnessed also his engraced affect in the midst of the loss of his wife, and in a battle of his own with cancer. His faithfulness to God in the endurance of suffering, like that of Job's, has expressed that he makes more of the glory of*

---

1. Some of the themes in this essay are expanded in W. Ross Hastings, *Theological Ethics: The Moral Life of the Gospel in Contemporary Context* (Grand Rapids: Zondervan, 2021).

God than he does of his own suffering. In this, he has deeply impressed me. Above all else, it is impossible to know Jonathan without hearing clearly from his heart and speech his passion for Jesus, for the kingdom of God, for the glory of the triune God in his work in the creation.

Many ethical issues have surfaced in the midst of the COVID-19 pandemic. These include how seniors should be treated in their care homes, who should get vaccines first, whether vaccines that have required stem cells from voluntarily aborted fetuses should be administered to people, whether democratic governments can or should legally impose lockdowns, whether government ministers should take trips to holiday resorts when travel has been restricted for the population, and so on. Jonathan would no doubt be pleased if Christian ethicists would engage with these ethical issues. I believe Jonathan would discourage a casuistic approach to these issues. Rather, I think he would urge the Christian community to discern ethical guidelines and practices that are grounded in the biblical narrative. Then he would encourage the kingdom community and its people to engage with the culture on these matters, such that the church overflows in its life and its practices into the world in a missional and non-oppressive manner. In a way that is life giving, that is shalom sharing, that leads to human flourishing.

The aim of this essay is limited. I won't even get as far as offering any detailed ethical judgments on these matters. I hope to offer something even more fundamental than principle. It is certainly assumed within the narrative arc of the biblical story, which is the final authority in our ethical thinking. It may be termed a metaethical perspective of the Christian faith, though I prefer the term theologico-ethical underpinning. It transcends both deontological (ethics according to rules) and utilitarian (ethics of calculation) approaches. I am referring to ethics as "Trinitarian," which also cascades into the question of what it means to be human persons.

Why is "Trinitarian" an appropriate and sufficiently broad category for ethics? Most crucially, this is so because of the inseparable intertwining of the Trinity and the gospel. The gospel is in its very essence the revelatory and redemptive acts of the economic Trinity. The union of the Son with humanity to live and die and rise again vicariously on our behalf the great objective reality which is in our personal history subjectively appropriated by the work of the Spirit, bringing us into union or participation with Christ. The twin graces of justification and sanctification come to us within that union. Justification enables the ethical life to be pursued in peace with God, within the prior acceptance of God. Sanctification includes our moral formation and actions. Ethics apart from that union becomes moralism and legalism, at best. Within the life of participation in who Christ is for us, by the Spirit who is in us, ethics is part of the shalom that the gospel brings. Thus, there cannot be such a thing as legitimate ethics apart from the gospel of God's unconditional love for humanity, the expression of that love in the history of Jesus Christ (the *ordo historia*), which then by the Spirit, through faith, becomes the history of those who believe (*ordo salutis*). "Trinitarian" indicates that an ontology of love is at the center of the universe and that God is *for* humanity and creation. We are not left alone in the moral quest. And what the God of love commands is good, and good for us. And he does not command without empowering us. Trinitarian ethics thus implies grace-filled ethics, ethics in the context and ethos of the gospel. Specifically, it does justice to the reality that the triune God is the norm, the ground and the power of ethics, as has been outlined by Geoffrey Bromiley[2] and Dennis Hollinger.[3]

But if "Trinitarian" is an appropriate and sufficiently broad category for ethics, it remains to show that it is *the most fitting category* for Christian ethics. Why for instance is *theological* ethics or *biblical* ethics not sufficient? The truth is that to be truly theological in the Christian sense is to be christological and pneumatological and therefore Trinitarian. To use the term *theological* ethics could also be interpreted as implying (rightly) that the final authority in ethics is the Holy Scriptures, which orthodox Christians believe to be the inspired written word of God. This statement does not, however, resolve all theological issues. The Scriptures are only authoritative as the church, *enabled by the Spirit*, seeks to interpet it appropriately. The matter of interpretation requires a listening voice towards the Spirit-dependent scholarship of the church which has occurred in the church in its historical depth and in its geographical width. What's more, many of the ethical issues we face today were not heard of in biblical times—in vitro fertilization, stem cell usage, iPhones, Twitter manners, creation and deployment of nuclear weapons. Rather than offering an approach to ethics that is restricted merely to issues addressed in the Bible, or even to handle ethical discernment merely by using a proof text approach, the Trinitarian narrative arc of Scripture provides an

---

2. Geoffrey Bromiley, "Ethics and Dogmatics," in *International Standard Biblical Encyclopedia* (San Francisco: Harper and Row, 1987), 2:186-90.

3. Dennis P. Hollinger, *Choosing the Good: Christian Ethics in A Complex World* (Grand Rapids: Baker Academic, 2002), 64-68.

interpretive framework for ethical reflection by the power of the Spirit in every age. My point is simply that the terms "theological" and "biblical" with respect to ethics are enriched by the greater gospel specificity and dynamic power that "Trinitarian" carries.

One of the greatest challenges in the field of ethics or the "moral field" is its situational and complex nature in the in-between time of the kingdom of God. We often cannot know the answer in advance of the situations we encounter, as almost every encounter in which we are called upon to make ethical decisions is unique (not to be confused with the situation ethics of Joseph Fletcher for whom "love" was the only rule, who excised the moral content out of love . . . "it can't be wrong when it feels so right" or "how can love ever be wrong?"). This requires that the moral subject be in communion with the persons and work of the holy Trinity, yes, attentive to Scripture, and yes, aware of all theological truth, but in need always of the dynamic enabling of the triune God in the ecclesial community that is his image.

Having voted for "Trinitarian" over "theological" or "biblical" ethics, the question arises as to why Trinitarian surpasses the three traditional categories used for ethics, even if it may employ them. The first is the *deontological* approach to ethics championed by Immanuel Kant in philosophical ethics, and his belief in the categorical imperative. Its greatest downside is neglect of community, of persons as persons-in-relation. It expresses an individualism of the "I think, therefore I am" kind, the kind of individualism rampant for example in end-of-life issues, and in sexual fulfillment narratives in our time. It is implicitly expressed in strands of both Reformed[4] and Catholic evangelical ethics.[5]

The successor to Kantianism is the *utilitarian* theory of ethics, that is, the invocation of means and ends. The greatest downside of this system is the neglect of the person, who is treated as an amorphous part of the collective, the kind of ethics that has characterized the treatment of seniors in care homes during the COVID-19 pandemic. Frustration with both the divine command and utilitarian theories and even proportionalism, which lies between them, has led to the development (some would say the

---

4. John Calvin's use of virtues in interpreting the Decalogue using synecdoche in *Institutes of The Christian Religion*, trans. H. Beveridge (Grand Rapids: Eerdmans, 1995), II.8.9, pp. 169–70, and his union-with-Christ emphasis argues for ethics well beyond the deontological.

5. See Norman L. Geisler, *Christian Ethics: Contemporary Issues and Options*, 2nd ed. (Grand Rapids: Baker Academic, 2010).

recovery) of *virtue* or *character* ethics, sometimes also called *narrative* ethics in the sense that the narratives of a community shape the virtues and character of its members. A primary influence in the renaissance of this now flourishing field in anglophone philosophy since the 1970s, and then in Christian ethics, has been Aristotle. The principal idea here is that the cultivation of character guarantees the correct ethical action in the moment of decision.[6] The telos for Aristotle was living well and *eudaimonia*, a Greek word meaning well-being, happiness, or human flourishing.[7]

Despite this recent surge of interest in virtue ethics within academic evangelical theology, there are a number of reasons why I think it is inadequate as a theological ethic that is distinctively Christian. I contend that a fully Trinitarian ethic does not rule out divine command, nor even on occasion the employment of utilitarian approaches. It also most *definitely* incorporates virtue ethics,[8] but nevertheless transcends them all. It transcends character ethics because the category of *person* derived by way of analogy from Trinitarian and specifically christological personhood is larger and more fundamental than character. The Chalcedonian definition of Christ centered on the concept of personhood, and it prepared the way for the analogy between divine and human personhood that is crucial to the question of what it means to be human. There is a human person, Jesus, who is first a divine person in the very Godhead! The relationship between divine and human personhood is one based on analogy (not univocity). It lies in the "radical and dynamic continuity between the divine and the human that is the event of Christ."[9] Christ recapitulates our personhood as the new Head of humanity. The continuity between divine and human personhood was expressed formally through various expressions of the analogy between divine and human personhood in the Orthodox, Catholic, and Protestant traditions in these various terms: *analogia entis* (analogy of being), *analogia fide* (analogy of faith), *analogia*

---

6. Thomas Aquinas borrows but commandeers Aristotle in this regard. See Fergus Kerr, "Doctrine of God and Theological Ethics according to Thomas Aquinas," in *The Doctrine of God and Theological Ethics*, ed. Alan J. Torrance and Michael Banner (London: T&T Clark, 2006), 71–84, esp. 77.

7. Aristotle, *Nichomachean Ethics*, trans. T. H. Irwin (Indianapolis: Hackett, 1999), bk 2, xv.

8. Jonathan R. Wilson, in *Gospel Virtues: Practicing Faith, Hope, and Love in Uncertain Times* (Eugene, OR: Wipf & Stock, 2004), illustrates the pursuit of particularly *Christian* virtues, and he does so within a participatory framework.

9. Alan Torrance, *Persons in Communion: Trinitarian Description and Human Participation* (Edinburgh: Bloomsbury T&T Clark, 1996), 209.

relationis (analogy of relationships), and *analogia entis personalis* (analogy of personal being).

It is not surprising therefore that the core essence of our salvation is the personalizing of the converting human person, through the "personalizing activity of the Word and Spirit of God," as T. F. Torrance has said. He points out that we as human beings are *persona personata*, that is we are personalized persons who are personalized by him who "alone is personalizing Person, *persona personana*."[10] The believer by grace participates in the Son, through the Spirit. Restoration of personhood is thus the core of the gospel.[11] Miroslav Volf, summarizing the Orthodox theology of Metropolitan Zizioulas, perceives that after the fall "human personhood is perverted, so that it exists only as 'individuals.'"[12] This is an important distinction. Individuals remain image-bearers in some sense as part of God's creation; however, they lack the animating breath of the Holy Spirit, unable to participate in the life of God. "For these reasons, human beings can become persons only in communion with the personal God, who alone merits being called a person in the original sense."[13]

The primacy of our being as persons means that character thus belongs within personhood and not the other way around. Trinitarian, person-centered ethics transcends virtue ethics because participation of the Christian in the virtues of God cannot happen apart from ecclesial and personal participation in the life of God, in Christ and by the Spirit.[14] It integrates but transcends the other ethical theories because it more intentionally and repletely grounds ethics within theology and the gospel. The dangers of ethical pursuit apart from relationship with God have been highlighted by Bonhoeffer.[15] Stated positively, the ethical life flows

---

10. T. F. Torrance, *The Trinitarian Faith: The Evangelical Theology of the Ancient Catholic Faith* (London: Bloomsbury T&T Clark, 2000), 230.

11. Torrance, *Trinitarian Faith*, 230.

12. Miroslav Volf, *After Our Likeness: The Church as the Image of the Trinity* (Grand Rapids: Eerdmans, 1998), 81.

13. Volf, *After Our Likeness*, 83.

14. Fergus Kerr writes a compelling case that the exposition of "virtue ethics" in Thomas Aquinas in the *Summa* is grounded in a theology of participation and contemplation of the divine beatitude. Fergus Kerr, "Doctrine of God and Theological Ethics According to Thomas Aquinas," in *The Doctrine of God and Theological Ethics*, ed. Alan J. Torrance and Michael Banner (London: T&T Clark, 2006), 71–84, esp. 82–83.

15. Dietrich Bonhoeffer, *Ethics*, Dietrich Bonhoeffer Works 6 (Minneapolis: Fortress, 2008), 21–22.

from participation in Christ who has died and now lives for us and in us by the Spirit. It flows from life together in the ecclesial community and its practices of word and sacrament and discipline, enabling us to live into the story that shapes us. It flows from life in the Spirit who incorporates us and empowers our formation by imparting love and all the virtues, the spiritual dynamic for the moral ethic. It flows from and to the Father who with the Son and the Holy Spirit is the source of love and holiness and justice.

To be sure, moral character is part of personhood, and formation of godly and just character is very important. However, the broader category of persons suggests an inherent relationality with God and neighbor that is not adequately accounted for in character or virtue ethics.[16] Personhood allows for ethical action that is the product of character within, but it *also* allows for the guidance and empowering of the Holy Spirit, and of hearing the word of God from outside of ourselves. We are persons of character, not characters. We are persons in union with Christ able to function in an evangelical manner rather than a legal or merely introspective way. We are able to be *and* to do *and* to speak ethically into our societies.

Even with respect to the critical consideration in ethics of how we know what we know, that is epistemology, a "Trinitarian" way of doing ethics is helpful. A Trinitarian ethic means knowing within the Trinitarian hermeneutical circle. This is a theme that has been developed by Jens Zimmermann in *Incarnational Humanism*,[17] an incarnational-Trinitarian theory, which proposes a personalist and intersubjectivist ontology, ethics, and hermeneutics in dialogue with Dietrich Bonhoeffer. Such an incarnational-Trinitarian model is explicitly theological, epistemologically communal, directively ethical and aesthetic (here, in dialogue with Von Balthasar). This aesthetic aspect has echoes in the work of Jonathan Edwards on virtue. Beauty as a characteristic of virtue and ethical life stems directly from the God who, as Edwards described him, *is* beauty, the triune God who is the supreme harmony of all.[18]

---

16. My gratitude for the work of Bethany Murphy in her editorial preparation of parts of this article for *Crux* magazine. See W. Ross Hastings, "Personhood: The Core of Human Identity," *Crux* 57 (2021): 11–18.

17. Jens Zimmermann, *Incarnational Humanism: A Philosophy of Culture for the Church in the World*, Strategic Initiatives in Evangelical Theology (Downers Grove, IL: InterVarsity, 2012).

18. See Jonathan Edwards, *Religious Affections* (Mineola, NY: Dover, 2013), 238,

The Trinity viewed as differentiated persons of irreducible identity expressed through the axiom of "appropriations" of roles, and also one in essence and communion (undivided nature and acts of God, coinherence), speaks to moral formation and ethics as being both personal and communal or ecclesial. Human persons are neither collectivist nor atomistic. They are communal and personal. These Trinitarian aspects of personhood and community are vital in consideration of many ethical issues.[19]

Lastly, ethics as Trinitarian offers a foundation for engagement of the church in the public square. Just as the Trinity is *communio in ekstasis*, a communion which overflowed in love to create and redeem the world, so the church as the icon of the Trinity, ecstatically moves out from its own inner being to speak graciously and evangelically in the public square, upending its narratives and offering shalom and human flourishing in engraced obedience to the divine command.

In sum, the Trinitarian caption is the most comprehensive, most evangelical, most personal, most communal, and most participation-based model, one which includes virtue ethics but clarifies its source in union with Christ and offers the category of personhood as larger than character though inclusive of it.

---

for just one example.

19. For more on the implications of the communal and personal nature of Trinitarian sexual ethics, see Hastings, *Theological Ethics*, ch. 8.

The Fact of Jesus

Stanley Hauerwas

In his fine article "From Theology of Culture to Theological Ethics: The Hartt-Hauerwas Connection," Jonathan Wilson rightly demonstrates how influential Julian Hartt was for my theological formation.[1] I want to use this opportunity to expand on Jonathan's insights about Hartt as well as how Hartt's work has shaped how both Jonathan and I have done theology.

I had Mr. Hartt my first year (1962) at Yale Divinity School for systematic theology. Robert King was my preceptor in the course. Under the influence of Hartt, King was writing his dissertation on agency. I call attention to King because much of what I learned from Hartt that year came through King, who later became a dean at Millsaps College in Mississippi. What I learned from Hartt and King about the relation of existence and essence has stayed with me.

Hartt's lectures were mesmerizing. He delivered them with what appeared to be few notes. He would think hard about one thing out loud, only to remind himself of what he also wanted or needed to say about another point. His lectures were brilliant, but many complained it was no easy thing to follow him. You learned it made little sense to try to keep notes on his lectures. You might take down a striking sentence here or there but he soon disabused you of any idea that this course was going to be information.

He organized the course around the Apostles' Creed, which he made to come alive. For example, his account of God the Father challenged

---

1. Jonathan R. Wilson, "From Theology of Culture to Theological Ethics: The Hartt-Hauerwas Connection," *Journal of Religious Ethics* 23 (1995): 149–64.

those like myself who assumed that to call God Father depended on our experience of having a father. Hartt was quick to tear such a view apart. You know God is the Father only because Jesus is the Son. He then suggested that move would call into question the assumption that the family is a given.

It was impossible to put Hartt into a category. He was certainly not a liberal theologian, but that does not mean he was conservative. Rather he was able to help us see the radical character of theological convictions that had been lost by a church that had sold its soul to the status quo—which was assumed to be the result of Christian influence. The chapter in *A Christian Critique of American Culture* entitled "The Life of the Church in Christian Civilization" could have been written by an Anabaptist.

Hartt was polemical, but he rarely named his opponents. Hartt's sophisticated account of the character of civilization makes no reference to Niebuhr's *Christ and Culture*.[2] One cannot help but think he would have had quite critical views about Niebuhr's famous five-part typology, but he was more interested in critiquing the project of the Christian attempt to convert the gospel into the pieties of contemporary culture. Yet Hartt maintained that God could and does use even the compromised church as a witness to a world that is death-determined.

The radical character of his position was evident in his reflections on death. He wrote tellingly about how the kingdom of God stands over against the kingdom ruled by death. With his usual powerful prose, Hartt observes we do not "enter the Divine Kingdom merely by dying. Death as an escape hatch from the travail and guilt of life is surely the most hideously bewitching counterfeit of all."[3] The phrase "merely by dying" could be written only by one who believes we have been given lives of joy through cross and resurrection.

Jonathan rightly suggests that Hartt's influence on me is clearly evident in my insistence that the gospel is best understood as a practical exercise. I learned from Hartt that theology is first and foremost a practical discipline. Though the course was labeled systematic theology, Hartt's lectures were an exemplification of his conviction that Christian theology was a practical discipline.

---

2. H. Richard Niebuhr, *Christ and Culture* (New York: Harper & Row, 1975).

3. Julian N. Hartt, *A Christian Critique of American Culture: An Essay in Practical Theology* (New York: Harper & Row, 1967), 173.

This was confirmed by the publication of Hartt's *A Christian Critique of American Culture*, which was not published until 1967.[4] When the book came out, I immediately read it from cover to cover. Like the lectures, the arguments in the book were thick and often heavy going, but I loved it. It confirmed what I thought I had learned from the lectures—that is, that the truthfulness of the Christian faith is fundamentally a practical exploration.

I took several seminars with Mr. Hartt. I remember one seminar in philosophical theology in which we engaged in an investigation of the concept of religion. Hartt was obviously not a Protestant liberal, but he forced us to attend to the serious claims of those philosophers and theologians who seemed to think an account of religion was a necessary preliminary if more specific theological claims were to be meaningful. I did not realize at the time how deeply l was drinking from Hartt's well.

Drawing on what I had learned from Mr. Hartt, I applied to do a PhD in Christian ethics at Yale. I did so under the assumption that the surest way to avoid formalism was to study ethics. Of course, that was a mistaken assumption, particularly given the dominance of Kantian and analytic modes of ethics which try to establish ethics as an autonomous discipline. Hartt's work made it necessary to challenge the kind of ethics found in books like Frankena's *Ethics*.[5]

Jonathan's insightful account of Hartt's influence on me is accurate and instructive. I certainly recognize that Jonathan's characterization of what I think is in fact what I think, given not only what I think but also how Mr. Hartt taught me to think. Rereading Jonathan's article, however, sent me back to reread *A Christian Critique*. It quickly became evident—an evidence I am sure Jonathan knows well—that Hartt's influence on me goes far beyond the attempt to collapse any systematic/practical dualism. In fact, I find it hard to see any position I have taken that is not already in Hartt's book.

The book is full of striking sentences that I wish I had written. For example, consider these sentences: "The Gospel begins and ends with an uncompromising declaration that certain things are facts, that is, that certain things have happened. The Gospel is just as uncompromisingly insistent that anybody who knows these things had better do something

---

4. Hartt, *Christian Critique*.
5. William Frankena, *Ethics* (Englewood Cliffs, NJ: Prentice-Hall, 1973).

about his situation now."[6] "Certain things are facts" is Hartt's way to resist making Jesus the exemplification of a philosophy of life that is more basic than Jesus's cross and resurrection.

The "facts" that are Christ cannot be known without proclamation. That is why for Hartt, Christian theology is first and foremost the announcement that the kingdom of God is present. Accordingly the gospel is "indigestible" as an element in cultural philosophies.[7] Jesus is at once the one who proclaims the kingdom come and the one who is that kingdom. Those that would distinguish between faith in Jesus Christ and the faith of Christ are making a theological distinction that is unreal. What these christological observations make clear is that Hartt's emphasis on the practical character of the theological enterprise is determined by the "fact" of Jesus being who the church proclaims.

I should like to think these observations sound familiar to those who have read me or Jonathan Wilson but have not read Hartt. The truth of the matter is that I have thought I had learned these fundamental theological moves from Barth, but it turns out Jonathan's recovery of Hartt reminds me that before Barth, there was Hartt. I remember, however, that our textbook in Hartt's systematic course was a volume of the *Dogmatics*. I think it was II/1.[8]

Though I had drawn on Hartt's title when I wrote "A Christian Critique of Christian America," I assumed the ecclesial presumptions I was developing were more radical than Hartt's. I thought, for example, that Hartt would not write this sentence: "The first task of the church is not to make the world more just but to make the world the world." I was stunned, therefore, to read Hartt's claim that Christian criticism "must begin with the life of the church itself. In the church itself opinion often enough parades as truth and expediency as wisdom; and status is precious there as on the outside; and self-aggrandizement has legion forms and the virulence of plague."[9] Hartt continues observing that exactly because the church confesses her sins, she makes it possible for the world to see God's grace.

Hartt's ecclesial reflections are tough. There is not a sentimental bone in Hartt's body. Nowhere is that better seen than in his discussion of what

---

6. Hartt, *Christian Critique*, 129.

7. Hartt, *Christian Critique*, 126.

8. Karl Barth, *Church Dogmatics* II/1, trans. G. W. Bromiley et al. (Edinburgh: T&T Clark, 1957).

9. Hartt, *Christian Critique*, 409.

he identifies as the ontological givens, that is, mortality, love, creativity, anxiety, and guilt.[10] For example, Hartt observes that we no longer love ourselves adequately when we discover that such a love is not reflected in the world beyond ourselves. We end up hating the world because the world, that is, other people, fail to reflect what we regard as our ego's self-value.[11] Such an account was sorely needed given the still-frequent celebration of love as the essence of what Christianity is about.

Julian Hartt's work is filled with insights about God, the world, and our relation to ourselves, God, and the world. It is no wonder, therefore, that Jonathan found in Hartt's work the way to do theology without apology. Like Hartt, Jonathan's work is filled with insights made possible by the recognition that Jesus is a "fact." That it takes some time for us to live into the truth that is Jesus. We are, therefore, indebted to Jonathan for the recovery of Hartt as well as for the power of his own work.

---

10. Hartt, *Christian Critique*, 216–20.
11. Hartt, *Christian Critique*, 217.

Speaking Words against Whiteness

Remapping the Message of Reconciliation

WILLIE JAMES JENNINGS

For the love of Christ urges us on, because we are convinced that one has died for all; therefore all have died. And he died for all, so that those who live might live no longer for themselves, but for him who died and was raised for them. From now on, therefore, we regard no one from a human point of view; even though we once knew Christ from a human point of view, we know him no longer in that way. So if anyone is in Christ, there is a new creation: everything old has passed away; see, everything has become new! All this is from God, who reconciled us to himself through Christ, and has given us the ministry of reconciliation; that is, in Christ God was reconciling the world to himself, not counting their trespasses against them, and entrusting the message of reconciliation to us. So we are ambassadors for Christ, since God is making his appeal through us; we entreat you on behalf of Christ, be reconciled to God. For our sake he made him to be sin who knew no sin, so that in him we might become the righteousness of God.

—2 COR 5:14–21[1]

---

1. This chapter uses the NRSV translation for Scripture references, unless otherwise indicated.

THE RACIAL CHRISTIANITY THAT we all have inherited has never known what to do with this passage of Scripture. More centrally, that racial Christianity has not known what to do with the language of reconciliation.

God has reconciled the world to Godself and therefore we should be reconciled to one another.

This common way of summarizing this text is not wrong. It simply is a line that does not lead us anywhere. This common line of thinking about reconciliation shows our inability to grasp what the thick message of reconciliation invites us to see and to do. For a long time, I have been known to say that Christians in the West, especially Christians identifying as white, should refrain from using the language of reconciliation.

God has reconciled the world to Godself and therefore we should be reconciled to one another.

I never meant by this that we all should abandon the doctrine of reconciliation or deny the message of reconciliation as articulated in this text. I was simply pointing to a history of turning the language of reconciliation into the language of whiteness.

God has reconciled the world to Godself and therefore we should be reconciled to one another.

In this regard, that means turning the language of reconciliation into a wish for toleration and even a dream for peace and thereby into a tool for cultivating and maintaining control—maintaining a racial status quo (politically, socially, economically, geographically) that conceals the ongoing formation of white identity and white hegemony. The language of reconciliation has been turned in our time into a tool of white supremacy.

God has reconciled the world to Godself and therefore we should be reconciled to one another.

I, like so many others, have been frustrated by the use of the language of reconciliation to protect what Robin DiAngelo has now famously termed white fragility.[2] That is, the fear that so many white people feel when they experience the de-centering of white life and the psychic pain they experience when the avenues to re-center white life are cut off from them. Now, this criticism of reconciliation language is not new; it has been with us now for a while, but what so many church communities and so many ministers have not been able to do is render the language of reconciliation as a tool against whiteness and, even more importantly, render that language as a tool in the fight against anti-blackness *and* as a

---

2. Robin DiAngelo, *White Fragility: Why It's So Hard for White People to Talk about Racism* (Boston: Beacon, 2018).

compelling vision not simply for tolerance, but for thick and revolutionary life together now. In so much of the Christian imagination, reconciliation remains at the level of a theological slogan.

God has reconciled the world to Godself and therefore we should be reconciled to one another.

I would like to engage in a bit of remapping of the language of reconciliation in this brief essay in order to get at the thickness of the message and the possibilities of life inside the message. I want to focus on three points on this map. First, a new kind of becoming; second, a different kind of ambassador; and third, a life aimed at joining.

The message of reconciliation begins in the body of Jesus where we are offered a new reality of becoming—moving from death to life.

For the love of Christ urges us on, because we are convinced that one has died for all; therefore all have died. And he died for all, so that those who live might live no longer for themselves, but for him who died and was raised for them.

It is the gift of this becoming in Christ that frames the message of reconciliation, and it is the struggle against racial becoming that frames our work and our lives at this critical moment. We who inhabit the Western world stand in the long legacy of a world transformed and forced into a single path of becoming—becoming mature, becoming human, becoming visible, becoming significant, becoming important, becoming worthy of being heard. That path of becoming in the West formed with white bodies at one end, black bodies at the other end, and all flesh placed in the middle. It necessarily invited everyone to move as best as one could toward whiteness.

As I noted in my recent book, *After Whiteness*, all of Western education exists inside a deformed vision of formation, a diseased image of what the educated state looks like.[3] That image drives so much of the educational endeavor of the Western world, and it is the image of a white self-sufficient man who embodies three demonically derived virtues: possession, control, and mastery. To become him has been the implicit dream of Western education, a dream born of the colonial masters who sought to prepare their children to rule and not be ruled, to win and not lose in the serious competition for resources and power. To determine one's fate, one must become this man individually and collectively as a people.

---

3. Willie James Jennings, *After Whiteness: An Education in Belonging* (Grand Rapids: Eerdmans, 2020).

All peoples made subject to the chaos of colonialism found their ways of becoming—becoming mature, becoming leaders, becoming elders—short-circuited by a racial becoming bound to an economic becoming. All were placed on a path of productivity to yield a humanity that would be recognized and respected. So many peoples found themselves caught up in nationalist projects in order to be seen and heard. This is not new news. What is yet to happen, however, is for this news to make its way fully into church communities and the ways we vision growth and formation.

The message of reconciliation begins with a new word about our becoming—a word that disrupts racial becoming by interrupting the smooth narration of growth and maturity that moves us along the path toward whiteness. That path has woven our vision of salvation, and of the good life, and of the mature life not only inside a capitalist logic but also inside a logic that makes no room for the Spirit's guidance. Racial becoming reduces the Spirit to our servant who helps us and our children to become self-sufficient, and in control, and in possession, and with some measure of mastery of something (e.g., lawyer, doctor, entrepreneur, scientist). And the aim of all of this is to become white men. Of course, not actual white men, but the white man dreamed up by the colonial master as he imagined his future in his children.

The language of reconciliation speaks disruption. We speak it into the places and spaces where people make and execute and live their plans for what they will become and who they will be—*we are convinced that one has died for all; therefore all have died. And he died for all, so that those who live might live no longer for themselves, but for him who died and was raised for them.*

This disrupting word breaks open life encased in racial becoming and places in the heart of our lives a crucial orientation toward the Spirit of the living God, asking the Spirit again and again to guide my life and to guide our lives. That plea for guidance must not be made generic, or docetic, or nebulous. It is guidance away from racial becoming, away from the dreams of the colonial masters. Which brings me to the second point on the map: becoming a different kind of ambassador.

We are ambassadors for Christ. It is fundamentally a participatory reality. We are inside the message of reconciliation, which means we are inside the incarnate way of the incarnate God. Jesus of Nazareth is God entering fully into the reality of the creature and learning the way of the creature from the inside. It is from the inside, as a learner, that God is revealed. It remains a profound challenge for Christians to understand the way of our witness of reconciliation. The colonial legacy we inhabit taught us that only a talking, teaching, evaluating, judging Christian is one who is giving witness to the message of God's reconciling love. Christians give witness to this reconciling God and this God's way of love. This is true, but it is a truth woven in the listening and the learning.

Reconciliation is about a productive silence that emerges after we have said the words "teach me your ways and show me your world so that I might be with you." And then we listen, and we learn and *in this way* the witness of reconciliation begins. We are ambassadors—we give witness. But the question is, what is the character of our witness? And here we must challenge what I have called the pedagogical imperialism within which whiteness formed, whereby the whole world was imagined by the colonial Christian as needing always and forever to be student to be taught, and the Christian to always and forever to be the teacher. It is that pedagogical imperialism that rests powerfully inside whiteness, driving people to imagine themselves always at the center.

We are ambassadors of the reconciling God, but that does not mean we are the center of things. It has been almost impossible for white Western Christians to imagine a non-centered positionality from which to think and live the reconciling life. Christians are not those who exist in some middle social, political, or economic position. This is why it is such a profound mistake and failure for us to imagine ourselves existing in some fictive middle position between liberal and conservative, trying to bring peace between two warring sides, and trying to create a space where liberals and conservatives can meet in common cause. We are ambassadors of a God who has joined those always at the margins *and* joined those who are aiming to be at the center. That joining collapses the distance between them in God's own body. The triune God is the moving center, tasking us with following the Spirit into the inner spaces of peoples' lives to give witness to divine love through our love of them. Which brings me to the third point on the map: a life aimed at joining.

God is making God's appeal through us—please be reconciled to God. This is not meant to be a theological slogan but a way of life where we join with God and call others to life together with God and with each other. This is life formed *for* reconciling community and *in* reconciling community, and it has been an elusive dream. One of the most powerful forces that has always challenged the formation of reconciling community has been the sovereign couple. The book of Acts shows us an example of that sovereign couple in the story of Ananias and Sapphira, who withheld their resources for the sake of their own life together.

> But a man named Ananias, with the consent of his wife Sapphira, sold a piece of property; with his wife's knowledge, he kept back some of the proceeds, and brought only a part and laid it at the apostles' feet. (Acts 5:1–2)

It is precisely the power of the sovereign couple that confronts the ambassadors of the reconciling God with their most powerful opponents, because the sovereign couple are ambassadors themselves. They represent a god who is in service to them. The sovereign couple forms community that encircles them, enhances them, speaks of the joy of their life together, turns everyone toward the quest of also becoming like them, becoming couple, and thereby becoming the source of all new life. The sovereign couple positions itself as the true incarnation of the divine life. Coupling has always had power. God gave it such. But coupling has always sought more power than it should. And it is understandable. In the face of creaturely vulnerability, creaturely fragility, and creaturely weakness, coupling suggests a way to keep such creaturely realities at bay in a space made by two called home, called safe, called secure. But the reconciling God found in Jesus took back the power that did not belong to coupling. Jesus is the place of home, of safe, of secure—not the couple. And this reconciling God found in Jesus will create a community formed in Jesus's name that will be the place of home, of safe, of secure. The couple will exist, but it will exist *for that community*. The reconciling community will not exist for that couple.

In our day and in our moment, the sovereign couple reigns supreme. Too many communities that name the name of Christ have made themselves the servants of the couple. Their entire life is geared to cultivating, bathing, powering, manicuring, feeding, and entertaining the couple and their children. Whether gay or straight, young or old, the couple has drained all the energy from the work of reconciliation and told the community to be reconciled to a faith formed for coupling. If the sovereign couple reigns supreme, then in our day whiteness guides its deliberations and its decisions. It is the couple shaped in whiteness that lies at the heart of white supremacy, anti-blackness, and the thwarting of a revolutionary vision of life together.

The couple shaped in whiteness is any couple and every couple, whether white or not, that imagines home and safety and security inside the dream of the colonial master, inside life made possible by the white self-sufficient man who embodies control, possession, and mastery. The sovereign couple shaped in whiteness is the couple that thinks its world from its own centered existence and therefore has no real need for the message of reconciliation unless it has to do with their own quality of life. Yet God also seeks to make God's appeal *through the couple*. The couple is to be turned outward to the forming of a community, to a life of ambassadorial existence where they together seek to learn and seek to live a revolutionary life together with others and not for themselves. They seek to form a life of home, of safe, of secure in Jesus and with others.

My mapping of the message of reconciliation is not complete. This is only a brief signaling of a few crucial stops along the journey. However we map the journey of reconciliation, the path must clearly mark an exit from a theological slogan and an entrance to a new life together with the living God. I end with a poem written as I settled into the insolation that came with the pandemic.

Us Too

Would that the Two be broken
Replaced by a Too that refuses
collapse. Us too! This lovely grand terror
Would steal into the intimate nation
Of duo and destroy the temple that
All imagined eternal.

Every movie, book, poem, story, epic
Lie that worships the I/Thou removed
From expensive pedestal and taken
Outside. From there we would give them to
seventeen-year-olds with the urgent
Instruction: Go find some good dirt where
Something can take root, spit into the dirt
three times and bury this idol. Watch It take
Root, soon it will sprout a large bush
With hundreds of small leaves. These
Leaves are more potent than any Cannabis.

Eat them, give them to your friends and
Your enemies but not your parents—
Another plant is being prepared for them.
Once the leaves enter your bloodstream
You will have a new obsession—the many.
But not one at a time. Together will become

New terrain from which to dream joy, to
Know the journey's middle and end inside
A tentacled hope that cannot be carried in
Matching baskets—this lasting love defies
Exhaustion because it resists isolation, its
Serial focus brings the clarity that makes
Loving one truly possible but never ever
The point.

Loving one in the many will never degenerate
Into loving the many in the one, that
Laziness banned by the shout of voices
Internalized—Us Too! Then children
will lean no longer on feeble nuclear love
Already exhausted by limited kin. They
Feel now the cords of life itself extended
Endlessly around the world, always ready
To be touched by their touch.

Invitation

Slowing, Silence, and Solitude

Chris Hall

I FIRST BECAME FRIENDS with Jonathan Wilson during the time we spent together as graduate students at Regent College in Vancouver, BC, in the late 1980s. If memory serves me correctly, we first met in our German class as we studied to prepare for admittance into doctoral programs in theology. German verbs were not only what we talked about. God was often a topic in our conversations, as were our families and our hopes for the future. Over time our friendship deepened.

Thankfully, our friendship has continued across the years. I smile when I think of the occasions we often connected during summers in Vancouver. Sometimes I would teach in the Regent College summer school program, and during these weeks in Canada it became a tradition of sorts between us to make sure we had at least one dinner together when my wife Debbie and I would catch up on the news with Jonathan and Marti.

Jonathan occasionally attended the evening lectures I gave at Regent. I would spot him in the audience, listening intently, sometimes a sly grin on his face as he prepared to ask me a hard question. He delighted in doing that, but always with a sense of fun and genuine interest. I think he also liked to see me squirm a bit as I struggled to come up with a coherent response.

I recall a summer some years ago when I was teaching at Regent. Jonathan and I were eating bag lunches together, seated on a bench outside of UBC. During our conversation I received a very difficult email regarding a situation at Eastern—one that contained hot anger over how

I had handled a situation there as provost. When I read the email, I felt physically ill because of the difficult road ahead the email indicated.

Jonathan could tell something was terribly amiss and simply listened as I shared the rocky situation and relationship. He listened discerningly, with sensitivity, support, and calm. He created space in his life for me—a listening space—an ability Jonathan had nourished in the time Jonathan spent in silence, solitude, and prayer with God.

So, in this essay, I want to share a bit about the spiritual disciplines of slowing, silence and solitude. With the permission of HarperOne, I'm drawing on material from *A Different Way*, a new book of mine to be published in the summer of 2022. I do so with gratefulness for the hours Jonathan and I have spent together listening and talking with each other over the years.

As I write my mind is drawn to Jonathan's daughter, Leah Wilson-Hartgrove, and her husband, Jonathan, both former students of mine at Eastern. I see the lively, probing mind of Leah's father reflected in both, as well as all three's commitment to social justice on a wide variety of issues.

Jim Houston once commented to me years ago that "spiritual formation is the slowest of all human movements." He's right.

The TGV

Deb and I walked up to the train platform and there she was, the TGV. The TGV is France's bullet train, *le train de grande vitesse* ("the train of great speed"). It looked like a long bullet, sleek and streamlined.

We stepped on board, settled in our seats and waited excitedly. Soon we'd be traveling at 120 miles per hour through the French countryside. I'd never traveled that fast while still on the ground, and wondered what it would be like.

The train started to move, and slowly made its way out of the station. As it gained speed, we felt little movement inside the cabin, although the countryside outside the window began to speed by faster and faster. When we reached top speed, my eyes hurt if I tried to focus on houses or trees; we were simply moving too fast for our eyes to track with our speed. We gave up trying to enjoy the scenery. Our speed in effect blinded us to what was present right outside our window. The sound of the train traveling at high speed didn't prevent conversation, but it did make it difficult. Things were too loud and too fast for us to do much else than sit and look at one another. Yes, we reached our destination very quickly. We just didn't see much along the way.

Our experience on the TGV is a parable of sorts for the pace at which many of God's image-bearers are leading their lives in the twenty-first century. Our lives are moving at TGV speed, but God moves at a much slower pace. How ironic that we can live at a pace where, in a manner of speaking, we leave God behind. If we move too fast in too loud an environment, we'll miss much along the way, inattentive to the gifts that God sprinkles through each day.

There are beauties and wonders very near us that we only see and appreciate if we slow down and quiet down, gifts such as "a perfect rose or the scent of honeysuckle, the embrace of a friend, the taste of bacon."[1]

The Rhythm of Jesus's Ministry

Jesus's ministry demonstrates a very distinct rhythm, one that illustrates the importance of slowing, solitude, and silence in a spiritually healthy and mature image-bearer's life.

As Jesus is the model for us, his image-bearers, surely following his example, the manner in which he lived, and the habits and practices that characterized his life, is the heart of wise spiritual formation. In a nutshell, if Jesus lived a paced life, with significant times of solitude and silence as regular markers of his life's rhythms, can we ignore his practices and hope to live our lives well with God?

Jesus was an extremely busy man, sent by his Father to accomplish the most important work in the history of the world. For Jesus, there was always something to do, someone to heal, something to teach, someone to exorcize and free from the power of evil. Luke describes Jesus's work in Luke 5:15. "Yet the news about him spread all the more, so that crowds of people came to hear him and to be healed of their diseases."[2]

Still, Jesus never seems rushed as he carries out his Father's work. He doesn't work at a frenetic pace. He moves through each day focused on whatever his Father offers him that day; his path and field of vision are straight and clear. On Jesus's way into Jerusalem, for instance, he *sees* the

---

1. Joyce Huggett, *The Joy of Listening to God: Hearing the Many Ways God Speaks to Us* (Downers Grove, IL: InterVarsity, 1986), 72.

2. This chapter uses the NRSV translation for Scripture references, unless otherwise indicated.

tax collector Zacchaeus in a sycamore tree and invites himself over for dinner that night (Luke 19:5–6).

Pause and reflect: *What or whom might I see if I lived a more paced life, transitioned from rushing to walking, from frenetic activity to a slower-paced rhythm through my day? Why have I chosen to move at such a rapid rate through my day, rushing from one thing on to the next? What am I hoping to accomplish? Take time to ponder the pace of your life and how things came to be this way. If I lived at a slower pace, might I actually accomplish more than less, regarding the important things of my life?*

Let's look again at Jesus's life. Luke points us to two specific practices that made all the difference for Jesus. After describing how busy Jesus is in Luke 15:5, Luke writes in the very next verse: "But Jesus often withdrew to lonely places and prayed" (Luke 5:16). These three practices—solitude, silence, and prayer—provided the hidden supportive scaffolding for Jesus's active ministry.

The rhythm of Jesus's ministry is clear: intense, focused, paced ministry, followed by withdrawal into silence, solitude, and prayer, and then return to intense, focused ministry. The question facing all of us is plain. We dare not avoid it. If Jesus withdrew regularly into silence, solitude, and prayer, can we imagine we will live or love well apart from the very practices that nourished him? If Jesus never rushed, what can I learn about the dangers of hurry and the blessings of slowing?

Think of Jesus's relationship with one of Jesus's best friends, Lazarus. Jesus receives word from Mary and Martha that Lazarus is ill. "Lord, the one you love is sick" (John 11:3). Mary and Martha want Jesus to hurry to address this dire circumstance, but Jesus remains where he is for "two more days," for he discerns God's deeper intent for this perilous situation. "Lazarus is dead, and for your sake I am glad I was not there, so that you may believe. But let us go to him" (John 11:14–15). Jesus knew what to do and when to do it. His heart, mind, and will were in tune with his surroundings and the people he loved, not because he was a divine computer, but because of the fundamental rhythms of his life.

Pause and reflect: *"What needs to open up in me?" I ask myself. "What noises and voices are echoing through the corridors of my mind and heart that need to be stilled? What truth is the Lord asking me to settle on, like a hen softly resting on her eggs? What might birth within me if I would simply slow down, quiet down, and settle down? Are there possibilities and prayers incubating in me that are waiting for the right environment to be birthed?" Might the same be true for you?*

Slowing, silence, and solitude offer a framework for discerning the influences—positive and negative—affecting how we think and live, and the power of some to deflect us from the values of the kingdom of God.

Each day through different media we hear voices, read words, and see images that affect us consciously and subconsciously. Some are quite positive. Others less so. Neil Postman points to Aldous Huxley's warning in *Brave New World*:

> What Huxley teaches is that in the age of advanced technology, spiritual devastation is more likely to come from an enemy with a smiling face than from one whose countenance exudes suspicion and hate. In the Huxleyan prophecy, Big Brother does not watch us, by his choice. We watch him, by ours. People will come to love their oppression, to adore the technologies that undo their capacities to think.[3]

Uncle Screwtape writes to Wormwood in C. S. Lewis's *Screwtape Letters* that mental laziness—a laziness fostered by our own attachment to the glowing screen—can easily lead to spiritual destruction: "You will no longer need a good book, which he really likes, to keep him from his prayers ... a column of advertisements in yesterday's paper will do." Once trapped by laziness,

> you can make him do nothing at all for long periods. You can keep him up late at night, not roistering, but staring at a dead fire in a cold room. All the healthy and outgoing activities which we want him to avoid can be inhibited and *nothing* given in return. . . . The Christians describe the enemy as one "without whom Nothing is strong." And Nothing is very strong: strong enough to steal away a man's best years, not in sweet sins but in dreary flickering of the mind over it knows not what. . . . It does not matter how small the sins are provided that their cumulative effect is to edge the man away from the Light and out into the Nothing.[4]

With every hour on the TV or our favorite website, media debris slowly drifts to the floor of our conscious and unconscious mind. So, periodically, the floor needs sweeping. Slowing, solitude, and silence provide the opportunity.

---

3. Neil Postman, *Amusing Ourselves to Death: Public Discourse in the Age of Show Business* (New York: Penguin, 1986), 155.

4. C. S. Lewis, *The Screwtape Letters* (San Francisco: HarperSanFrancisco, 2001), 19-20.

Slowing increases our awareness of, as Joyce Huggett puts it, the "pools of silence" God offers us every day. "Whilst washing up, ironing, hoovering [vacuuming], dusting, gardening, walking to the post, driving to the shops, or traveling by public transport . . . I would try to listen to God as intently as in my place of prayer. It worked." Slowing and silence increase our ability to "see" what is right in front of us, sprinkles of God's blessing, care, and love. False attractions and diversions, many fostered by immersion in technological media, numb our awareness of the beauty of the common.

Huggett suggests the helpful method of the "godly pause." "When taking paper out of my typewriter or making myself a cup of coffee or waiting at traffic lights, I would turn my mind God-wards quite deliberately. Often God would communicate his presence to me in some felt way."[5]

Mary Pipher reminds us that most "real life is rather quiet and routine. Most pleasures are small pleasures—a hot shower, a sunset, a bowl of good soup or a good book. Television suggests that life is high drama, love and sex. TV families are radically different from real families. Things happen much faster to them. On television things that are not visually interesting, such as thinking, reading, and talking, are ignored. . . . Instead of *ennobling our ordinary experiences*, television suggests that they are not of sufficient interest to document."

Yes, there is a phrase to remember. Slowing, solitude, and silence grow our ability to ennoble "our ordinary experiences."

Learning to Live a Different Way in Contemporary Society

In the introduction to Richard Foster's chapter on learning to meditate on the Bible in *Celebration of Discipline,* Foster writes this: "In contemporary society our Adversary majors in three things: noise, hurry, and crowds. If he can keep us engaged in 'muchness' and 'manyness,' he will rest satisfied."[6]

Ponder with me, for a moment, the influence of "crowds." Our family, peer group, local community, work environment, and national context influence us on a daily basis. A firm step away from the crowd every now and then helps us to regain our focus. A key question to ask is this: "*Is my*

---

5. Huggett, *Joy of Listening*, 171–72.

6. Richard J. Foster, *Celebration of Discipline: The Path to Spiritual Growth* (San Francisco: HarperOne, 2018), 15.

normal environment helping me to love other people or not?" To be more specific, are the "normal" aspects of my environment, say my cultural context, from the perspective of the kingdom of God really "abnormal" at best and sinful at worse?

I think of the history of slavery in the United States and its racist remnants. For hundreds of years racist perspectives and actions toward African Americans, Native Americans, Asians, and Hispanics have characterized American society. They still do. Yet the deaths of precious image-bearers like Trayvon Martin, George Floyd, and Breonna Taylor have focused American's attention on the evil of racism. Americans are increasingly willing to admit that what seemed "normal"—whites are superior—is an absolute horror.

Pause and reflect: *What aspects of American culture considered as "normal" might you identify as "abnormal" from the perspective of Jesus and his kingdom? What comes to mind for you? Of course, this question applies to other cultures as well.*

Foster also mentions noise and hurry as devilish tools and tactics. How so? Noise distracts. Noise drowns out. Noise diverts. From what? From the most important things. Distraction diverts our attention from what really matters. If loving God and neighbor are to be pursued above all things, should we be surprised that the devil uses noise to divert and distract us from our highest calling?

Uncle Screwtape warns his nephew Wormwood that he must never allow those he tempts to experience two things: music and silence. Indeed, noise "alone defends us from silly qualms, despairing scruples, and impossible desires. We will make the whole universe a noise in the end. We have already made great strides in this direction as regards the Earth. The melodies and silences of Heaven will be shouted down in the end. But I admit we are not yet loud enough, or anything like it. Research is in progress."[7] It's fair to say that the devil's research is bearing abundant fruit. We have entered the noisiest period in human history. The devils couldn't be more pleased.

Hurry Sickness

What about hurry? Of all that Foster might have chosen to highlight the demonic, why would he choose hurry as one of the big three? ("noise,

---

7. Lewis, *Screwtape Letters*, 119–20.

hurry, and crowds") John Ortberg provides a succinct and wise answer. "Love and hurry are fundamentally incompatible. Love always takes time, and time is one thing hurried people don't have."[8]

We are just now recognizing something that God has known for a long time. *Psychology Today* defines hurry sickness as "a behavior pattern characterized by a continual rushing and anxiousness; an overwhelming and continual sense of urgency." It's a sickness "in which a person feels chronically short of time, and so tends to perform every task faster and to get flustered when encountering any kind of delay."[9]

A national survey in *USA Today* "revealed that the vast majority of Americans feel they are busier this year than last year and they were busier last year than the year before, and for better or worse, the pace of life is speeding up to make us feel trapped in a 'time crunch.'"[10]

I recently listened to a short talk by Tony Campolo on the Red Letter Christians website. Tony commented on the coronavirus pandemic's isolating effect. Yet Tony believed the new pandemic environment might offer unexpected benefits. He encouraged listeners to consider how slowing and silence might be very good things to experience, though initially somewhat uncomfortable.

Campolo spoke of attending a conference in Florida at which Bill Gates was speaking. To no one's surprise Gates was extremely excited about new computer advances that enabled ever faster access to information and the processing of that information. A man in the audience from an Indian background raised his hand and asked Gates a simple but direct question: "Mr. Gates, how can you help the people in my village to slow down?"

Yes, rapid access to information has helped many. Thousands of lives have been saved through the speedy dissemination of knowledge on a global scale. Yet there are some things—some learnings—that simply can't be rushed. When we try to rush them, life blows up in our face.

The simplest things in life teach us this lesson. A cake must be baked for a sufficient time at a precise temperature. If we remove it too quickly from the oven in our desire to taste its sweetness, all that reaches our eager

---

8. John Ortberg, *The Life You've Always Wanted: Spiritual Disciplines for Ordinary People* (Grand Rapids: Zondervan, 1987), 83.

9. Rosemary K. M. Sword and Philip Zimbardo, "Hurry Sickness," *Psychology Today*, Feb. 9, 2013, para. 1, https://www.psychologytoday.com/us/blog/the-time-cure/201302/hurry-sickness.

10. Quoted in Sword and Zimbardo, "Hurry Sickness," para. 4.

palate is uncooked dough. Insufficiently baked cake may deceive us with its golden-brown surface, but thorough baking demands time and patience.

I remember the excitement I experienced as a little boy living in Phoenix. I had just bought a pack of carrot seeds for fifteen cents. I tilled a small patch of soil in the backyard carefully, watered it, dropped my carrot seeds into the ground, and covered them gently.

How hard it was to wait for the carrots to grow! Each day I cultivated my little garden, eagerly waiting for the shoots of my carrots to break the soil's surface. "What's going on down there?" I asked myself. "This is taking too long. Is something wrong? Maybe I should take a look just to make sure everything is all right."

I succumbed to temptation and hurriedly dug beneath the surface. There were my carrots. They had just begun to develop. And my impatience had snuffed out their burgeoning life.

So, I'd like to pose some hard questions. "How fast are you moving? Do you need to slow down to reach your destination safely and to enjoy the view along the way?" I think of my experience on the TGV.

How might we regain our center, our grounding, our balance? Our internal gyroscopes are wildly spinning. How can we reset them by the power of the Spirit?

John Ortberg asked a trusted friend—my guess, it was Dallas Willard—what he needed to do to be spiritually healthy. The answer? "You must ruthlessly eliminate hurry from your life." "That's a good one," John replied. "What else?" "There is nothing else. You must ruthlessly eliminate hurry from your life."[11]

"Ruthlessly" is quite an adverb. I looked it up. Here's the definition: "without pity or compassion; mercilessly; unsympathetic." So, if I'm understanding Ortberg's mentor correctly, I must be ruthless with hurry in my life. I must not make excuses for why I hurry through day after day. I must show hurry no compassion. I must kill it. How about you?

How do we know if we have hurry sickness? Ortberg lists a number of symptoms of hurry sickness that are worthy of our attention. I found I had a number of them. I must have hurry sickness.

1. Do you find yourself constantly speeding up your daily activities?
2. How about multitasking? I recall pulling up at a red light and noticing a good friend in the lane next to me. He had the day's paper spread

---

11. Ortberg, *Life You've Always Wanted*, 76–77.

over his steering wheel. I honked my horn, gave him a concerned look, and self-righteously wiggled my finger: "Naughty, naughty."

3. Do you ever count the number of cars in front of you? "Sure," I say to myself. "Who doesn't?" If you move beyond counting cars to change lanes, having carefully computed the fewer cars or the fastest lane, you might well have hurry sickness. Ouch. I feel my temperature rising. Is that a fever I sense?

4. How about looking for the fastest checkout lane at the grocery store? I do this all the time. Not only do I look for the fastest lane—Ortberg may have the same problem—but I find myself competing with folks in the line I thought was going to be slower than mine. I just did this the other day at Wawa, a local convenience store. I felt a sense of disappointment as the person who was where I would have been checked out first. I had lost. I probably have hurry sickness.

5. How about putting your clothes on inside out or backwards? You could be in trouble. I seem to do this all the time. I thought I did so because I'm old. Maybe my diagnosis is wrong.

6. Have you ever slept in your daytime clothes to save time in the morning? Oh my. Call the doctor.

7. Do you have a hard time saying no? Yes. I'm a people-pleaser. I don't want to let people down. What are the hidden costs lurking every time I say yes?

8. Are you so tired at the end of the day that you have no time, energy, or love for those who matter most to you? Ortberg calls this sunset fatigue.

What happens to us when hurry sickness remains undiagnosed and continues for a lengthy period of time? We burn out. We crumble. We disintegrate. We get depressed. Our nervous system implodes. Consider the case of Juanita Rasmus.

Juanita is the co-pastor of St. John's United Methodist Church in downtown Houston. In her book *Learning to Be: Finding Your Center after the Bottom Falls Out*, Juanita talks about "the stress of living in a do-do-do world." For a number of reasons, Juanita found herself enmeshed in a pace of life and list of demands that ultimately proved too much for her and her nervous system. Finally, Juanita crashed. She experienced a severe nervous breakdown.

"Friends and family reflected on how wound up I was," Juanita shares. "Relationships suffered—I didn't have time to 'waste' talking to friends about getting together. I had things to do and places to go. Though I valued my friendships, my to-do list took priority over my to-be list. I was running on empty. And since I was meeting my deadlines, for the most part, I never noticed the growing problem."[12] Suffice it to say, Juanita's body did. She crashed into a significant, life-changing depression.

Thankfully, Juanita recovered and is ministering again today. Part of Juanita's process was *extended periods of silence and solitude*. "Silence is amazing," Juanita writes. "It's like a marinade to put on chicken, fish, or beef. There are times when I'm like the fish in marinade, easily overcome by the silence."[13]

As Juanita spent time in solitude, her self-awareness grew and matured. "In the silence the nuances of my personality have been revealed for what they are. . . . Marinating in the silence is allowing me to see me. This is heavy shit, but I don't feel punishment, which is what I've always expected in these moments. I feel regret, remorse, and a bit disoriented by my new awareness, but believe it or not I also feel a great deal of gratitude."[14]

Juanita was helped by Richard Foster's words concerning busyness: "Busyness is not of the devil. It is the devil."[15] In silence and solitude, Juanita learned to slow down and quiet down. Her spirit has been renewed; her body has been healed. She has recovered and is in a much better place than when she ministered to others in such a frenetic, driven manner.

Juanita's prayer: "Okay, Lord, marinate me in your silence so that I'm transformed into something fulfilling, life-giving, and memorable."[16] You might try praying Juanita's prayer with her. Is the Lord inviting you to silence, to extended periods of quiet and solitude when you can simply marinate in the wonder, beauty, and love of God?

I'm trying to live, think, and work more slowly. As I walk from my office to another room of the house I purposely walk slowly. As I sit at my desk writing, I'm gradually learning to slow down. Occasionally I simply sit and ponder. During Zoom calls I work at growing my attentiveness, focusing on the person across from me and not on the next call to be

---

12. Juanita Sanders, *Learning to Be: Finding Your Center after the Bottom Falls Out* (Downers Grove, IL: InterVarsity, 2020), 8.

13. Sanders, *Learning to Be*, 122.

14. Sanders, *Learning to Be*, 123, 125.

15. Sanders, *Learning to Be*, 126.

16. Sanders, *Learning to Be*, 123.

accomplished. I'd like to say I've moved from speed to slowness, but I'm not there yet. I am taking steps in that direction, though, and they seem to be adding up.

I'm developing a new habit—slowing. Am I accomplishing more than I did in my hurried moments? Maybe. Maybe not. I do sense I'm living, thinking, and acting in a healthier way. How patient Jesus has been as he waited for me to come to my senses. I can hear him saying, "You were always in such a rush. Why? I never lived that way myself, yet I accomplished what my Father asked me to do. Do the same with me. Don't get ahead of me. I'm a slow walker."

I remember teaching in the Cursillo Movement in Geneva, Switzerland, one weekend in the early eighties. At the beginning of the retreat, we collected wristwatches from retreatants as they entered through the monastery door. They looked anxious as they dropped their watches into a box for safekeeping. "We'll keep track of time for you," we assured them. "You don't need to worry."

We also gently asked folks to observe silence from Friday evening through Saturday lunch. We considered our request as a gift, for most of these retreatants lived very busy lives. Some were leaders in worldwide corporations such as Caterpillar. Others worked at the United Nations, World Health Organization, or the World Trade Organization. Their lives were very noisy and busy, even before the age of email, Twitter, Facebook, and Instagram.

In a nutshell, we gave our new friends three gifts: the gift of slowing, the gift of silence, and to a certain degree, the gift of solitude. By the time of their last communion service together on Sunday afternoon, they were changed people, some of them in tears over what they had experienced.

Pause and reflect: *Are there people, problems, relationships, and issues—maybe three or four—that silence and solitude might shift to the center of my awareness for the next few years, if only I would slow down and quiet down? How might my horizons expand, and my understandings deepen if I was simply patient enough to stay put in a quiet place long enough for the learning to occur? What do you think you might see or learn if you periodically visited a quiet place for prayer and reflection?*

Silence and solitude grow our attentiveness. They broaden our field of vision to what really matters and what doesn't. To whom or what have I given my attention this past month or past year? Why have I done so?

To develop focus and dissipate distraction, though, *requires an environment that sifts out influences that deflect our attention from what really counts*. As our eyes clear, what will we see? Who will we see? What needs? The blurriness of eyes too long clouded by high intensity foolishness demands a healing, quiet environment conducive to clarifying and expanding our vision.

The Desert Dwellers

Christian history is filled with image-bearers who have asked these same questions. Many in the communion of the saints can help us as we seek a different way. The desert dwellers have helped me. Perhaps they can help you. Wise examples and prudent imitation can move us to a better, wiser place.

From the late second century into the fourth, a stream of Christians made their way out to the Egyptian and Judean deserts. Why would they do such a thing? What did they hope to find there? What did the desert represent to them? What were they seeking in the bleak, seemingly godforsaken hotbox of the Egyptian desert? Women as well as men made their way to the desert. Why would they think this bare, boring furnace might serve well as a learning space for mind, heart, soul, and body?[17]

At first glance, the desert dwellers seem to be turning their backs on Christ's teaching to be salt and light to the world (Matt 5:13-16). Is such actually the case? Or might spiritual light flash in this most unlikely environment? Might life in the desert offer a variety of possibilities and opportunities for service and spiritual growth, opportunities more difficult to discover or embrace in an urban or country setting?

Picture the desert as "a space in which obedience to truth is practiced." Parker Palmer notes the *importance of space* in the lives of the desert dwellers and directs our attention to a well-loved desert "abba" or "father," Abba Felix. "Abba Felix and his fellow seekers left the crowded cities to meet truth in the desert, one of the most open and spare spaces on earth. They went there not only to enter an outer space free of the cities' clutter, but also to open up an inner space of heart and mind, free of inward noise. In desert emptiness the soul is able to settle on truth, to concentrate on that which is essential to salvation."[18]

---

17. I first encountered the idea of the desert as a "learning space" in Parker Palmer's book *To Know as We Are Known: Education as a Spiritual Journey* (San Francisco: HarperOne, 1993), 69.

18. Palmer, *To Know*, 69.

Consider for a moment the distinctive, beautiful, and harsh geographical space Christian desert dwellers inhabited day in and day out. The desert offered ancient Christians desiring to enrich their relationship with God intense, unremitting solitude and silence.

In their desert environment, these ancient Christians learned to finely attune their ears to Scripture, to the voice of God in prayer as they continually prayed the Psalms, to their habitual thoughts and temptations, and most of all, to the call to love God and love neighbor. They viewed with suspicion anything or any person that distracted, disrupted, or diverted them from their fundamental call to love.

In their thinking and practices, the desert dwellers married love and truth. Basil the Great, one of the great church fathers who spent significant time in the desert, comments that "one cannot approach the knowledge of the truth with a disturbed heart."[19]

Pause and reflect: *What's disturbing your heart or mind today? Perhaps you're feeling a general sense of unrest, uneasiness, discomfort, or confusion. Is the Holy Spirit nudging you to a different way of thinking and living, an unexpected and invigorating way of reconfiguring your life as a conduit for the Spirit's love?*

A desert environment, either literally or figuratively, can help us in this new construction project, as unpromising as it appears at first glance. "What can grow in the desert?" we ask. "Tumbleweed? Cacti?" Still, when the rains come, desert flowers appear, even on the surface of a cactus.

Is the Spirit gently tapping you on the shoulder? "Hey, friend. Might it not be time for you and I to get to know each other? And dear one, for you to get acquainted with yourself? Allow me to guide you to a learning space that has helped other image-bearers to know me, and to know themselves."

For some, the desert's silence and solitude served as a magnet, raising the cracked filings of their personalities, habit patterns, and sins to the surface of their awareness. "Ah, so this is who I am. Who would have thought?"

Pause and reflect: *Crazy voices inspire crazy lives. Can I pry just a bit? Whose voices have you listened to over the course of your lifetime? Why these particular voices? If you listed on a piece of paper the personalities, books, films, television programs, and music that have shaped your life and*

---

19. Basil is quoted by Tito Colliander in *Way of the Ascetics: The Ancient Tradition of Discipline and Inner Growth* (Crestwood, NY: St. Vladimir's Seminary Press, 1985), 28.

your response to life's opportunities and challenges, what titles, names, and ideas would appear on your list?

Whose voices are you listening to in this present moment? Are they bringing perspective? Peace? Or confusion? Craziness? Worry? Are they nurturing love or fomenting suspicion and anger? The voices we habitually listen to may be positive or negative influences. What effect are they having on you—or me?

Folks journeyed to the desert in their search for the silence and solitude necessary to surface key influences, people, and powers in their cultural environment that had hindered their life with God. There was time to focus in the desert and no need to rush, for where was there to rush to? Opportunities for diversion or distraction were minimal, if not nonexistent. In time, attentiveness to deeper, more important matters increased.

"Why did they do this?" Thomas Merton asks. Merton believes these Christians increasingly discerned the society in which they lived had, quite frankly, lost its mind. "Society—which meant pagan society, limited by the horizons and prospects of life 'in this world'—was regarded by them as a shipwreck from which each single individual man had to swim for his life. . . . These were men who believed that to let oneself drift along, passively accepting the tenets and values of what they knew as society, was purely and simply a disaster."[20]

"They knew they were helpless to do any good for others as long as they floundered about in the wreckage. But once they got a foothold on solid ground, things were different. Then they had not only the power but even the obligation to pull the whole world to safety after them."[21]

Merton's words resonate with those of the apostle Paul in Rom 12. "Don't let the world squeeze you into its own mould, but let God remould your minds from within" (Rom 12:2 PME). The great temptation, one that often lurks below our direct consciousness, is to drift mindlessly with the broader cultural consensus, passively floating downstream, without heeding the white water ahead.

The desert dwellers spotted the rapids and scrambled to shore. Or, to use Paul's metaphor, they sensed the tightening grip of a cultural consensus opposed to their deepest desires and values and the teaching of Jesus; it was time to flee, many felt. To remain locked in their culture's corroding environment was to surrender their mind and heart to insanity. For the

---

20. Thomas Merton, *The Wisdom of the Desert* (New York: New Directions, 1970), 3.

21. Quoted in Pete Greig, *How to Pray: A Simple Guide for Normal People* (Colorado Springs: NavPress, 2019), 47.

desert dwellers, and it seems for Paul, a basic premise is this: a society can lose its mind. To help it, we may need to leave it, if only for a time.

What may surprise some is that when the movement to the desert reached its peak in the fourth century, the Roman world had become increasingly Christian. No longer was the church a minority community existing in a hostile cultural context. For in AD 312, Constantine converted to the Christian faith and subsequently emblazoned the cross on his legion's shields. Soon many conversions occurred, some genuine, and some politically expedient. Many Roman senators, for instance, knew which way the wind was blowing and exchanged their pagan gods for the God of the Christians.

Sadly, though, with the conversion of Constantine, the spiritual strength present in the Christian community during the sporadic, though extremely intense persecutions of the mid-third and early fourth centuries, began to dissipate, almost imperceptibly, as the Christian faith became culturally dominant. For some, the cross was viewed more "as a signal of temporal power" than redemption.[22]

Literal martyrdom largely ceased as Christianity was accepted in the Roman Empire of the fourth century, a culture that had shortly before Constantine's time not hesitated to persecute Christ-followers. Some Christians perceived the need for a new type of martyrdom or witness, a bloodless one. The geography of the desert offered the opportunity for its development. Why a new martyrdom? Desert dwellers knew there was something in them that needed to die, something that needed to blossom, and a witness that needed to be borne.

It's very difficult to discern how our environment is affecting us. How is the "world" squeezing us into its "mould"? (Cf. Rom 12:1–2 Phillips.) The desert dwellers purposely moved to a learning space that reduced the "world's" vice-like pressures.

Ponder what learnings can only arise in a desert environment. What might we learn that only a desert environment can teach us? What about ourselves, the world, evil, sin, love, and God? How might the sands of the desert hone our lives and our character? How might the desert teach us to love God and neighbor more deeply, wisely, and effectively?

Many of us have never lived in a literal desert environment. Some, like me, may have spent time in a desert state such as Arizona and experienced the desert directly. Others have never had the opportunity or desire. No

---

22. Merton, *Wisdom of the Desert*, 3.

problem. We can validly expand the boundaries of a "desert" environment to include the various expanses and circumstances of our lives.

Have we not all lived in learning spaces in which the demands of the desert apply? A cracked, abusive family environment is a desert. A long stretch in a lonely hospital room is a desert. A business that has failed is a desert. The reduced capacities of old age—physical, emotional, intellectual, spiritual—are all a desert. The searing pain of loss is a vast desert. Life's inevitable disappointments are a desert, as are our disappointments and disillusionments with God. "Anything but this, Lord. Anything but this," we cry. And the Lord gently responds, "Ah, my child. For a time, this must be the only thing."

Yes, we will all experience the desert. It is inevitable. So, rather than resisting, let's enter the desert together. What will we learn here that we can learn nowhere else? The desert strips, the desert cracks, the desert demands, the desert trains. We must not idealize the desert. It is a dangerous place that demands constant attentiveness from those who would live there or even occasionally visit.

At first glance, it seems the desert offers so little. "Lord, why would you bring me to this place, of all possible places? What you teach me here, in my desert experiences?"

Initially, it seems the desert would be the least likely space to nurture our relationship with God. Yet there is a beauty, clarity, and focus the desert offers. "I offer you nothing," the desert says, "but a lonely space, a learning space. Come and dwell here. There is little here to distract you, little to divert your attention, little to entertain. Who will you meet here? You will encounter the real you, and by God's grace, the real Jesus. This will be a very good thing. You will meet the One who can teach you what you need, what you can safely set to the side, and most importantly, how to love."

Thank you, Jonathan, for your friendship and your life. You have spent extended periods of time in the "desert." You have learned to slow down and quiet down. You have embraced what the Lord has offered you for your gift of years. You have modeled for me a wise, loving life. I'm thankful.

Pursuing Theology's Primary Mode

Jeffrey P. Greenman

A COUPLE OF MONTHS into my first semester as a first-year student in theological college, a group of newfound friends gathered for a potluck supper. I was surprised to discover that the mood of the gathering matched the grey, drizzly autumn weather that had begun to settle in. Mostly I listened.

People talked about what had brought them to the college. They had enrolled with high hopes for maturing in their Christian faith—finding biblical insight, personal development, spiritual growth, renewal in their ministry, clarity about their God-given vocation. Those themes, in fact, were central in the college's promotional materials and reputation. As we finished off the casseroles and headed into dessert, we went around the table taking stock of what we were experiencing. People admired their professors. They appreciated the opportunity to learn. They loved the community life with their fellow students. Chapel services were a highlight. But what emerged was a growing sense of frustration.

Our table talk became "Why are we doing what we're doing?" My peers were not seeing the relevance of the material we were required to learn for their current lives and future ministries. The dominant pedagogy was lecture. Vast amounts of new theoretical content was being presented, oftentimes quite quickly. We wanted to trust that what was being said was good and important, but how did it apply to our lives? Monologue was preferred over dialogue. Just keeping up with the reading took all one's energy. There were gripes about one particular assignment that called for writing up chapter summaries of an immensely long, boring textbook. Everyone felt that exercise was a waste of time. It wasn't a book that anyone would ever use again. Anxiety about grades was rising. "This isn't the sort of thing we came for" could be the summary. Disappointment was in the air.

My potluck friends were not asking "Why haven't we arrived yet at what everyone is hoping for?" We knew that we had just begun. Rome wasn't built in a day. Rather, the question really was "If this is the path we're on, are we heading to our destination?"

What dawned on me that night was an insight about education that has stayed with me since: ends and means need to be aligned. We felt in our bones a disconnect between our learning goals and the methods being used in the classroom. A year later, I took a splendid course about learning and teaching for which I wrote an essay on the use of lectures in higher education, with reference to the purposes of theological education. That course set me on a lifelong journey of learning about what makes for deep and significant learning, and about what teaching has to do with it.

What my peers were expressing was a heartfelt yearning for a deeper and more integrated Christian faith that made coherent sense of their lives and their world. No one was hoping to become a professional exegete or theologian. They trusted their teachers, and therefore were open to learning assorted -isms and -ologies in hopes of some practical payoff from an academic adventure into unknown territory. Yet they hungered not merely for new information with which to think about the faith, but for compelling ways to experience the faith personally and to live the faith authentically. Their desire was for the kind of transformative learning that I have expounded elsewhere as "the rich intersection of knowing, being and doing as expressions of human life, encompassing the cognitive, affective and behavioral domains of learning."[1] My central question throughout three decades as a classroom professor and academic administrator has been "What enables or prevents this kind of whole-person, life-changing learning?" This question immediately raises the issue of how our teaching methods in theological education might align or misalign with the goal of holistic, transformative learning that fosters a deep and integrated faith.

---

1. Jeffrey P. Greenman, "Head, Heart and Hands: The Promise of Holistic, Transformative Learning," in *Serving God's Community*, ed. Susan S. Phillips and Soo-Inn Tan (Vancouver, BC: Regent College Publishing, 2014), 88–96, esp. 88.

Theology's Primary Mode

An article by one of the most influential thinkers about theological education helps us to understand what is at stake. At the end of a distinguished teaching career, Edward Farley pinpointed the problem with "a prevailing pedagogical paradigm."[2] Farley explains in a compelling *mea culpa* that his core mistake as a classroom professor was the result of a misconception about theology's genre, which led naturally to his adoption of a flawed pedagogy. His article has helped me to grasp what was going on at the potluck supper.

According to Farley, his approach to teaching repeated the dominant model inherited from his own graduate school experience. This model defined theology as scholarship, which is presented to students as a sophisticated academic field. Teaching is directed toward students becoming inducted into the field. The main focus is acquiring a new vocabulary and gaining certain advanced skills of interpreting written texts.

To expand on Farley's frame, in this approach, the student is largely considered an empty vessel to be filled up with the expert's knowledge, an approach that Paulo Freire has called "the banking model."[3] The students' life situation and personal-spiritual needs are not given priority. In fact, they are decontextualized from their life situations, and transferred into a space construed as the expert's territory; significant disorientation and confusion often ensue.

The big mistake for which Farley issues his *mea culpa* was "focus on the field rather than on the students' eventual use of it."[4] He came to see "that most of my students will not imitate, repeat, or even be very interested in the contents and issues of my teaching as they pursue their career choices and lives in everyday-life situations."[5] In other words, he realized that there was a major disconnect between the student goal and the teacher's focus and methods. Farley came to understand that what was needed was not primarily better or different methods, but a better and different definition of theology's genre.

---

2. Edward Farley, "Four Pedagogical Mistakes: A *Mea Culpa*," *Teaching Theology and Religion* 8 (2005): 200–203. Farley's *Theologia: The Fragmentation and Unity in Theological Education* (Philadelphia: Fortress, 1983) is a classic.

3. Paulo Freire, *Pedagogy of the Oppressed* (New York: Continuum, 1970), 58.

4. Farley, "Four Pedagogical Mistakes," 200.

5. Farley, "Four Pedagogical Mistakes," 200.

Farley defines "theology's primary mode" as "thinking (inquiring, assessing, apprehending, clarifying) the manifest realities with which faith has to do in the situation in which faith has to live."[6] In this mode, theology belongs fully and properly to the whole people of God, not merely to academic specialists, and the need for theologizing arises in and for a wide variety of settings: "personal situations, familial situations, political situations, global crises, congregational situations."[7] (We should add workplace and neighborhood situations.) This type of theological engagement is situated literally everywhere that the people of God find themselves—in congregations, homes, workplaces, or the public square. In this paradigm, theology-as-scholarship becomes a derivative, secondary, and (when done well) supportive resource for Christians pursuing theology—"the thinking life of faith under the Gospel."[8]

The implications are far reaching: a recasting of theology as first and foremost a practice of the believing community of faith, the kind of thinking required by God's people toward faithful gospel-shaped action in the world. This means that every Christian is a theologian in the primary sense of the word.

It also overturns the dominant pedagogy of theological education. Teaching is reoriented toward apprenticing Christians in the art of theologizing (reflecting, discerning, coming to insight) rather than introducing methods or "covering" content. It is reconfigured to address the disconnect wherein students find themselves capable of "doing" theology-as-scholarship but incapable of "theologizing" about their situations in life under the gospel.[9] It orients those of us who labor diligently in theological education to the unsettling challenge of the proverbial student who passed all their exams but flunked life.

Farley's provocative article provides categories for describing the frustrations felt at the potluck supper. My friends couldn't see how theology-as-scholarship could address their life situations. They were looking for wise guidance toward their own theologizing, an ability to think Christianly and act faithfully in their contexts and callings, but instead

---

6. Farley, "Four Pedagogical Mistakes," 201.
7. Farley, "Four Pedagogical Mistakes," 203.
8. Farley, "Four Pedagogical Mistakes," 202.
9. Farley's distinction is reminiscent of a comment made by J. I. Packer. When asked what was distinctive about the vision of Regent College, he replied: "At Regent we desire to teach more than just the doctrines of Christ. We want people to study the difference that Christ makes to everything."

were caught up in priorities inherited from the academic guild. Could things have been done differently?

Reoriented Priorities

Farley's *mea culpa* essay includes a confession: "I must acknowledge that I do not know what a theological pedagogy ordered by the primary mode of theology would look like."[10] Yet the issue is crucial. He warns that unless we discover a "theological pedagogy oriented to theology's primary meaning," theology "will remain scholastic in setting and the arcane possession of a handful of Christendom's scholarly specialists."[11]

The reminder of my essay will explore Farley's challenge. What are some priorities for theological pedagogy if we were to pursue theology's primary mode? I will pick up from some clues offered by Farley.

Farley rightly identifies the issue of the predominantly scholastic setting of theology-as-scholarship. Theology in that mode is practiced in the classrooms of formal educational institutions, including seminaries. This means that the training of future pastors, who will become teachers of their faith to their congregations, is under the umbrella of a schooling paradigm. Education is equated with schooling.[12] In this paradigm, the focus is on the teacher's instruction rather than on the student's learning, on informational inputs rather than life-changing outcomes. According to Perry Shaw, in this approach "a premium is placed on the accumulation of information, and this priority on head knowledge is subconsciously transferred to ministry."[13] Consider how often congregations organize their adult education programs around classrooms with passive learners parked in chairs arranged in rows that face forward to focus on a teacher who presents information through lecture. In one of my former congregations, the program offered a progression through "basic, advanced, and elective courses" listed as 101, 201, 301, and 401, mimicking the nomenclature of an undergraduate university degree program. Such is the dominance of the schooling = education paradigm. Yet given the

---

10. Farley, "Four Pedagogical Mistakes," 203.

11. Farley, "Four Pedagogical Mistakes," 203.

12. For a thorough critique of the schooling paradigm, see Ted Ward, "Schooling as a Defective Approach to Education," *Common Ground Journal* 11 (2013): 28–31.

13. Perry Shaw, "The Hidden Curriculum of Seminary Education," *Journal of Asian Mission* 8 (2006): 23–51, esp. 28.

academy's deep separation of theory and practice, professors-as-theoretical-specialists oftentimes offer little help relating their abstractions to life. Their proposals for complex personal or social issues, or core contextual challenges facing the church, can be stated confidently yet merely reflect their own cultural, disciplinary, or personal biases rather than the workings of a mature Christian mind. In other words, it is not uncommon for skilled practitioners of theology's secondary mode to be unskilled at practicing theology's primary mode. At the same time, they decry the church's disinterest in theology-as-scholarship. Condemnations of the church's anti-intellectualism abound. The sentiment appears to be, "If only the church had a properly learned clergy, who cared more about our academic interests and talked more like we do, everything in the church would be better." In my experience, it is more accurate to recognize that many "ordinary" Christians would be highly interested in theology-as-reflection-on-life-under-the-gospel, with its offer of exploring the direct bearing of their faith on every aspect of their daily lives, if they were given the opportunity to explore it.

This allows us to circle back to my friends' grumblings at our potluck supper. What was the deeper root of their frustrations? Theology-as-scholarship performed in a schooling paradigm is an inadequate method of addressing the desire for whole-person, transformational learning toward a deep and integrated Christian faith. The end and means do not align. Building on Farley, the core problem involves attempting to fit the church's classic formational goals (growth into Christlikeness, spiritual-moral maturity, cultivation of godly wisdom, discernment of vocation) inside the assumptions, structures, methods, and values of theology-as-scholarship. What if we reversed the logic? What if we reconceived the role of the theological academy inside the church's classic formational goals? What if theological learning was repositioned to become a servant of the church's call to "reflective engagement with situations under the Gospel"?[14]

Farley hints at the shift this reversal implies: "Primary theological pedagogy does not so much abandon texts, Bible, or doctrines as re-situate them. In this situation, they are not so much theology's aim and object as its perspective-determining contents and utilities."[15] Theology's reconceived primary mode places a high value on equipping students with substantive knowledge of Scripture and the church's doctrinal heritage

---

14. Farley, "Four Pedagogical Mistakes," 201.
15. Farley, "Four Pedagogical Mistakes," 203.

because they are what Farley calls "perspective-determining contents." In other words, Scripture and doctrine are the essential intellectual substance required to foster the depth of Christian mindedness or biblical mindedness needed for "reflective engagement with situations under the Gospel." There is a profound challenge in shaping a Christian mind amidst the varied pressures toward conforming to the world's ways rather than to the gospel.[16] Indwelling the Christian tradition takes attention, time, and sustained energy, just as a jazz musician learns the melodies and rhythms of the standard repertoire from the acknowledged masters, listening deeply and practicing for hours and hours. Improvisation is possible only through being steeped in the jazz tradition. In this frame, the church's intellectual tradition becomes a fundamental resource for the church's contemplation, reflection, and action. Students are invited to become steeped in its habits of mind and heart. The indispensable work of biblical and theological specialists emerges as equipping the whole people of God for their own improvisational work of theologizing in everyday life.

Farley "insist[s] that theology in its primary mode is both rigorous and complex."[17] In my experience, it is a self-involving activity that proves to be far more personally, spiritually, and intellectually demanding that doing theology-as-scholarship (which encourages subjective detachment). According to Farley: "In a Christian setting contemplation or theological thinking faces the rigors in thinking of, from, and under the Gospel, and as it thinks from, toward, and in situations and contexts."[18] This approach embraces complexity: interpreting wisely the meaning of the gospel and one's contextual situation toward wise, Holy Spirit-aided discernment of their relationship for the sake of faithful action in the name of Christ and of embodying the reality of the kingdom of God. This is the church's enduring theological task. Farley wants us not to miss the fact that this is a complex and rigorous process. It calls for the church's deepest thinking.

Therefore, theology's primary mode, with its emphasis on gospel-centered reflection toward action, involves recalibrating the meaning of rigor. In theology-as-scholarship, academic rigor is defined in

---

16. See Rom 12:1–2. For more on the notion of the Christian mind, see Jeffrey P. Greenman, "Faithful Christian Learning," in *Liberal Arts for the Christian Life*, ed. Jeffry C. Davis and Philip G. Ryken (Wheaton, IL: Crossway, 2012), 81–89.

17. Farley, "Four Pedagogical Mistakes," 203.

18. Farley, "Four Pedagogical Mistakes," 203.

quantitative terms to the perceived value of "more"—more technical jargon, more pages of reading, more footnotes, and more deference to existing scholarly discourse. Theology-as-reflective-engagement shifts the focus to intellectual rigor, attending to the quality of thinking involved in Christian reflection on situations under the gospel. There are biblical texts to consider, and texts from Christian authors across the ages, but the focus is in thinking deeply, critically, and carefully, with insight that leads to wise judgments.

Although Farley does not emphasize it, in theological terms the pursuit of theology-as-reflective-engagement is necessarily communal. The biblical picture of wise discernment is never centered on the lone, heroic individual, but grounded in the church's shared life of prayer, worship, and service. Whenever we focus attention on individuals facing choices or decisions in their contexts, we need to resist the pull of our individualistic culture by reminding ourselves that biblical anthropology holds that human beings are always persons-in-community, and that followers of Jesus share in the body of Christ with sisters and brothers.

It is beyond the scope of this essay to provide a detailed account of the practice of Christian discernment at the core of theology-as-reflective-engagement. Let me simply suggest some key questions that pertain to the kind of theologizing under discussion. Is this possible action consistent with who we are and what we want to become, as people who confess that Jesus is Lord? What is God already doing in this situation? What evidence is there of God's truth or power or judgment in operation? What evidence is there of fallen rebellion or idolatry in this situation? Does this situation have any parallels with situations found in the biblical story? What potential exists in this situation for Christlike service of our neighbors? What opportunities exist in this situation to demonstrate the reality of the kingdom of God?

Life under the Gospel

In this brief essay we have explored Farley's redefinition of theology as "the thinking life of faith under the Gospel." It is critical to notice the primacy of the gospel in this account, which stands over against highly abstract and heavily systematized understandings of theology. For Jonathan Wilson, like his mentors Julian Hartt and Stanley Hauerwas, "the Gospel is determinative for theology" and "the intellectual work of theology should be done not for its own sake but for the sake of the behaviour of church and Christian."[19] Confident in the truth and power of the gospel, Wilson argues that "in Jesus' words and deeds the Kingdom of God is a reality in which we are to live."[20] My potluck friends were eager to discover what it means to live more fully into the reality of the gospel that is truly good news for an upside-down world, that turns the world right side up and offers a life that is truly life.[21]

May our every pedagogical endeavor be born of that desire, and cultivate it to the glory of God.[22]

---

19. Jonathan R. Wilson, "From Theology of Culture to Theological Ethics: The Hartt-Hauerwas Connection," *Journal of Religious Ethics* 23 (1995): 149–64, esp. 153.

20. Jonathan R. Wilson, *God So Loved the World: A Christology for Disciples* (Grand Rapids: Baker Academic, 2001), 26.

21. Wilson, *God So Loved*, 25.

22. I am deeply grateful to my friend and colleague Lucila Crena for her feedback about an earlier draft of this chapter.

Earthing Heaven Now

Jim Purves

IN THIS ESSAY I invite you to journey with me, exploring the relationship between heaven and earth. More specifically, to reflect on the way we conceive of the presence of God and his rule, at work in and through the lives of Christians, impacting upon the earth. My motive is simple and practical, just as it has been a compelling concern in the thought and writing of Jonathan Wilson. We want to help the contemporary church be more effective: to do what she exists for. The redemption of creation requires the church to understand her agency in bringing heaven to earth. I will contend that we who are the church need a larger, reconstructed and reenergized vision of the way that God would work in and through us. We need this in order to better fulfill our mission, bringing hope and healing to God's creation, of which we are an integral part.

It's fashionable, these days, to declare that the mission of God—and the kingdom of God—is neither defined by nor contained within the ministry of the church. Sounds good, where we understand by this that God is bigger than the church. It can, however, also sound like an admission of failure. When Cyprian of Carthage famously declared in the third century AD "No salvation outside the church," it was not only a declaration against heretics. It was also a declaration of confidence: that the church really matters. That the church, as the body of Christ, really can do great things. Does the church still really matter today? Can the church still do really great things? Is there still something really special about Christians? Are we different from others—and are we called to achieve something that others cannot achieve—or not?

A historic, biblical perspective would be that all people are created in the image of God. What does that imply? It doesn't mean that everyone has the kind of special relationship with God that Christians are meant to have, through faith in Jesus Christ. Truth is, though, most Christians seem to impact the earth, for good and for bad, just like other people. At one extreme, some of us may be "all will be dissolved by fire" people, who assume that everything will be destroyed in the end days and then replaced or at least renewed, with the coming of a new heaven and a new earth. This might lead some into thinking, in turn, that the pollution and destruction of ecological equilibrium doesn't really matter, because we've concluded that everything is going to be wiped out by God anyway.

At the other extreme, there are those who see that what we've got around us, here and now on earth, really does matter. People who feel that it's important to care for God's earth. People who readily associate with a "creation care" project or are activists in a "justice for all" campaign. Now, that's not to say that any of that is wrong: it's great. But lots more people than Christians care about planet Earth. While we can affirm that something of the image of God is in everyone, it leaves us with the question "What's special about Christians?" Is it just that they are "going to heaven"?

There is a challenge, for those of us who self-identify as Christians, in claiming that we have a special relationship with God: that we are "saved." What practical difference do we make? Born again. Redeemed and sanctified. Shouldn't we make a bigger difference than other people? Shouldn't there be something special going on?

Many of us Christians don't necessarily see it that way at all. What they see, when looking in the mirror, are bruised goods. Grateful sinners, saved by the power of Jesus Christ's sacrifice for us. Snatched from the brink of hell. Not worthy in any way. We wretched creatures are indistinguishable from the other sinners around us. Is that the way it is for you? Is that the way it's meant to be?

Should it be that we are to make a difference, instrumental in the mission of God upon earth? What should that look like? Let's approach this by reflecting on some problems that have come from the way that Christendom came to perceive the relation of heaven to earth. We can look at how that affects how we perceive ourselves; and how it can misshape our witness as Christians. Then we can go on to try and put together a better way of seeing things.

When the Cord Was Cut

Bible-believing Christians are often a lot less Bible-believing than they think they are! Deeply embedded cultural and philosophical influences warp our thinking far more than we realize. It started way back, when Christianity spread out of its Hebrew culture and into the Greco-Roman world.

The Hebrew Bible is about the rule of God—the kingdom of heaven—coming to earth. The story of the Hebrew people, Israel, is about a community called to bear the distinctive presence of God upon them and with them. The God of heaven manifesting his presence among us here and now. Carmen Joy Imes, in her recent study of what it means to bear God's name, traces how a deeper understanding of our Hebrew heritage draws us into recognizing how we might do this. As God put the divine name upon the Israelites and blessed them, he did so in order to bring the values and practices of his rule into this world.[1] The people of Israel were constituted by God to bear the name. As Christians who follow Israel's Messiah, we share in that identity given by God.

But the cord was cut early on, in the development of Christianity and the church. Greco-Roman thought was saturated in a worldview that separated an ideal world, hidden in heavenly places, from the rough and tumble of a corrupted creation: a creation that is but a shadow of a pure, heavenly reality. Then bring Jesus Christ into the equation. When the Christian message moved out of the God-shaped thinking of the Hebrew mind, it moved the focus away from the message of how heaven comes to earth through the presence and person of Jesus Christ. Instead, it dragged Christian imagination into a world of thinking where there was a clear-cut separation of things above, in heaven, from things below, on earth. Heaven became where Jesus now lives and where we properly belong, not here on earth. Living here on earth became a second-best option, albeit one we can enjoy at times. The Christian message became warped by a Greco-Roman worldview. The cord between heaven and earth was cut.

J. Richard Middleton, in his exploration into this departure from a Hebrew mindset, a departure that distorted a proper understanding of biblical truths through accommodating them within the mindset of the Roman Empire, notes how "the holistic and this-worldly character of God's purposes" came to be sidelined.[2] This was not good. A biblical

---

1. Carmen Joy Imes, *Bearing God's Name: Why Sinai Still Matters* (Downers Grove, IL: InterVarsity, 2019), 85.

2. J. Richard Middleton, *A New Heaven and a New Earth: Reclaiming Biblical Eschatology* (Grand Rapids: Baker Academic, 2014), 58.

mindset should help us perceive that "redemption consists in the renewal of human cultural life on earth rather than our removal from earth to heaven."[3] That got lost.

The rapid growth of the Christian church through the three centuries after Jesus Christ's death and resurrection, married to the adoption of Christianity as the prevalent religion of the Roman Empire in the fourth century AD, witnessed a mutation in Christian understanding of the relation of heaven to earth. No longer was heaven perceived as the presence of God come to earth through the ministry of Jesus Christ. Now heaven became a distant, perfect, ideal place: an ethereal location for deceased souls to be transported to, far from the stormy, shadowy, sinful realm of earth. The earth ceased to be viewed as the environment where Christians, called to bear the likeness of Christ, are to be God's emissaries, commissioned to bring present healing and earthly transformation. The cord between heaven and earth, established in Hebrew thinking within Israel, was well and truly cut as the gospel was reinterpreted within a Greco-Roman mindset.

What effect did this come to have on the way that Christians understood their witness and mission upon earth?

Who Pulls the Strings?

One immediate effect of envisioning and configuring heaven as cut off from earth was the way in which an understanding of God's involvement in our lives came to be viewed. This became evident in the teachings of theologians operating with a Greco-Roman mindset. Anselm of Canterbury, a leading thinker of the eleventh century, argued that in imagining that God exists at all, we allow for the possibility of his existing; this prepared the way for Descartes to affirm, in the seventeenth century, that humanity's intellectual facility validates our personal identity: "I think, therefore I am." The intellect, in the realm of ideas, could deduce truths about both God and people. So it was that in the thirteenth century the Italian philosopher and theologian, Thomas Aquinas, could shape five "proofs" for the existence of God that would continue to be taught, as a means of forming faith, through to the present day. In the first proof, he argued that all movement has to begin with a Mover; and that this Mover must be God. In the second, he argued that everything has to be brought

---

3. Middleton, *New Heaven*, 58.

into being by a Cause; and that Cause is God. Third, he argued that the whole cosmos has to have some point when it begins. That point—which has to be outside of time—lies with the Creator of the cosmos. Fourth, he concluded that because people argue about goodness, recognizing that there are various degrees of goodness around us, there must be an ultimate good: God. Fifth, because life seems to be shaped towards some end or goal, there must be an intelligent designer shaping this end. All very neat. Both the existence of God and the identity of people could be affirmed by the operation of our intellect. The existence of God—and heaven—could be validated by intellectual process. Heaven, an abode of ideas. Heaven and earth could exist apart from one another, through our thoughts.

Now, all that might be very fine, from a Greco-Roman mindset. But it made the demonstration of God's reality, through a sensory engagement of heaven with earth, an irrelevance for those who had intellectual capacity. Certainly, the superstitious and the less capable might search for signs and immediate demonstrations of divine activity. Sacraments would mediate God's grace into our lives. But the perfect realm of heaven would only be reached by us beyond this present existence; and perceived, for now, by those who refined their thoughts, focusing on a perfect heaven of abstract doctrine and ideas.

Both deism and theism flourished in such an environment. A politicized church served as the mediator of God's grace. God was properly viewed as either detached from his creation, albeit interested in what was happening; or active through a mysterious causality of divine providence, ever confounding or confusing mere mortals. Worship God and obey the king! The church would care for our souls, guarding them for a final journey to heaven. The king or governments would control, under God, life here on earth. God had established it that way. The church would help, through its ministrations, to sustain everything in good condition. Does not God validate such order to life? As Cecil Frances Alexander's hymn, penned at the height of the British Empire, declared,

> All things bright and beautiful,
> All creatures great and small,
> All things wise and wonderful,
> The Lord God made them all.
>
> The rich man in his castle,
> The poor man at his gate,

> He made them, high and lowly,
> And ordered their estate.[4]

Political stability and the status quo could be protected, so long as the cord between heaven and earth remained severed, replaced with an understanding of God and heaven held well apart, albeit claiming that all is well under God's sovereign plan and so long as the means of grace are present, to be imparted to humankind.

Restoring the Image-Bearers of the Triune God

The Messiah came and violated the good order of things. The Messiah of Israel, proclaiming the advent of the kingdom of heaven upon earth, bearing the name of God and leading God's people, had declared,

> The Spirit of the Lord is upon me, because He has assigned me to bring good news to the poor. He has sent me to proclaim pardon to prisoners and recovery of sight for the blind, to send out the broken in forgiveness and proclaim a season when God shows favor.[5]

The expectation found within the Hebrew Scriptures is that Israel's Messiah would commence the rule of God upon the earth, enabling God's people to fulfill their divine destiny, extending the rule of God to all the nations of the earth. The Messiah would bear the presence of heaven here, on earth. A conquest would, however, be necessary. There would need to be a defeating and routing of forces that opposed the presence of heaven on earth, resisting God's rule. An understanding of how the Messiah would equip and enable people to do this, as image-bearers of God, would be essential. Where the presence of heaven was to be manifested and multiplied across the face of the earth, there would need to be an equipping of people. People would need to be equipped to bear the name of Jesus Christ. Just as Jesus bore his heavenly Father's image, in and through his humanity here on earth.

In the Gospel accounts, the teaching of how this advance of the kingdom of heaven takes place is unveiled. Jesus Christ makes it clear. Jesus offers an applied interpretation of Old Testament law, worked out and

---

4. Cecil Frances Alexander, "All Things Bright and Beautiful," from *Voices of Praise: For School and Church and Home*, #238, https://hymnary.org/hymn/VoP1883/238.

5. Luke 4:18–19, my translation.

demonstrated in his practices as a human being. He marries convictions and practices together and insists that a true knowing of God leads to action that pleases and honors God. The presence of heaven upon earth is to find expression in and through practices of our lives that demonstrate that we are image-bearers of God, in Jesus's name. That has implications for us now, today.

We need to rediscover and reaffirm our identity, as Christian disciples: our identity as image-bearers of the triune God. Broken sinners we may well be; but by the presence and power of the Holy Spirit working in and through our lives, we can be mended and then carry healing to others. We can be mended as people. We can be mended as communities of people who bear the name of Jesus Christ. We can be mended to be more effective image-bearers of our Father in heaven by replicating the manner in which the Son, Jesus Christ, looked to be filled and enabled by the Holy Spirit, in order to bring the presence and power of the kingdom of God to earth. Earthing heaven, here and now.

There are two focal points that we need look to in pursuing this path of earthing heaven here and now. The first is an ethical one. There is a need to continually look to interpret the teaching of Jesus within our changing culture and context, in a way that gives expression, through our practices, to the actualizing of kingdom convictions in our lives. Jonathan Wilson, in highlighting an understanding of church as a community of practice, living for God's kingdom purposes, has given good voice to this needful emphasis,[6] joining other contemporary Baptist voices such as William James McClendon Jr.[7] and Glen Stassen and David Gushee.[8] Doctrine, abstracted from the practices of everyday life, betrays an absence of heaven come to earth. Instead, with lives rooted in Jesus Christ, the manifestation of heaven upon earth needs to be evidenced among us through the intensified infilling and workings of the Holy Spirit in our lives. Intellectual process remains important, as it is an aspect of our humanity; but it must issue in practical expression and action through our

---

6. As in Jonathan R. Wilson, *Why Church Matters: Worship, Ministry and Mission in Practice* (Grand Rapids: Brazos, 2006).

7. Building on his early collaboration with James M. Smith, *Understanding Religious Convictions* (1975), McClendon set practices as the foundation for understanding Christian convictions, as expressed in *Ethics* (Nashville: Abingdon: 1986), the first of his three-volumed *Systematic Theology*.

8. In their seminal work *Kingdom Ethics* (Downers Grove, IL: InterVarsity, 2003).

lives, as our heavenly Father looks to give expression to divine presence in us, as image-bearers in Jesus's name.

A second focus must also be further pursued, though. One that is easily omitted. A focus, arising not out of Greco-Roman thought and not easily accommodated through our intellectual process; but a focus that is powerfully Hebraic, importing significant emphasis in bringing physical expression to the presence of heaven upon earth. In part it found expression within the Radical Reformation among the Anabaptists of Central Europe. These disciples would migrate in large numbers to the New World, carrying a vision of community that expressed the teachings of Jesus Christ in fellowship together, in a manner that was distinctively different to the ways of wider society.[9] More recently, it has found expression in the exponential growth of both Pentecostal and charismatic dimensions to Christian faith in every part of the world.

The writings of Bill Johnson, senior pastor of Bethel Church in Redding, California, attracts little attention in scholarly circles; yet is one example of teaching focused on the bringing of heaven's presence to earth now.[10] Dependent on the power of the Holy Spirit to manifest works of healing, deliverance, and miracles among those who are image-bearers of God in Jesus's name, ministries such as Johnson's are at the forefront of contemporary church growth. As mission and ministry advisor to a national church network in Scotland, I see the real need for a new appreciation of how we might better learn from those who are acting as conduits of earthing heaven through signs and wonders. We need to have church that expresses both ethical authenticity and spiritual power released upon earth, bearing witness to Jesus Christ as Lord. Failure to address this dimension of Trinitarian image-bearing impoverishes us all.

Jonathan Wilson has served us well, earthing heaven among us. May his work continue to feature among the writings of those who herald the presence of heaven on earth, through practices that we pursue as image-bearers of the triune God.

---

9. As is given expression in Harold S. Bender's classic paper, *The Anabaptist Vision*, (Scottdale, PA: Herald, 1944).

10. Bill Johnson, *Experience the Impossible* (Minneapolis: Chosen, 2014).

Eating the Peaceable Kingdom

Margaret B. Adam

The wolf shall dwell with the lamb,
and the leopard shall lie down with the young goat,
and the calf and the lion and the fattened calf together;
and a little child shall lead them.
The cow and the bear shall graze;
their young shall lie down together;
and the lion shall eat straw like the ox.
The nursing child shall play over the hole of the cobra,
and the weaned child shall put his hand on the adder's den.
They shall not hurt or destroy
in all my holy mountain;
for the earth shall be full of the knowledge of the Lord
as the waters cover the sea.

—ISA 11:6–9[1]

Edward Hicks's paintings of the *Peaceable Kingdom*[2] show wild, domestic, and human animals relaxing comfortably together, without

[1] This chapter uses the ESV translation for Scripture references, unless otherwise indicated.

2. I will continue to use *kingdom* language beyond references to Isaiah and to Hicks's artwork, throughout the essay. I appreciate concerns that affirming kings and

predation, conflict, or carnivorous consumption. Hicks was a sign-maker by trade, a preacher by vocation, who produced sixty-two paintings that illustrate his interpretations of Isa 11:6–9, over the course of his life. Early on, he was appreciative of William Penn's efforts toward a peaceable kingdom brotherhood in the agrarian Pennsylvania colony; but Penn's treaty with the Lenni Lenape indigenous people failed (at great cost to the Lenni Lenape), the divisions among Quakers intensified, and Hicks doubled down on inward peace.

Hicks's cousin, Elias Hicks, was a prominent Quaker preacher who advocated a quietism theology of internal-controlled passions and a personal salvation.[3] Edward preached this message too, using verbal and visual imagery of nonhuman animals as allegorical representations of human animal passions. His *Peaceable Kingdom* nonhuman animals lived together, without conflict, illustrating the human animal need for internal humility and calm in order to experience true peace. The artistic cohabitation of wolf, lamb, leopard, kid, lion, calf, bear, cow, ox, child, and asp illustrates Hicksian hope for the spiritual development of human animals and their quelling of internal animal natures, in heaven if not on earth.[4] Elias and Edward critiqued the more urban, Orthodox Quakers for clinging to the distractions of worldliness and of unnecessary doctrine. The Orthodox Quakers critiqued the Hicksians for their resistance to creeds, biblical infallibility, and the evangelical movement.[5] The Hickses were not peaceable promoters of their message: their diatribes led to the 1927 Great Separation. Edward was especially provocative because he engaged in artwork (generally viewed as idolatry by Quakers), his biblical

---

kingdoms as the nature of the divine identity and relationships affirms oppressive power structures within fallen creation. At the same time, I am not aware of another human-animal governmental structure that escapes the abuses of power, and Scripture seems to use this imagery to connote a generous, loving, and providential monarchy better than any in creation. My hope is to associate eschatological peace with images of peaceable relationships beyond creatures' capacity to establish.

3. As Elias Hicks explains, "These scripture testimonies [Isa 11:6–9] give a true and correct description of the gospel state, and no rational being can be a real Christian and true disciple of Christ, until he comes to know all those things verified in his own experience, as every man and woman has more or less of all those different animal propensities and passions in their nature." Elias Hicks, *Letters*, 231–23, cited in David Tatham, "Edward Hicks, Elias Hicks and Jon Comly: Perspectives on the Peaceable Kingdom Theme," *American Art Journal* 13 (1981), 36–50, esp. 46.

4. Tatham, "Edward Hicks," 43.

5. Thomas D. Hamm, "A Protest against Protestantism: Hicksite Friends and the Bible in the Nineteenth Century," *Quaker Studies* 6 (2002): 175–94, 179.

interpretations in sermons and on canvas were highly unconventional, and he depicted specific opponents as allegorical animals who needed to be humbled (like the lion who, as Hicks described, gave up his diet of violence in order to eat straw like the ox).[6] Hicks himself spent little time on conciliatory gestures with others; his ethics of peace looks inward toward personal reconciliation and the light of heaven.

While Hicks[7] put scant effort into peacemaking with his Quaker opponents, he expressed no interest at all in making peace with the actual farmed animals who modeled for his allegories of human spirituality, the animals he regularly consumed. He joins a host of Christians (before and after his lifetime) who appreciate *Peaceable Kingdom* imagery without considering potential ramifications for daily life relationships between human animals and the farmed animals they eat. Yet, visions, allegory, and analogies are necessarily connected to the figures on which they expand. Human animals need familiar reference points in order to imagine what they do not know. Visual and rhetorical descriptions of the extra-ordinary combine the probable and the improbable in order to point toward the thus-far unknowable.[8] The vision of the *Peaceable Kingdom* depends on common knowledge of these on-the-ground, vegetarian, non-agonistic nonhuman as models of the harmonious human and nonhuman relationships to come. Otherwise, the image of wolf, leopard, lion, and bear lying peaceably with lamb, kid, and cattle would not indicate anything out of the ordinary.

The lamb, kid, and cattle illustrate peaceableness not simply because they do not kill and eat other animals, and not simply because they seem calm and nonaggressive. They are models of peace also because their lives are relatively free from stress, hunger, confinement, and loss. They exhibit in their calmness the peace of their relationships with their farmers. The *Peaceable Kingdom* presumes that everyday farmed animals are comfortable and well cared for. Reconciliation with potential predators expands their peaceful lives beyond a baseline of thriving, to a supernatural life of certain safety, contentment, and companionship.

That baseline, harmonious, farmed animal existence (to which the predators humble themselves in the *Peaceable Kingdom*) has changed

6. Eleanore Price Mather, "The Inward Kingdom of Edward Hicks: A Study in Quaker Iconography," *Quaker History* 62 (1973): 3-13, esp. 11-13.

7. From here on, Hicks refers to Edward, not Elias.

8. Even the strangest creatures in Revelation are made up of imaginable, recognizable parts and features.

radically since Isaiah, since Edward Hicks, and since the mid-twentieth century. The previously presumed common knowledge about peaceable farmed animals no longer describes the relationships between farmed animals and farm workers in contemporary farming systems. It is not that farmed animals have become violent or that farm workers are abusive, but farmed animal living conditions have changed significantly. We know more and more about the emotional, cognitive, and physical desires and experiences of farmed animals; but at the same time, the majority of farming systems focus more on efficient production than on farmed animal thriving.[9] Ninety-nine percent of farmed animals in the United States, and over seventy percent in the United Kingdom, are farmed in systems that constrain their access to family (to suckle and raise their children), social groups, and the out-of-doors; their freedom to engage in species-specific activities (foraging, grazing, dust-bathing, playing); their freedom from mutilations (tail-docking, disbudding, beak-clipping, and castration[10]); and their chance to live closer to their lifespan than, for example, six weeks (chickens) or six months (pigs). An up-to-date *Peaceable Kingdom* painting would need to show reconciliation between wild animal predators and farmed animals *and* between human animals and farmed animals.

Christians who eat—all Christians—are implicated in present day agricultural systems. All Christians are directly and indirectly tied up in damaging, counter-peaceable relationships with farmed animals, as well as with the human animals who work on farms, slaughterhouses, and processing plants; who own and manage and work in retail companies; and those who purchase and consume animal products.

The *Peaceable Kingdom* images present Christians with daunting challenges. It is hard enough to imagine eschatological human animal relationships with each other that avoid lying, strife, and abuse of power; it is harder still to imagine nonviolent relationships between wild animal predators and farmed animals. It might be most difficult of all to imagine life so peaceable that human animals do not consume any farmed animal

9. All farmers care about their animals, and some smaller farms excel at providing improved welfare conditions, often for fewer animals and with a higher cost for farmed animal products. Many smaller farms are in a position to provide more opportunities for peaceable farmed animals lives, but they are subject to financial pressures that inhibit those changes. Retailers, consumers, and government policies must provide the necessary additional support for farm workers and farmed animals.

10. These are standard practices to address real animal husbandry challenges. There are alternatives, but they require financial investment and revised practices.

products, let alone high levels of farmed animal products at mass production inexpensive prices.[11] These are all marks of the peaceable kingdom in which, through Christ's reconciliation of the cosmos, God's order is regained and completed, natural violence is overcome by the salvation of creation, and no human or nonhuman animals need to consume any others in order to thrive. The sharp discrepancy between the peaceable kingdom and everyday life challenges Christians to examine what relationship there might be between eschatological images and a Christian ethics of peace. What does it mean for Christians who eat to make peace?

If peacemaking means effecting the peaceable kingdom here and now, then clearly it is impossible. Systems of farming, policies, social traditions, and economic necessities stand in the way of efforts to make peace in the style of the *Peaceable Kingdom*. We have no divine agency to change the natures of wild and farmed animals; human agency is not enough to reshape creaturely patterns of consumption into a *Peaceable Kingdom* pattern of creaturely coexistence. Creation is mired in the effects of our systemic sin; and we are responsible for practicalities, risk management, and realistic expectations. Current patterns of food production and consumption are already firmly established. Eschatological images of noncarnivorous, non-commodifying, multispecies, nonviolent cohabitation reach too far beyond human/animal peacemaking efforts even to consider.

In fact, it *is* impossible for Christians to make peace—at least not the true, lasting, persevering-love, *Peaceable Kingdom* sort of peace. The peaceable kingdom is not a mission plan to be accomplished over the course of five or fifty years. Human efforts alone do not create peace or make it happen. There is one peacemaker, Jesus Christ, who as the fully human and fully divine creator and savior of creation *is* peace, "in whom all things hold together" (Col 1:17). Christians—imperfectly human and not at all divine—can claim to be agents of peace only to the extent that they reflect, anticipate, cooperate with, and witness to the perfect peace that Jesus Christ has effected and is effecting in and for creation. Our job is to participate in the peace that Christ creates and redeems, by witnessing to the peace that we cannot make happen on our own.

---

11. There are, of course, many Christians who do not consume farmed animal products, or who consume farmed animal products only from farms that offer improved welfare conditions; but these are the minority, and the majority of Christians in the United Kingdom and United States consume large quantities of inexpensive animal products from animals with poor welfare conditions.

Christians witness to peace by recognizing the discontinuities between eschatological images of the end of creation and the life we know right now in the midst of not-yet-completed creation. Somehow, Christians need to embody, enact, and demonstrate Christ's kingdom, even though it is Christ's agency alone that renders the kingdom accessible. The challenge of making connections between human animals' interactions with farmed animals now and the relationships of the eschatological peaceable kingdom is the same challenge of all Christian ethics: to live as if the peaceable kingdom is here, even though it appears not to be, and we cannot make it happen. We are constrained by finite resources, by economic and social necessities, and by frailty and death, but we can still notice and point out glimpses.

Christian saints and heroes of the faith offer these glimpses in a wide range of particularity. Their lives together construct a kind of peaceable kingdom image, illustrating how they model extraordinary witness to the presence of divine peace through their relationships with other human and nonhuman animals. These relationships may not effect broad and visible change, but they do display the impossible peace that is both possible and eschatologically established. The saints respond to the ultimate reconciliation in Christ, by living improbable, impractical, and implausible lives of peaceful interactions with the human and nonhuman animals they meet. Christian hagiography is full of stories about saints who communicate with nonhuman animals, give glory to God with them, heal them, and share company and resources: for example, Saint Anthony Abbot and a pig, Saint Anthony of Padua and fish, Saint Modestos and oxen, Saint-Mungo and a bird, Saint Cuthbert and otters, Saint Melangell and hares. These are stories of peace-revealing, in companionship, not consumption.

The kingdom of peace calls all of creation to respond as if Christ's peace is real in all their relationships: with God, with each other, with nonhuman animals, and with the whole created cosmos. Christians frequently note saintly patience, fortitude, faithfulness, and peaceableness as virtues worth emulating, at least to the degree possible by less-saintly human animals, but there is something about the saints' miraculous acts of peace that warrants emulation as well. It is not necessary to reproduce saintly communication with nonhuman animals in order to witness to the peace they reveal. It is enough to imagine and proclaim that there is more than brokenness and death.

For Christians, this means living into ever-more peaceable relationships, especially where they seem improbable, impractical, and implausible. It means learning "to anticipate that ultimate communion with animals by changing our present attitudes, practices, and policies."[12] It means learning about the needs and desires of farm workers and farmed animals, in order to provide moments of relief, comfort, and pleasure. It means asking some human animals to pay more for dairy products from a farm where the calves stay with their mothers until they are weaned, while providing other human animals with affordable, accessible, healthy foods. It means supporting farmers who are trying to improve their farmed animal opportunities to thrive, when the improvements seem impossible. It means meeting farm workers and farmed animals to learn about their desires and delights and finding out how to contribute to their well-being. It means searching for some small gesture to suggest that realistic limits to farmed animal flourishing or to human animal humble generosity are not Christ's limits.[13] "The resurrection of Christ reveals that this fallen world is not all there ever has been and will be."[14] Christ's death and peacemaking resurrection establish the peaceable kingdom, the Holy Spirit expand our imaginations for peace beyond our low expectations. The Eucharist reveals the already and still coming peace that explodes the limitations of finance, convention, consumption, and death.

To be a peaceable kingdom witness, eat the body and blood of Christ who ends death.

Learn to eat like a saint who embraces nonhuman animals as members of the creation Christ is redeeming.

Eat in community with other human animals and together develop peaceable kingdom imaginations.

Eat like a lion who humbly eats straw with an ox.

Eat as if the peaceable kingdom is here.

---

12. Stephen H. Webb, "Ecology vs. the Peaceable Kingdom: Toward a Better Theology of Nature," *Soundings: An Interdisciplinary Journal* 79 (1996): 239–52, esp. 247.

13. To learn about farmed animals and how they are farmed, see David Clough et al., *The Christian Ethics of Farmed Animal Welfare: A Policy Framework for Churches and Christian Organizations*, https://web.archive.org/web/20211201155658/https://www1.chester.ac.uk/sites/default/files/CEFAW_PolicyFramework_DigitalDownload.pdf. To learn about animal theology and ethics, see David Clough, *Systematic Theology*, vol. 1 of *On Animals*; and *Theological Ethics*, vol. 2 of *On Animals* (London: T&T Clark, 2019).

14. Jonathan R. Wilson, *God's Good World: Reclaiming the Doctrine of Creation* (Grand Rapids: Baker Academic, 2013), 254.

The Practice of Walking as Theological Knowing

An Experimental Journey

Mike Pears

THIS ESSAY IS ABOUT walking, or more specifically about the relationship between walking and knowing as a way of theological reflection. The essay itself is more like a walk than a structured argument. While I have an overall direction in mind, I respond to things glimpsed down interesting-looking side streets and investigate things that have caught my attention along the way. This walk is not akin to a journey taken along a well-marked trail or footpath where the route is clearly signposted and trodden down by the many feet that have gone before. This walk is shaped by my own experience of close-on four decades of urban wandering in the cities in which I have lived and ministered.

The essay is to honor and pay tribute to someone who has faithfully walked his own pathway with God—friend and colleague Jonathan Wilson. Meeting with Jonathan a few years ago seemed one of those chance encounters that are so characteristic of the journey on foot. For me, this encounter has brought a gift of friendship, stimulating conversation and active partnership in a shared journey with God. For you Jonathan, my hope is that there are plenty more fruitful paths to travel, both for yourself and together.

As far as I can remember, my practice of urban walking has been motivated by the desire to become more deeply immersed in the places in which I, and my family, have lived and ministered. Walking evokes a certain kind of anticipation that something unexpected might turn up—a fresh insight provoked by a chance encounter, some previously unknown niche or creative piece of street art, some new insight to the character of the place, and a hope that I might somehow glimpse the Spirit of God beckoning me to pay deeper attention to a particular situation.[1] My motivation, as far as I can tell, has been to gain a richer sense of the reality of the place itself, a better understanding of what is actually going on in the neighborhood—and a conviction that the best way of accomplishing this is to travel on foot. In the early years of ministry in Peckham, Southeast London, I walked out of instinct. Where possible I walked to meetings and pastoral visits, often leaving time to take the long way round or leaving space for a chance meeting with someone along the way—time to amble along rather than walk at full speed. Our part of Peckham was dominated by brutalist-style architecture where large blocks of flats were connected by raised platforms and internal corridors making it possible to walk for miles without descending to ground level. With the benefit of hindsight, I realize now that my younger self was rather naïve and un-self-aware so that my view of the place was through the relatively unfiltered perspectives of a young, middle-class white man just out of university (studying physics). However, the years of walking, in all weathers, through corridors, up back streets, through parks, down main roads at all times of day and night had a gradual transformative effect on me personally. I have come to slowly understand that walking is, in a significant way, related to knowing, that somehow the rhythm of walking, the practice of putting one foot in front of the other, the vulnerability of being lost or finding oneself out of place in a city, opens one's eyes to things that would otherwise be difficult to comprehend.

This sense of knowing through walking is well described by Robert Macfarlane in his beautifully written book *The Old Ways*. "From my heel to my toe is a measured space of 29.7 centimeters or 11.7 inches. This is a unit of progress, and it is also a unit of thought."[2] Macfarlane's writing reveals his understanding that the rhythmic physicality and the emplaced experience of walking are intricately linked to processes of thinking and understanding. I appreciate the turn of phrase he uses in referencing an

---

1. The idea of "glimpsing" the Spirit of God is presented by John V. Taylor in *The Go-Between God* (London: SCM, 1972), 8–18.

2. Robert Macfarlane, *The Old Ways: A Journey on Foot* (London: Penguin, 2013), 27.

idea made famous by Rousseau "that cognition is both motion-sensitive and site-specific."[3] We should take care, however, not to misrepresent or romanticize the experience of walking-as-knowing as if it were a kind of avant-garde spirituality. Walking is mundane, natural, even boring . . . it is, of course, pedestrian in all senses of the word. At times, walking through a seemingly endless suburbia or with aching feet through an unattractive urban green space with no café in sight, I have had to question whether this "walking thing" is actually working. In Macfarlane's words, "sometimes walking is the mind's subtle accomplice; at other times its brutal antagonist."[4]

Over the years my own habit of walking has evolved into a more deliberate attempt to explore ways of theological knowing guided by the sense that the experience of walking the city opens insights and spurs to theological reflection which cannot be gained simply through book-based study. As an immersive, embodied practice, walking as theological reflection draws on a more varied epistemology than a purely rational approach.

This understanding has been developed through reading the growing literature on theology and ethnography which challenges the dominant position in Western theology of the epistemology of the intellect. In this context "ethnographic methods provide a path by which truth emerges, rather than a way to apply truth."[5] As with urban walking, ethnographic practice "primarily utilizes an inductive method" whereby "it seeks to discover what truth or valuable insight is found within specific locations—discovered in communal and individual stories, cultures, practices, and experiences."[6] Thus, what distinguishes between an everyday stroll and the practice of walking-as-theological-knowing is a kind of keen attentiveness to the situation alongside an intuitive reflexive sense of self. Christian Scharen and Anna Marie Vigen's description of a researcher might equally apply to an urban walker in that they "assume the posture of a learner who wants to be taught rather than that of an expert who possesses the crucial theory for analyzing what is going on or what is really real."

I like the analogy of the bird-watcher in relation to the "posture of the learner," especially as used by Rowan Williams to evoke the patient

---

3. Macfarlane, *Old Ways*, 27.

4. Macfarlane, *Old Ways*, 28.

5. Christian Scharen and Anna Marie Vigen, eds., *Ethnography as Christian Theology and Ethics* (London: Continuum, 2011), 17.

6. Scharen and Vigen, *Ethnography as Christian Theology*, 16–17.

expectation of the prayerful disciple. In the context of this reflection, the idea of observing through binoculars is somewhat problematic in that it suggests the objectification of the subject. Nonetheless it evokes a sense of patient expectation which captures the essence of urban walking.

> The true disciple is an expectant person, always taking it for granted that there is something about to break through from the master, something about to burst through the ordinary and uncover a new light on the landscape. The master is going to speak or show something; reality is going to open up when you're in the master's company and so your awareness (as has often been said by people writing about contemplative prayer) is a little bit like that of a bird-watcher, the experienced bird-watcher, who is sitting still, poised, alert, not tense or fussy, knowing that this is the kind of place where something extraordinary suddenly bursts into view.[7]

The posture of the learner, which is characterized by attentive expectation, can be understood then to relate not only to a sensitivity to the "natural" social-cultural landscapes through which one is walking, but also to the possibility of encounter with the Spirit of God. One might glimpse, as it were out of the corner of the eye, the presence of God in a happenstance encounter on the road. Or one might sense the hospitable presence of the Spirit in the space of meeting between the self and another, for example, in the unexpected meeting with the man serving tea from his roadside van or the homeless person busking in the underpass.

These ideas and their associated experiences are some of the points where my own journey converges with that of Jonathan's. There is, I think, an interesting resonance between the notion of an inductive sensibility to place with the possibility that God may be witnessed there, and Jonathan's exploration of kingdom realism. Jonathan calls our attention to the "reality of the kingdom of God" that is "here and now."[8] Thus a deeper awareness of our "situatedness" will involve not only being attentive to our own social and cultural location. It also calls us to be alert to the reality of God's presence and activity in everyday life. In reality, to become more aware of our own situatedness is no straightforward thing and will necessarily involve a deepening reflexive understanding about

---

7. Rowan Williams, *Being Disciples: Essentials of the Christian Life* (Grand Rapids: Eerdmans, 2016), 2-3.

8. Jonathan R. Wilson, *God So Loved the World: A Christology for Disciples* (Grand Rapids: Eerdmans, 2001), 26.

the ways in which our own social location affects the things we see and understand, especially our view of others and our understanding of God. Growing in self-awareness should not be confused with a short reflexive exercise undertaken, for example, to fulfill the requirements of some academic assignment.

The kind of self-awareness we are talking about is a lifelong journey (a walk) that can entail a habitual practice of moving bodily out from the security of one's customary social location and into the worlds and social spaces of others—neighbors and strangers alike. It might sound obvious to say that such a change of social location must involve moving one's own body across the social and cultural boundaries that hem us in through the course of everyday life. For example, such boundary crossing could involve walking down a street you would normally avoid, eating in a café that is somehow outside of your comfort zone, or accepting an invitation to be a guest of a person of another religion. The effect is to cause a sense of being out of place. It is probably more sensory than cognitive, that is, more of a feeling than a rational understanding and in this sense, one might describe it as a form of sensory-knowing. The consequence of this de-centering experience can be to open one's eyes to other ways of seeing the world and indeed of understanding God. It can expose previously unacknowledged prejudice in ourselves and even our (unwitting) complicity in unjust social relations. In my own journey, some such out-of-place experiences have included surprising moments of encounter with the Spirit of God and have become an important part of what I would describe as my ongoing conversion.

Of course, the simplest way to undertake such a relocation is to walk!

On returning from Vancouver in 2000 to Bristol in the West of England (the city which had been our family home for many generations) I began to explore more deeply the practice of urban walking by inviting individuals or groups to walk together across various cities in the United Kingdom and then reflect theologically on what we had seen.

Passing through a gate one day on one of these extended walks across the city I observed that the person I was walking with changed in his demeanor from thoughtful and attentive to his surroundings into a mode of relaxed conversation completely unrelated to the purpose of our walk. I asked him what had happened: "Oh . . . this is one of my favorite places in the city. If the weather is nice my wife and I often come down here to walk in the evening." The familiarity of the place had caused him to change his mode of observation, in effect he stopped noticing.

This story draws to our attention an important quality of place and ways in which we might be better equipped to "see" what is going on in places. The quality of place in question is that the meanings that are inherent within places are most often hidden from us. Even though these meanings are replete with the power relations that govern our everyday lives, the place itself may present to us a kind of opaque surface or hard veneer that is difficult to penetrate or make sense of. As witnessed on this walk through the gate, familiarity tends to enhance the sense of opaqueness. Indeed, it has been a common refrain by those participating in urban walks that "although I know this place well, I'm not sure what I am meant to be seeing." The urban walker might find some help in this conundrum by thinking about the position or point of view from which they are looking, their positionality.

The positionality of the theologian is discussed by Michel de Certeau in his intriguing—though difficult to understand—text on "everyday life." Famously Certeau imagines a view of the city from atop the World Trade Center. The elevation "transfigures him into a voyeur. It puts him at a distance. It allows one to read [the text of the city] . . . looking down like a God."[9] Certeau contrasts this elevated view to that of the "ordinary practitioners," the "walkers" who "live down below." Through their embodied navigation of the city these ordinary people follow an "urban 'text' they write without being able to read it."[10] According to Certeau, for those who live down below the city is unseeable:

> Escaping the imaginary totalizations produced by the eye, the everyday has a certain strangeness that does not surface, or whose surface is only its upper limit, outlining itself against the visible.[11]

There may be a correspondence between Certeau's words and the experience of the person in my previous story of passing through the gate into, what was for him, a familiar space. Certeau provokes us to consider how the everyday experience of the city is characterized by blindness, of how we are generally unaware of the "certain strangeness" that is constantly around us. The practice of walking does not in itself open our eyes to that strangeness; the "manifold story" that Certeau describes

---

9. Michel de Certeau, *The Practice of Everyday Life*, trans. Steven Rendall (Los Angeles: University of California, 1984), 92.

10. Certeau, *Practice of Everyday Life*, 93.

11. Certeau, *Practice of Everyday Life*, 93.

as embodied in the streets, is not that easy to discern. In fact, it seems that the very nature of "place" is to hide from us the sense of meaning and the values invested in the everyday experiences of the city and of its built environment beneath a hard veneer of normativity. It is as if the place itself resists attempts to a deeper understanding by presenting to us everyday experience as "common sense" or "taken for granted" realities.[12] Like my companion we might, on passing through a gate, come to better understand the occluding influence of the familiar, but that in itself does not open our eyes to the "manifold stories" of urban places. In truth, this business of "doing theology from the street" (what is popularly referred to as "incarnational theology") is more difficult and often more frustrating than at first conceived. Yet it is precisely the acknowledgment of this difficulty, especially in the growing realization of our own limited sight, that is a necessary part of learning the craft.

Walking as a theological practice has helped me to better appreciate the challenges of associated with an embodied or contextual approach to theology. However, the theme is far from new and as I am now immersed in the life of the IBTS Centre[13] I find myself surrounded by a rich tradition of Baptist theologians who have grappled over the years with these very issues. An important voice in this regard is that of James McClendon who has been a significant theological presence for many years at IBTS.[14] Baptist theologian and McClendon specialist Ryan Newson has taken up this theme of positionality in relation to theology in the works of Mc-Clendon. In a recent lecture he stated that

> A baptist approach to theology ... will not proceed "from above," discovering truths from abstract or theoretical heights that are then "applied" to the world. The notion that Christians either could or should get their theology in order first *and then* move to engage the world is illusory—and likely leads to putting off "engagement" or "participation" or even "ethics" indefinitely.[15] But so

---

12. Tim Cresswell, *In Place / Out of Place: Geography, Ideology, and Transgression* (Minneapolis: University of Minnesota Press, 1996), 17–20.

13. International Baptist Theological Study Centre, Amsterdam. See https://www.ibts.eu/.

14. IBTS is associated with the McClendon Chair, which has been established at the Vrije Universiteit, Amsterdam. See https://mcclendonchair.com/.

15. This is partly why McClendon famously begins his systematic theology with ethics: not because it is more important than other loci of investigation, but because it has so often been neglected or deprioritized in the history of Christian theological thought. See James William McClendon Jr., *Ethics*, vol. 1 of *Systematic Theology* (Nashville: Abingdon, 1986), 39–41.

too is it illusory to think that Christians can abandon the work of theology altogether. Rather, on this view theology is done *as one lives* in the world, or perhaps as one proceeds along the way, participating and arguing and contributing to the life of the city. It is at the borders of encounter that we discover the (fluid, shifting) points of convergence and divergence between us.[16]

Since those early days of wandering the streets of London almost four decades ago, the conviction that theologizing should somehow be embodied has not diminished. I hope that it has matured and that (to put it in academic terms) my methodology and methods have been somewhat refined. Of significant help in this respect has been the growing engagement amongst practical theologians with qualitative research in general and ethnographic methods in particular.

Mary McClintock Fulkerson has been an especially helpful conversation partner in my own theological journey. In *Places of Redemption* she talks about her own experience of walking for the first time into the Good Samaritan Church, a small multiracial church in a working-class area of a small southern city.[17]

> I notice a thin white man sitting twisted in a wheelchair, parked next to a short man who looks like he has Down syndrome. As I approach the man in the wheelchair, my body feels suddenly awkward and unnatural. When I get in his immediate vicinity, I realise I do not know where to place myself. . . . My height feels excessive and ungainly. I tower over this pale man strapped in the wheelchair. Do I kneel down? Bend down to be face level with him? Speaking to him from above feels patronizing. Or is it the crouching down that would be patronizing? My hand moves to touch his shoulder, as if to communicate, "I care about you, despite your mildly frightening, contorted body and guttural gurgling sounds." But I withdraw my hand quickly, wondering if this, too, would be a sign of condescension. What was it like to be unable to command a safe space with your presence, to be vulnerable to the groping of other people's hands.[18]

---

16. Lecture attended online through Vrije Universiteit Amsterdam on Nov. 13, 2020. See also Ryan Andrew Newson, *Inhabiting the World: Identity, Politics, and Theology in Radical Baptist Perspective* (Macon, GA: Mercer University Press, 2018), ch. 5.

17. Mary McClintock Fulkerson, *Places of Redemption: Theology for a Worldly Church* (Oxford, UK: Oxford University Press, 2007), 4.

18. McClintock Fulkerson, *Places of Redemption*, 5.

She describes the sense that arises from this encounter as a wound—a sense of disjunction, brokenness, a feeling of strangeness.[19] It evidenced "a broader social 'unaccustomedness' to black and disabled bodies" and unaccustomedness which she attributes to an obliviousness, and in particular obliviousness that comes with dominance.[20] This kind of "not seeing" belongs not only to the individual but is a shared experience of the (white) social group; it is an obliviousness that goes with power.[21]

The recognition of blindness is itself a profound and unsettling experience—it may be that the only indication of blindness is the sense of disturbance (being bothered)—the sense that we have bumped into something because we did not see it and still do not know exactly what it is. In my own journey of theological reflection, including that of walking, the insight so eloquently put by McClintock Fulkerson has had a profound personal effect—once again, I might almost say that it has been some kind of conversion. To put it bluntly, it is a change of position from "there is nothing to see here . . . I know all about this place" (the problem of familiarity) to "there is a lot to see here—if only I weren't so blind." The problem is not so much that there is nothing to see—it is, in McClintock Fulkerson's words, a problem of reflexivity: my blindness prevents me from recognizing what is right in front of me.

Poignant for me is the recent controversy in Bristol surrounding the removal of the statue of Edward Colston—toppled and thrown into the harbor during a Black Lives Matter demonstration.[22] As a regular walker in that city and someone with an interest in exploring urban landscapes, including the ways in which "whiteness" (that is, a white way of seeing the world) was embedded in the city, I had walked past that statue many hundreds of times without a second glance! Though it is uncomfortable to admit, I confess that I just did not see this statue nor pay attention to its disturbing significance. In hindsight, now that the issue has been so clearly addressed, it is hard to understand how and why the presence of the statue remained uncontested and generally unnoticed by so many of Bristol's residents.

These disturbing reminders of blindness seem to be frequent in my own experience and I would suggest are to be expected, and even

19. McClintock Fulkerson, *Places of Redemption*, 15.

20. McClintock Fulkerson, *Places of Redemption*, 15.

21. McClintock Fulkerson, *Places of Redemption*, 19.

22. BBC, "Edward Colston Statue on Display in Bristol Exhibition," *BBC*, June 4, 2021, https://www.bbc.com/news/uk-england-bristol-57350650.

embraced, by those who espouse kingdom realism. The experiences cajole and provoke me into understanding that I too must be one of the blind disciples traveling with Jesus on the road (Mark 8:14–38; Luke 9:51–10:37). As a reader I can no longer stand in haughty judgment of those apparently slow-to-learn disciples as if their blindness were inexcusable on their part—"How could they be so dim-witted when the kingdom is right in front of them?" My superior objectivity is being taken from me and I must confess that if I was in their position, I would no doubt also be addressed by Jesus with "Do you not yet see!" (Mark 8:17–21). Thus, my urban walking is not simply reduced to an exercise of ethnographic observation or of psycho-geographical exploration, rather it is also framed as a journey on the Way; in this instance, the Way to Jerusalem.

There are, however, in these walking narratives places of profound hope—that those who were blind now do see, whether on the road to Jericho (Luke 10:21–23, 33–35) or on the road to Emmaus (Luke 24:31–32). And it is noteworthy that in each case the experience of eyes being opened are in the context of encounter with Christ, whether Christ in the other as represented by the Samaritan in Luke 10 or around the bread broken in Emmaus in Luke 24.

McClintock Fulkerson is again eloquent in her explanation about how those who suffer from non-seeing are brought to a new condition of sightedness. In her terms, "the transformation of obliviousness and its social harms is best imagined as the creation of its opposite: 'a shared space of appearance' . . . a place to be recognised and to recognise the other."[23]

My hope in writing this essay is that those who are friends and colleagues of Jonathan, and readers of his work, will perhaps be stimulated by the resonances between the idea of walking as a theological practice and with Jonathan's understanding of kingdom realism where "the kingdom of God is a reality in which we are to live."[24] Walking as I have described it might be one way of going about what Jonathan points to as an essential part of our theological task, which is "not to conjure up the past or anticipate the future but to discern the present work of God." Quoting Julian Hartt, he states that "the primary goal of that theology

---

23. McClintock Fulkerson, *Places of Redemption*, 21.
24. Wilson, *God So Loved*, 26.

called Christian is to amplify the power to see God in all things and thus to participate in the superabundance of his being."[25]

In the course of this essay, I have introduced you to some of the companions who have stimulated my thinking and practice in relation to walking as theological knowing. It has been a delight and privilege in more recent years to encounter on the journey another noteworthy companion whose has inspired by his company and conversation. Thank you, Jonathan!

---

25. Jonathan R. Wilson, "From Theology of Culture to Theological Ethics: The Hartt-Hauerwas Connection," *Journal of Religious Ethics* 23 (1995): 149–63, esp. 154.

A Gospel of Fukushima

Three Vignettes and One Hope, Ten Years after the Triple Disaster

Soohwan Park

"Can I go with you next time when you go to Fukushima?"

Back in summer of 2012, Jonathan asked me this question. I had already concluded a one-year-long missiological experiment project in Fukushima and delivered my findings to the relief agencies whom I was advising during the initial relief period in 2011—this story was published by *Christianity Today* in July 2013.[1] I hesitated to answer his question because I had no plan to do another missiological or theological project. I just wanted to go and hang out with people in Fukushima. At that time I did not imagine I would create another experiment, nor did I know what saying yes might entail.

And little did I know that we would end up in a marriage covenant together after that year.

---

1. Soohwan Park, "Redeeming Disaster in Japan," *Christianity Today*, July–Aug. 2013, https://www.christianitytoday.com/ct/2013/july-august/redeeming-disaster-in-japan.html. In this article I place the testimonies of local churches in the face of triple disaster of Fukushima in the larger contexts of the global Christian movement of disaster relief in the last seventy years. Alongside this article *CT* published in the same edition an interview with Japanese theologian Atsuyoshi Fujiwara which gives a larger context of Japanese Christian history, dating back to the sixteenth century's Catholic mission and martyrdom in Japan and how it shaped a Japanese culture of resilience and high view on suffering.

Jonathan came to Fukushima that fall soon after I had a retreat in Fukushima with Midori, my ministry friend, Japanese translator, and cultural coach. We went around by bullet trains, local buses, and foot, walking for miles. We listened to stories and ate with people. Some stories made us weep and others gave us joy. Jonathan and I went back again and again. Some years I went back without Jonathan. Other years I took a small team from a local church in Vancouver. I repeated my journey, going to the same local churches and meeting the same people year after year. But the pandemic and global travel restrictions finally stopped me from paying my annual visit to Fukushima in the early spring of 2020.

It is only in the last few years that the focus of this second missiological experiment has started to emerge, not in the form of questions, but in the stories of three pastors. Just like the first accounts of the Gospel and epistles, I wanted to capture the stories about Jesus through the lens of these people; how their faith in Jesus shapes their convictions and feeds their inner strength to do what they do everyday in Fukushima.

I call this *barefoot theology* as these pastors work under the unprecedented challenges of the triple disaster; earthquake, tsunami, and the ongoing nuclear crises. Such theological grounding forces them to go beyond the textbooks of formal training and prior ministry experience. It demands that they imagine new practices of mission out of Fukushima as they get a glimpse of the kingdom unveiled in the light of Easter hope breaking through the darkness of the most pressing nuclear and ecological crises today.

Story 1: Life in a Place of Death

Ken Nishiono graduated from a seminary in southern Japan on March 10, 2021, just one day before the disaster. With no clear future plans but a servant heart and able body to serve, he started working as a volunteer in a national NGO, responding to the disaster. In the following year he met his future wife, Seiko, at a youth conference in Fukushima. He then moved to the city of Iwaki, to work together with her at a local church relief center where she had been already working.

After Ken and Seiko got married, they continued to work in the relief project for two more years until they moved in 2015 to a smaller town on a hill called Miharu, about fifty kilometers east of Fukushima Daiichi, to accept a call to pastoral ministry.

Iwaki is on the coast and had the lowest level of radiation in Fukushima, while in the eastern part of Fukushima, where Ken and Seiko moved, higher levels of radiation have been detected, especially around the mountains. Most young people, especially families with young children, left Fukushima soon after the disaster. They feared raising children, especially girls, with the potential stigma of Fukushima. Even seventy some years after the Hiroshima atomic bombing, the country still lives under the fear of radiation. "The fear of Fukushima" isn't going to go away for a long time.

But Ken and Seiko moved to Miharu with a newborn baby and a second one on the way to take the baton from a retiring pastor at a local Baptist church with a small, aging, declining congregation and a large church property to manage. Ken began to rejuvenate the congregational life out of traditionally inward looking churchgoers. He built relationships with neighbors and became involved in community organizations.

While working in relief, Ken experienced burnout a couple of times, wondering why he wouldn't get to "preach the gospel" but only to meet the physical needs of people. When he recovered from the burnout, he was able to renew his calling as he recovered a deeper meaning of his labor. He recalls his work experience being transformed when he realized that "relief work is a very special ministry, it isn't just a means to get to people so that I could preach."

Having had this experience, Ken and Seiko knew that they would need a lot of patience and capacity to see this as a marathon, not a sprint. They began to learn about the church's ministry and their local community. Their third and fourth children came along. Soon the excitement of a growing family with young children became more challenging as they received a devastating diagnosis of their second child, Guillain-Barré syndrome, a rare neurological disorder. While adjusting to this new reality, their third child developed a urinary tract infection, which needed doctors' attention regularly in her early years. Long-distance trips to hospitals became a regular routine added on top of a busy pastor's working life, especially during the summer and rainy season when the church's large property requires many hours of maintenance with few volunteer help and no resources to hire workers.

Jonathan and I recently had a chance to speak with him at a virtual meeting to commemorate ten years after the triple disaster. I asked him the hard question, "What has given you the most joy in your ten years of ministry? What is your secret to being there in Fukushima for ten years?"

He responded in his usual, quiet, but assertive voice with frequent pauses. He is excited about the new opportunity that he can exercise leadership in the community organization to meet all of his neighbors who might never step into the doors of the church building. Most of all, his deepest joy comes from raising his four children with his wife in Fukushima as a sign of true hope in Jesus Christ. They know their family life, planted among atheist or Buddhist neighbors, would be the clearest witness to the gospel of Jesus they could make: a burden he joyfully carries everyday. Ken shares the secret to his joy, a daily prayer and recitation from a psalm:

> Praise be to the Lord, to God our Saviour,
> who daily bears our burdens. (Ps 68:19)[2]

Story 2: We Japanese Must Repent

It is a widely-known fact that Japanese culture does not value the role of women in public. In Japanese *Christian* culture, it gets even worse. When I first met Toyomi Sanga, a co-pastor and wife of the senior pastor at Grace Garden Chapel in Koriyama city just a month after the triple disaster, I knew something extraordinary was happening in that church. This husband-and-wife team of pastors has been working together, *planting a garden* through a disaster recovery ministry. The name "Grace Garden" came from the famous passage in Jer 29:5 and 7, a passage given by Toyomi's father at their wedding before they moved to Koriyama to work with this church.

> Build houses and settle down;
> plant gardens and eat what they produce.
> Also, seek the peace and prosperity of the city to which I have carried into exile.
> Pray to the Lord for it, because if it prospers, you too will prosper.

Koriyama, a midsize city, located sixty kilometers east of Fukushima Daiichi, quickly became a major city after the triple disaster due to its Shinkansen (bullet train) connection to Tokyo. The largest evacuee shelter in Fukushima was set up in Koriyama, near this church. The influx of tens of thousands of evacuees quickly changed the life of the city and the

---

2. This chapter uses the NRSV translation for Scripture references, unless otherwise indicated.

life of the congregation. Soon after they began the relief work, Toyomi and her team decided to focus on helping families, especially mothers and young children, settle down and reestablish life in this new landlocked city, away from their ruined homes on the coast. Over the years, the church has served through afterschool programs, parental education events, youth band festivals, gospel choir concerts, and more. Their primary focus is to raise up a new generation that will build Fukushima again.

Most importantly, the church is doing this ministry by empowering their own youth to play a major role in the long-term work of disaster recovery.

Toyomi's son is a remarkable example. Akito spent all his teenage years doing disaster relief along with his parents and his friends. When I first met him, he had just finished elementary school. His first year of middle school was spent mostly at home, church, and evacuee shelters. Before the triple disaster his desire was to study hard and go to a good university in Tokyo or another big city and move out of Fukushima. Transformed by his volunteer experience, he decided to study psychology and social work at Fukushima University so that he could become professionally equipped to contribute to a long-term recovery in Fukushima. During my last visit to Fukushima two years ago, I had a chance to sit down with Akito and his friends over dinner to hear their stories. Not only his vocational choices, but also his faith, were deeply shaped by the disaster. When I asked him what he thought of Fukushima's future, he answered,

> It's like the story of the blind young man in John's Gospel (ch. 9). It's not his sin that he was blind, but it is to glorify God. It is not our fault that we live in Fukushima or that Fukushima had the terrible disaster. Some say we are cursed, and others urge us to escape from here. But I believe we are blessed to live in Fukushima and serve hurting people here, because we know Jesus and we have hope in him.

Ten years have passed since the triple disaster, but Toyomi's conviction stays the same. In my first meeting with her ten years ago, she shared with tears in her big eyes, "Recovery is not the big issue. We Japanese must repent first. Repent of our greedy lifestyle, our sinfulness, stubbornness away from God. The continuing radiation is a reminder of our sin." Tears in her eyes spoke louder than her words because I know it is her yearning for her own people to acknowledge that there is no true happiness by seeking human achievements of material success and wealth without Jesus. Japanese Christians do not believe that the disaster was brought by the wrath of God. It is rather an outcry for a search of meaning and hope in the perfect storm like this.

Recovery from the earthquake and tsunami was completed rapidly after the disaster in Miyagi and Iwate, two prefectures north of Fukushima, which were affected much worse by the earthquake and tsunami than Fukushima. After all, Japan is known for its efficiency and highly developed technology in disaster preparedness and recovery. However, the ongoing nuclear crises from the crippled Fukushima Daichii have made Fukushima recovery much harder and a more complex journey for everyone at every level of society, from worries over agricultural produce—Fukushima was once the "breadbasket"—to alternative energy and economic revitalization, let alone ecological restoration. Japan's nuclear experts warned of wear and tear on the plants and the potential for disaster, but they were ignored by greedy corporate leaders and politicians. Ordinary people are paying the human and cultural cost at the expense of today's youth and their future.

"Fukushima has the highest rate of suicide and solitary death in Japan now," Toyomi told me and others who gathered on an online platform to pray for Fukushima for tenth commemoration. "Now is the most important time for the church to rise up and demonstrate our hope in Christ, to show why the life in Christ is meaningful and worth living."

A ministry veteran with three decades of team ministry with her husband, she does not stop at pointing out the devastating aftermath, a silent tsunami of mental health crises in Fukushima. But she continues with excitement in her voice,

> The pandemic has closed down the whole world, but it has opened up Fukushima to the world. Before the pandemic, we were cut off from the rest of the world, and people were afraid of traveling to Fukushima. But now, we are playing on a level field. Everyone gathers for church online. Our church started seeing people joining from all over the world and we now have a virtual global outreach service regularly. We believe the hope of future is indeed coming from Fukushima.

Grace Garden, by God's grace, is building an eternal garden city on earth.

Story 3: Ecumenism—The Way of the Suffering God

Eiji Sumiyoshi was hesitant for a couple of weeks after the triple disaster. Originally from Tokyo, he and his family moved to Nakoso Christ Church in Fukushima fifty kilometers south of Daiichi power plant just a few years prior to the disaster. His family and friends back in Tokyo kept calling him to leave Fukushima but he was unsure what he should do. Then he saw in his dream one night that Jesus was carrying the cross and walking into a burning Fukushima Daiichi power plant.

Jesus turned, looked at him and asked, *"Why are you abandoning me?"*

He woke up the next morning and repented of his indecisiveness and confessed to his congregation the following Sunday. Changed by his dream and conviction that Jesus was calling him to stay in Fukushima, he opened his church for relief operations for the community. Then he began to worry about his denomination's ethos of suspicion of anything that smacks of "social justice," since he comes from one of the more conservative, evangelical denominations in Japan. Serving the hurting community with practical materials in a time of disaster could be seen as sidelining from "the real ministry" of the gospel. Having studied widely on Japanese sociopolitics in the light of a theology of suffering shaped by a Korean pastor and freedom fighter, Rev. Chu Ki-Chol, Sumiyoshi was keen on working out his own theology of mission appropriate for disaster-stricken Fukushima. However, the denominational position was something that caused him to hesitate once again.

The divide between social and evangelical lines of denominations has been deep in Japan, a country with a tiny Christian population, for the last hundred years, just like the rest of the Protestant church. One good thing that the triple disaster brought to the church in Japan is that this thick wall between the Evangelicals and the liberals is breaking down and unity and collaboration among local churches is becoming a norm in city after city in the disaster-stricken areas. Each group discovered, in the face of the disaster, that they did not have the whole gospel. They needed more than social change or individual salvation. Church leaders are coming together to pray and to organize around local issues despite denominational differences.

One year after the triple disaster, I attended a theological symposium in Tokyo as the first commemoration. One of the most prominent Japanese theologians, Hideo Ohki, former president and professor emeritus of systematic theology at Tokyo Union Theological Seminary, spoke. He analyzed how sociopolitical events transpired by a natural disaster could influence a theological trajectory of the church in Japan in his profoundly convincing essay with a subtitle of "Theologize Japan, Do Not Japanize Christianity." He used the example of the Kanto earthquake in 1923. The largest natural disaster in Japanese history until March 2011, it took over one hundred thousand lives in Tokyo and surrounding areas.

> In the period leading right up to that earthquake, Japan had been victorious in wars with China and Russia. Fought on the side of the English, French and American Allies in the World War I, and enjoyed the prosperity of Taisho Liberalism. However, the Anglo-Japanese Alliance that had supported newly developing Japan was decided against in 1921, and officially terminated on August 17, 1923. Just fifteen days later, the Great Kanto Earthquake destroyed Tokyo, turning it into a scene of disaster and misery....
>
> In 1933, ten years after Tokyo was destroyed, Japan left the League of Nations and its seat as a permanent member and joined Germany, where Hitler had come to power, to form the Axis powers, thus cutting off the rudder of destiny and moving on its disastrous course towards August 15, 1945....
>
> In the very year of 1933, with his "Theological Existence Today" Barth stood against "German Christians" who were connected to Hitler. However, a bizarre phenomenon took place. "As if nothing had happened," using Barth's expression, Japanese churches on Sunday kept their worship services with the vertical relationship (with God) in a spiritual catacomb, so to speak. And they could not help but obey the national policy during the weekdays in militarist Japan. The dualism resulted from misusing the "transcendence" of Barthian theology.... I cannot help but feel that God is pressing us to reform the post-war Protestant churches in Japan through the great earthquake that also shook us from the foundation.[3]

For the last ten years, my interaction with Sumiyoshi has been always around the empirical findings of his work of serving tsunami victims or evacuees from near nuclear ground zero, reflections on his reading of the Scripture, and theological imagination around what could be done to rebuild Fukushima. Sumiyoshi once elaborated his discovery

---

3. Hideo Ohki, "The Reformation Pressed upon Us by God: Thinking Theologically of Japan," in *A Post-Disaster Theology from Japan: How Can We Start Again?*, ed. Atsuyoshi Fujiwara and Brian Byrd, Theology of Japan Monograph 6 (Saitama, Jpn.: Seigakuin, 2013), 59–61.

of the deeper meaning of the whole gospel with two wheels of a vehicle: evangelism and social ministry to go hand in hand in order for kingdom work to move forward.

Shaped by a mystical experience of encountering Jesus in his dream, his social outreach is embedded in his understanding of the of the cross and the hope of resurrection. Sumiyoshi's theology of suffering has been influenced largely by the Korean martyr of the twentieth century, Rev. Chu Ki-chol, who stood against the emperor worship imposed on Koreans and Japanese during Japanese colonization. Deep down in their hearts, Japanese Christians know the high cost of following the suffering God as the Lord and King in the face of deadly disasters or under totalitarian rulers of the world because of their history of Christian martyrdom, which we know well from the movie *Silence*, based on the novel by Shusaku Endo. Simply, this gospel of Fukushima is at odds with the gospel of healthy and prosperous life we foreigners have tried to export to Japan and elsewhere in the twentieth century.

Sumiyoshi is moving closer and closer to Fukushima Daiichi as he continues to follow Jesus into the flames.

Three years ago Sumisyoshi and his wife took me and Midori to Futaba, a town just eleven kilometers south of the power plant. It is one of the areas that had just opened after the government declared in haste that decontamination was complete so that they could shift their resources to new building projects to host the 2020 Olympics. Very few people have returned, and community and social infrastructure were nonexistent. With no prospect of future jobs or economic revitalization, schools and cultural recovery aren't even on the map. To this date less than 20 percent of the population has reclaimed residency in these areas.

He showed us a home that was badly damaged by the earthquake, for which he had started fundraising for major renovation work. He and some of his colleagues had started repairing the building as part of their ongoing prayer ministry. "This is going to be a house of prayer to welcome lonely and broken people who have no hope elsewhere but to return here. When the renovation is complete, we will open a church and it will be called Futaba Hope Church." He then handed gloves and cleaning tools to me and Midori as a gesture to invite us to participate in this prayerful ministry of repair.

This year was the tenth Easter since the triple disaster in Fukushima. Sumiyoshi opened the church for a small gathering for the first time for local returnees. I was imagining that had it not been for pandemic travel restrictions, Jonathan and I would have been there. We *will* be there one day to celebrate the Easter Sunday in Fukushima.

Barefoot Theology and the *Ground-Up* Kingdom

My ten-year experiment in Fukushima of following these three courageous and resilient pastors has taught me one thing about the gospel of Jesus: it is about the lived conviction of a hope we do not see in the presence of impossible contradictions of the world.

I have seen time and again that Fukushima, in its forgotten silent suffering, cries out for a new gospel story to be written for our century. A gospel that grounds us in the broken world we live in, and that takes our blurry vision of kingdom from the ground, to unwavering resilience of ordinary faithful people to be present with an Easter hope among suffering neighbors.

An Intentionally Disciplined Way of Life and the Ministry of Spiritual Direction

Susan S. Phillips

Jonathan Wilson wrote of the need for confession and repentance, for our own sakes and for the sake of the watching world. Confession and repentance, he claims, would require "an intentionally disciplined way of life that makes such practices integral expressions of life together with God and one another, not a marketing program or public relations ploy."[1] These are inviting and cautionary words. The intentional and confessional way of Christian living is and has been a narrow, less traveled road.

In this essay I reflect on how the ministry of spiritual direction is informed by what we know about the arts of self-examination and spiritual guidance as they were practiced in earlier times, including during what some have called "the long fifteenth century" from which came Protestant reforms and Ignatian spiritual practices.[2] Though these contemplative practices have been taken up by a minority within the church during any particular period, they have provided steady enrichment to souls and the church through the ages, and are core to the ministry of spiritual direction.

1. Jonathan R. Wilson, *Living Faithfully in a Fragmented World: From "After Virtue" to a New Monasticism*, 2nd ed., New Monastic Library: Resources for Radical Discipleship (Eugene, OR: Cascade, 2010), xix.

2. John Van Engen, *Sisters and Brothers of the Common Life: The Devotio Moderna and the World of the Later Middle Ages* (Philadelphia: University of Pennsylvania Press, 2008), 307.

Ancient philosophers endorsed the character-shaping practices of self-examination and guidance of conscience, while sixteenth-century Christians advised that those practices might or might not be true spiritual disciplines in keeping with the Reformation. Insights from history about these practices shed light on what I've witnessed in the spiritual formation programs of New College Berkeley, specifically small group spiritual direction and the spiritual exercises of Ignatius of Loyola (the thirty-week format).[3]

A person who spent a year in the exercises wrote:

> [The spiritual exercises] encouraged me to finally begin a really regular prayer practice which has led me to a faithful trust in a spiritual world that holds me and is always there for me whatever happens. To honestly share with others all of our paths of consolations and desolations as we grappled with what the stories from our traditions really mean to us today, was an incredible gift. My confidence in the Spirit has blossomed. Through this experience I feel I have finally developed a more personal relationship with Jesus, grounding my spiritual ideas in the realities of his life. Through prayer and meditation I have responded to the events in his life with a recognition of their truth in my own psychological struggles today. For me, Jesus and the Christian message are much more real now than they were before.

Prayerful self-examination and guidance are fully integrated with reflection on Scripture (especially the narratives of Jesus's life) in these year-long, covenanted groups. As the person above wrote, one's own spiritual ideas and experiences become grounded in "the realities of his [Jesus's] life."

Like other Christian ministries, New College Berkeley found the years around the new millennium to be a dry time spiritually for many people of faith. We read Willow Creek's *Reveal* study in which the researchers studying evangelical megachurches reported their finding that a significant number of churchgoing, mature Christians feel spiritually undernourished.[4] The researchers determined that one-on-one spiritual guidance would be helpful for those members of congregations, while

---

3. For a more detailed analysis of the research from these New College Berkeley groups, see my article "Together in Prayer: The Art and Gift of Group Spiritual Direction," *Crux* 49 (2013): 12–23. The thirty-week spiritual exercises program is also called the "Nineteenth Annotation" because Ignatius mentioned the possibility in a footnote with that number.

4. Greg L. Hawkins and Cally Anderson, *Reveal: Where Are You?* (South Barrington, IL: Willow Creek Association, 2007).

small fellowship groups were recommended for the less mature, but also spiritually stagnating, Christians.

We responded to this need for spiritual nourishment by offering year-long (nine-month) spiritual direction groups and the thirty-week spiritual exercises, with some people remaining in the direction groups for many years. We've also created focused groups for mature women, young adults, clergy, undergraduates, and graduate students at UC Berkeley, as well as groups specifically for Black, Indigenous, and other students who are People of Color.

A senior minister who participated in the weekly spiritual exercises wrote: "Learning to picture myself among the disciples, walking the dusty Galilean roads and listening to the Master, I have gained fresh perspective on the Gospels and seen my preaching and ministry enhanced. . . . My prayer life is richer. My ability to listen to God's word is keener."

In the spiritual direction groups and the spiritual exercises (the latter includes regular, private spiritual direction as well as group direction), the focus is on how the person is experiencing God's grace, or longing for and not experiencing it. A junior at UC Berkeley reflected on his experience in spiritual direction this way: "[Group spiritual direction was] really helpful for undergrads especially—in a time where reflection may be scarce in our busy lives, but also a really transformational time of life. . . .[It] required me to reflect on the ways that God was working in my life (taking time to notice these) as well as places he might be calling me into."

Spiritual direction is a countercultural commitment to contemplative listening for God with another person or persons. Its roots are ancient.

What we call "spiritual direction" was significant in the lives of some Christians five hundred years ago, including small, devotional communities of lay people. In fact, the self-examination and interpersonal guidance crucial to spiritual direction—and so needed today—have been present for millennia in the practices of persons and communities committed to spiritual and moral formation.

Practices of Self-Knowledge: Administrative and Medical

Today, practices of self-examination and guidance of conscience have been primarily relegated to secular professionals, at great loss to the church. Though professionalized forms of these practices are little more than a century old, secular forms of these practices are not new.

In lectures delivered in 1979 and 1980, the French social theorist and historian of ideas Michel Foucault addressed the development of the modern self as influenced by Classical moral practices and Christian spiritual disciplines, an analysis useful to Christians, even though embedded in Foucault's overarching critique of religious belief and authority. His distinctions among administrative, medical, and religious practices of self-care are especially enlightening in our increasingly secularized society.[5]

The Foucauldian analysis is critical of the techniques of social control embedded in devotional practices, yet differs from the Protestant theological critique of these practices. Both critiques illuminate the contemporary retrieval of the Christian practice of spiritual direction in our self-help age, Foucault by drawing our attention to the possibility of camouflaged power dynamics, and the Reformers by affirming the centrality of Jesus Christ as known through Scripture and the indwelling of the Holy Spirit.

Foucault claimed there is ancient precedent for contemporary administrative and medical uses of self-examination and guidance of conscience, two essential instruments for the cultivation of self-knowledge and virtue. In the Hellenistic world, certain educated people[6] engaged in daily self-examination in order to discover how they were progressing in self-control and their performance of duties. For example, Seneca in *De ira* (On anger, a first-century Latin guide to mastering one's passions) wrote:

> What could be more beautiful than to conduct an inquest on one's day? What sleep better than that which follows this review of one's actions? How calm it is, deep and free, when the soul has received its portion of praise and blame, and has submitted itself to its own examination, to its own censure. Secretly, it makes the trial of its own conduct. I exercise this authority over myself, and each day I will myself as witness before myself. When my light is lowered and my wife at last is silent [!], I reason with myself and take the measure of my acts and of my words. I hide nothing from myself; I spare myself nothing. Why, in effect, should I fear anything at all from amongst my errors whilst I can say: "Be vigilant in not beginning it again; today I will forgive you."[7]

---

5. See Michel Foucault, "The Hermeneutics of the Self," in *Religion and Culture: Michel Foucault*, ed. Jeremy R. Carrette (New York: Routledge, 1999), 158–81.

6. Including Pythagoreans, Stoics, and Epicureans.

7. Michel Foucault quoting Seneca; audio from the Howison Lectures at UC Berkeley, 1980. See also Foucault, "Hermeneutics of the Self," 164.

Foucault called this an administrative approach to self-examination. Seneca, the Stoic, took stock of his day, weighed it morally, and determined whether his actions warranted praise or blame. Then, duly self-examined, he faced the next day with a clean slate, lessons learned, himself forgiven. Note how behavior-focused and solitary the process is. Seneca was his own manager, engaged in an autonomous practice of self-guidance. The danger in administrative forms of self-help is radical autonomy entailing no corrective input from outside oneself.

The classical expression of self-examination and guidance could assume a medical form as well. In an example also quoted by Foucault, Serenus, a young friend of Seneca's who was hoping to alleviate his moral malaise, sought the philosopher's advice, saying, "Why . . . should I not confess to you the truth, as to a doctor? I do not feel altogether ill but nor do I feel entirely in good health."[8] The two men then engaged in an ethical, behavior-focused conversation about Serenus's use of his property, his way of speaking, and more. Serenus rendered himself a patient so that he might receive a prescription for living and relief from his dis-ease, thereby becoming an independent, self-managing person. In the medical forms of these disciplines, the peril is one of passivity.

We see in the administrative and medical approaches to disciplines, the contrasting dangers of radical autonomy and passivity. These dangers are present in the administrative and medical forms of self-examination alive and well today. We take on-line personality inventories, dwell in siloed social media, and curate ourselves for presentation. The proliferating field of coaching offers instructional benefits similar to those Serenus was seeking.

Christian Practices of Self-Examination and Interpersonal Guidance of Conscience

It's the searching, God-cultivated soul that we encounter in spiritual direction. As we meet, the curated self quickly fades in the atmosphere of prayer, confidentiality, and honest self-disclosure.

---

8. From Seneca's *De tranquillitate animi* (On tranquility of mind), quoted by Foucault, "Hermeneutics of the Self," 166.

Our Forefathers and Foremothers

We have exemplars of religious self-examination and interpersonal guidance in Scripture—for instance, King David examined his heart with moving and poetic pathos, and disciples and acquaintances sought Jesus's guidance. Paul asserted that "everyone ought to examine themselves before they eat of the bread and drink from the cup" (1 Cor 11:28), and James instructed us to "confess . . . sins to each another" (Jas 5:16).[9]

By the first century, Christian ascetic and monastic texts linked self-examination and the guidance of conscience. These Christian texts, like those of the Hellenistic schools, embraced humility and right detachment (mortification) for the sake of perfection (sanctification). In the Egyptian desert, people seeking deeper spiritual experience sought out holy hermits who listened to the insights gleaned from self-examination and then offered guidance. This practice was transmitted to Celtic Christians who, in turn, transmitted it to other Christians.[10]

The Christian linkage of self-examination and spiritual guidance introduced contemplation and devotion into the classical disciplines, moving them from administrative or medical practices of self-help to religious, penitential disciplines. Critics feared that people might turn to their confessors in a medical, spiritually mediated way, abdicating their active, moral responsibility before God and others. Ideally, true confessions were obediently uttered to God in the presence of the spiritual director—a formative relationship.

Foucault saw the spiritual disciplines of self-examination and guidance as central to "the pastorate of souls"[11] within the hierarchical structure of the medieval church and, at times, in more spontaneous and egalitarian forms in communities.[12] The Middle Ages saw the formation of small groups of Christians concerned with "conversion," the turn toward a more devout form of life.[13]

---

9. This chapter uses the NIV translation for Scripture references, unless otherwise indicated.

10. See, for example, Annemarie S. Kidder, *Making Confession, Hearing Confession: A History of the Cure of Souls* (Collegeville, MN: Liturgical, 2010).

11. Foucault, "Hermeneutics of the Self," 144.

12. Such as the late-fourteenth-century *Frères [et Soeurs] de la Vie* (Brothers and Sisters of the Common Life, also known as the *Devotio Moderna* movement).

13. Van Engen, *Sisters and Brothers*, 18.

A contemplative, devotional thread of influence extended from the urban, lay women's communities of the Beguines of the early thirteenth century to the Reformers of the sixteenth century. The Beguines "helped shape a new model of discipleship and of spiritual direction, contributing to the flowering of lay manuals for spiritual directors emerging in the late thirteenth and fourteenth centuries." The manuals were written in the vernacular, seemingly aimed at all Christians and encouraging them "to serve as spiritual directors to one another."[14]

The thirteenth-century Beguine writers Hadewijch of Brabant and Mechthild of Magdeburg wrote about detachment from things not of God through self-examination, confession, and moral guidance, all conducted in the light of Christ's life and passion, and with the aid of imaginative prayer with the stories of Jesus's life. Such practices are to prepare the believer for intimacy with God through Christ's self-giving love.[15]

Also influenced by these lay communities was the movement of spiritual reform in the Low Countries known as the Modern-Day Devouts.[16] The society began in the late fourteenth century, comprised of semi-monastic communities devoted to teaching.[17] The Devouts were not focused on church reform, religious orders, social estates, kingdoms, and statutes, but rather on "knowing, examining, caring for, and methodical re-making of the self" in this world.[18] They engaged in a communal, intentionally disciplined way of life, and they serve as an inspiration to those of us hoping to cultivate lives of Christian discipleship.

"The so-called modern devotion . . . was adamantly opposed to the rote observance of prayers and rituals and highly distrustful of all external expressions of faith."[19] This was a voluntary, "companionate" society, an *amicitia socialis* composed primarily of the laity, though in the men's houses there were also some clergy. This arrangement strikes a resonant note with the groups within New College Berkeley's ministry, in

---

14. Kidder, *Making Confession, Hearing Confession*, 73.

15. Kidder, *Making Confession, Hearing Confession*, 74.

16. See Kidder, *Making Confession, Hearing Confession*, 76, and Van Engen, *Sisters and Brothers*, 307. These groups are known by several names: the Brothers and Sisters of the Common Life, the Modern-Day Devouts, or the New Devotion (*Devotio Moderna*).

17. See Carlos M. N. Eire, *Reformations: The Early Modern World, 1450–1650* (New Haven, CT: Yale University Press, 2016), 107.

18. Van Engen, *Sisters and Brothers*, 303.

19. Eire, *Reformations*, 107.

which there is a predominance of lay people, along with some clergy, all participating in self-examination, confession, and guidance (though not in shared residence or mission).

As a teenager Martin Luther was a boarding student at a Devout school in Magdeburg. He was influenced by their piety and remained a defender of their society against Catholic and Protestant criticism.[20] Both John Calvin as a teenager and Ignatius of Loyola in his late thirties studied at the Collège de Montaigu,[21] where they were shaped by Devout thinking and austere spiritual expectations of Scripture reading, devotional writing, and self-examination.[22] These three men, who have so profoundly influenced modern Christianity, were immersed in devotional environments where interest in governing one's soul for the sake of God's indwelling was joined by a desire to be known within a relationship of care.

The Foucauldian warning is that self-examination and guidance of conscience always stand in danger of becoming instruments of socialization or its more muscular cousins, indoctrination and subordination. Therefore, the disciplines must be regularly examined and corrected. This is as true today for religious forms of the disciplines as it was five hundred years ago when people in the church sought reform.

A Reformed criticism leveled against the medieval church in Europe was its administrative exercise of the confessional. The Fourth Lateran Council's decree of 1215 required people to make confession to a priest of the church prior to Lent in order to be in good standing to receive the Eucharist at Easter, and the church, at its worst, allowed an obligatory and rote approach to participating in the sacrament.[23] There may be danger when a spiritual discipline becomes regularized, and the church is always reforming in part because structures can calcify, thus stifling the flow of life they were intended to serve. When self-examination is cursory *or* overly scrupulous, authentic self-disclosure and receptivity to God wither.

By the early 1500s the clergy and laity of the German church observed more frequent penance and private confession. Martin Luther met with Johann von Staupitz, the vicar general of the Augustinian order and dean of Wittenberg University, as his confessor and spiritual guide,

---

20. Van Engen, *Sisters and Brothers*, 306–7.

21. Desiderius Erasmus, too, spent time in a Devout boarding school and also at the Collège.

22. Van Engen, *Sisters and Brothers*, 317–18.

23. Kidder, *Making Confession, Hearing Confession*, 105.

sometimes confessing to him "at least weekly, often daily, and on one occasion for as long as six hours."[24] We assume that this was not a merely administrative exercise in self-examination, for Luther claimed that without it, "I should have sunk in hell."[25] However, despite Staupitz's encouragement that Luther surrender to the mystical environment of God's loving presence, Luther was caught in an obsessive scrupulosity that had a non-relational, possibly administrative, astringency to it.

Unable to divert Luther from his preoccupation with his sins, Staupitz turned him toward biblical studies. That is where Luther found grace, for "no works of merit, excessive penances, painstaking scrutiny of the conscience for nearly forgotten sins to be confessed in order to be forgiven had brought him peace. That came only from a faith that was born in the hearing and study of God's word."[26] Grace was found, in part, through the wisdom and loving care of a spiritual director who helped Luther move beyond obsessive self-examination.

The Christian tradition also has often employed healing imagery for growth facilitated by practices of self-examination and guidance. It is said that by the sixteenth-century in Europe the sacrament of penance and private confession were common, "and parishioners and monastics alike made use of its presumed healing and medicinal power."[27] A follower of Luther's wrote that true penance "is not satisfaction for past sins, but medicine against those of the present and future."[28] However, the Devout way was not intended as the administrative deploying of strategies for self-improvement; it was based in a relationship with God and community. Neither was it medicinal, entailing a passive surrender of personal agency.

The sixteenth-century Christian critique of self-examination and guidance of conscience stood on other grounds than those Foucault articulated, yet there is alignment in the concerns. Proclaiming "the priesthood of all believers," the Reformers sought to democratize relationships of interpersonal guidance,[29] and Reformed corrections allowed a believer

---

24. Kidder, *Making Confession, Hearing Confession*, 105.

25. Kidder, *Making Confession, Hearing Confession*, 104, quoting Roland Bainton, *Here I Stand: A Life of Martin Luther* (Nashville: Abingdon, 1950), 45.

26. Kidder, *Making Confession, Hearing Confession*, 108.

27. Kidder, *Making Confession, Hearing Confession*, 105.

28. Quoted in Kidder, *Making Confession, Hearing Confession*, 126, quoting John T. McNeill, *A History of the Cure of Souls* (New York: Harper, 1951), 179, quoting Martin Bucer, *Buceri Scripta Anglicana fere omnia* (Basel: Ex Petri Pernae Officina, 1577), 319.

29. For example, the Second Helvetic Confession (ch. 14), from the Reformed

to confess to a minister or to a lay person. Both Luther and Calvin urged people to meet with their pastors for spiritual comfort, but to do so freely and as needed. Confession was voluntary and could be made to any church member.[30] While not formalizing confession in the church, Calvin wrote that he would prefer confession to "no discipline at all."[31]

Five hundred years ago Martin Luther (1483-1546), John Calvin (1509-64), and Ignatius of Loyola (1491-1556) were contemporaries, and we are their spiritual heirs. They, like many Christians today, lived in an environment of rapid cultural change, political turmoil, devastating epidemics, and competing ecclesial reformations. Each of these agents of church reform—Ignatius within the Roman Catholic church and Luther and Calvin separating from it—emphasized aspects of Christian spirituality relevant to spiritual direction: attention to fostering personal relationships with God through interior piety, biblical rootedness, and devotion, which blesses the church and transforms the world.

The practical process of growth in righteousness was aided by small group meetings of the laity for "mutual exhortation, edification, and confession."[32] Under the leadership of Calvin and others, church members were visited annually by elders to give an account of their faith. Pastors were encouraged to submit to small-group, peer supervision in "the company of pastors."[33] At their best, these practices promoted sanctification by encouraging devotional self-examination and spiritual guidance.[34]

---

tradition (drafted in Switzerland in 1562), Christian Classics Ethereal Library, https://www.ccel.org/creeds/helvetic.htm.

30. Howard L. Rice, *Reformed Spirituality: An Introduction for Believers* (Louisville: Westminster, 1991), 126.

31. Rice, *Reformed Spirituality*, 127.

32. Kidder, *Making Confession, Hearing Confession*, 211.

33. Kidder, *Making Confession, Hearing Confession*, 212.

34. In the Reformed tradition people have continued to derive comfort and encouragement from speaking honestly and confessionally to another believer. An English Puritan advised that "when the soul is in the dark, and her own light shines not, she may do well to get a guide, and to take heed to borrowed light, until the day dawn and the day-star arise in her own heart" (in Rice, *Reformed Spirituality*, 135, quoting Francis Rous, "The Mystical Marriage," in *Treatises and Meditations* [London: Robert White, 1657], 702). Also in seventeenth-century Puritan circles, self-examination through private journals became a recognized and popular practice. Often these journals were confessional, and they were also prayerful engagements with Scripture, places where Luther's lively Bible would "lay hold" of souls. Journaling with prayerful self-examination and in preparation for spiritual direction is a common practice today, and is a core practice in the Ignatian spiritual exercises.

Soul Care in Spiritual Direction

The sixteenth-century Reformers remind us that we are the church reformed, always being reformed, according to the word of God.[35] The contemporary retrieval among Protestants of the practice of spiritual direction is part of that ongoing reformation as people seek spiritual thriving.

Like the Lutherans and Calvinists, the Jesuits endorsed small, confessional, accountability groups. Ignatius developed spiritual exercises to help people find the right sort of detachment so that they might experience more fully their attachment to God. This marks a shift away from a sin-focused theology that stresses management or medicinal cure, toward a vision of mystical oneness with God. This vision animates the spiritual lives of people today who seek to follow a contemplative, devotional path through the landscape of the world, like the college student in a New College Berkeley direction group who said he was learning to be an "open-eyed contemplative."

Another person in one of our spiritual direction groups wrote:

> I realize what a privilege it really is to hear the honest inner struggles of dedicated people. . . . [It was] a place to regularly practice thinking about and sharing the very personal things related to my spiritual development. . . . [This discipline] allowed me to think about and explain my inner life to a group of people in a Christian language that is a good foil for my tendency to think so much in psychological terms. Having lived a life with very few close friends that I have opened up to, this has provided wonderful validation and support.

As Jonathan Wilson cautioned, there is the danger that even self-examination done with religious hope and discipline might be taken up in an administrative way that is empty of an awareness of God's Spirit. In Christian spiritual direction the intent is one of discipleship: listening to God in prayer and Scripture with a spiritual director (possibly in a group setting), for the sake of following Jesus to the completion toward which God's grace draws us.

A directee in a group wrote:

> I found close, intimate fellowship with a group of Christians who listened, prayed and supported me without offering advice or criticism, and withheld judgement. . . . The benefit of the [group] will last a lifetime. It helped me to recognize how God

---

35. *Ecclesia reformata semper reformanda secundum verbum Dei.*

speaks into my daily life. It helped me recognize that the things that gnaw, interrupt and irritate me are opportunities to let God step into. It filled me with wonder and gratitude that God was with me in those moments and wanting to help me. I felt closer to God in that struggle.

The directee experienced a deepening relationship with God, though life has not become more manageable or problems easily cured.

Foucault differentiated among kinds of practices of self-examination and guidance. In addition to the administrative and medical, he proposed an additional form, one that is religious and pastoral. Drawing on biblical writing about shepherds tending their flocks, he wrote that the shepherd saves his flock through "constant, individualized and final kindness. . . . Shepherdly kindness is much closer to 'devotedness.'"[36] In a similar key, an early Jesuit recommended that spiritual directors offer "instruction when in doubt, strength when weak, encouragement when wavering, consolation when arid, calm when tempted, guidance when in danger, and, in general, direction in the right way."[37]

While spiritual direction has always been—and will remain—a practice embraced by a minority of Christians, for the past twenty-five years spiritual direction has been flourishing in many parts of the world as an intentionally disciplined way of life. Spiritual directors help people—individuals and groups—attend to God's presence and call. Today spiritual direction is often offered by lay people, and "while this practice has continued from its ancient roots in Eastern and Celtic expressions to modern monastic communities and the Roman Catholic Church, Anglican and Protestant churches have begun to recover it more fully only in the past twenty years."[38] The practice offers the possibility of self-examination and guidance in conscience such that the soul is cultivated, creatively and correctively, by God's amazing grace.

---

36. Foucault, "Hermeneutics of the Self," 138.

37. John O'Malley, *The First Jesuits* (Cambridge, MA: Harvard, 1993), 139, paraphrasing Gaspar de Loarte's *Exercicio dela vida Christiana* (Cagliara, It.: Sembenino, 1567), fols. 5–7.

38. Kidder, *Making Confession, Hearing Confession*, 236.

Embracing Partnership

Terry Smith

OF THE MANY THINGS *that I share with Jonathan Wilson, one of the most precious is a similar journey, shaped by parents with a heart for what was known back then as "foreign missions." And while Jonathan was led into the pastorate and the academy, I went overseas. By God's grace, our paths on this journey converged nearly twenty years ago around partnership in mission. Jonathan has been a "force majeure" in our understanding of true partnership. It has been my honor to work with Jonathan and learn from him as our Senior Associate for Theological Integration at Canadian Baptist Ministries (CBM). As colleagues, we have sought to enable our Baptist churches to engage in genuine partnership as equals with their brothers and sisters in the global South.*

In 1971, Professor Emeritio Nacpil of Union Theological College in Manila, Philippines, wrote an article in *International Review of Mission* entitled "Mission but Not Missionaries." He expressed a feeling shared by many Christians in what was formerly known as the developing world that missionaries from the West had failed to follow the biblical teaching of partnership by stifling the growth of the truly indigenous church. His call for a missionary moratorium would have, as its outcome, greater maturity for indigenous churches that would have a say in what they wanted to become. "The most missionary service a missionary under the present system can do in Asia is to go home. And the most free and vital and daring act the younger churches can do today is to stop asking for missionaries."[1]

Such tensions are not infrequent within partnerships. Theological differences, patterns of colonialism, arrogance, disregard, economic disparity, etc., have contributed to a painful strain in interchurch relations across cultures. Although Nacpil's opinion was not endorsed by the churches of Asia, it demonstrated a common frustration when mutuality in partnership is absent. The risks of non-biblical models of partnership are great. Churches, mission agencies, and receiving bodies need the solid basis of the Scriptures to help frame their collaborative endeavors.

We are familiar with partnerships in mission across national, ecumenical, denominational, and international divides, where collaboration in witness, proclamation, and social engagement is a viable option. Yet a cursory reading of most English-language translations of the Scriptures might lead one to suspect that it was not part of early Christian thinking. But that is only if we judge the importance of the concept of partnership by the extent to which the word is used in our English translations, where partnership barely registers on the scale.

Yet partnership is a deeply biblical concept, often associated with the Greek word *koinonia*.[2] In Protestant theology, this Greek word has usually been understood as fellowship. But the word "fellowship" fails to convey the powerful resonances and sense of personal engagement in a shared activity that the word partnership does. If we understand *koinonia* to mean partnership as well as fellowship, we will have a better understanding of the nature of our shared life in Christ and what Christian discipleship can be.

Among twenty-three English versions of the New Testament,[3] only seven use the word "partnership" anywhere at all, and even then, its

---

1. Emrito P. Nacpil, "Mission but Not Missionaries," *International Review of Mission* 60 (1971): 356-62.

2. Common interpretations include and have been translated in the New Testament by such words as association, communion, fellowship, close relationship, generosity, a sign of fellowship, gift, partnership, or contribution.

3. These include: Darby Translation (DT), Bible in Basic English (BBE), English Standard Version (ESV), Good News Bible (GNB), Complete Jewish Bible (CJB), Douay Rheims (DR), New Jewish Publication Society (NJPS), English King James Version (KJV), The Message (M), American Standard Version (ASV), New American Standard (NAS), Revised Standard Version (RSV), New International Version (NIV), Today's New International Version (TNIV), New Jerusalem Bible (NJB), New Living Translation (NLT), 21st Century King James Version (KJ21), Amplified Bible (AB),

use is infrequent.[4] That said, the concept is more frequently conveyed in many recent English-language versions. Instead, fellowship, sharing, communication, contribution or communion, are much more prevalent. The most frequent translation, "fellowship," is deeply rooted in the English-language Christian tradition. Commonly, the notion of Christian fellowship is somewhat more inclined to assume a passive notion of "being together" rather than a more active "participating in a common enterprise."

But *koinonia* can take on a tangible expression as a practical act of generosity, as we will see in the case of the collection for the church in Jerusalem in its poverty stricken condition.

For the apostle Paul, *koinonia* expresses the believers' sharing and participating in the gift and the work of Christ and of the Holy Spirit (1 Cor 1:9; 10:16; 2 Cor 13:13; Phil 2:1; 3:10) and in giving and receiving material resources (2 Cor 8:14; 9:13; Rom 15:26). He uses the word *koinonia* as a holistic concept, describing the sharing in the gospel. It describes not only a state of being in relationship with one another and with the gospel, but also the dynamic of action that that relationship entails. *Koinonia* is a life shared in Christ.

In 1979, Letty Russell encouraged the use of "partner/partnership" as a translation for *koinonia*. He saw this word as being beneficial in numerous contexts, ranging from Christian cooperation to partnership in marriage.[5]

The words "partner" and "partnership" have assumed more positive attributes than were previously held by the terms "fellow" and "fellowship." In a specifically Christian context, *koinonia*'s translation as "partnership" offers a broad sense of what is meant in the shared life in Christ, a more active, engaging relationship of participating together, working together and not simply just being together.

It is interesting that the earliest and most frequent usage of the words derived from the root *koinos* should be found in the Letters to

---

Contemporary English Version (CEV), Holman Christian Standard (HCS), New Century Version (NCV), Wycliffe New Testament (WNT), Young's Literal Translation (YLT), and New Revised Standard Version (NRSV).

4. These include: New Revised Standard Version (1989), English Standard Version (2001), New International Version (1978), Today's New International Version (2005), The Message (2002), Revised Standard Version (1952), New Jerusalem Bible.

5. Letty Russell, *The Future of Partnership* (Philadelphia: Westminster, 1979). He also identified a number of negative connotations of the word "partner."

the Corinthians where Paul develops his clearest ecclesiology. One biblical scholar, in 1934, claimed that *koinonia* was "*l'idée maitresse de toute l'épitre*" (the overarching idea of the epistle).[6] The foundation of Paul's call to love and order in the church is *koinonia* with Christ (1 Cor 1:13-17).

Because of his certainty of their union with Christ, Paul encourages the church to practice gratitude and praise, in spite of their own chaos. He longs to be a co-partner (*sun-koinonos*) with them in the gospel (1 Cor 9:23). A union between Christ and the believer leads to partnership with one another. The emphasis is upon the shared benefits of the gospel, with Paul and all believers as equals.

In 2 Cor 8:4, we see the first employment of *koinonia* in reference to the financial generosity of the collection for the church in Jerusalem. Because the believers are in spiritual union with Christ and with one another, Paul invites them to share in the material needs of the church in Jerusalem. This occurred during a time of great famine that happened in the reign of Claudius.

The first mention of the collection appears in 1 Cor 16:1-4, where Paul gives the Corinthians directions on how it should be made. The project had been introduced earlier and the Corinthian church had seemingly written a letter to Paul asking questions. The church was asked to appoint representatives to take the collection to Jerusalem along with letters of recommendation. According to 2 Cor 9:2, the Corinthians responded initially with zeal but then seemed to regress.

A significant portion of 2 Corinthians (chs. 8 and 9) is devoted to instruction about the collection project. It was important that Corinth make a strong statement regarding the collection. It would not only be a statement of material help, but would also demonstrate Paul's apostolic authority, both in Corinth and Jerusalem, bridging Jewish and Gentile believers. Using gentle but firm words, he seeks to inspire the congregation to complete a task they have begun. He had already expressed his confidence in their earnestness (2 Cor 7:14-16).

He then speaks of the generosity of the Macedonian churches, an example to follow (2 Cor 8:1-7). Their generosity is born out of the grace of God and the testimony thereof (v. 1). The divine grace given to the Macedonian church flowed through them to the church in Jerusalem.[7] The Macedonian *koinonia* took place in the midst of their own poverty

---

6. Quoted in John Michael McDermott, "The Biblical Doctrine of Koinonia, Part II," *Biblische Zeitschrift* 19 (1975): 79.

7. See F. F. Bruce, *1 and 2 Corinthians*, New Century Bible Commentary (Grand Rapids: Eerdmans, 1971), 220.

and hardship,[8] due in part to the exploitation by their Roman conquerors, to the civil wars and the reality of persecution (1 Thess 2:14). Despite the Macedonians' deep afflictions, joy and poverty combined in the life of the believer, which led to an abundance of generosity in *koinonia*.

For Paul, the Macedonians surpassed the basic rule of sharing their resources in proportion to their financial ability. They exceeded their ability. And they gave of their own free will. Such is the mark of Christ followers (2 Cor 8:5). They begged Paul for the privilege of participating in the collection for Jerusalem. Their *koinonia* was not a passive sense of camaraderie but rather a strong act of sharing material possessions, proof of true Christian partnership.

The word used to describe the collection, *diakonia*, carried a connotation of waiting on tables and providing for sustenance. In this regard, *koinonia* and *diaconia* converge to provide for the suffering brothers and sisters in Jerusalem. Giving first to the Lord, then giving money to others, demonstrated that there was no dichotomy. Service to God and to those in need are part of Christian obedience. So the Macedonians gave themselves first to Christ, then to Paul and his team, and to those members of their community set apart for Paul's service in the work of spreading the gospel.

Paul urged Titus to go to Corinth and complete the collection that he had initiated (2 Cor 8:5). He employs the example of Jesus, who, though he was rich, became poor for the sake of the Corinthians (2 Cor 8:9), so they might become rich through his poverty.

In Christ's incarnation, *kenosis* (Phil 2:5-8), he placed himself in a position of equality with human beings so that they might share in his mercy. Such self-sacrifice incites faithful obedience for the recipients of Christ's mercy because they have received a gift that they cannot repay.

Paul's use of the incarnation in the context of the collection is clear. The Corinthians are materially rich, just as Christ was divinely rich. They should follow in his footsteps. The logical conclusion, basing the collection on the model of the incarnation, should lead to self-sacrificial action, not out of obligation.

Paul refused to issue an order (2 Cor 8:8) for fear that it would remove the spontaneity that he was trying to stir up. The collection would be proof of their love. He wants to avoid any unnecessary perception of coercion. His sole goal is to honor God and demonstrate a willingness to partner with the church in Jerusalem. Therefore, Paul urges them to complete what

---

8. See 1 Thess 1:6; 2:14-16; 3:3-7; Phil 1:28-30; Acts 16:20-24.

they had started, their desire to do so having already been present. He encourages them to give in proportion to their wealth (2 Cor 8:12).

Then comes the guiding principle of equity in partnership: not contributing so much that they would be left in distress, while the Judeans would live in laziness or luxury (2 Cor 8:13–15). Equality plays on two levels: material equality, whereby the needs in Jerusalem would be met by the abundance of the Corinthians' contributions; and spiritual equality, through the realization of the abundance of God's grace towards them.[9] The collection should lead to "equality" among the churches, not that this is the purpose of the collection. But a certain "realignment" among the churches was important. This balance had been disrupted because, although there is abundance in Corinth, there is need in the church of Jerusalem.

Paul suggests that the abundance of the Corinthians and other gentile churches should make up for the needs of the Jerusalem congregation, thereby reestablishing the balance of equality among the churches. But Paul also speaks of how an abundance in the Jerusalem church can supply the need of the church in Corinth. "If you do this . . . ," we can hear him say, "your abundance is applied to their need and their abundance is applied to your need; there will be equality." Thereby, the gentiles meet the economic need of the church in Jerusalem, whereas the Jerusalem church meets the spiritual need of the gentile churches.[10]

Herein lies the principle of mutuality in partnership: a double equalization process, whereby the deficiency of one was met by the abundance of the other, and vice versa. Corinthian abundance is in giving to the church in Jerusalem, while being deficient in fully grasping the grace of God in Christ. The Jerusalem abundance was their spiritual richness, understanding their blessing in Christ, but their deficiency was brought on by the circumstances of the famine and their material poverty. The invitation is for sharing in the needs of the poor, bringing relief from the burden of want or famine. The Corinthians should give to the poor in Jerusalem, and in the same way, the Jerusalem church should share their spiritual wealth with the church in Corinth.

Regrettably, little is known of the Corinthian response to Paul's invitation to partnership. Much later, in a letter to the Corinthians written by Clement of Rome in AD 96, Clement makes mention of their past

---

9. See Rom 15:27.

10. Frank J. Matera, *II Corinthians: A Commentary*, New Testament Library (Louisville: Westminster John Knox, 2003), 193.

generosity: "You had no regrets when you have been charitable, being ready for any good deed."[11] This may be an allusion to Paul's call to make a substantial contribution to the needy brethren in Jerusalem.

In his treatise on economic *koinonia*, Lindy Scott outlines nine lessons from this act of solidarity:

1. The primary motivation for Christians to share is the fact that Jesus first shared the spiritual riches with them.
2. Subjectively, Christians should share according to their financial ability. The important statistic is not the total amount but the amount given compared to the total amount available.
3. Objectively, economic *koinonia* should flow from richer believers to poor, wherever believers do not have the necessities of life.
4. Economic *koinonia* is not to be confined only locally, but extended globally.
5. Economic *koinonia* is an expression of God's grace flowing through his body and visible evidence of the love among Christians.
6. The sharing of material possessions should be totally voluntary, not commanded or enforced.
7. Christians should eagerly seek out those who need their support.
8. Relief of material needs is not divorced from devotion to God, the former being an expression of the latter.
9. Economic *koinonia* often involves one's presence as well as one's presents.[12]

Paul's ultimate focus is God. He will cause growth and transformation in the life of the church. In addition to supplying the needs of others, their partnership will result in thanksgiving: First, the Corinthians will praise God for the chance to partner. Second, those in Jerusalem will praise God because of the favor he has shown through the Corinthians. And third, thanks to God for the gift of salvation. In sum, participation in the collection for the church in Jerusalem results in a profound union between the churches in Corinth and Jerusalem.

---

11. Quoted in Lindy Scott, *Economic Koinonia within the Body of Christ* (Mexico City: Kyrios, 1976), 132.
12. Scott, *Economic Koinonia*, 136–39.

The collection is a test of the character of the Corinthians. Do they fully grasp the implications of the gospel they confess? This is the gospel, uniting Jews and gentiles, rich and poor, west and east, north and south.

By responding generously, the Corinthians would establish their obedience to the gospel and their partnership, or *koinonia*, with the believers in Jerusalem. And the believers in Jerusalem would reciprocate because of the grace of God demonstrated through their generosity.

For Paul, the collection is God's work. It was God's grace at work that led them to extraordinary generosity. Now he tells them that the same grace will enrich them so that they can give generously as well. This generosity will in turn lead others to praising God. From start to finish, the partnership, or *koinonia*, is God's work, beginning with his grace and ending in thanksgiving to him.

Although these two chapters (2 Cor 8–9) are an appeal for money, they also provide a theology of partnership, rooted in the grace of God revealed in Jesus Christ, which allows and empowers people to be generous with each other.

As we partner with churches in global discipleship, we would do well to model and encourage the principles of *koinonia* from the apostle Paul and the church in Corinth. We invite churches to join in serving and giving for the sake of their brothers and sisters in the global South. And, as we live out *koinonia*, giving and receiving, not just financial resources but gifts of grace and faith.

Rethinking "Church and University"

A Call for Christ-Centered Formative Education

L. GREGORY JONES

FORTY YEARS CAN BE forever, or it can pass by in a blur. For the Israelites in the wilderness, it seemed like forever. A thirty-nine-year-old adult Israelite in the wilderness would never have known home, even a home of oppression and slavery. It must have seemed as if they had been navigating wilderness forever.

Yet in the grand sweep of the world, forty years is a blur. It is a mere blip in the history of the cosmos, barely enough time for a sequoia to begin to grow towards its majesty. In the span of a life, forty years can seem like yesterday.

It was forty years ago that Alasdair MacIntyre published *After Virtue*.[1] It was a book that rattled the conventions of moral philosophy and theology. It seems like MacIntyre's argument, and his emphasis on themes like traditions, virtues, narratives, and practices, has been around forever. Such themes have influenced the thinking, teaching, and writing of Jonathan Wilson over the course of his distinguished vocation.

Yet it seems like a blur since Jonathan and I first met almost four decades ago and began discussing MacIntyre, Hauerwas, and the shape of Christian theology and ethics. Jonathan and I forged a lasting friendship as we wrestled with important ideas and shared commitments. The time has flown by since we were beginning to imagine our vocations as

---

1. Alasdair MacIntyre, *After Virtue* (South Bend, IN: University of Notre Dame Press, 1981).

Christian scholars who wanted to serve both the church and the university. It feels like I have known Jonathan forever.

Almost four decades ago Jonathan found himself drawn to the work of Julian Hartt, an exemplary but too often neglected scholar who had embodied a Christian scholarly vocation in the university. He sought as his dissertation advisor Thomas A. Langford Jr., who embodied a similar vocation at Duke. I have learned much from Jonathan's early work with Tom Langford as they reflected together on Julian Hartt's life and legacy, including Hartt's important book *Theology and the Church in the University*.[2]

Hartt's life and work represent an admirable witness of how Christian scholars can make a difference in universities, whether in formerly "Christian" universities such as Yale or public ones such as the University of Virginia, as does Langford's life and work at the ambiguously "Methodist" context of Duke where Jonathan and I met.

Yet the frameworks in which Hartt and Langford lived and navigated now seem as if they come from a different world that disappeared a very long time ago. It seems like forever since words like "church," "university," and even the "and" between them could be used as if we would know what we are talking about.

Four decades since Jonathan and I first met, I wish we could start again in graduate school to revisit the question of what it means for Christians to form and be formed by a life of learning and a desire for God, and what kinds of institutions can do that most faithfully and effectively. I suspect in the 2020s Jonathan and I would think of MacIntyre's famous opening pages as less "extreme" and more a foretaste of the fragmented world in which we now live—or perhaps simply as an accurate description.

Jonathan has devoted much of his life to cultivating Christian wisdom about the times in which we live—as a scholar, a teacher, a pastor, and a guide. Taking Jonathan's own life and legacy as a touchstone, I want to revisit the phrase "church and university" to suggest ways Christians can navigate our current wilderness in faithful and fruitful ways. I don't know how long the current wilderness will last. Yet the call to focus on the promised land could not be more urgent.

---

2. Julian N. Hartt, *Theology and the Church in the University* (Philadelphia: Westminster, 1969).

Rethinking "Church and University"

The great Czech playwright, activist, and statesman Vaclav Havel offers a vivid metaphor for the era in which he lived, a metaphor that has continuing relevance for us. Rather than the wilderness or MacIntyre's fragments, Havel describes us as living in the "rubble" of modernity. Writing more than two decades ago, in 1994, Havel writes,

> I think there are good reasons for suggesting that the modern age has ended. Today, many things indicate that we are going through a transitional period, when it seems that something is on the way out and something else is painfully being born. It is as if something were crumbling, decaying and exhausting itself—while something else, still indistinct, were rising from the rubble.[3]

Writing in 2021, it feels indeed as if we are living in rubble, and it is still hard to imagine what might be rising from it. Yet Jonathan Wilson's life and legacy offer us an imagination for rethinking university, church, as well as the "and" that we have so often taken for granted. I will take each word in turn.

University

Jonathan and I have spent our adult lives in a variety of academic institutions, from the more established to those more on the edges. When we first met at Duke, Jonathan was coming from Regent College in Vancouver, a school that now seems established but that began as a creative experiment and continues to offer insights and practices for Christians around the world.[4] Over the years, he has taught at a variety of Christian institutions of theological education, ranging from the more established Westmont College to Acadia Divinity College and his alma mater Regent itself. He has also been a lecturer and advisor to institutions around the world.

---

3. Vaclav Havel, "The Need for Transcendence in the Postmodern World," delivered in Independence Hall, Philadelphia, July 4, 1994, http://www.worldtrans.org/whole/havelspeech.html.

4. For an instructive history of Regent and its role in creating a new model of "Christian study centers" around the United States, see Charles Cotherman, *To Think Christianly: A History of L'Abri, Regent College, and the Christian Study Center Movement* (Downers Grove, IL: IVP Academic, 2020).

As Jonathan's experience attests, we are in a time where new experiments are needed for Christian learning around the world. Forty years ago, the term "university" seemed so natural and well-established that we assumed we knew what we were talking about. It had a coherence, even a permanence, that most people took for granted. Some prescient leaders like James Houston at Regent anticipated the crumbling of modernity, and even the fragility of well-endowed and long-established universities such as Oxford and Cambridge, Harvard and Yale, as well as more recent places like Duke. But those of us who have lived inside such institutions have felt the crumbling even as these institutions have been able to mask the crumbling with large endowments and the weightiness of history (especially those that have existed for centuries). Yet the crumbling has only intensified in the wake of the multiple pandemics of 2020 and 2021.

Not everything is doom and gloom. Elite universities will continue to exist, and some even thrive, in the midst of the rubble. But people are beginning to ask not only about purpose—"What is a university for?"—but, more fundamentally, about identity—"What is a university?" To be sure, issues about "purpose" have become more relevant as people have been questioning the cost of higher education, the growing problems of student debt, and issues about whether students are actually being educated either for character and wisdom on the one hand, or for skills needed for jobs on the other.

But the deeper questions about identity are also being pressed as new models and ventures have been launched to great fanfare and some success. The variety of institutions providing education has multiplied in recent years, as have the modalities of their pedagogies. Even institutions with hefty endowments find themselves struggling with business models that seem increasingly outdated and unsustainable.

What counts as a university? Harvard has been the model for modern higher education, especially in the United States, but what does that mean for a small Christian college, a regional public institution, or a flagship state institution that now receives less than 10 percent of its funding from public sources? How do institutions like Southern New Hampshire University, Western Governors University, or Minerva fit into the landscape? As small schools struggle to survive, do they have a viable future?

The challenges include broken business models, dysfunctional accreditation processes and regulations, and growing distrust in the industry and between faculty and administrators. They also include questions about the role of technology in teaching and learning, the relationship between conveying information and developing skills, and whether classical notions of truth, goodness, and beauty have a place in the contemporary university.

Questions of a university's purpose offer opportunities for Christians in higher education and for Christian institutions, even if the landscapes have changed rather dramatically in recent decades. But the deeper identity questions about universities suggest the need to reassess Christian engagement with higher education more generally. Universities have existed for a millennium, and Christian emphases on formative education go back to the early church and to Israel before Christ. We have a large stake in universities as we go forward, but not necessarily much of a stake in the "modern" version of universities. Christians are well positioned to lead the way in new forms rising from the rubble of modernity.

Church

Forty years ago, when Jonathan and I were beginning our theological and academic vocations, the "church" seemed relatively stable. To be sure, there was the perpetual problem of the disunity of the church understood at a global level, but "denominations" within Protestantism and orders within Catholicism all seemed relatively stable—even if rarely in conversation with each other. The "church" in discussions of the church and the university was typically meant to refer to denominations and their relative commitments to colleges and universities they had founded. Even some of the new experiments on the edges such as Regent College were strongly connected to a denominational movement (in its case, the Christian Brethren).

Most mainline denominations had already loosened their ties with stronger institutions, even as more evangelical denominations began to clutch on to theirs more closely. The secularization of higher education was becoming a broader topic in the 1990s, prompted especially by major books by leading scholars such as George Marsden's *The Soul of the American University* and James Tunstead Burtchaell's *The Dying of the Light*.[5]

---

5. George Marsden, *The Soul of the American University: From Protestant Establishment to Established Nonbelief* (Oxford, UK: Oxford University Press, 1994); James Tunstead Burtchaell, *The Dying of the Light: The Disengagement of Colleges and Universities from Their Christian Churches* (Grand Rapids: Eerdmans, 1998). A broader account of forces in higher education that led to secularization, and a valorization of

Yet much of the conversation presumed greater stability about the existence of denominations as sponsors of higher education than would be warranted over the next two decades. Now, it is very difficult to know even how to think about Christian engagement with higher education given the weakening of denominations (mainline and otherwise), the rise of megachurches, the emergence of nondenominational congregations and networks, and internal fights within Roman Catholicism. Many "church-affiliated" or "Christian" institutions have had to seek new sources of funding to replace what once had been provided by denominations and sponsoring congregations.

Church-based institutions have increasingly rebranded themselves in distinction from the denominations and churches that founded them, whether doing so through formal separation or informal messaging. For example, Duke University remains formally a United Methodist university, but it means very little outside of its ties to its Divinity School and to a lesser extent Duke Chapel. Many institutions have formally severed their ties with their founding bodies, including especially colleges and universities that had been affiliated with the Southern Baptist Convention prior to its split.

The problem of "church" is increasingly compounded by the brand damage to the term "Christian" in the United States in recent years. This damage has been caused both by moral failures of church leaders and the increasing co-opting of "Christian" frames in partisan politics on both the far left and the far right.

Christ-centered people will continue to congregate in communities that shape and form us for discipleship and enable us to worship the triune God. But they will likely have networks and patterns very different than those developed in modernity. Again, there are significant opportunities for us, but just relying on denominations and the term "Christian" would distract us from the opportunities.

The world has changed significantly in forty years.

---

the "research university" in general, is found in Julie A. Reuben's instructive book *The Making of the Modern University: Intellectual Transformation and the Marginalization of Morality* (Chicago: University of Chicago Press, 1996).

And

There is much to commend the use of the word "and" as an alternative to "or." It suggests that there is room for connection rather than opposition, and that connection will likely be beneficial for both entities being linked. In recent years we have seen a flourishing of those "and" connections: faith and work, faith and leadership, the church and the university, faith and learning, the church and business, and the list goes on.

Yet even in stable times, the "and" suggests coherent entities that are being linked together, rather than mutually implicating engagements that depend on as well as provide deeper interconnections. From this perspective, we do better to think less of "and" relationships and more of "faith-animating" relationships or "Christ-centered" implications.

This would be true in any time. In a world where terms such as university and church are undergoing significant questioning and the institutions to which they refer are in significant need of repair, innovation, and new experiments, we can no longer afford to continue conversations as if the world remains similar to where it was in 1981, much less in the middle decades of the twentieth century.

Whither, then, conversations about Christians in higher education?

A New Calling: Christ-Centered Formative Education

An underlying problem of the assumptions about "the church and the university" over the last century is that we have too often lived and acted as what Stanley Hauerwas and Will Willimon identified in the 1980s called "practical atheists."[6] Charles Taylor later broadened this diagnosis in *A Secular Age*. At the heart of Taylor's diagnosis is that, whereas at the beginning of modernity everybody assumed there was a God (so "atheists" were more likely deists), at the end of modernity everybody—including religious people—lives and acts as if there is no God.[7] If we are to take into account all that has changed institutionally in universities, churches, and denominations, we also need to take broader account of the failures of Christians to live and act as if God continues to be active in the world, in institutions, and in our lives.

---

6. Stanley Hauerwas and William Willimon, *Resident Aliens: Life in the Christian Colony* (Nashville: Abingdon, 1989).

7. Charles Taylor, *A Secular Age* (Cambridge, MA: Harvard University Press, 2007).

As Christians navigate the complicated new terrain that we find ourselves on in the 2020s, I suggest that we need to focus our attention on Christ-centered formative education. The term "Christ-centered" is a way to move us away from terms that are more easily capable of being domesticated into "this-worldly" terms and focus on vocation, institutions, and witness in relation to the God who continues to redeem us, institutions, and the world through Christ by the power of the Holy Spirit. As I use the term, being "Christ-centered" presumes that we are centering our lives in the One whom God raised from the dead. It also conveys a presumption that the Holy Spirit is at work in the world, and in human life, "making all things new" by conforming us to Christ—the One in whom, as John 1 and Col 1 illumine, the creation came to be.

What would Christ-centered formative education entail? I briefly outline three dimensions to which we ought to devote our attention, resources, and focus.

First, we need to invest in those colleges and universities that still have an identifiably Christian identity and focus as "Christ-centered institutions." These have significant potential for the future, especially as institutions that show how and why a coherent faith-animated orientation provides coherence and the centrality of truth, beauty, and goodness for our world and formative education of students. Such institutions, especially universities that have sufficient diversity of vocations and areas of study, can offer creative solutions to endemic problems and offer a renewed vision of life abundant.

Second, there is an important role for Christian witness in secular contexts, both through "study centers" and individual scholarly and pedagogical leadership. The Christian study center movement has offered important networks and visibility for Christ-centered scholarship across diverse disciplines and important settings for vocational discernment and Christ-centered formative education. Too often Christians have underemphasized the importance of institutions and networks, yet institutions and networks were central to the spread of early Christianity—especially empowered by a sense of "Easter hope" and "Pentecostal power." Individual Christian scholars, particularly those who are influential in particular disciplines, such as Francis Collins or John Polkinghorne in the sciences, or George Marsden in history, or John Witte in law, or Sarah Coakley in theology, can have a powerful witness in the broader secular academy.

Third, this is a time for Christians to prioritize new experiments—sometimes at a bold scale—to offer new possibilities for formative education. This is as important for K-12 education as for higher education and professional education more generally. What would a Christ-centered Western Governors University look like? A Christ-centered Khan Academy? Something not yet even imagined?

The spread of early Christianity was significantly dependent on innovative commitments to new institutions, new networks, and new patterns of formative education. Those innovative commitments were quite surprising to the Greco-Roman world, and enabled Christians to provide leadership in education, in health care, and in the major intellectual debates of the day.[8]

This suggests that Christian leaders, intellectuals, and donors will need to develop new wineskins for the new wine which God is preparing for us. If we continue to use old wineskins, and prepare for 1950 in case it ever returns, we will likely see Christ-centered influence diminish significantly in higher education, in Christian communities, and in broader cultures and the world.

We can't afford to live as practical atheists anymore, or to prepare for a world that no longer exists. Forty years may seem like yesterday as well as forever ago, yet we are called to focus on the promised land of God's reign. Jonathan Wilson's life and legacy offer a faithful witness from which we ought to learn as we imagine a bold future for Christ-centered leadership and discernment.

---

8. See C. Kavin Rowe, *Christianity's Surprise: A Sure and Certain Hope* (Nashville: Abingdon, 2020), for an illuminating overview of the power of Christianity's "surprise" and its innovative experiments and impact.

Equipping the Saints

Marilyn McEntyre

And he gave the apostles, the prophets, the evangelists, the shepherds and teachers, to equip the saints for the work of ministry, for building up the body of Christ, until we all attain to the unity of the faith and of the knowledge of the Son of God, to mature manhood, to the measure of the stature of the fullness of Christ.

—EPH 4:11–13[1]

STANDING AT A PULPIT or a podium or on a stage with a microphone, those of us who preach or teach have probably wondered at least for a fleeting moment, "What am I doing here?" There are a lot of ways to answer that question. They're all verbs: inviting, challenging, testifying, guiding, directing, correcting, modeling, inspiring, reminding, reframing. Or, more boldly, prophesying, unveiling, awakening. Comforting and afflicting. And we are equipping the saints.

"Equipping" is a rich way to think about the work we've been called to. "Equip" comes from an Old Norse term that meant to fit out or load a ship. Load up for the journey. Put in supplies. You equip the crew by giving them what they need: food, goods to sell, emergency equipment,

---

1. This chapter uses the ESV translation for Scripture references, unless otherwise indicated.

navigational instruments, weapons, maps. Basic necessities. To do that, if you're the quartermaster, you have to know what *is* necessary. You have to know something about the route and weather patterns, about storage space and the shelf life of each provision; and, if you're wise, something about the crew itself—their appetites, allergies, perhaps, age and strength and temperament and training. You have to know what specific dangers they might encounter—who might attack them (pirates? A great white whale?) on the high seas. They need maps and instruments and rules of conduct, emergency training and a common language. And stories and music and a few quiet spaces.

The metaphor of outfitting a ship for its voyage opens a wide avenue of reflection on the work we have done, and continue to do as preachers, teachers, liturgists, scholars, and writers who have at some point said to God, "Here am I. Send me." It raises questions: if our work is to equip others for their journeys, what food will nourish them? What maps may help them? What creature comforts will sustain their spirits? What hardships must we help them anticipate? And what do we know about the conditions of the journeys that lie ahead of them? What do the saints need now? And what do we, who stand with them in the need of prayer, need in order to sustain clarity and kindness as we try to stay faithful to our calling?

The list might be very long. Or short: what the "saints" need, and what we need, might be easily summarized by the deep truth that we need the love of God and neighbor, grace and mercy, guidance and hope. But each September as the beginning of the school year rolls around and I prepare for classes, or when I talk with pastors preparing for a new season of preaching or Bible study, the question arises with a certain urgency: what do the students need now, in this season of their lives, amid the urgencies of this particular historical moment? The people in the pews? The adults saying yes in midlife to a new direction or vocation? How can we equip them for their journeys?

What follows is my "quartermaster's" list—those things I hope we can offer them as we try to deepen our own receptivity to the voice of the Spirit who has called us to this work, knowing we can't give what we haven't first received.

They Need Comfort

It's a dark time. Deep political division; unchecked lies, misinformation and disinformation; the brutalities of late-stage predatory capitalism; war-making with weapons that wreak lasting destruction on soil and infrastructures, food systems and families; polluted oceans and parched land and melting ice caps are a lot to take in at any age. Young people in particular need some assurance that life on this planet, as swiftly as it may change, and as starkly, is worth living. Suicide is the second leading cause of death among people ages ten to thirty-four. The false comforts of glib euphemism or denial or cheap optimism are ineffectual and temporary. They blow away in the first wind like dandelion seeds. This is no time for mere cheerful admonishments or sentimentalities about hope that a new day will dawn. It's a time to offer the deep comfort of real hope—the kind of hope that has the courage to learn what we may not want to know and that is inseparable from a longing for justice. Real hope is scandalously particular: it has not only to do with believing in the new Jerusalem, but also with supporting viable peacemaking in the present one; not only with the many mansions that await us, but also with transitional housing for those living on the streets they travel daily.

The saints need the comfort of authentic community and need to know how to foster and sustain it as they rise to the daily challenges they face—shopping for food with an overstretched budget; ministering to a child with special needs; bearing the unbearable sorrow of unreachable relatives in Gaza or Guatemala or in detention centers. They need to be gathered and held, at least for a time, in a shared space—a fold—where a strong gate protects them while they lay their burdens down. They need hymns and cohousing and shared meals and Sabbath gatherings.

When Baby Suggs, the aging preacher-prophet in Toni Morrison's remarkable novel *Beloved*, goes to the woods for a "calling"—a revival meeting in the truest sense—those who, with her help, have crossed the river and escaped enslavement come with her as a grateful, sorrowful congregation in deep need of comfort and healing. What is surprising and memorable about the comfort she offers is that it comes not in soothing words of reassurance, but in forceful imperatives: "Let the children come! . . . Let your mothers hear you laugh! . . . Let the grown men come! . . . Let your wives and children see you dance!" And then to the women, "'Cry,' she told them, 'for the living and the dead. Just cry.' And the women let loose." What happens as she calls them is a remarkable testimony to what comfort looks like in a beloved community:

> It started that way: laughing children, dancing men, crying women and then it got mixed up. Women stopped crying and danced; men sat down and cried; children danced, women laughed, children cried until, exhausted and riven, all and each lay about the clearing damp and gasping for breath. In the silence that followed, Baby Suggs, holy, offered up to them her great big heart.[2]

In that clearing in the woods—a space made sacred by Baby Suggs's prayer—her suffering people enter into the great hospitality and permission of divine grace offered not as doctrine, but as invitation and command, a little like Jesus's life-changing imperatives: Rise up. Take up your bed. Go your way. Come forth. The deep reassurance of these restorative moments—the comfort they offer the afflicted—comes almost as admonishment, and admonishment as empowerment.

They Need Protection

"Hide me in the shadow of your wings," the psalmist writes, "from the wicked who do me violence, my deadly enemies who surround me" (Ps 17:8–9) and repeatedly, "Evildoers assail me." They still do. Many among us are victims of domestic violence or mass shootings; of state-sponsored terrorism or inhumane policies or insidious propaganda. We have all become "target markets" in this era of "late-stage predatory capitalism," and targets of nearly constant electronic surveillance. Some need protection from racist police violence. Some need the literal protection of sheltering church buildings like Mouhamed Soumah who lived in sanctuary in a Quaker meeting house for two years under threat of deportation or Vicky Chavez who lived with her two daughters inside a Unitarian Church for more than three years. Some need to be hidden in homes. Many others need pro bono legal representation. Or the protection teachers and professors provide by equipping students with deep understanding of how the law works, how to discern reliable faith testimony, how to make sound arguments, how to recognize manipulation and falsehoods. How to read in ways that protect them particularly from the dangerous misreadings that have turned the living word into a lethal weapon.

2. Toni Morison, *Beloved* (New York: Knopf, 2006), 104.

They Need Biblical Literacy

They need theologians and readers of the biblical texts who refuse oversimplifications and poor translations, who can not only tolerate ambiguity but also welcome it as a humbling reminder of mystery and the limits of human reason. They need to *be* those readers. They need tour guides to take them on the six-thousand-year journey through texts that are ancient and alien, filtered and refracted through translations that are not all equally accurate. They need to be equipped to see through flat-footed literalism and anachronistic misreadings. There need to be some among us who can read Greek, Hebrew, and Aramaic and share the fruits of that language study, knowing where a translator's word choice may make the difference between confusion and a precious moment of insight. They need to be invited again and again into Scripture as a hospitable space for reflection that transcends our own parochialism and prejudice and frees us from contemporary bias so that we may enter a place where the voice of God can still be heard in the wilderness and where we finally meet the "word within a word, unable to speak a word" whose native language is silence. They need to be helped to dwell without anxiety in the tensions between stories of tribal warfare and the call to be peacemakers and to think historically, critically, and resiliently about how the great story of salvation is refracted through human consciousness like light through a prism. They need some understanding of how the Bible intersects and coexists with other sacred texts—the Koran, in particular these days, as Muslims are maligned and persecuted, and the Talmud. They need to be equipped to read like serpents and live like doves.

They Need Good Reading

They need us to teach it and practice it, model it and encourage it. They need reading groups and poetry workshops where a few may pause together over a word or phrase and ponder its facets and possibilities. They need to be amazed by the power and pervasiveness and consequence of metaphor—to recognize it all around us—the militaristic metaphors in medicine, the paternalistic metaphors in political propaganda, the ways metaphor can soften and sentimentalize where we need a sharp critical eye or can direct fierce attention to what might have been buried in abstraction. They need to notice when a word choice may change our fundamental understanding of how things happen—what difference it makes to say, for instance, "Those who had been enslaved regained their freedom," rather than "The slaves were freed." They need, as Ezra Pound put it, to "go in fear of abstractions,"[3] seeking and insisting on the accountability of concrete particulars, resisting words like "development" or "security" or "philanthropic" until their applied meaning and implications are explored. They need us to equip them with reading skills and practices that help them notice how techniques serve purposes and help them cultivate the patience to pay attention to techniques. Not only in classrooms, but in the pews, they need to hear good reading—slow, clearly enunciated words read with the kind of comprehension that honors the importance of musicality to meaning. Sentences that do their work with elegance and economy and emotional nuance and surprise, clarifying or illustrating or introducing or summarizing. They need the critical tools that will help them read poetry differently from prophecy or myth or history or open letters (or emails or headlines or op-eds). They need to be helped to widen the range of their curiosities so as to widen their capacity for engagement with the world around them—to be authorized and enabled to read a critique of legislative process or an explanation of the fallacies of the "free market" economy or an analysis of factors contributing to climate change.

They Need Scientific Literacy

We all do. That's the point. People in pews and classrooms, even if they failed—or never took—geology or biology or chemistry need to understand basic science as a part of our call to be stewards of this precious planet—as the Book of Common Prayer so beautifully puts it, "this fragile earth, our island home."[4] Ignorance about pesticides or pharmaceuticals or about the way a virus works, and a vaccine, when information is available and accessible, becomes culpable at some point in adults who vote and buy and have opinions in public. Pastors and English teachers and lay leaders who come to church after a week of managing a beauty salon may not see science education as their calling, but Paul's admonishment to the Thessalonians to "encourage one another and build one another

3. Ezra Pound, "A Few Don'ts by an Imaginiste," *Poetry: A Magazine of Verse* (Mar. 1913): 200–206, esp. 201.

4. "Eucharistic Prayer C," in Episcopal Church, *The Book of Common Prayer and Administration of the Sacraments and Other Rites and Ceremonies of the Church: Together with The Psalter or Psalms of David* (New York: Seabury, 1977), 70.

up" (1 Thess 5:11) surely includes equipping one another to live in the world responsibly and generously, using and sharing its resources wisely and knowing something about how, exactly, to care for the widow and the orphan if the widow lives in a food desert with no car and the orphan is living where the water is laced with lead. The saints are also citizens, inhabitants of "two cities." As responsible citizenship requires participation, participation requires reliable information. So those of us who lead in faith communities need to help equip others to make informed decisions about things that for many make the difference between life and death.

Minimal scientific literacy doesn't require a course or a textbook or even a subscription to the *Smithsonian*. It requires leaders and teachers who can simplify without dumbing down—who can devise homely analogies and memorable object lessons, and who can help show how knowing some science can make us more effective at loving one another as we decide what's in the food basket we deliver or when to speak up at a city council meeting about sewers.

And as we come to terms with our own need for enough scientific literacy to equip others with needful awareness, we also need to be willing to call out and identify pseudoscience, so often practiced in the service of profitable lies, and to correct misinformation and disinformation where we can.

They Need Correction

Sometimes people are just wrong. All the good-willed nonviolent communication in the world won't make a falsehood into a truth or neutralize racial invective or excuse abuse. Sometimes what can be forgiven should still not be excused. I was edified years ago, when I attended Quaker meetings for a time, to discover that Quaker meetings have a "committee on admonishment." These are usually elders, designated to notice where harm is being done within the community and take aside those doing it and help them correct course and make amends. It takes a certain courage these days to correct, since tolerance and inclusiveness are so urgently needed as correctives to intolerance and exclusion. For some of us the hardest challenge of leadership is finding the courage to correct. But Paul makes it clear—again to the Thessalonians—that elders and leaders and teachers should "admonish the idle" (1 Thess 5:14) and to the Corinthians he writes tenderly, "I do not write these things to make you ashamed, but to admonish you as my beloved children" (1 Cor 4:14).

If we are to equip the saints to grow in faith and grace, we need to pray in real humility for the grace to admonish with both courage and tenderness where we see wrongdoing. It's hard to do this without self-righteousness, or at least the appearance of it. It's as necessary as it is hard. Uncorrected, dogs bite and children bully and adults can do great and lasting harm.

I was well into adulthood before I realized that meekness and gentleness and respect for elders didn't entitle me to be silent in the face of wrongdoing and that there are times when neutrality is complicity. I had to learn to complain, trying to complain in the right places, to people who could change policy or correct an injustice. Challenging a colleague's unfair practices or wanton ineptitude isn't as rewarding as other forms of pastoral care, but occasionally just as necessary. That said, though, it can only rightly be done if the background music to the confrontation scene is the hum and beat of prayer that continues without ceasing.

They Need Prayer

We all do, of course. And we need to keep learning to pray and sharing that learning and praying—grace before meals, breath prayers as we enter the lecture hall or sanctuary, public prayers that bless our gatherings, deep silent prayers on wakeful nights, prayers at the bedsides of the dying and over newborn children and prayers as we watch news from war zones we can hardly bear to witness. To equip the saints is to pray for them without ceasing, lifting them up as they come to mind in the course of an ordinary day and setting aside time for focused intercession.

We are entrusted to one another, and they to us in a particular way by calling. To equip them is to live for them, to open our hearts and homes to them, to ground them and engage them and encourage them and gather them, to pray for them and with them, and finally, as we raise our bowed heads and recognize in every face the radiance of Christ-light, to give them reason to rejoice.

Celebration

Dalit Christian Theology

Chandra Mallampalli

Having Jonathan Wilson as a friend and colleague at Westmont College is one of the most treasured experiences of my adult life. He possesses a rare combination of personal warmth, intellectual curiosity and depth, and concern for the poor and marginalized. I recall our lengthy conversations about the state of the church, our nation, and academia. It was refreshing to converse with someone who still believed that we needed to take the teachings of Jesus seriously—indeed, that God expects us to put them into practice, both in our daily lives and in the way we engage and influence our national culture. For too long, Christians have imbibed the realist paradigm extolled by theologians like Reinhold Niebuhr, which essentially confines "gospel virtues" to the realm of interpersonal ethics, while validating the militarism and greed that drives American society as mere expressions of the inherent selfishness of nations. I miss those conversations. Jonathan's voice finds particular relevance today in light of the rise of Christian nationalism in America and the support Evangelicals are extending to some of the most reprehensible politics in our nation's history.

As I considered how best to honor Jonathan in this Festschrift, I decided to submit an essay arising from my own specialization in the history of Christianity in India. This essay concerns the plight of India's Dalits (formerly known as "untouchables"). Dalits (which literally means "broken," "crushed," or "oppressed") are those who occupy the lowest and most menial occupations in Indian society and have suffered a long history of abuse, exploitation, and discrimination. Many converted to Christianity in hopes of escaping the stigma of untouchability and finding greater acceptance and self-dignity. Dalit Christians of the early twentieth century lived in the shadows of two towering personalities, those of Mohandas K. Gandhi and B. R. Ambedkar. Jonathan's pacifism resonates with many aspects of Gandhi's principles of nonviolence and his willingness to apply them in the struggle against British colonialism. Gandhi, however, supported India's caste system and advocated peaceful, nonpolitical, and gradual remedies for the plight of Dalits. Ambedkar sharply opposed Gandhi's approach and advocated for legal and political solutions for Dalits. Ultimately, it was Ambedkar who would win the hearts of Dalits. Even Dalit Christians gravitated toward Ambedkar, but this, as we shall see, is because his methods reminded them of the radical love that Jesus would offer on their behalf. In the pages that follow, I outline some of the major tropes of Dalit Christian theology, an attempt to interpret the Christian faith in light of Dalit experiences and their quest for liberation and dignity. This theology from below, however, had to contend with the theology being espoused by elite, educated Christians, which in the Dalits' view only reinforced upper-caste domination.

During the era of Indian nationalism and in decades following Independence, Indian Christians felt uniquely burdened to demonstrate their devotion to Indian nationalism.[1] Many embraced the project of Indianizing Christianity. They wanted to purge the church of its foreign complexion and reframe it in ways that reflect the religious culture of what had become the dominant religious tradition, Sanskritic Hinduism. Such impulses in Indian Christian theology begin in the late nineteenth century and extend well into the twentieth. It includes efforts of theologians such as Vengal Chakkarai Chetty (1880–1958) to produce an authentic, indigenous Christian theology by harmonizing it with Hindu philosophical thought. In *The Unknown Christ of Hinduism*, Raimundo Pannikar points to a living presence of Christ in Hinduism and espouses the cross-fertilization of theology from many religious traditions.[2] The theologian M. M. Thomas attempted to move Christian theology beyond an enclave that isolated it from developments within other faiths, including the renaissance occurring within Hinduism.[3] Other attempts to indi-

---

1. Most of this essay is drawn from my forthcoming book, *South Asia's Christians: Between Hindu and Muslim* (New York: Oxford University Press, forthcoming).

2. Discussed in Peniel Rajkumar, *Dalit Theology and Dalit Liberation: Problems, Paradigms and Possibilities* (London: Ashgate, 2010), 34–35.

3. See M. M. Thomas, *The Church's Mission and Post-Modern Humanism* (New

genize Christianity trace back to early-twentieth-century figures such as Sadhu Sundar Singh, the Sikh convert who became an itinerant Christian guru in the tradition of Hindu world renouncers. Singh is known for his desire to preach "the water of life in an Indian cup," a phrase denoting his attempted indigenization of Christian ideas.[4] Theologians comprising what came to be known as the "Rethinking Christianity" group in Madras explored a similar project of streamlining Christianity with Hindu heritage and traditions.

From a Dalit perspective, such endeavors to Indianize Christianity are problematic. Indianizing had become synonymous with Sanskritizing and Hinduizing. Such a project only reinforced the primacy of Brahminical knowledge and upper-caste dominance.[5] Mass movements of conversion among Dalits and tribals had yielded a church consisting of as many as 70–80 percent of *avarnas* (outcastes); and yet the church in India was led by caste elites who were doing most of the theologizing. This elitist impulse has a deep history across South Asia's Christian traditions. The Syrian Christians function as a caste community in Kerala claiming Brahminical roots.[6] Roman Catholics since the days of Robert de Nobili were fixated on converting the upper castes. Nobili and his associates claimed for themselves Brahmin status. Even the Lutheran Pietist missionaries who followed Ziegenbalg's lead adhered to theological perspectives that ended up accommodating caste distinctions within the church.[7] Each of these historical instances of accommodation laid foundations for upper-caste dominated traditions, whose church pews consisted primarily of low caste and Dalit peoples. The twentieth-century project of Indianizing Christianity simply added another ideological layer to what was already an elite-driven church.

Delhi: CSS and ISPCK, 1996), 25–27. Discussed in K. P. Kuruvilla, *The Word Became Flesh: A Christological Paradigm for Doing Theology in India* (New Delhi: ISPCK, 2002), 149–50.

4. A. J. Appasamy, *Sundar Singh: A Biography* (Cambridge, UK: Lutterworth, 1958), 189.

5. Sathianathan Clarke, *Dalits and Christianity: Subaltern Religion and Liberation Theology in India* (New Delhi: Oxford University Press, 1998), 41–43.

6. Nidhin Shobhana, "Caste in the Name of Christ: An Angry Note on the Syrian Christian Caste," Round Table India, Mar. 21, 2014, https://www.roundtableindia.co.in/caste-in-the-name-of-christ-caste-in-the-name-of-christ-an-angry-note-on-the-syrian-christian-caste/.

7. Rajkumar, *Dalit Theology*, 25–29.

Asserting Difference from Hinduism

Dalit Christian theology emerged as a powerful critique of this impulse to adapt the gospel to upper-caste culture. As Indian nationalism increasingly became a Hindu nationalism, it tended to invalidate or marginalize the aspirations and experiences of Dalits.[8] In response, Dalit theologians developed a theology that employed and interacted with the symbolic resources of their own communities. An important strategy was to differentiate Dalit religion from so-called Aryan, Sanskritic, or Brahminical religion. This was Ambedkar's approach, and others have since followed suit in different ways. In his book *The Confusion Called Conversion*, Ebe Sunder Raj argues that untouchable and tribal peoples of northeast India have never belonged to Sanskritic culture. Similarly, South Indians of Dravidian origins were not originally practitioners of Sanskrit-based religion. They worshiped different gods, adhered to different rites, and observed their own festivals. Indo-Aryan migrants from north India eventually drew South Indians into the orbit of Brahminical religion and its priestly order. They did so by forging powerful bonds between Brahmin missionaries (as Sunder Raj calls them), South Indian kings, and temples. Kings legitimated their rule by patronizing temples, while Brahmins provided ritual services as priests. The differentiation of labor that arose within this "sacred complex" became the caste system.[9]

Another iteration of this strategy of differentiation is presented Kancha Ilaiah's depiction of the plight of "Dalitbahujans." This term, coined by the politician Kanshi Ram, envisioned a united political movement consisting of all Dalit communities along with other Syrian Christians from the Sudra caste. In *Why I Am Not a Hindu*, Ilaiah narrates his experiences as a Dalitbahujan.[10] He stresses the difference between his familial customs and those of Hindu society. In addition to recounting the long history of oppression and discrimination that he and his fellow caste members

---

8. Clarke, *Dalits and Christianity*, 40.

9. Here, he cites the anthropologist L. P. Vidhyarti. Ebe Sunder Raj, *The Confusion Called Conversion* (New Delhi: TRACI, 1988), 39, 68–71. See also James Massey, *Roots: A Concise History of Dalits* (New Delhi: ISPCK, 1994).

10. The term "Dalitbahujan" encompasses all groups classified either as Scheduled Castes, Scheduled Tribes, or Other Backward Castes. It combines the term "Dalit," which includes only the untouchables, with the term "Bahujan" a term popularized by Kanshi Ram and meaning literally "majority." Kancha Ilaiah, *Why I Am Not a Hindu: A Sudra Critique of Hindutva Philosophy, Culture and Political Economy* (Calcutta: Samya, 1996), viii.

(Kurumaas) suffered under caste Hindus, Ilaiah describes how every dimension of his caste culture can be differentiated from Hindu culture. These domains of difference include family relationships, the roles of women, deities, dietary habits, sexual mores, occupations, and education. Based on such differences there are no grounds, Ilaiah argues, for regarding Dalitbahujans as part of the Hindu fold. Attacking the Hindutva-inspired co-opting of his caste into the Brahminical social structure, Ilaiah writes:

> The question is what do we the lower Sudras and Ati-Sudras (whom I also call Dalitbahujans), have to do with Hinduism or with Hindutva itself? I, indeed not only I, but all of us, the Dalitbahujans of India, have never heard the word "Hindu"—not as a word, nor as the name of a culture, nor as the name of a religion in our early childhood days.... But today we are suddenly being told that we have a common religious and cultural relationship with the Baapanoollu [Brahmins] and the Koomatoollu [Baniyas]. This is not merely surprising; it is shocking.[11]

The tools that Ilaiah employs to explain why he is not a Hindu are not centered on academic-sounding distinctions between different classes of people, but on the power of storytelling. This approach is similar to that taken by the Roman Catholic Dalit author Bama. In *Karukku*, she narrates her life, skillfully weaving together her individual experiences and those of her community. Like Ilaiah, she eschews an academic presentation of Dalit experience, preferring instead to narrate pain, trauma, and humiliation in different episodes of her life.[12]

Ilaiah's reasoning taps into a tradition of non-Hindu confessionalism reflected in the work of anti-caste reformers such as Jyotirao Phule, B. R. Ambedkar, or E. V. Ramaswamy Naicker. The goal of this strategy is to differentiate Dalits from Hindu society while at the same time establishing them as people of the soil, indeed as the original inhabitants of India who had been colonized by the Aryan other.

The strategy of differentiating Dalit or Dalitbahujan identity from Hinduism does not come without risks. By forging a broad network of solidarity that stresses difference from Sanskritic society, they increase their capacity to counter Hindu majoritarian politics with an alternative politics tailored to their interests. At the same time, the system of affirmative action benefits those Syrian Christians who remain Hindu.

11. Ilaiah, *Why I Am Not*, xi.
12. Bama, *Karukku*, trans. Lakshmi Holmstrom (New York: Oxford University Press, 2012).

Dalits feel pressured to accept a Hindu identity in order to gain access to reservations in employment and education. This structural incentive undermines their politics of difference. For all practical purposes, the system of reservations has functioned as a form of inducement and a means for retaining Syrian Christians within the Hindu fold. Brahmins and other upper castes have long employed strategies of co-option and assimilation in order to thwart rebellious assertions of difference among lower castes. By denying reservations to those who leave Hinduism for Islam or Christianity, a Hindu majoritarian state has found yet another a means of co-opting Dalits.[13]

With an eye to recovering suppressed Dalit particularities and asserting their difference from dominant castes, Dalit theologians draw upon the symbolic resources of Dalits to formulate their theologies. This sets them apart from Indian Christian theologians who made Sanskritic concepts and categories their primary reference point. The theologian Sathianathan Clarke draws upon the centrality of goddess worship and drum beating in the lives of South Indian Paraiyars. In an earlier era, missionaries would have dismissed goddess worship as demonic. From the standpoint of Dalit theology, however, the veneration of Ellaiyamman represents an "alternative mode of religion making."[14] Paraiyars believed that Ellaiyamman protected the boundary that separated their village domains from those of caste Hindus. This deity, notes Clarke, "shields and polices the geographic, social, and cultural space of the Paraiyar from the continuous colonizing proclivity of the caste peoples."[15] Whereas some local myths link Dalit goddesses to the Hindu divinities Shiva and Vishnu, Elliayamman remained independent. This shows the desire of Paraiyars to be "distinct, different, even separate" from Hindu society.[16] The veneration of Ellaiyamman is embedded deeply into the oral traditions of the Paraiyars, including songs and stories that make derogatory references to caste Hindus.

Paraiyars also differentiated themselves from Hindu society through their use of the drum. At marriage processions, ceremonies that invoke divine grace in everyday life, exorcisms, dances, and public declarations,

---

13. Their strategy of co-option has also included their incorporation of Ambedkar into their "pantheon of great men." See Christophe Jaffrelot, *Dr. Ambedkar and Untouchability: Analysing and Fighting Caste* (London: Hurst, 2005), 145–47.

14. Clarke, *Dalits and Christianity*, 128.

15. Clarke, *Dalits and Christianity*, 102.

16. Clarke, *Dalits and Christianity*, 103.

drum beating is central. The sound of the drum is related to the Pariayar culture of oral transmission. Because it conveys meaning through sound as distinct from a written text, the drum differentiates Paraiyars from upper-caste, literate elites. For Christian theology to speak to Dalits, it needs to penetrate this subaltern (non-elite) interior of Pariayar experience. Upper castes withheld from Paraiyars the sacred word by denying them access to Sanskrit texts. Excluded from temples and the sacred knowledge arising from Sanskrit, Paraiyars found in the drum the mediating presence of the divine. Within the context of Dalit theology, Clarke makes the case that the drum signifies the "immanental presence of God" in Christ, and a powerful symbol of liberation for Paraiyars.

Dalit Liberation

In addition to drawing upon the unique experience and symbols of Dalits, Dalit theology is committed to their liberation. The project is not merely incarnational (that is, rooted in Dalit localities and experiences), but is also emancipatory. It is a theology inspired by Latin America's liberation theology. Originating in the work of the theologian Gustavo Gutierrez, liberation theology called for a radical reading of the Bible through the lens of Marxist notions of class struggle and revolution. Such a reading drew liberationist themes from the story of the exodus and portrayed Christ as the liberator of the oppressed. Liberation theology applied this reading of the Bible to the sociopolitical struggles of poor and oppressed Latin American peoples. Eschewing notions of salvation that were focused on the afterlife, liberation theology fused its doctrine of salvation with a praxis focused on challenging structures of inequality. Dalit theology does similar things, but tailors its liberationist vision to the context of Hindu caste oppression (as distinct from postcolonial Latin American struggle). The theologian Arvind Nirmal describes the profound *pathos* that defines Dalit consciousness:

> My dalit ancestor did not enjoy the nomadic freedom of the wandering Aramean. As an outcaste, he was also cast out of his/her village. . . . When my dalit ancestor walked the dusty roads of his village, the *Sa Varnas* also tied an earthen pot around my dalit ancestor's neck to serve as a spittle. If ever my dalit ancestor tried to learn Sanskrit or some other sophisticated language

the oppressors gagged him permanently by pouring molten lead down his throat.[17]

The memory of such experiences and their present-day reality are powerful shapers of Dalit Christian consciousness. They inform the quest for liberation that runs through their readings of the Gospels. Jesus is not a detached guru of contextual Indian Christian theology, but the one who was subject to humiliation and crucifixion at the hands of the religious establishment of his day. Dalits—who are similarly crushed, broken, and humiliated—see both their experiences and their emancipation in the crucified Jesus.

The connections Dalits draw between their brokenness and the wounding of Christ's body resonate with powerful motifs of African American theology. This resonance is particularly strong in connection to the violence that both Dalits and African Americans face from whites or upper castes. Throughout their history in the segregated American South, Black Americans were victims of lynching, instances where a group of whites would hang a Black person publicly for alleged crimes without a trial. The theologian James Cone draws a parallel between the lynched African American body and the suffering of Christ. The poetics of Black preaching and the Black literary imagination saw the immediate resemblance, Cone observes, between the cross and the lynching tree. They portrayed Christ as the "first leaf in a line of trees on which a man should swing."[18] Christ, then, became the first lynchee, and the lynching of Blacks became occasions where Christ was lynched again.[19]

This identification with the suffering Christ is a salient feature of Dalit theology as well. Dalit theology recognizes Jesus as a Dalit. The lowly birth, humiliation, and crucifixion of Jesus resonate with Dalit experience. Like African Americans, Dalits routinely are victims of atrocities and instances of humiliation, primarily by members of upper castes. India's National Crime Records Bureau indicates that a crime is committed against a Dalit by a non-Dalit every sixteen minutes. This includes rape, violence, stripping and parading naked, seizing of land, and restricted

---

17. Arvind P. Nirmal, "Towards a Christian Dalit Theology," in *A Reader in Dalit Theology*, ed. Arvind P. Nirmal (Madras: Gurukul Lutheran Theological College and Research Institute, 1990), 60–72, 61.

18. James H. Cone, *The Cross and the Lynching Tree* (Maryknoll, NY: Orbis, 2011), 96.

19. Cone, *Cross and Lynching Tree*, 96.

access to water.[20] Dalit theology looks to Jesus as the one who embodies their pain and subjugation and opens the path for their liberation. The Son of Man's "rejection, mockery, contempt, suffering, and finally death" (Mark 8:31) occurred at the hands of "the dominant religious tradition and the established religion." In this manner, Jesus underwent Dalit experiences as the "Prototype of all Dalits."[21]

In terms of their politics, Dalit Christians are inspired by the leadership of the Dalit reformer, Bhimrao Ramji Ambedkar (1891-1956). Unlike Gandhi, who advocated gradualist change based on persuading upper castes to treat Dalits better, Ambedkar, a Dalit himself, insisted on legal and political solutions for Dalits. Following Ambedkar's lead, Dalit Christians have been staunch advocates for extending affirmative action benefits to their community. So inspired have they been by Ambedkar that they are inclined to view his methods as the praxis that flows from their liberation theology. In Ambedkar and Jesus, they find a special affinity, so much so that some theologians, like L. Jayachitra, read them in a complementary manner. Just as Jesus confronted the hypocrisy, purity laws, and exclusionary practices of the religious establishment of his day, Ambedkar attacked Brahminical laws of purity as practices that oppress and exclude Dalits. Jesus called for an "inclusive temple" and displayed a special concern for the poor. Similarly, Ambedkar decried the religious basis of caste discrimination, prohibitions of intermarriage and inter-dining, and discriminatory practices that reinforced economic backwardness among Dalits.[22] Fired by this dynamic and contrapuntal reading of Jesus and Ambedkar, Dalit Christians are inspired to confront caste-ism within the life of the church and in the society at large. The radical social critique rendered by Dalit Christians through novels, poems, plays, and artwork is fired by a similar imagination.

---

20. Arundhati Roy, *The Doctor and the Saint: Caste, Race, and "The Annihilation of Caste"; The Debate Between B. R. Ambedkar and M. K. Gandhi* (Chicago: Haymarket, 2017), 21.

21. Nirmal, "Towards Christian Dalit Theology," 66-67.

22. L. Jayachitra, "Jesus and Ambedkar: Exploring Common Loci for Dalit Theology and Dalit Movements," in *Dalit Theology in the Twenty-First Century: Discordant Voices, Discerning Pathways*, ed. Sathianathan Clarke et al. (New Delhi: Oxford University Press, 2010), 121-36, esp. 124-25.

For God So Loves the World
(Thank You, Dr. Jonathan Wilson)

Jennifer Harvey

I GAVE MY FIRST paper at the American Academy of Religion (AAR) when I was a second-year doctoral student studying at Union Theological Seminary. I was really nervous. My nerves were partly about it being my first AAR presentation, of course. But they were also because I was giving my paper in the AAR's "Lesbian and Feminist Issues in Religion" section.

I'd been out as a lesbian for about three years at that point. I'd thus already done some really hard things—like leaving my marriage to a kind and supportive husband, coming out to my large (and mostly evangelical) family and all my friends, and sitting down in repeated small groups with members of the church I was serving as an assistant pastor—senior pastor at my side—to explain why I'd needed to take a short leave of absence.

But still, presenting in this formal scholarly way felt like a whole new level of vulnerability and visibility; a major amplification of "coming out."

I was ready. But I was really, really nervous.

It would be impossible to overemphasize, then, how physical were the feelings of warmth and connection and care that began to wash over my entire being after I stepped up to the podium to begin, took a deep, adrenaline-laced breath, looked out into that intimidating audience of scholars, and saw a familiar face I hadn't seen in years.

There was Jonathan Wilson. He was sitting right there, in the second row; really close to the podium! He was looking at me with total joy and happy anticipation. He had a big smile on face. His eyes were shining. Love seemed to be just pouring out of his heart.

I couldn't believe what I was seeing. But I knew exactly what I was feeling as I took in his beautiful presence. I was feeling (again) the manifestation of what it really means when we mean it when we say "God so loves the world."

Let me back up. Jonathan had been my theology professor back when I was a student at Westmont College. That had been more than ten years before the moment I just described—the memory that came over me immediately and viscerally when I learned Jonathan was turning seventy and I was being given the opportunity to celebrate his life and his work by writing about him.

As I began to reflect on how I might contribute to this celebration of Jonathan's journey, I realized this memory captures what Jonathan's willingness to walk with me during a raw but beautiful, painful but formative period of my life has meant in the larger arc of my own. I also realized that sharing it, and some of what led to it, were the only way I could hope to convey why and how I cherish this devoted Christian, loving and beloved teacher, deep and authentic thinker and scholar, even though I have not seen or spoken to him in person for—once again—more than ten years now.

Despite the years of remove, Jonathan Wilson remains one of a handful of people in my life journey from whom I directly learned, and also experienced, what "God so loves the world" really means when we mean it when say it; when "God so loves the world" is more than a mantra and never a litmus test, when it's proclaimed in faithful response to a reality that is already manifest and the temptations to make ourselves arbiters of its reach and implication are resisted as a spiritual discipline.

God so loves the world. The whole world. Including you. And, also, including me.

Let me back up again. As I do so, it dawns on me that this is a narrative I've never even shared with Jonathan. It's one of those stories you tell to make sense out of some part of your experience you only find words for—however inadequate they remain—long after you already know how it all turns out. It's a story you can only tell after you know it's going to be okay; or at least as "okay" as anything in this mortal coil can ever really be. Because at the time I was living this story, I certainly did not know any of that. At the time it was scary and hard and very, very lonely.

But whether he consciously realized it or not, Jonathan was always there. And that mattered centrally, not only in why everything did ultimately turn out "okay," but also in how and why I remained (and remain!) a Christian.

I grew up steeped in white Evangelical Christianity. Bethel Baptist Church sat at 1801 S. Logan Street and, on a slow week, my family was there at least three times. Denver's Christian radio station, KWBI, played in our living room day in and day out. On Saturday the voice of James Dobson—of *Focus on the Family*—seeped through the speakers as my siblings and I listened to *Children's Bible Hour*.

Billy Graham was a family hero. Images of him adorned our home. My grammy especially loved him. She'd read and reread his books, which always sat stacked on her headboard. One of the highlights of my teenage life was being old enough to be a counselor when the Billy Graham Crusade swept through Denver in 1987. For ten nights I got to stand on the field of Mile High Stadium as thousands of people, tears streaming down their faces, came out of their seats to greet us counselors who stood waiting to walk each precious one of them through the Jesus Prayer to be born again.

Bethel Baptist, where my grammy was the pianist for decades and taught Sunday school to each of my six siblings, was the sun around which we orbited, and white Evangelical Christianity was more than a belief system. It wasn't only about going to church or following strict moral codes. This was an ethos and world, an encompassing culture and community. It was the ecosystem through which I came to know and understand myself as a self and make sense out of my relationships with others.

In this formation, "God so loves the world" became my fundamental existential framework; always the thing I knew to be most true. Despite being able to see in retrospect the persistent exclusions in what that meant to or how it was being used by the community that raised me, I assumed God so loves the world meant the *whole* world. As in, God so loves *all of us*.

So off I went to Westmont College. I was an eighteen-year-old who'd picked my school for a muddled set of reasons. The main one had to do with the exceptional quality of Westmont's women's soccer program, which was unusual in the early 1990s (that's a whole different story that someday I'll tell). At Westmont the "God so loves" framework through which I understood my very existence began bumping right into some of the deep contradictions inherent to white Evangelicalism's claim to preach God's love, contradictions I hadn't ever really seen before.

I would quickly find it impossible to look away.

My first year, I volunteered at a local Salvation Army homeless shelter. On Sunday nights I'd leave campus with a student ministry group and serve soup after the mandatory church service. For some reason I felt compelled to begin spending more time in that space and began going downtown more often and on my own. I'd talked at length with the people I met there, many of whom were homeless.

Learning about poverty and profound economic injustice for the first time rattled me. The juxtaposition of such suffering with my own daily life couldn't have been starker. I'd get on the college shuttle after these experiences and ride back up into the wealthy hills of Montecito, where an overwhelmingly white student body, who also claimed to believe God so loves the world, had parked very expensive cars. All I could see were contradictions.

At the same time, I was falling in love with the study of theology, a discipline I hadn't known existed before I went to college. (Guess with whom I was studying! I'll come back to that shortly.) Soon I was asking gentle but probing questions about the ways I'd been taught to understand the Bible. I noticed things the Bible didn't seem to actually say, despite the fact I'd always been told it did. I started noticing the Bible said a lot of things I hadn't heard anything about, some of which raised questions about the wealth ensconced on our rather self-righteous, devout, lily-white campus.

I did well in these classes and turned out to be an excellent theology student. I got high grades. Professors in the department reached out, wanting to mentor me. I declared a religious studies major even though I had no idea what I'd do with such a thing.

But the further in I got, the more cracks and crevices manifested. I would sit in my classes, one of the strongest students in the room, and the debate might turn to questions like what kind of leadership was permissible for women to have in "the church." Given the gender configurations at Bethel—where women couldn't even serve communion—these debates weren't new to me. But something else soon was. New was the dawning awareness that such debates sat adjacent to questions about my right to be in that theology classroom at all and conferred upon the debaters the presumed right to render a verdict on whether my excellence meant anything.

I noticed that some of the same students insisting women couldn't be ordained were folks who'd drive their Mercedes Benz right past homeless families hunkered down and hungry on the streets of Santa Barbara. I could scarcely tolerate the absurdity of this moral positioning.

Essentially, I was realizing there was an emperor who had no clothes and discovering myself to be someone unwilling to pretend that he did. Such realizations weren't merely intellectual (though they were that). This wasn't just a faith crisis (though it quickly became that). Rather, all the threads that wove through my understanding of God, threads that held me together as a self, bound me to a community and rooted me in a world, were being strained. They ruptured and split more completely with each passing semester.

Dislocation eventually came to fully characterize the primary way I experienced my relationship to the community I'd been formed in, and eventually to the church specifically and Christianity more broadly. It was a terribly exciting and breathtakingly, heartbreakingly terrifying time.

Of course, as it turns out, Christianity is really diverse. And at some point, in all of this rupturing and unraveling, I would be offered a life-changing introduction to liberation theology. Anyone reading this celebration of Jonathan Wilson's vocation—wherever they may locate themselves theologically—knows that the basic premise of liberation theology is pretty simple. It's this: God so loves the world *really does mean* the whole world. In turn, this means God cares about every single part of our lives as human beings. And this means God cares about human suffering—all of it—including the massive suffering caused by sexism and racism, economic oppression and homophobia, colonialism and so much more. Then here came the kicker for me: if God cares about the suffering of these "-isms," suffering caused by profound and pervasive injustice, then by sheer force of logic God has to be a god of justice.

My trips down to the Salvation Army became theologically sensical; God hated homelessness and wealth accumulation that turned a blind eye to it. My classroom experiences where the denigration of women was legitimized by debates over women's capacity to lead were thrown into sharp relief. I began to understand them for what they were—straight-up sexism.

By every measure the most important intellectual encounter I would have in this period of time was with the work of James Cone, who also wrote that, yes, God is a God of justice, but went on to be more explicit. Cone wrote that if God is a God of justice, then God has to be Black because Black people are the oppressed of the oppressed in the United States.

For other reasons of my own biography, growing up in bussing, integrated, but racially tracked public schools in Denver, Colorado, Cone's writing changed everything about how I understood my own life, relationship to Jesus, humanity and relationship to country and church, as well as my own call. Everything I've lived vocationally in my thirty years of life since those undergraduate years—as a pastor, teacher, activist committed to anti-racism and racial justice—and the complex and deep ways I theologically identify as a Christian still, go back to this point in the story.

This is one of those stories that's like the movie where you already know the ending is happy, but as you rewatch it the near misses along the way where everything could turn out horribly still make you hold your breath. And without Jonathan Wilson (and two other Westmont faculty—Diana Butler Bass and Brad Berkey), the point in my story that has been everything to what has mattered most in my life just wouldn't have come to be.

The truth is I could have never even read or accessed Cone—nor taken him seriously—were it not for Jonathan, who trusted me enough to actually teach me theology and was invested in a belief that I had a right to my own mind and soul-discernment as I engaged it, thought about it, wrestled with it.

I distinctly remember sitting in class with Jonathan and talking about John Yoder's *The Politics of Jesus*.[1] I was enthralled and captivated. My mind was blown. Here was a book giving permission to imagine I could actually take the words of Jesus as seriously as I was inclined to. I could actually believe they might mean what they seemed to me to so clearly say, despite the way doing so put me at cross-purpose with the politics of white Evangelicalism.

It was also not lost on me even then that Jonathan was taking some risk—not necessarily by teaching that text but (in a place like Westmont) by being willing to be clear that he actually believed Yoder's theological vision should have a claim on who we were as a people; that he (Jonathan) actually believed these things to have truth.

I distinctly remember reading Jurgen Möltmann, and for the first time realizing theological thinking and attempts to discern what might

---

1. The devastating revelation of Yoder's violations of women throughout his career cannot go unmarked here, even as I neither know what to say about it nor how Jonathan has himself wrestled with it, though I am certain he has wrestled with it and with no small amount of pain and sadness.

be theologically true involved more than simply pulling biblical quotes from a text and claiming to "apply them" to things. (I was never able to look at our soccer team's T-shirts, which quoted Phil 4:13, "I can do all things through Christ who strengthens me," on the back, quite the same way.) I remember the thick, complex discussions in class about what Jesus's death meant or might mean, how we might or could ask questions about that meaning.

Even when I wasn't sure how Jonathan thought about Möltmann's assertions himself, the permission that was given, granted, insisted upon by this vibrant, energetic, passionate, and kind teacher to take Möltmann seriously and ask my actual questions—questions that in other spaces would have been shut down before they were fully articulated was, quite simply, like drawing in oxygen-rich fresh air for the first time. Even when his own theological claims or conclusions differed from where I might land (or think I was landing), Jonathan's affirmation and respect for my integrity of mind, his assumption I had my own relationship with God and that his conclusions were not the arbiter of that was . . . well, there are no words for what I learned from that.

My last year or so at Westmont was the most difficult one. I was falling in full-fledged love with feminism, contending with the communal consequences of my growing refusal to make myself smaller simply because I was a woman. I was writing things for the student newspaper about economic injustice and racism that made people mad (and would probably embarrass me today). I was in open conflict with my parents and church community at home who couldn't understand me, and I was increasingly treated by my student peers (and many faculty) at Westmont as someone existing on a continuum somewhere between enigma and pariah.

But I was okay. Because, even when I wasn't in class with him in a given semester, Jonathan was there, in that community. And I always had an experience of feeling seen, affirmed, supported, loved. Even on my most angry days and during the most lonely ones, that such a wise and kind human had the audacity to support and nurture me—even when he differed from or disagreed with where I was in my thinking, was everything. It not only let me know I was truly "okay." It was theological: it was an experience of what it means when we mean it when we say "God so loves the world. As in all of us."

This is to say nothing of the times as graduation came close that Dr. Jonathan Wilson, as the hold that liberation and Black and womanist theology had in my life became increasingly clear to him, would pull me aside and say, "There is a place for you" and "It might be Union Theological Seminary." This is to say nothing of what it meant for a professor at an evangelical Christian college to dare affirm Union as a place that was, itself, a Christian community; a place for me where I might find community and a safer place to explore and grow; to be faithful to God and to my call.

Besides helping me access the theology that helped me continue to journey as a Christian, Jonathan literally helped me find a seminary community where the life-transforming, conversion-furthering journey that began in those amazing classes with him could continue and continue and continue, as it has ever since.

I could not be more grateful for this human, this teacher, this scholar, this Christian. There simply aren't words for any of this.

There are only memories that convey in Technicolor how this faithful Christian of integrity and love has lived out his call and his vocation; and I am more than confident that mine is only one memory among thousands of students who have had the gift of walking with Jonathan Wilson.

Which brings me back to that AAR encounter.

The period when Jonathan's ways of being and teaching and mentoring accompanied me on that difficult journey, and the time when he made sure my journey as I departed Westmont pointed in a direction where I might continue to grow and be nurtured—all of these Westmont years—unfolded long before I came out as a lesbian.

So many other parts of my story emerged and grew while I was at Union. They could only have emerged and grown there because they wouldn't have been safe anywhere else. My relationship with my own evangelical identity (and community) continued to change dramatically in that time, and I remained palpably grateful for Jonathan having supported and loved me at a time when so much was unraveling in my relationship to Christianity but/and in ways that helped me continue to knit the pieces back together at an equally robust pace.

When I finally came out, the experience was the equivalent of finally being able to fully believe and trust that God so loving the world actually did really include me—as in the actual, full, created-by-God me. But even as I knew coming out to be right and true, and that I was a *beloved* child of God and created in the image of the divine, when I would reflect on all that had brought me to this point in my life, I would sometimes experience a soft but persistent nagging worry. Perhaps what I knew in my life to be an experience of God's presence in/with/through my journey would be felt as a kind of a disappointment to Jonathan and the other small number of brave and loving souls at Westmont who had cared for me so well. What if they knew the turn my story had taken? If they knew that on top of everything else I'd been through with them at Westmont, *I was also gay*.

It's none of those souls' fault that I worried about this. Even in the most inclusion-aspiring, justice-seeking, creation-as-good versions of Christianity and church, the experience of being gay or lesbian (let alone transgender) is difficult, and one can feel ever contingent.

And I don't want to imply that I would think about this too often or worry about it too explicitly. I had field exams to prepare for after all! I was busy coming into my own as a junior scholar who had a passion for theology and a clarity that God's love manifests in the form of a commitment to justice that lays a call on each of our lives to seek to make real God's just reign in a world of aching, sinful, human-caused suffering.

But still, my convictions that God so loves the world and that I, like all of us, am called by the divine to respond to that manifest reality in ways that contribute to the flourishing of the world, is the only reason I ended up in the academy as a scholar and teacher at all. My relationship to Christian community, including the ones that formed me and the ways they have struggled to love LGBTQ+ people, has always remained a point of self-reflection and care. Which is to say, I wondered sometimes whether this teacher who was so beloved to me would have been disappointed in how my story had turned out; the turn it had taken.

And then, Dearest Jonathan, you were there in the second row. You were looking at me with total joy and happy anticipation. You had a big smile on your face. Your eyes were shining. Love seemed to be just pouring out of your heart. I felt sure you came looking for me—giving my presentation in the "Lesbian and Feminist Issues in Religion" Section of the AAR—specifically so that I would know that you were proud of me even still. There you were seeing me, affirming me, believing and trusting I had my own walk with God, even if it looked different than yours or wasn't what you'd expected.

And so once again I experienced what it means when we mean it when we say "God so loves the world. The whole world. As in *all of us*." I knew what it meant because there you were again, just living it. Not a litmus test, just a response to the reality that is already manifest.

Dearest Jonathan, there are no words for the gift of having that experience. There is only "thank you."

God's Work Is to Redeem Creation

Jonas Kambale Musamba

THE QUESTION IS RELEVANT and interests researchers of the holy books: why does God intervene in human life? Many people have talked about it. Even Professor Jonathan talked about it. I want to show Jonathan Wilson's contribution to this interesting question. Jonathan and I talked a lot about it during our doctoral ministry program from 2010 to 2016 in Kenya, where Jonathan taught us the courses on reflecting theologically. I was very interested in Jonathan's reflections because he taught us how we can still think about God in all situations. The main question is to find who God is in the situation we are facing. In all, God is the Creator of everything, and he is the one who maintains creation.

I was very interested in Jonathan's book about creation: *God's Good World: Reclaiming the Doctrine of Creation.*[1] I want to reflect on what I learned from Jonathan for this Festschrift, where we want to thank God for all he does through his servant Jonathan R. Wilson.

I began by trying to understand Paul's writing to the Romans:

> The creation waits in eager expectation for the sons of God to be revealed. For the creation was subjected to frustration, not by its own choice, but by the will of the one who subjected it, in hope that the creation itself will be liberated from its bondage to decay and brought into the glorious freedom of the children of God. We know that the whole creation has been groaning

---

1. Jonathan R. Wilson, *God's Good World: Reclaiming the Doctrine of Creation* (Grand Rapids: Baker Academic, 2013).

as in the pains of childbirth right up to the present time. (Rom 8:19–22)[2]

This passage confirms that redemption is not only concerned with humans; the whole creation is waiting for the revelation of God's sons. We understand that the whole creation will be renewed from all suffering according to God's plan. This redemption is both christological and eschatological. Indeed, redemption is coming through the deliverance, which is already taking place in Jesus Christ, and it will be completed in the forthcoming arrival of Jesus, when the true nature of the sons of God will be revealed in the new creation. It is this conviction that justifies the Christian hope, a very important element in the Christian faith.

Speaking about creation in the light of Paul's view, Jonathan shows that God's work is to redeem creation. He emphasizes it as follows:

> If the work of the Father, Son, and Spirit is the work of redeeming creation for its telos in New Creation, in the midst of a world that has fallen away from its telos, turning from life to death, we who believe that the Father, Son, and Spirit redeem creation for New Creation live with tensions and difficulties. One of the most significant is what is traditionally called the problem of evil. Another way to state the challenge to Christian convictions is to call it the problem of suffering. There are many complications when we look closely at these "problems": the problems of natural and moral evils; the problems of just and unjust suffering. The challenges are also diverse.[3]

Jonathan reminds us that the world has turned from life to death, inheriting the problem of natural and moral evil. Other problems in this fallen creation include just and unjust suffering. We found the response to these issues in the idea of redemption in the new creation. To render redemption more comprehensive, Jonathan has provided an account of Christian thinking and living in the midst of evil and suffering. Christian faithfulness in the midst of evil is comprised of two stories, two practices, and two prayers.

---

2. This chapter uses the NIV translation for Scripture references, unless otherwise indicated.

3. Wilson, *God's Good World*, 217.

Two Stories

In speaking about two stories, Jonathan means the story of the fallen world, which concerns turning away from the telos of creation that is life, and the story of creation, which concerns redemption towards the telos of life as revealed in the new creation. The difficulty for believers at this time of evil in our world is the fact that we are not able to separate the story of the fallen world from the story of creation.

The first story, which is far more frequently preached in the church, concerns the fallen world and explains the origin of evil. This story shows how evil has become the characteristic of the world. Following Jonathan, we understand that "the 'world' is subordinate to the fallen world."[4] We notice that there is a correlation here with the Jewish belief that states that when the human fell, his sin affected not only himself but also the whole of creation. This idea is very clear in Gen 3:17, where we see God cursing the ground because of human sin. It is this passage to which Paul refers when he says in Rom 8:20 that "creation was subjected to frustration."

But who has subjected creation to this frustration? The immediate response is Satan, who seems to have been the one who deprived the world of its perfect character as the place of human peace and well-being. The second response could be Adam, who subjected the world to futility when he ate the forbidden fruit. But the majority of biblical scholars agree that the one who subjected the world to frustration was God himself.[5] The reference to Gen 3:17 shows this clearly, where God curses the ground. But, the earth's curse was caused by human sin, which is the beginning of the story of evil. Thus, it is evil which caused the alienation of the whole creation. The animate and inanimate features of creation lack peace and perfection that God intended for them.

The second story is the story of the redemption of creation, which is the elimination of the fallen world. Indeed, creation strives towards the objectives that God had assigned to it. It awaits redemption. In addition, the arrival of Christ, the Redeemer, gives a new justification to this waiting. Because of Jesus Christ, creation can recover the true potential that human disobedience frustrated. Christ institutes in the new creation the new humanity of the "children of God." In him, the human, who has

---

4. Wilson, *God's Good World*, 219.

5. John Ziesler, *Paul's Letter to the Romans*, New Testament Commentaries (London: SCM Press, 1989), 220.

returned to a subsidiary relation with God, is able to subject creation to his useful work, which has been his proper vocation since the beginning. The new humanity will be revealed to creation as God's image-bearers, bringing God's protective authority over all creation. This eschatological reality can be lived now as well as in the future. Christians can already start to show their good dominion over the rest of creation.

The first story shows how the present world is dominated by evil and this evil dominion leads to death. The second story shows that all creation is waiting for redemption. This understanding helps us understand the "why" of human atrocity towards other humans and towards all creation. It will also help us know that in Jesus Christ there is the reality of the creation's redemption in the new creation.

Two Practices

The stories of the fallen world and of the redemption of creation should be held together in our living and our thinking in the midst of evil. This reality leads to what Jonathan calls the two practices: presence and patience.[6] These practices are done by God's grace and by faith in Jesus Christ the Redeemer.

In fact, Jesus Christ is the manifestation of God's presence that came towards humankind and the fallen world. He is the continuation of all God's revelation to humanity beginning with Adam in the garden of Eden. God came to search for Adam and Eve after their sin (Gen 3), he came to Abram and called him (Gen 12), he revealed himself to Moses and came down to deliver the Israelites from Egypt (Exod 3), and in Jesus God came to all humanity and all creation for redemption. He will come to reveal the reality of the new creation (Rev 21). So, God is present with humanity in the midst of evil. But the presence of God transforms the reality of evil, humiliates it, and triumphs over it. This "transformer-presence" and triumphal presence is manifested in the crucifixion and resurrection of Jesus Christ.

This divine presence is justified by the fact that God does not keep his anger forever (Ps 103:9). If God did maintain his anger forever, he would destroy his work. He punishes in order to save. He wants to lead creation to the goal that he fixed. This leads to the second practice: patience. This patience is resourceful. It gives to the world a supreme and

---

6. Wilson, *God's Good World*, 219–22.

decisive possibility of the mission of God's Son, the firstborn of the new creation, in whom the believing human becomes a new creature (2 Cor 5:17). Jesus is the chief of the community of those who have become his brothers and sisters by adoption and who constitute the church, which is his body.[7]

In this way, redemption is the object of the second practice of patience. It will not be redemption with regards to sin only, but also a participation in God's glory. It is redemption when the glory of the Creator will appear to complete the new creation. The new humanity and the new creation will correspond: new heavens and new earth (Isa 66:22; Rev 21:1). Ernest Best notes:

> We can appreciate the point that a new universe and a new humanity go together: a perfect universe requires perfect men ... and perfect men require a perfect universe in which to exercise their perfection. The fate of the universe depends on man, and his fate depends on that of Jesus in the cross and resurrection (Rom 5:12–21; 6:1–11).[8]

This relationship between humanity and creation gives hope to both. The reality is that if a human is saved, then through him the creation is also saved. If humanity is freed from death, which is the punishment of his sin, then creation will also be freed from destruction. It is for this reason that the whole creation waits in hope and patience for the new creation. The creation waits with patience for God's sons to be revealed because in the present period, as Best has written, where the old and Nnw age exist simultaneously, the fact that Christians are God's children is not apparent. However, when the new age is manifested, God's children will exercise a new lordship over creation.[9] Then, creation will attain God's original design and enjoy the redemption and splendor of the children of God.

It is thus important to see God's presence in Jesus Christ and then to overcome evil power by the power of Christ who is always present among us.[10] In this way, we will manifest our participation in the redemption of

---

7. Franz J. Lienhard, *L'Epître de Saint Paul aux Romains* (Paris: Labor et Fidès, 1995), 126.

8. Ernest Best, *The Letter of Paul to the Romans* (New York: Cambridge University Press, 2008), 99.

9. Best, *Letter of Paul*, 98.

10. Wilson, *God's Good World*, 220. Wilson emphasizes that those who are present in the midst of great, inexplicable suffering and horrors to care for victims are engaged

creation. It is this Christian participation in the redemption of creation that constitutes patience. Jonathan qualifies this patience as a primary mark of God's work in the world. God is a God with patience. He took time to form a nation through whom the Savior Messiah came to us. And following the coming of the Messiah, God continues to work patiently.[11] God's patience is also for human salvation.

The Second Letter of Peter instructed and encouraged Christians in this way (2 Pet 3:8–15). The apostle Peter encouraged people who were disappointed by the fact that the forthcoming arrival of Jesus seemed to be taking a long time. We note in Peter's words that God is patient not in anticipation of human destruction, but in anticipation of human repentance which leads to salvation. This is why Peter refers to the writings of Paul, which say that the Lord's patience means salvation. In this case God's patience is a response to evil. And this teaches us to also be patient regarding evil while waiting for God's salvation.

Nevertheless, as Jonathan notes, we must not understand patience as passivity or an excuse for inaction, denial, or withdrawal. The same God who is patient is the One who became incarnate and dwelt with us, the One who proclaimed healing and liberation, and the One who denounced injustice. The key to the practice of presence and patience is located within the story of God's redemption of creation, not within the rule of the fallen world.[12] The practices of presence and patience lead to action, an action of redemption. In other words, these practices form virtues that sustain Christian witness and help us wait while transforming the world.

Two Prayers

The two prayers that Christians pray in the midst of the fallen world and in facing evil are very clear in two passages: Ps 13:1–2 and Rev 21:20. These prayers are "How long?" and "Maranatha," or "Come, Lord Jesus." These two prayers explain the fact that Christian witness is formed by presence and patience.

---

in this practice and bearing witness by their presence even when the limitation of resources and circumstances allows them only to be present.

11. Wilson, *God's Good World*, 221.
12. Wilson, *God's Good World*, 221.

The first prayer, "How long?," expresses the lament of victims. This prayer forces victims who are experiencing pain to direct their doubts, struggles, anxieties, frenzy, and failure to God. In so doing, lament is properly centered on God, who alone brings life in the midst of death, who alone brings evil to account without doing evil, who alone changes the world not just for the better but for a new creation in Christ.[13] "How long?" is the expression of faith in a God who intervenes in human life and also an expression of the patience that the human has in waiting for redemption. "How long?" expresses that God is the only One who can redeem the world and change the situation.

The second prayer is "Maranatha," or "Come, Lord Jesus." This prayer is a prayer of hope that reminds us of the fact that in the midst of the fallen world and the rule of death, we are caught up into a greater story of the most real world: the redemption of creation in the new creation. We read these words in Rev 22:20: "He who testifies to these things says, 'Yes, I am coming soon.' Amen. Come, Lord Jesus." This prayer concerns the messianic promise, which includes peace, shalom. We know that shalom concerns all of creation. Thus in suffering, Christians are called not only to hope and pray for the presence of Jesus, but also to hope that the presence of Jesus makes all things be under his authority. This prayer is a call to Jesus to inaugurate his kingdom, where he will reign in peace, justice, and love for the well-being of humanity and all creation.

"Come, Lord Jesus" refers to the redemption of all creation, which waits with patience for the revealing of the sons of God. It concerns the reality of God's liberation and the reality of shalom. The presence of Jesus is considered as redemption itself and the complete reversal of the situation. As Paul said in his First Letter to the Corinthians (15:22–28), all things will be under the authority of Jesus. Here all things means all creation. So creation is waiting for this day of redemption. All things are made by him, all things are sustained by his word, and all things are for his glory, and so also all things will be redeemed by him.

We say that God's work is to redeem creation. For Jonathan, Christian faithfulness in the midst of evil is comprised of two stories, two practices, and two prayers. Together, these three help humans in the midst of suffering understand that all things are still in God's control. We wait for God's redemption, which was inaugurated by Jesus Christ and will be complete in his forthcoming fulfillment of the new creation.

---

13. Wilson, *God's Good World*, 223.

A Note of Thanks for the Scholar's Gift

Peter Harris

Dear Jonathan,

I am delighted to contribute to this Festschrift for the very un-Anglican number of two reasons, but then as the first time we met was at a Baptist college I hope you won't disapprove. I will return to those reasons in a while, but first of all I want to recall our initial encounter at Carey. I understand how you were feeling on that day rather better, now that I have lost Miranda, but even so I just hope that I wasn't insensitive; it was only a few months after your great loss of Marti. I don't believe I was, but then there are no travel guides to the land of grief. Sometimes those who haven't yet been there, however empathetic they are, can very understandably struggle to grasp just how harsh and inhospitable a landscape it can be.

I think your grief shaped our conversation. It was intended to be about your work on creation which, at Loren Wilkinson's urging, I had read and appreciated greatly and so I was looking forward to meeting you and gaining your insights. But even before we began talking, you suggested that we might simply listen to Palestrina for five minutes. We did, and the music baptized our conversation. In a season of life when my days were rammed with meetings, often back-to-back and typically only separated by rattling bus/metro/subway/underground trips, it taught me how important it is to stop and to reflect with music like that filling the air. It was a very physical reminder that time itself is a created gift of God, to be celebrated and honored when you are spending that time with people who are themselves God's own creation and who are often deeply immersed in experiences which are very different from your own.

Now to my two reasons. Firstly, I am glad to be contributing to this book because the work of serious and rigorous biblical and theological scholars, such as you are, is an essential companion and resource for all of us who are engaged in the calling of what James Davison Hunter[1] has called "faithful presence" in creation; for anyone who is given to serving and conserving all that God has made (Gen 1:31). That may seem an unlikely affirmation from someone like myself, more drawn to the work of an activist than that of a scholar, but if you are putting great energy into a journey it is only wise to be sure it is begun in the right direction. If it isn't, not only is the energy wasted, but your efforts will take you far from where you wish to go. As the raw material of our work is God's handiwork, any attempt to transform it without wisdom will likely do more harm than good, even with the best of motives. To take up another of the great descriptions that we could apply to lives given to serving and working in God's creation, we need good guides for "a long obedience in the same direction," Friedrich Nietzsche's words so wonderfully taken up by another particularly good guide for such work, our mutual friend Eugene Peterson. We are finding ourselves in great company in this letter, aren't we? Although I am not so sure it would be very cheering to chat to Nietzsche, so we will let that pass . . .

The second reason that I am glad to contribute to these pages is that by its nature a Festschrift is a testament to long relationships. Some contributing here may know you only through your writing, but in my case the connection is personal. Over recent years you have truly become a valued part of the A Rocha family worldwide, even though the role has never been formalized as far as I know. Certainly, *God's Good Creation* is important reading for many in the A Rocha family, but we were friends before that. And, of course once Soohwan became an international trustee, and then went on to lead the board, there was grace in the way you simply assumed that you too had joined in with the effort, even without portfolio. So, we have spent time together in Kenya, Portugal, United Kingdom, Canada, and probably elsewhere that I have forgotten, and each time the conversation has been rich. Knowing of your wisdom, a couple of

---

1. James Davison Hunter, *To Change the World: The Irony, Tragedy, & Possibility of Christianity in the Late Modern World* (Oxford, UK: Oxford University, 2010), 368.

years ago Miranda and I came to dinner with you both so we could mine your insights about impending retirement. I am only sorry that I can't salvage too much of it. We must gather around the table again for a new conversation.

So, let us return to the importance of a biblical theology of creation and some of the essential insights that I believe emerge from your writing that can orientate those who work for its flourishing.

As the title of *God's Good Creation* suggests, the efforts of anyone who cares for God's world are worth it because creation is good; indeed, God calls it very good as he surveys its totality in Gen 1:31. There are many ironies in the fact that Christian appreciation of that goodness has not led to a correspondingly urgent, universal, and committed response to creation's current distress and despoliation. Perhaps our prevailing absence from the ranks of those who have been so active has given rise to a particular conflict, or difficulty, among those who wish to plead the cause of "the environment"? In the secular societies that now dominate the global economy, and the secular organizations that dominate the world of "nature conservation," it is proving highly problematic to establish a value for nature. Without a clear idea of why nature matters, it is hard to see how the world can go beyond the current perspective that sees "the environment" as merely a series of connected resources for short-term economic growth. Alternative views that aim to attribute an intrinsic value to nature would seem to hold very little persuasive power if we are to judge by the impact that they have on either our patterns of economic behavior or the principal metrics upon which decision-makers draw.

However, in your writing and speaking you have shone a light on why creation reflects our Creator and so how we can know it is very good. That alone should give true orientation to those who believe in the Creator. Orientation is one thing, but we have to recognize the widespread loss of nerve that the gospel will *work*. Its wisdom and hope have been relegated, for all practical purposes, to being merely "inspirational." So, your true audience should be seen as not only the usual green suspects but anyone who has anything to do with the material, with matter, which is all of us, every day. Although it might seem as though farming, fishing, manufacturing, and consuming are religiously neutral acts, insofar as they deal with a material reality God has declared good, they are not. And you have insisted that we have to do with God's good creation at every turn of our lives.

It might seem as though there is now such a widespread indifference to "religious" thinking of that kind throughout the Western societies where you have primarily been working that the outputs of a theologian would be irrelevant. However, they are surely important because the decisions being made about the nature of nature, or if you like about why matter matters, are the deep consequence of assumptions and choices that are absolutely "religious" in character. Often those choices are not as lucid and coolly rational as we pretend, rather taken up by a kind of osmosis from prevailing culture. If nothing else were to reveal the falsity of a distinction between "faith" and the various kinds of skepticism or indifference that pass for rational, then a casual search of the public reasons that all those who are endeavoring to impact "the environment" for good or ill give for their actions quickly reveals the omnipresence of belief statements and value judgments in the discourse. It is also very clear that as those choices and decisions play themselves out in the world with technologically empowered consequences, how we understand the world to be rapidly becomes highly transformative, and so our beliefs make an immediate difference, whether or not they wear formalized labels.

Our present cultural incoherence in the face of the urgent necessity to establish a value of nature that can serve as a bulwark against the rising tides of monetization and sheer destruction clearly reveal that what we value is never arbitrarily attributed from our necessities and desires. Rather, the value we place on nature will flow from how we understand the world to be, both empirically and by the faith positions we hold. Those positions in turn prove, more often than not, to be biographically germinated from deep and hidden soils, rather than philosophically or religiously constructed from square-off materials that lie in the daylit ground of our public choices.

It is true that some contemporary assertions of value seem to chime more readily with Christian understandings of why the creation is good, and of how that goodness relates to the Creator's own. Nevertheless, if they actually have different foundations, they can prove as fragile as more utilitarian approaches which make no pretence at acknowledging needs beyond our own. So, to say that in order to establish creation's worth it is enough to extol its beauty, or to argue that nature must be protected because we feel awe and wonder when we are in the wilderness, merely leaves us with prior and urgent questions about our own identity. If we are simply a collection of atoms in a determined reality, then our assertions of value are by necessity of the same random character. So even if there is a convergence of perspectives with a Christian insistence that nature matters beyond its value as raw material for human well-being, that merely defers the difficulty. Of course, a purely anthropocentric view of the value of nature, established on the self-evident observation that it provides us with "ecosystem services," is far from a Christocentric idea that assigns a sacred character to creation. It does however have the virtue of coherence with the overall and persistent religion of our times, which could perhaps be characterized as a blend of hyper-individualism and relict Renaissance humanism.

Whatever the shortcomings of contemporary assertions of nature's value, and lest we become complacent, it is important to remember that your work has been primarily directed towards the Christian community and to our own need to "reclaim the doctrine of creation," as your subtitle had it. Yet within that community itself our practical indifference, for the most part at least, to the ecological crises of our times undermines any claim to credibility with those who have given themselves to caring for creation for much longer, and with far more commitment, than so many Christian believers. In our own Christian community we need to acknowledge that there have been a lot more talking the talk than walking the walk. The reasons for that go beyond the purview of this letter, but it can be seen most clearly at both ends of a spectrum of Christian presence, both personally and institutionally. That spectrum runs from boardrooms and investment decision-makers at one end, to, at the other, the hardscrabble daily lives of the poorer Christian communities in the global South where biodiversity is most concentrated. You have eloquently shown how within the church we have witnessed a corrosion of biblical and creational understanding as we have floated in the waters of Western values. We ourselves suffer widespread damage when we put our personal needs to the top of our agenda rather than conforming our desires, our thinking and all our relationships, including the one we inevitably have with creation, to the character of our Creator. If we elevate our personal story above the story of the cosmic redemption in which we find ourselves, we lose our sense of what matters to God and are left with a worthless quest to establish what should matter to us. In the daily work of nature conservation, such confusion is a great and practical problem. Recent days of COVID-19 revealed to the general public how medical practitioners have always had to make tough choices if treatment resources are limited. What value is a new heart against ten thousand vaccines? Similarly, in the acutely resource-constrained world of nature conservation, what is the value of a program to "save" one iconic species such as a snow leopard compared to undramatic and hidden square miles of fungi in the soil, a web of life for everything around?

Your work has mattered, and we are profoundly grateful to know that it will endure. I write to thank you now and to urge you to continue to encourage and orientate us all as you have so faithfully done these seventy years.

The Church as Embodied Witness

Philip D. Kenneson

I HAD THE PRIVILEGE and pleasure to learn alongside and from Jonathan Wilson when we were both graduate students thirty-five years ago. One of the great blessings of those years was to be surrounded by fellow students like Jonathan who had a deep love for and abiding commitment to the church. Jonathan's subsequent ministry as a gifted teacher and writer has borne out what was always the case: Jonathan desired his life, regardless of what he was engaged in, to be in service to three inseparable things: Jesus Christ, the gospel of the kingdom, and the church. As a result, Jonathan has devoted much of his life to encouraging real communities of disciples to bear embodied witness to God's present-yet-still-coming reign of shalom.

The enduring challenge, of course, is discerning in any particular time and place what bearing such embodied witness might look like. For this short essay, and in honor of Jonathan's life and work, I would like to rehearse a bit of the story of one congregation that has sought over the last several decades to do precisely that: discern together what being a sign, foretaste, and servant of God's reign of shalom might look like on the Near Eastside of Indianapolis. I do so not because they have it all figured out; they would be the first to admit that they surely don't. But perhaps their struggle to more faithfully live into God's mission in and for their neighborhood can be used by the Spirit to stir our own imaginations about ways in which we too might participate in God's good work of healing and wholeness.

Englewood Christian Church was founded in 1895 and grew quickly in the early twentieth century to the point that, around 1970 (and before the notion of "megachurches" was commonplace), it was a congregation of about 1100 people. In fact, it was one of the largest in the country at the time. As was the case with many major cities, the demographics shifted during the second half of the twentieth century as many families and churches left the cities for the suburbs. Englewood made the decision to remain in the city; however, its membership shrank to about 250 members and it came to be viewed primarily as a mission outpost for the suburban churches. As a result of this well-documented "white flight" that took place across urban landscapes all across the United States, this congregation found itself in what was widely regarded as a blighted neighborhood, surrounded by neglected and abandoned property.

The congregation's decision to remain and be a presence there was not an easy one. What would it mean to remain? Who were they now? What they soon became was primarily a service agency. Suburban churches would drive in on weekends and do service projects. Englewood had a food pantry, a furniture pantry, and a clothes pantry where urban residents could receive secondhand castoffs from their now distant suburban neighbors. The church was full of old furniture and clothes. What the congregation realized over time was that this "service agency" mentality was not really helping their neighborhood, nor was it really bringing a greater measure of wholeness and human flourishing to anyone involved.

At this point, the congregation made the decision to step back and ask themselves some difficult questions. But first they needed to create space for serious conversation around who the church is called to be and who God was calling them to be as a congregation in that specific place. Not so long ago it was commonplace for churches to have Sunday evening services. Englewood decided that this Sunday evening time was their best opportunity to gather and talk as a family. So about twenty-five years ago they began a conversation every Sunday evening about fundamental things: the nature of the gospel and the church, who they were and who they were called to be, and what it might mean to live out the gospel incarnationally in their own particular time and place. That Sunday night conversation continues today.

It would be a grave mistake, however, to romanticize these weekly conversations. They were difficult and contentious. They discovered when they began asking fundamental questions that they didn't actually agree on many matters that they had assumed they did. As the conversations continued and got more difficult, they worked diligently to be open and honest with one another, but there was no denying how challenging, even painful, all of this was, and they lost a number of members. Over time, those who remained began to come to a working consensus about their God-given calling: God was calling them to be a part of God's mission and to be a sign, a foretaste, an outpost of God's reign in that neighborhood. They began to ask questions about what that might look like. And they began to ask what it might mean for their embodied witness if they truly believed God had given them all the gifts they needed to be faithful coworkers with God in that place.

At this point, the congregation had fewer than 200 members—a small congregation by most standards. But because they believed God had given them what they needed to be who they were called to be, they began paying greater attention to what was right in front of them. They began to notice, for example, that they were in a neighborhood that itself had many gifts even though very few people recognized them as such; instead, nearly everyone thought their blighted part of the city had little or nothing to offer. So Englewood began a number of initiatives they hoped would help them see their neighbors and neighborhood differently. They held neighborhood meetings, listening and taking inventory of the manifold gifts at hand. Rather than hiring a youth minister as their second staff person, Englewood hired a member of their congregation who was good at construction to be a development organizer. Equally important, in 1995 Englewood started a nonprofit Community Development Corporation (ECDC).

As they began focusing on paying attention to what God was already doing in their neighborhood and what gifts God had already given them, they also began asking questions about how those gifts matched the needs of their neighbors. They heard that an older, single mother in their congregation was living on minimum wage and was about to be evicted from her house. The congregation asked themselves: What gifts and assets do we have as a congregation to address this situation? After deliberating, they took one of the abandoned houses near the church, removed the furniture being stored there, and completely renovated the house. The woman and her family moved into what was essentially a brand-new house. And then they realized two things: one, there were all kinds of people in the neighborhood who needed better housing; and two, all these run-down properties in the neighborhood that had seemed liked problems now appeared as assets. So they began to see part of their mission of shalom-making as providing both good housing and good work for people through refurbishing neighborhood houses.

Over the years they have completely refurbished forty houses within a two-block area of the church. As a result, more members of the congregation began moving into the neighborhood surrounding the church property. Today, about three-fourths of the congregation lives within a four-block radius of the church. Together they seek to be an incarnational presence in that neighborhood. And that they are. They have also done repair work on over two hundred additional houses in the neighborhood. With ECDC serving as an employer, neighbors are granted an opportunity to enhance their skills and to do meaningful work.

The church was also gifted a few years ago with an old public elementary school that sits adjacent to its property. Considerable resources were devoted to transforming the former school into much-needed housing; it now contains thirty-two units of mixed income apartments, with a dozen of those units reserved for those coming out of homelessness with some form of mental illness or physical disability. Other tenants pay affordable, below-market rates, while others pay market rates, yet all are living together in the same space. ECDC has also renovated other nearby buildings, creating about seventy affordable senior apartment units. Many of these environmentally conscious apartments were designed to generate more energy than they use.

One final aspect of this congregation's creative foray into neighborhood housing is worth noting. Not only has the congregation provided housing and opportunities for meaningful work to their neighbors, but because these properties are owned by ECDC, they also control the cost of this housing to ensure it remains affordable. Likewise, they have control over who their tenants are, ensuring it continues to be a mixed neighborhood and thereby resisting the neighborhood's gentrification.

In addition to housing, the congregation has also been a force for good in the neighborhood when it comes to education. In the mid-1990s, two women in the congregation decided they would like better day care and pre-K options for their children. A lot of young working mothers lived in the neighborhood, and there were limited options for their children. Because the church's sizable building was mostly unused during the week, the women asked if they could use a room so they could teach their children and other neighborhood children. This was the seed that over time has grown into Daystar Childcare and Infant Learning Center, one of the top early childhood programs in Indiana. Daystar not only offers affordable education each day to over two hundred children from ages six weeks to twelve years old, but it has also received national accreditation and the State of Indiana's highest quality rating. They also employ forty people full-time, paying them a livable wage, which is no small achievement given their commitment to offering affordable education to low-income neighbors. Even though churches in Indiana who run such programs are not required to be licensed, all of Englewood's teachers are licensed and the program voluntarily meets all state regulations. They also seek to be a good neighbor by offering children enrichment opportunities. Annually they take one hundred children on a three-day camping trip, giving parents a much-needed break while offering many children their first opportunity to experience nature in this way.

This congregation for many years, through its CDC, has also run a mowing service, cutting lawns and landscaping a number of city parks. This small business allows them to hire low-skilled workers and offer them a living wage. In this and other ventures, Englewood thinks about and practices economics unconventionally. When people are hired, they have a frank and open conversation about how much they need to earn to live. And then ECDC tries to meet that. This means that people working the same jobs may not make the same amount, with some workers actually earning more than their supervisors. Likewise, income levels and salaries can fluctuate over time, depending upon current financial obligations. If some employees have student loans to pay, they might make more until those loans are paid off, at which time they may agree to take a reduction in pay to support others. This countercultural approach to economics focuses attention on how much people need and not on finding one's identity and worth in one's annual income. Such an approach is rooted in trust, since people are simply asked to be honest about how much they really need to live.

This posture of trust and risk is also displayed in the congregation's willingness to dream boldly about new ways they might be an instrument of God's work of shalom. For many years, ECDC has been instrumental in renovating abandoned commercial property and transforming it into opportunities for new, locally owned businesses. Today you will find a small Mexican restaurant in a refurbished house, a print shop and artist collective in a former warehouse, a coffee shop in a repurposed historic lodge building, and a space where custom woodworkers design and sell contemporary furniture.

More recently ECDC has partnered with an even wider array of community groups, seeking creative and redemptive ways of transforming some of the neighborhood's largest abandoned commercial properties into assets that support human flourishing. For years they had dreamed about how they might redeem a huge abandoned factory that had once been a major employer in the area, but like many abandoned properties, the site was contaminated. Rather than seeing this as an insurmountable problem, Englewood chose to keep dreaming and planning and seeking more partnerships. As a result of that careful planning, creative financing, and cooperation from many stakeholders, this property that was for many years little more than a visible scar, a daily reminder of how their neighborhood had been abandoned, has been transformed into one of the Near Eastside's greatest assets. It is now home to two fine schools, including the Englewood campus of Purdue Polytechnic High School, an innovative project-based high school that seeks to ready a greater number of under-resourced young people for college and beyond. Another part of the property houses a sixty-thousand-square-foot state-of-the-art hydroponic farm, owned, in partnership with ECDC, by an international company with expertise in such farming. This venture has created local jobs, sells to local retailers, and also provides healthy produce for distribution to those who would not otherwise have access to it. These examples are further powerful testimony to what can happen when the Spirit is at work in and through a community who believes God has given them everything they need to flourish.

This brief sketch of Englewood only touches on some of the ways this relatively small congregation is seeking to bear witness to God's reign of shalom on the Near Eastside of Indianapolis. One can't live in that part of town and not know about this congregation, but few people outside their little corner of the world know much about them. This congregation doesn't like to talk about themselves and they are nervous when people try to hold them up as a model for anything. They are simply seeking daily to be faithful to their calling to be an agent of God's life-giving Spirit in their surrounding neighborhood. They are quick to say they are not doing this work by themselves; rather, they are always seeking to cooperate with what God is already doing in their midst, which usually means partnering with other community organizations in the area. They don't begin any venture without being in conversation with their neighborhood, trying to be good neighbors rather than saviors. By God's grace and the Spirit's patient work through them over decades, this congregation serves as a visible, embodied sign of God's reign, leading people to ask all kinds of questions, such as "Why are you here?" and "Why are you doing this?" Such questions create a most fruitful dynamic within which to talk about the good news of Jesus Christ.

Yet even if we are wise not to make Englewood a model to emulate, there is still much about their embodied life that can stir our imaginations. They are, by God's grace, a beautiful incarnational presence in their neighborhood. They come alongside people of all ages, help them recognize their gifts, and then encourage them to put those gifts to work in life-giving ways. They are also deep and patient learners, and their life together is organic, slow, and messy. They once devoted an entire year to studying the book of Ephesians, imagining together what it might mean for their daily lived experience if God really is making known the manifold wisdom of God through the church. Their deep learning is also enhanced by wide reading, which is aided by their own very fine publication, *The Englewood Review of Books*, where they encourage thoughtful and imaginative engagement with important voices across a wide theological and ideological spectrum.

Englewood's willingness to wrestle with difficult challenges and then risk putting that learning into action has real-life implications for every sphere of life, including economics and the shape of daily work. Those thoughtful decisions and practices have a shalom-making ripple effect across their congregation and into their local neighborhood and community. That wrestling and learning always takes place in collaboration, not only through their congregational conversations and partnerships with other neighborhood leaders and groups, but also through larger networks of congregations and intentional communities from whom they continue to learn. Englewood's approach to everything always begins with what God has already given rather than in terms of what they might feel compelled to do. They are constantly asking: If God really has given us everything we need, indeed, an *abundance—more than what we need—*here in this place, how do we best use those gifts to join God's mission in the world? Theologically speaking, that's a very sound place to start, and perhaps other congregations would do well to begin conversations amongst themselves about what their embodied life together might look like in their places if they began there as well. My hope and prayer is that in sharing a bit of their story, more people might be inspired to seek ways to live out God's call to be a foretaste of God's reign of shalom in their own neighborhoods, seeking creative ways to be used by God's Spirit to bring a greater measure of healing and wholeness to a broken world.[1]

---

[1]. For those interested in learning more about the Englewood story, esp. concerning the central role of regular and deep conversation for their life together, see esp. two books by C. Christopher Smith, founding editor of *The Englewood Review of Books* and member of Englewood Christian Church: *The Virtue of Dialogue: Conversation as a Hopeful Practice of Church Communities* (Englewood, CO: Patheos, 2012) and *How the Body of Christ Talks: Recovering the Practice of Conversation in the Church* (Grand Rapids: Brazos, 2019).

Learning to Be a Missional Church

Rob Filgate

I was on my way to meet some of the young leaders in my church when I noticed that my front pocket was growing hot. This had happened before (a few times) and I immediately recognized the source of the heat. I had put my phone in my pocket without first turning it off. So, I reached into my pocket, pulled out my phone, went to turn it off, and noticed that it had somehow opened my contacts and the name on the screen was Jonathan Wilson. I hadn't been in contact with Jonathan since my ordination four years earlier.

Jonathan had been a professor of mine and his teaching and his life had deeply impacted me. Consequently, I had asked Jonathan to speak at my ordination on Vancouver Island in 2012. Eight months later I ended up moving to Wales to pastor a Baptist church in the market town of Cardigan, just a few miles down the road from the site where the 1904 Welsh revival began. In the gap of time and with the activity of life, I had lost touch with Jonathan. Now, here he was unexpectedly on my screen.

I continued on to my meeting and forgot about the "pocket dial" until later that evening when the odd incident came to mind. Something about seeing Jonathan's name on my phone seemed providential, and I wondered if he still had the same contact info. I decided to send a brief email and to my surprise (and delight) he responded right away. I was even more surprised to hear that he was coming to the United Kingdom in a few week's time. And even more surprised to hear the reason he was coming to the United Kingdom—he had remarried, and his wife, Soohwan, had an A Rocha board meeting near London. This seemed to be shaping into a real "God-incidence." We quickly made arrangements and Jonathan and Soohwan came to West Wales to stay with us for a few nights. That visit (followed by two more visits) would have a greater impact than I could ever have imagined.

I had moved to Wales with my wife, Andrea, in 2013 to pastor a Baptist church in Cardigan. The calling to come to Wales was clear but the true purpose of our calling here still remained a mystery. God had made it clear to me at the start of my pastoral ministry that I was to call people to worship and to live holy lives. So, in this small church in rural Wales I did what I know how to do and God was gracious to us and the church began to grow. We saw people come to faith and even baptized whole families. In a country where churches were in steep decline, our church was growing. But something wasn't quite right.

Mount Zion Church was a traditional Baptist church with a big heart for people. But we were experiencing the tension that comes with a growing church—new Christians with no church background were expected to adopt the traditional ways of doing church. I concluded that some of the traditional ways needed to change. When I came to Wales I had no intention of transitioning a church, and no experience in being part of that kind of change. But I had a growing sense that God was setting us up for something. At first, I thought the needed transition was to go from a traditional church to a more contemporary church. A transition in style, not substance. I couldn't have been more wrong. The transition needed was much more foundational than that.

Around this same time, I discovered that the denomination was seeking ways to counter the rapid decline of members and churches (on average, the Baptist Union of Wales had been closing one church per week) and I began to meet with some of the denominational leaders. We were on a similar quest, but they had a much larger task. The denomination was seeking a path for change and knew that mission had to be part of the solution. They were a few steps ahead of me, but still without answers.

This was about the time that my pocket began to heat up. God was at work. Jonathan and Soohwan came to Wales and we had a wonderful visit. It was great to reconnect and grow our relationship and also to seek some wisdom from both of them. It was during our conversations that I began to see things differently. I don't remember an exact moment, but I realized that God had not called me to Wales to transition a traditional church to be a more contemporary church. God had called me to Wales to come alongside a traditional Baptist church to help us to become more missional. Everything changed in that moment. I wasn't even sure what it meant to be "missional" and I certainly didn't know how to be part of such a paradigm shift.

It was during Jonathan's next visit a year later that we went for lunch one day after dropping Soohwan of at Ffald y Brenin retreat center for the afternoon, and I continued to share the story of Mount Zion Church with Jonathan. The church was still growing numerically but I was struggling with helping the church become more missional. At the time we were considering moving from the little redbrick church building that we had outgrown to the local high school hall and some people were struggling with the idea of a move.

Jonathan listened patiently as I talked, paused thoughtfully when I had finished, and then asked me if I knew Cam Roxburgh. I had meet Cam a few times but had not kept in touch and had no idea what Cam was up to. Jonathan didn't expand much but simply said, "I think you should contact Cam and ask him about Forge Canada."[1]

I contacted Cam and asked him about Forge Missional Training and after a few FaceTime calls things began to come into focus and I realized that this missional training wasn't just for me or for Mount Zion Church, but this was a way forward for the whole denomination. The next move was to introduce Cam to the director of mission for the Baptist Union of Wales.

A number of years earlier the Baptist Union of Wales made the bold move to create a position titled director of mission. Simeon Baker, the director of mission, had been searching for a way of engaging more of our churches missionally. For years he had been looking for a process that would fit the Welsh context. Wales has a unique culture, and the church in Wales has a very unique culture—one that looks skeptically on any type of program that comes from the outside.

Especially if the outside source is England or America.

But the Welsh look kindly on Canadians. They even like our accents. So, missional training from a Canadian source had a chance to be accepted. And a training "process" had a much better chance of acceptance than an imported, ready-made program. Of course, the process of accepting *anything* in the Baptist context takes many meetings and is slow by any standard. We met with Cam (online and in person) over the next

---

1. See Forge Global, "Our Story," n.d., http://www.forgeinternational.com/about#our-story.

two years and finally, the Baptist Union of Wales entered into an official partnership with Forge Canada in the autumn of 2020.

It was a minor miracle that both the Welsh- and English-speaking wings of the Baptist Union agreed to fund the two-year training process. The likelihood of this was truly nonexistent when we started discussing the possibility, but God was at work. And against all the odds, we began the training with nearly twenty churches and over a hundred participants. Ten months into the training and we are already witnessing a noticeable impact in Wales. To be more specific, I'd like to share the impact that the Forge Missional Training has had on my leadership and the church I pastor.

I love my church. We care about the community God has placed us in and desire to be "missional." We are devoted to prayer and we embrace opportunities to invite friends and family to church (Back to Church Sundays, Carols by Candlelight, Easter, baptisms). We hold three specific outreach activities to serve the local community each year, and we have seen much fruit from these efforts. But is that what a missional church is?

Each time we planned a mission event, a small number of our "mission-minded" people participated, leaving mission to those few "called" ones. Inadvertently, we were sending the message that mission is optional. We were sending the message that not everyone is called to live missionally—some people are called to serve in other areas. We had reduced mission to be a program or ministry of the church that some people engaged in.

We needed what Forge Canada calls a "renewed theological vision of the church on mission." We needed a greater understanding that mission is not just an action we participate in, but an attribute of God. God is missional in nature and in action. *Missio Dei*—the God of mission. The mission of God is what unifies the Bible from beginning to new beginning. And we are invited into this great story. We are a chosen people, being conformed into the image of Christ, taking on the nature and character of our heavenly Father. We are becoming missional in nature because God is missional in nature.

I began to realize that we had embraced a management model of mission. We put mission into our terms. We had a mission mandate from God and in response we were going to manage mission and do missional things for God rather than join God in his mission. Christopher J. H. Wright has said, "It's not so much the case that God has a mission for his church in the world, as that God has a church for his mission in the world.

Mission was not made for the church; the church was made for mission. God's mission."[2] We had it backwards. We thought God had a mission for us to reach our community and we had to somehow figure out the best way to do that. Being missional meant doing missional things. But we weren't starting from a right understanding. We were asking church questions, not God questions. Questions like "God, how can we attract more people to our summer outreach events?" and "How can we encourage our members to invite their friends to the Christmas carol service?"

If you start with the wrong questions, you will likely end up with the wrong answers.

If indeed the promise of Jesus in Matt 9 is true, the God of mission is at work in his world and the harvest is plentiful. It's the workers who are few. It's the workers who are distracted by many things and not going into the harvest field. We were working diligently at what we thought we should be doing, but not stopping to ask God, "Where is your harvest field? Where are you at work and how can we join you?

The kingdom reality is that God is at work in the world and has a church for his mission. It is his mission and we have been set apart (called to live holy lives) for the purpose of being sent back in to the world. This sending is at the very heart of the Father. As the Trinitarian formula goes, the Father sent the Son; the Father and the Son sent the Holy Spirit; the Father and Son and the Holy Spirit are sending the church to be a sign, instrument and foretaste of the kingdom. We have been sent, each one of us, to bear witness to "the most real world" (to use a phrase that I have heard Jonathan express on many occasions.) The most real world where Jesus is Lord, and where we are nourished by the word and where his church is being transformed into his likeness. Where, even in our weakness, we bear witness to the life giving power of the gospel, and in doing so bear witness to the reality of the kingdom of God in our midst.

The transition from a traditional church to a missional church is a slow and at times a painful process. Old patterns and understandings do not change without a fight. But we are learning to be a community of Christ followers who are learning what it means to join the God of mission. And I have been gaining a new understanding of what it means to pastor such a church. Many of the accepted patterns of Christendom are being challenged. Shifting our energies from a Sunday focus to an everyday, kingdom focus is a difficult step to take. The understanding

---

2. Christopher J. H. Wright, *The Mission of God: Unlocking the Bible's Grand Narrative* (Nottingham, UK: InterVarsity, 2006), 62.

that our neighborhoods are our mission fields and that God is at work in our neighborhoods is a difficult reality to live into. The shift from attending church to being a disciple of Christ is challenging. The traditional role of the pastor has been challenged as well—shifting from expert to equipper—and I'm having to learn new ways to equip people to faithfully participate in the mission of God.

I had no idea that reconnecting with an old friend would lead to the Baptist church in Wales pursuing a renewed theological vision of the church on mission. Or, to put it another way, "Who wouldathunk that a hot pocket would lead to the Baptist church in Wales heating up?"

Who can fathom the mind of our Lord?

Join with All Nature in Manifold Witness

Engaging the Soteriological Doxa of Secular Vancouver

Ross Lockhart

"As followers of Jesus Christ, we are situated in the world to be witnesses to the good news that in Jesus Christ God loves and saves the world."[1] I first came across Jonathan Wilson's work as a young pastor while serving a congregation in Northern Ontario. The remote yet beautiful environs of that ministry included winters so cold one was often left imaging a more urgent call to the mission fields of Hawaii. I was fresh out of seminary, armed with that heretically named degree "master of divinity," oddly implying that I had somehow *mastered* the eternal God through education. A little bit like a rematch at the ford of the Jabbok, this time with Jacob walking (rather than limping) away, holding on tightly to the champion's belt like a WWE superstar. No, as I was about to discover, pastoral ministry in post-Christendom required placing trust in divine agency, rather than human ingenuity, if one were to catch even a glimpse of the now, and not-yet, kingdom. Therein lay both the gift and dilemma that Jonathan Wilson's words presented. So much of my preparation for ministry was through the lens of a "religious professional." I was skilled in the latest exegetical tools and homiletical models for presenting the

---

1. Jonathan R. Wilson, *God So Loved the World: A Christology for Disciples* (Grand Rapids: Eerdmans, 2001), 160.

gospel to a receptive audience ... I mean congregation. My pastoral care was essentially "psychotherapy lite" with the appropriate head nodding and questions that a television news reporter asks, like "How did that make you feel?" Ministry in (formerly) mainline denominations was imagined as somehow static, even though we were already in a time of growing discontinuous change and desperately in need of adaptive leadership.

Being called to witness? That sounded more passive than my Christendom training suggested. Of course, there is nothing redeemable about "our ministry." As Andrew Purves argues, "Ministry kills us with regard to our ego needs, desire for power and success and the persistent wish to feel competent and in control."[2] Jonathan Wilson's approach to Christology, alongside the missional movement, awakened me to the witnessing/participatory nature of ministry that Purves so aptly describes as "the ministry of the church is our participation in the continuing ministry of Jesus Christ, to the glory of the Father, in the power of the Holy Spirit."[3]

It was on a return trip to Toronto that I happened upon Jonathan Wilson's *God So Loved the World* in a theological bookstore. It accompanied me on the long journey back north and became a welcome and familiar go-to resource in the pastor's study and pulpit. Little did I know that many years later I would end up on the University of British Columbia campus with Jonathan Wilson as a colleague and friend at nearby Carey Theological College. In fact, after his service at Carey concluded, Jonathan even moved in with us at St. Andrew's Hall with a lovely little office on the third floor. From that place, Jonathan influenced the developing Center for Missional Leadership, offering his wisdom, humor, and guidance alongside our Senior Fellow in Residence Darrell Guder. How could it be that two of the scholars who shaped my ministry and discipleship in print were now with me in person? It leads one, especially a Presbyterian, to

---

2. Andrew Purves, *The Crucifixion of Ministry: Surrendering Our Ambitions to the Service of Christ* (Downers Grove, IL: InterVarsity, 2007), xxi. To further drive home his point, Purves illustrates human limitations in ministry and our need to rely on the Holy Spirit when he writes, "It does not take us long to discover that we cannot heal the sick, raise the dead, calm the demonized, guide the morally afflicted, sober up the alcoholic, make the wife beater loving, calm the anxious, pacify the conflicted, control the intemperate, have answers to all the 'Why?' questions, give the teenagers a moral compass and preach magnificent sermons every week, all the while growing the congregation and keeping the members happy."

3. Andrew Purves, *Reconstructing Pastoral Theology: A Christological Foundation* (Louisville: Westminster John Knox, 2004), 10.

double down on the doctrine of providence! Indeed, with his keen sense of reading text and context, Jonathan helped further awaken my curiosity as a missiologist about what God was up to here in the secular, post-Christendom context of Vancouver to which we now turn.

The call to witness is central to the missional theology discussion that has shaped so much of the missiological discourse in North America over the last twenty years. Of course, the contemporary discussion on mission goes much back further, including as early as 1932 when theologian Karl Barth argued for a greater emphasis upon the missionary vocation of the church and the missionary nature of the triune God. David Bosch later described the shift as changing from a "church centred mission . . . to a mission centred church."[4] Barth's emphasis upon the Christian's vocation as witness has been a source of great encouragement for many who followed and explored more fully the impact of the *missio Dei* on church and culture.

When I first moved to Vancouver almost fifteen years ago, I had just completed my doctoral studies in homiletics and evangelism, eager to engage in a place that was known as the most secular part of Canada.[5] Yet, what I discovered here was even more challenging than I imagined. There was a reason, after all, that Vancouver and indeed all of Cascadia is known as a church planter's graveyard.[6] I came eager to engage in clever apologetics and ready to wade into deep and heated conversations with the new atheists that were a dime a dozen back in eastern Canada. But here, in this new space God had situated me for witness, I did not find angry atheists by and large. Rather, I found most of my neighbors were

---

4. Darrell Guder, "From Mission and Theology to Missional Theology," *Princeton Seminary Bulletin* 24 (2003): 36–54, esp. 43.

5. I encourage my students to acknowledge the different "secularities" in Canada. For example, Quebecois secularity, following the Quiet Revolution, is quite different with its hard-edged approach to religion, compared to the more laid-back secularity of the West Coast. Nevertheless, West Coast secularity regarding those who identify as "nones" is highest, as profiled in Joel Thiessen and Sarah Wilkins-LaFlamme's *None of the Above: Nonreligious Identity in the US and Canada* (Regina, Can.: University of Regina Press, 2020), 13.

6. Cascadia is the commonly used regional name for Oregon, Washington state, and British Columbia that share the Cascade Mountain range. A church-planting colleague in Portland told us how she loved to go to local coffee shops and play "spot the new church planter from Christendom Texas" in skinny jeans and a full sleeve of tattoos. "What they don't get is that the soil is different here in Cascadia. This is a church-planting graveyard if you don't come prepared." Jason Byassee and Ross A. Lockhart, *Better Than Brunch: Missional Churches in Cascadia* (Eugene, OR: Cascade, 2020), 3.

simply affable agnostics. "Hey, so you're like a spiritual person, that's cool. I think my grandma maybe went to church or something. Anyways, have a great Sunday—I'm off to cycle Stanley Park and then up Grouse Mountain this afternoon to ski." Um, okay. Once more, Jonathan Wilson's teaching offered me both gift and dilemma. He wrote,

> To carry out [its] mission in the world, the church must speak a language that the world understands. . . . To faithfully proclaim the kingdom, the church must know how the kingdom is present in a particular time and place. And it must proclaim that kingdom in an idiom appropriate to that time and place. But the church that is in the world for the sake of the kingdom is also not of the world. . . . This means that when the church faithfully proclaims the presence of the kingdom in the language of the world, it does not trim the gospel of the kingdom to fit the world's expectations.[7]

Later, I would better understand Wilson's cautionary remarks about trimming the gospel to fit the world's expectations through Darrell Guder's concept of reductionism. Guder argues that the fundamental form of reductionism is the "mission-benefits dichotomy that has established itself so firmly in the theologies and ecclesiastical practices of virtually all Christian traditions."[8] Indeed, there is the ever-present heretical danger of becoming "Marcion-like" by playing cut and paste with the Scriptures to suit our own desires. The latest "it church," with dry ice and lasers, preachers in skinny jeans and ironic facial hair, always on the knife-edge of inculturating *or* enculturing the gospel.[9] No, I had to let go of what I thought I knew about Christian witness in a previous context, still running on the fumes of Christendom, in order to respond to what God was already up to in the lives of those around me on the West Coast. It was at this time that I started to dive into the deep end of the missional theology pool, aided in large part by regular sushi lunches with Alan Roxburgh,

---

7. Wilson, *God So Loved*, 176.

8. Darrell L. Guder, *The Continuing Conversion of the Church*, Gospel and Our Culture (Grand Rapids: Eerdmans, 2004), 137.

9. Inculturation is a missiological term which refers to ways to adapt the communication of the gospel for a specific culture being evangelized. Enculturation, however, is a process of influence by the dominant culture upon an individual or community to imbibe its accepted norms and values so the individual or community is pressured to find acceptance within the society of that culture. For more, see W. Ross Hastings, *Missional God, Missional Church: Hope for Re-Evangelizing the West* (Downers Grove, IL: InterVarsity, 2012), 38.

who, along with his family, participated in the church I was serving at the time in Vancouver.

Within the missional theology conversation, influenced significantly by the work of the Gospel and Our Culture Network, I began to look with new eyes upon the context where God situated me for witness. Paying attention (or is it praying attention?) is a crucial missional practice. As Anne Lamott wrote recently, "Seeing is a form of pure being, unlike watching or looking at. Seeing is why we're here."[10] This new way of seeing took me back to the original challenge that Jonathan Wilson's work on Christology offered me as a young pastor. Was I ready to adopt a posture of humility in ministry, awaiting divine agency? Or was I going to continue to engage in a mechanistic, human agency driven model of change, a "de facto deism" that treats God like an absent landlord who rents the apartment but doesn't return to fix a leaky toilet? Indeed, the turn towards missional theology necessitated a posture of cooperating with the Spirit "to form witnessing communities that participate in the divine mission by living God's love in the way of Jesus Christ for the sake of the world."[11]

It took several years for God to help me unlearn and relearn patterns of witness appropriate for the West Coast, in light of the lessons gleaned from the missional conversation. In doing so, I did not leave behind my convictions or assurance of who Jesus Christ is for the sake of the world. Rather, building on Jonathan Wilson's exploration of Christology from multiple images,[12] the missional conversation offers a robust yet expansive understanding of the saving work of Jesus Christ. John Franke explains it this way:

> Missional Christology does not seek a single, normative theological conception of the person and work of Christ. It acknowledges the importance of plurality in Christological and

---

10. Anne Lamott, *Dusk, Night, Dawn: On Revival and Courage* (New York: Riverhead, 2021), 47.

11. John Franke, *Missional Theology: An Introduction* (Grand Rapids: Baker Academic, 2020), 86. Franke helpfully defines missional theology as "an ongoing, second-order, contextual discipline that engages in the task of critical and constructive reflection on the beliefs and practices of the Christian church for the purpose of assisting the community of Christ's followers in their missional vocation to live as the people of God in their particular social-historical context" (172).

12. Wilson, *God So Loved*, 134. Throughout the book Wilson juxtaposes and develops the richness of multiple soteriological meanings of the cross from Jesus as sacrifice, example, and victor.

theological construction while also affirming the centrality of the person of Jesus for all of life. It resists an "anything goes" approach that is characteristic of radical cultural relativism; instead, it affirms what might be called a "thick" or "convictional" plurality rooted in the Christian tradition. This thick plurality arises from the nature and character of God as a missionary, the unique role of Jesus in the mission of God, the witness of the Spirit to Jesus in the mission of God, the belief that God speaks in revelation, and the trustworthiness of Scripture as a faithful witness to that revelation.[13]

Driven, therefore, by the desire to engage and participate in the missionary work of the triune God, or as Jonathan Wilson would prefer, one God—Father, Son and Spirit,[14] we attend to the particularities and peculiarities of where we are "situated," in order to offer effective witness to who Jesus Christ is for the world—the same yesterday, today, forever.

While we could explore many different areas of what effective missional witness looks like in Vancouver, the limitations of this chapter enable us to focus on only one. While I have explored other missiological themes in Vancouver elsewhere in greater detail, from real estate to immigration to individualism, Jonathan's compelling work *God's Good World* led me instead to reflect on the high value that Vancouverites place on the environment.[15] Indeed, Vancouver is recognized as being distinctive from other regions of Canada in part due to its particular geography, climate, and culture.[16] Raymond Madden argues that "the relationships between humans and places are complex and multi-layered. Humans

---

13. Franke, *Missional Theology*, 161.

14. Jonathan R. Wilson, *God's Good World: Reclaiming the Doctrine of Creation* (Grand Rapids: Baker Academic, 2013), 71. Wilson notes, "I use the unusual and somewhat awkward phrase 'one God—Father, Son and Holy Spirit' to keep us mindful of the limitations of human language when directed to God. I do not use the more familiar 'Trinity' or 'Triune God' because I think that those terms have become so familiar that they are nearly empty of meaning. We confess 'one God—Father, Son and Spirit.'"

15. For a more fulsome exploration of other aspects of Christian mission in Vancouver, please see Ross A. Lockhart, ed., *Christian Witness in Post-Christian Soil: Coworkers with God in the Land of Hiking, Hipsters, and Hand-Crafted Lattes* (Eugene, OR: Cascade, 2021).

16. Home to over 2.5 million people, Greater Vancouver is known for its stunning natural beauty, being the birthplace of environmental groups like Greenpeace, and taking seriously the licence plate motto, "Beautiful British Columbia."

are place-makers and places make humans."¹⁷ Here on the West Coast of Canada the soaring tree-lined, snow-capped mountains sweep down majestically to the sparkling Pacific Ocean in Instagram-post perfection. And yet, surrounded by such stunning natural beauty, Vancouverites appear to be on a different page than John Calvin, who urged us to take a "pious delight in the clear and manifest works of God" in the "beautiful theatre" of creation.¹⁸ Our Christian ancestors sang "Join with all nature in manifold witness,"¹⁹ knowing that "nature" was doxologically charged where "the mountains and hills will burst into song before you, and all the trees of the field will clap their hands" (Isa 55:12).²⁰ In Vancouver today, however, those cherry blossoms in spring . . . well, they are *just* cherry blossoms. Period. Drawing on Canadian philosopher Charles Taylor's *A Secular Age*, Jonathan Wilson laments the "far-reaching and damaging effects of the loss of teleology" in what he describes as "the transformation of creation into nature."²¹ Wilson argues this turn to nature is the conviction that this world is all that there ever has been and ever will be. Echoing Charles Taylor, Wilson notes that even Christians in this "imminent frame" are conditioned to see the world around them within the self-governing norms of nature. What I have identified elsewhere as "Christian Functional Atheism,"²² Wilson describes in this way: "people are most often 'practical naturalists,' confessing belief in God and creation and afterlife while living as if this world were all there ever has been and ever will be."²³

What does Christian witness look like in a landscape where the Creator has not only gone missing, but creation itself has been domesticated as simply the beautiful backdrop of Canada's third largest city—a recreational playground for hiking and exploration without fear of the

---

17. Raymond Madden, *Being Ethnographic: A Guide to the Theory and Practice of Ethnography* (London: Sage, 2010), 37.

18. John Calvin, *Inst.* 1.14.20 (*Institutes of the Christian Religion* [Peabody, MA: Hendrickson, 2008]).

19. Thomas O. Chisholm, "Great Is Thy Faithfulness," in *The Book of Praise* (Toronto: The Presbyterian Church in Canada, 1997), #418.

20. This chapter uses the NIV translation for Scripture references, unless otherwise indicated.

21. Wilson, *God's Good World*, 37.

22. Ross A. Lockhart, *Lessons from Laodicea: Missional Leadership in a Culture of Affluence* (Eugene, OR: Cascade, 2016), 49.

23. Wilson, *God's Good World*, 38.

elements?[24] In his book *Cascadia*, journalist Douglas Todd suggests that environmentalism is the civil religion of the Pacific Northwest.[25] While people may not feel a bond to each other as closely here in Vancouver as they might to neighbors "back east" in the rest of Canada, there *is* a close bond with nature and human beings' responsible care for it.[26] Indeed, more than once I've quipped that "the hardest part about preaching heaven in Vancouver is that most people think they're already there!"

In response to this reality, Jonathan Wilson's work in *God's Good World* is an encouragement for us to find new and effective ways of translating the gospel in this context to share the saving work of Jesus with those whose default "civic religion" is reverence for nature. I was reminded of this recently when on a rare snow day in Vancouver I took my youngest child up to the local hill to toboggan. While there I struck up a conversation with the man beside me. He remarked on how nice it was for the kids to have a day off school. I agreed and noted how the snow reminded me of growing up in Manitoba. The man replied that he was born and raised in Vancouver and never experienced a "real winter." Other pleasantries were exchanged as we pushed our children on their sleds, until at one point he inquired, "So, what school does your daughter go to?" An innocent question. I replied that our kids went to the local Christian school. The other man's body language changed, however, becoming frostier than the snow falling around us. "Oh," he said, taking a step back and looking puzzled. "So . . ." he stuttered, "you're a Christian?" The way he asked the question made Christianity sound like a communicable disease. "Um, yeah, I'm a Christian," I replied with tempered zeal (like a good Presbyterian). He stood there quietly for a moment and continued, "I don't know any Christians. So, what *do* you guys really believe about climate change, anyways?" What began as a simple exercise of taking my daughter

---

24. It's ironic that our ancestors in North America, both settler and Indigenous, living with an enchanted worldview, often had more respect, even fear, of creation/nature, knowing that often people would go into the woods or mountains and never return. Where I sit and write this chapter is five minutes from the North Shore Rescue helipad where I regularly hear the team going up to look for flip-flop- and shorts-wearing naïve hikers who get lost in the snowy elevations of the North Shore Mountains.

25. Douglas Todd, ed., *Cascadia: The Elusive Utopia—Exploring the Spirit of the Northwest* (Vancouver, BC: Ronsdale, 2008), 18.

26. The limited scope of this chapter does not enable us to engage in a more fulsome theological discussion on whether there is evidence of Vancouverites exhibiting either pantheism or panentheistic viewpoints regarding nature, but it is worth further exploration.

tobogganing had now escalated into some off the cuff apologetics. "Well," I replied cautiously, "As Christians we believe God created everything in the universe, including the Earth, and that we are called to be good stewards of creation. As followers of Jesus, we believe in partnering with God to repair the world and are happy to work with anyone, no matter what their faith beliefs might be, to help take care of the planet." Not exactly sparkling evangelism, but it gave me time to continue the conversation and listen as he offered in return the various media-fueled stereotypes about Christianity not caring about the environment.[27]

Reflecting on this curious but not unusual experience, I realized that surely part of our Christian witness in this context involves the articulation of our shared concern for creation that identifies our common creatureliness. Jonathan Wilson thinks so, as he contends, "Let me say this strongly: we are not truly and fully human until we believe that we are God's creatures and trust in Christ to remove our inhumanity, free us from all that makes us less than human, and bear away the consequences of our refusal to acknowledge our creatureliness and trust in God for life."[28] Surely this move from excarnation to incarnation, made all the more challenging by the enhanced digital lives we've lived through the pandemic (including in Christian community), is a key aspect of Christian witness in the particular context of a highly individualized and isolated urban context such as Vancouver.[29] Our creatureliness binds us to one another in community. Tim Dickau, my colleague in the Center for Missional Leadership, who himself has been deeply influenced by Jonathan's wisdom, notes this essential role of a witnessing community, especially if it has developed a thicker, more porous life together. He writes, "Our formation in Christ takes place in the flow and rhythms of daily life in communion with others. Working alongside one another at a community meal . . . serving on non-profit boards together and playing soccer on a Sunday afternoon with neighbors can all become contexts of disciple-making, where the way of following Christ is 'caught' more than

---

27. Lockhart, *Christian Witness*, xiv.

28. Wilson, *God's Good World*, 41.

29. In its well-researched, detailed, and thoughtful report, the Vancouver Foundation released its findings regarding social isolation for residents, entitled *Connections and Engagement: A Survey of Metro Vancouver*, Vancouver Foundation, June 2012, https://www.vancouverfoundation.ca/sites/default/files/documents/VanFdn-Survey-Results-Report.pdf.

taught."³⁰ Missional theology can help place that common experience, or overlapping consensus, with neighbors into a larger framework of shared concerns and values. As Alan Roxburgh says, "God is about a big purpose in and for the whole of creation. The church has been called into life to be both the means of this mission and a foretaste of where God is inviting all creation to go."³¹

Leveraging the overlapping consensus of environmental concern with our affable agnostic neighbor offers us the ability to articulate the gospel through the lens of care for creation. Wilson reminds us regarding creation care that "a theology with a robust doctrine of creation would help us see that our environmental crisis is not rooted in our struggle to manage scarcity or to allocate resources properly in a zero-sum game; it would help us to see rather that our environmental crisis is rooted in our misuse and abuse of the superabundance provided by God."³² Again, returning to missional theology's emphasis upon the *missio Dei*, we can see how our witness is conditioned by trust in divine agency. Are we, in the words of Alan Roxburgh, becoming "detectives of divinity" or, per David Fitch's call, attending to God's "faithful presence"? Do we live missionally in a way that Jonathan Wilson asks whether a "precedence of the mission of God over the church's mission" is evident?³³ If so, maybe *this* is a gift for an exhausted yet environmentally sensitive Vancouverite when it comes to Christian witness? For those who are fully immersed in the "baptismal waters" of the soteriological doxa of environmentalism

---

30. Tim Dickau, *Forming Christian Communities in a Secular Age: Recovering Humility and Hope* (Toronto: Tyndale, 2021), 150. Tim adds, "In these contexts, the art of discipleship is observed, copied and practiced. Since many of these actions are public, those who are not yet followers of Christ can begin to find a place of belonging within the community and imagine what it might be like for them to join in living this way."

31. Allan Roxburgh and Fred Romanuk, *The Missional Leader: Equipping Your Church to Reach a Changing World* (Minneapolis: Fortress, 2020), xi.

32. Wilson, *God's Good World*, 23. Even the language of creation care is problematic, as Leah Kostamo reminded my students reading her book *Planted* in last year's Introduction to Practical Theology course at Vancouver School of Theology. Kostamo is a founder and spiritual care coordinator of A Rocha Canada, an environmental ministry on a farm in Surrey, BC, long supported by Jonathan Wilson. She noted her movement away from the language of "creation care" given the power and patriarchal tones, which risk leaning into an unhealthy understanding of language that leaves everything up to us as human beings to control.

33. Jonathan R. Wilson, "Beloved Community as Missional Witness," in *Christian Witness in Post-Christian Soil: Coworkers with God in the Land of Hiking, Hipsters, and Hand-Crafted Lattes*, ed. Ross A. Lockhart (Eugene, OR: Cascade, 2021), 169–80, 170.

in Vancouver, and who have been catechized in the doctrinal formula of Reduce, Reuse, and Recycle, is there anything more teleological to offer other than one's best efforts to save the planet? Thank God (literally) the answer is yes. As Wilson reminds us, missional witness offers hope to the world. Wilson writes that effective missional witness is "rooted in God's intention for all creation (by and for Jesus Christ—Colossians 1), the mission of God's people is to live in such a way that we participate in God's realizing of the telos of creation in new creation through Jesus Christ and bear witness to that telos as the Holy Spirit forms us, guides us, and equips us."[34] Christian witness in a fallen world, yet one not forsaken by God. For those living in this beautiful, beloved, yet broken world, there is hope. While honoring our neighbors' human-agency-driven mantra of reduce, reuse, recycle, Christians offer a more hopeful, divinely enabled response. Through *resurrection, redemption,* and *reconciliation* God is transforming the world in Jesus Christ through the Holy Spirit. And we get to participate. This good news, situated and translated into our context, joins our voice with the faithful through the ages in manifold witness whereby "a Christian doctrine of creation transforms this limited gratitude into limitless praise . . . in [Jesus] we see and participate in the redemption of creation for the new creation."[35]

---

34. Wilson, "Beloved Community," 175.
35. Wilson, *God's Good World*, 178.

Kingdom Realism

Gato Munyamasoko

FOR THE FIRST TWENTY-THREE years after I decided to follow Jesus, I thought my calling was simply to obey the Lord's commands in my own life and bring other people to Jesus. I became an evangelist in my home country, the Democratic Republic of Congo, to share the gospel with as many people as possible. This was good, but it did not lead me to think about the well-being of others or creation. It was as if "the kingdom of God" that Jesus talked about was only about being "saved." But once I came to learn about the integral mission of God—the word and deeds that cannot be separated—it changed my perception of the kingdom of God. This helped me to understand what God has intended for his people since the creation. During my ministry in the church, this led to a deep transformation of both myself and the flock I have been called to shepherd.

I want to give thanks for this new way of thinking that Professor Jonathan Wilson has helped to teach. Because of it, many people have been able to take steps out of poverty and gain a new standing in life. I have watched pastors change the way they were preaching. Because of this new understanding of the kingdom of God, Christians started organizing savings cooperatives in the Congo. Their small groups came together to form a big group, "Don't Sleep with Hunger When I Am Here," through which Christians share their resources in order to make sure their neighbors do not go hungry.

The notion of the kingdom of God is the object of many of Jesus's parables. In his preaching and the miracles he performed, Jesus shows us what it looks like to live in this new kingdom. The already-kingdom that is present by God's grace manifests the transformation of people who hear and accept the message of the kingdom.

This salvation brings a new relationship between God and his people. It changes the relationships between people who were estranged. But it also changes the relationship between humans and the creation. This is how Colossians explains the intention of God's kingdom:

> The Son is the image of the invisible God, the firstborn over all creation. For in him all things were created: things in heaven and on earth, visible and invisible, whether thrones or powers or rulers or authorities; all things have been created through him and for him. He is before all things, and in him all things hold together. And he is the head of the body, the church; he is the beginning and the firstborn from among the dead, so that in everything he might have the supremacy. For God was pleased to have all his fullness dwell in him, and through him to reconcile to himself all things, whether things on earth or things in heaven, by making peace through his blood, shed on the cross.
>
> Once you were alienated from God and were enemies in your minds because of your evil behavior. But now he has reconciled you by Christ's physical body through death to present you holy in his sight, without blemish and free from accusation—if you continue in your faith, established and firm, and do not move from the hope held out in the gospel. (Col 1:15–23)[1]

What Is Kingdom Realism?

Before we can understand the gift of kingdom realism, we must consider the recent comprehension of believers and pastors concerning the kingdom of God. In our context in Central Africa, the kingdom of God is most often preached as an invitation for people to be saved by Christ and have good behavior while waiting for the return of Jesus Christ. Once people are Christians, they are called to make other people disciples. But as Jonathan asks in his book *A Primer for Christian Doctrine*, "What does 'to make disciples' mean in a culture where there is deep poverty, disease, and suffering?"[2]

---

1. This chapter uses the NIV translation for Scripture references, unless otherwise indicated.

2. Jonathan R. Wilson, *A Primer for Christian Doctrine* (Grand Rapids: Eerdmans,

For too long the kingdom of God was understood to be a hope out of this world reserved for those who respect the word of God, pray, and worship on Sunday. But the reality of the already-kingdom did not lead Christians to think about the well-being of others as a mandate that is not separate from the gospel. This led to an understanding of "mission" that did not ask what the church can do to fulfill God's mission but rather what we could do to help get more people "saved."

Since the beginning of creation, God's mission has been about bringing shalom to his people and to creation. In his book *Changing Lenses*, Howard Zehr writes that "shalom defines how God intends people to live in a condition of 'all rightness' in the material world; in interpersonal, social, and political relationships; and in a personal character."[3] Kingdom realism is about pursuing the shalom God wants for all of us and considering its implications for all humans and the creation.

Where Kingdom Realism Starts

The kingdom of God is described in both the Old Testament and the New Testament. In the Old Testament, the kingdom of God starts with God at creation. Genesis 1:28 shows us how God blessed Adam and Eve and gave them authority to govern everything. If Adam and Eve were governing everything under God's direction, that means the kingdom of God was established.

In this vision of creation as God intended it, we see what shalom looks like in reality. Everything is created for the well-being of God's people. Shalom is not only the satisfaction of humans' needs; it is also the satisfaction of God's desire for people, land, and animals to be in a good relationship with God.

After the fall of Adam and Eve, God redeemed the humans by making clothes from animal skins. In Gen 3:21, the human beings found themselves naked and felt ashamed. But God reestablished a relationship with his people, demonstrating the character of God as the King of the universe.

Kingdom realism recognizes the fullness of salvation that God intends for his people and for the universe.

2005), 111.

3. Howard Zehr, *Changing Lenses: A New Focus for Crime and Justice* (Scottdale, PA: Herald, 1990), 132.

So the historical kingdom did not just start with Kings Saul, David, and Solomon. The kingdom of God was there—at least in concept—from a much earlier point in history. God was King from the start, and God was preparing his people to be a kingdom for many years before the political kingship was established. He told them through Moses that he wanted his people to be a "kingdom of priests and a holy nation" (Exod 19:5-6).

A priest has access to God and acts as an intermediary between the people and God. Jethro gave a concise account of a priest's role when he spoke to Moses and pointed out his primary responsibility (Exod 18:13-27). Israel, led and taught by God, would become a light to the nations. They would be able to do this because, as God said to them, "the whole earth is mine," so Israel is to be a holy nation as God is holy (Exod 19:6b). This consecration compels Israel to be set apart, different from other nations.

Just as God intends to set Israel apart as a holy nation, God also intends to set Israel free from the bondage of Egypt and its rulers. When the Lord says, "I have indeed seen the misery of my people in Egypt . . . So I have come down to rescue them from the hand of the Egyptians" (Exod 3:7-8), it is clear that God wants to bring Israel to the full life of shalom. God wants Israel to be set free from the slavery in which the Egyptians had bound them. He wants to deliver them to flourish spirituality, socially, economically, and politically.

By reading this passage and others passages in the Old Testament, we see that God wants to set up a kingdom where justice, peace, and love are taking place. When we read how the prophets advocate for the poor, the vulnerable, the widows, orphans, the slaves, and the needy while also rebuking those who are acting against the law of God, it is clear that God wants to establish a kingdom where people can become holy and also live in dignity.

In the New Testament context, we see this kingdom vision in the Lordship of Jesus. In Acts 2:36, the passage shows how Peter in his Pentecostal sermon says that God made Jesus Lord and Messiah. Tetsunao Yamamori and C. René Padilla, in their book *The Local Church: Agent of Transformation*, write that "the relation between the resurrection and exaltation of Christ and his enthronement as Kyrios is shown clearly in a passage in which Paul writes that the power of God in the lives of believers is the same as that which God ... put to work in Christ when he raised him from the dead" (Eph 1:20–22).[4]

The kingdom that Jesus proclaimed and embodied here on earth is now available to those who believe by the power of the Holy Spirit. If we study the Gospels, we can see that some people misunderstood the kingdom Jesus preached as a political movement that would put their leaders in power. In our time, people more often misunderstand the kingdom as a spiritual reality without any repercussions for our material lives. But if we read the Gospels closely, we find that the message Jesus preached and the life he lived both reveal the holistic salvation of kingdom realism. Just as the concern of God in the Old Testament was for Shalom and healing in all aspects of life, so too in the New Testament we see Jesus preaching and enacting a kingdom that brings wholeness.

Jesus came to rule a kingdom where the poor hear good news that salvation has come, but the poor also hear the good news that they will get what they need to survive and thrive. Jesus says he came that we might know the fullness of abundant life.

Kingdom Realism Must Reflect the Great Commission and the Great Commandment

In Matt 28:19–20, as Jesus inaugurated the kingdom of God and made disciples for the kingdom, he commissioned his disciples to continue to make disciples for the kingdom.

> Then Jesus came to them and said, "All authority in heaven and on earth has been given to me. Therefore go and make disciples of all nations, baptizing them in the name of the Father and of the Son and of the Holy Spirit, and teaching them to obey everything I have commanded you. And surely I am with you always, to the very end of the age."

The kingdom of God that Jesus preached is inclusiveness of all people. There is no distinction and favoritism. His mission was left to his disciples and those who will believe in their testimony, to make more disciples. They were to baptize and teach these new disciples to obey Christ. This is an eternal kingdom because Jesus promises to be with them always.

4. Tetsunao Yamamori and Rene Padilla, eds., *Transformation: An Ecclesiology for Integral Mission* (Barcelona: Kairos, 2003), 39.

Jesus also makes clear that the kingdom of God is for the transformation of those who claim to be disciples. We must respect the second Great Commandment, which is declared in Mark 12:31: "'Love your neighbor as yourself.' There is no commandment greater than these."

This commandment is really the reflection of what the kingdom must look like. And this is what Jesus came to accomplish in his death and his resurrection. Love will bring justice, forgiveness, compassion, solidarity, communion, service, and also humility. Jesus came to help us to live in peace with our neighbors in love.

Jesus came to inaugurate the kingdom through his death and resurrection. This is real and available to us. But it is also incomplete, as the kingdom is not yet fully realized in our world. Because Jesus will complete this work when he returns, we read in 1 John 3:2: "Dear friends, now we are children of God, and what we will be has not yet been made known. But we know that when Christ appears, we shall be like him, for we shall see him as he is."

Again, we have a "now" (we are the children of God), and we have a "not yet" (our future state). We are children of the King, but we must wait to see exactly what that entails.

God is the one who wants his people to be really delivered from all bondage. As he was concerned in the Old Testament to deliver his people Israel from the spiritual, social, physical, economic, and political oppressions they were facing in Egypt, God wants to continue leading his people by delivering them from all those aspects of bondage today.

God's kingdom is different from a secular kingdom or state. The ultimate kingdom realism of God will be when Jesus will return to inaugurate the new heaven and new earth. By being in the already while also waiting for the not yet, we live in obedience to God by being his faith disciples. We reflect our life as children of God by loving others and influencing others to join this God's kingdom.

Church Matters

Isaac Villegas

Late in September 2001, I walked up the hill from my dorm room to the Religious Studies department offices on the campus of Westmont College. I paused in the hall to sort through the chaos in my head, then knocked on Professor Wilson's door. My faith was still in shock after watching the Twin Towers crumble in New York City—the horrors of that attack, the devastation. Christian leaders had joined President Bush's promise to avenge the mass murders. A thirst for blood sacrifices, in the name of retributive justice, dominated the political discourse. Bush rallied Christian America with a call for a crusade: "This crusade, this war on terrorism," he announced a few days after the attacks.[1] His vengeful language echoed with Christendom's legacies of conquest and colonialism.

This Christian vision of US power, I discovered, had been dormant in the faith with which I grew up—a gospel latent with a theology of violence-as-last-resort, warfare as regrettable but necessary given the sinfulness of our world and our lives. I had a feeling that none of this fit with the Jesus my Sunday school teachers told me about, but I didn't know how to stick with a church that, from my experiences, chose the way of violence instead of the way of Jesus. The dissonance sent my faith into a spiral of confusion. To get my bearings, I knew I had to talk with Prof. Jonathan Wilson.

As an undergraduate student that fall, I was in Jonathan's seminar on theological ethics. The classroom became pastoral when I showed

---

1. See James Carroll, "The Bush Crusade," *Nation*, Sept. 2, 2004, https://www.thenation.com/article/archive/bush-crusade/.

up in his office. He welcomed me, listened as I struggled with my faith, and offered to accompany my search for a Christianity I could claim as my own. Over the semester and the academic year he introduced me to nonviolent theologies, to traditions of peace within Christianity. Between lectures he made time to meet and talk about other readings he had mentioned. His conversations guided me into theological landscapes where my faith could grow again.

That guidance was an important part of what has led me to where I've landed: a pastor of a Mennonite congregation, where I've served for fifteen years. On the occasion of Jonathan's seventieth birthday, and in celebration of his theological ministry, I'll highlight two important gifts Jonathan has passed on to me, which have shaped my life. First, he invited me into the Anabaptist vision for Christian faith; and, second, he taught me the theological significance of church life.

Anabaptism

My first memories of church return me to mass at a small parish in Lomita, California—a neighborhood where my immigrant parents started their lives together in this country. Later, our family wandered into charismatic and Pentecostal traditions—living room fellowships and storefront Christianities. By the time I arrived at Westmont College, I was awash with divergent expressions of the faith, a flow of ecclesial *mestizaje*. Yet, the people I was still in conversation with from those various traditions coalesced around the call to retributive violence after September 11, 2001. Jonathan provided a lifeline for my faith, as I flailed around, lost at sea. He told me about the witness of Anabaptist communities through the ages, people whose rejection of violence was internal to their Christian beliefs—not as an appendix to a statement of faith, available to accessorize a person's convictions. He turned my attention to the witness of Anabaptism, the ecclesial tradition that developed as the radical wing of the sixteenth-century European Reformations. I read the church history books Jonathan recommended, which opened up a world of lived theology that resonated with what I had been taught about the gospel. The stories provided glimpses of historical instances of the communal life of people committed to the nonviolent way of Jesus, even when their fidelity to their convictions led to their death, to their own crosses.

The Anabaptist movement helped me consider the possibilities of an incarnate faith that made central not only the death and resurrection of Jesus, but also his life—the life of Jesus as an invitation into the body of Christ, a people drawn together into the peace of the Holy Spirit. Anabaptism is a commitment to the institutionalization of the peace of Christ in congregational life, passed down through the generations in the ordinary fellowship of communities of worship.

After learning from the pages of books about this tradition of enacted faith and incarnate peace, I asked Jonathan if he knew of any of these groups in our city or nearby—because I wanted to experience this possibility for faithfulness as good news. Sadly, there were no such communities in Santa Barbara, but he told me about the varieties of Anabaptism, as living traditions, throughout the United States—including his years at a Mennonite congregation in Durham, North Carolina, while there for graduate school at Duke University. I tucked away that information for a later opportunity—and that opportunity for participation in an Anabaptist community came soon enough, when I relocated to North Carolina and joined a Mennonite congregation. Jonathan helped me to find an ecclesial home, to discover a sense of belonging in a church tradition. I'm indebted to him for my vocational discernment.

Church Matters

After I graduated from Westmont, at Jonathan's advice, I enrolled in the master's of divinity program at Duke Divinity School. I had no idea what I was doing with my life, nor did I have any concept for graduate programs of theological study. I did not grow up with an awareness of higher education. My parents didn't attend college, and we never talked about such things. But when Jonathan let me know that there was more schooling I could do, more classes I could take, more books for my life, I signed up for a trek from one coast to the other for three more years of theological study.

However, no matter how much I delighted in academic work (yes, *delight* is the right word; I was the type whose eyes would well up with tears of joy while reading volume 4, part 2, of the *Church Dogmatics* for Stanley Hauerwas's seminar on Karl Barth), I never lost sight of Jonathan's description of church life as the site for theology—that worship is theological discourse, that the practices of the church are theology made flesh, that there's nothing more theological than the church at prayer. Congregational ministry is the primary location for theological reflection. The centrality of worship practices is a theme Jonathan took up most explicitly in a book he published after I had graduated from seminary and had been called in a pastoral role—that is, *Why Church Matters: Worship, Ministry, and Mission in Practice*.[2] But that emphasis was there from the beginning—the church as the pulse of his theological vision. That focus was already implicit in his book on Julian N. Hartt, a revision of his dissertation: *Theology as Cultural Critique: The Achievement of Julian Hartt*.[3]

I read Jonathan's book on Hartt the summer after I graduated from college, as I fretted about what to do with my life. Through those pages I heard a clear articulation of church work as theological engagement with the world, a compelling vision that fixed my sights on the significance of Christian community. "The church is 'against' the world in so far as the world is built on lies and illusions and binds humanity in the kingdom of death," Jonathan writes of Hartt's ecclesiology. "But the church is against the world—and in the world—for the sake of God's creation, for the purpose of exposing the lies and illusions in order that humanity may see the real shape of the world, which is the kingdom of God."[4] Church is how we give ourselves to the unmasking of the delusions that chain us to death's dominion of our lives, he explains. The collective work of worship is a constant exposure of the forces of sin that oppress humanity—a condition that includes the church, a community inextricably part of this world. We begin to experience the life God wants for us as we confess our complicity in worldly patterns of self-destruction. Jonathan's language for this ecclesial posture is *witness*, which he develops from Hartt's corpus. "In order for the church to fulfill her vocation," he argues, "in order for the Gospel to be preached and the Kingdom to be witnessed, the church must continually assay civilization and the church's place in civilization."[5] The church proclaims the promises of God not through a claim to exceptionalism but through a life of confession and witness—to offer our

---

2. Jonathan R. Wilson, *Why Church Matters: Worship, Ministry and Mission in Practice* (Grand Rapids: Brazos, 2006).

3. Jonathan R. Wilson, *Theology as Cultural Critique: The Achievement of Julian Hartt* (Macon, GA: Mercer University Press, 1996)

4. Wilson, *Theology as Cultural Critique*, 96.

5. Wilson, *Theology as Cultural Critique*, 121.

posture of confession and repentance as our reception of God's transforming grace, for our lives as testimonies to the work of grace, in and beyond us.

"Hartt's ecclesiology," Jonathan notes, entails "a communal life which generates and sustains witness to the Kingdom of God in Jesus Christ."[6] His ecclesiology is christological. Church life is organized as a collective prayer for Christ's redemption of our world. And this faith is, Jonathan quotes Hartt, "something seen and something done," which involves us in arguments about society: "The Christian must be prepared to argue about the shape of the real world," Hartt claims, because "the revelation of God in Jesus Christ stands forth as a disclosure of the shape, the form, of the real world."[7] The gospel makes claims on our world, which we don't keep to ourselves; instead, according to Hartt, the gospel's claims on the world necessitates the publicness of the church's witness: "God requires the church to communicate the Gospel rather than to mutter to itself."[8]

The gospel is the redemptive act in the life, death, and resurrection of Jesus Christ—a redemption that has everything to do with our world. The church, I learned from Jonathan's reading of Hartt, lives as a witness to that gospel. The pastoral calling is to help organize the communal shape of that witness. This theological vision, which I've received from Jonathan, returns me week after week to experience the worship life of my congregation as awash with God's grace—and to receive that grace as our transformation from glory to glory, not only for our own sakes but for our lives to bear witness to God's love made flesh, for our lives to become good news for the world.

I have a folder in my file cabinet called "Prof Wilson." In preparation for this reflection, I read through my old notes from his classes—introduction to theology, contextual theologies, the doctrine of the word, theological ethics. When I revisited what I learned from Jonathan, I realized that I've internalized so much of his thinking. His methods of approach to theological matters have become part of my own habits, my own reflexes. I guess those files are probably redundant. But I think I keep them around as a kind of material testimony of my gratitude—a

---

6. Wilson, *Theology as Cultural Critique*, 108.

7. Julian N. Hartt, *Theology and the Church in the University* (Philadelphia: Westminster, 1969), 134; quoted in Wilson, *Theology as Cultural Critique*, 15.

8. Julian N. Hartt, *A Christian Critique of American Culture: An Essay in Practical Theology* (New York: Harper & Row, 1967), 231; quoted in Wilson, *Theology as Cultural Critique*, 102.

paper trail for my debts. To give an account of my pastoral life involves storytelling about Jonathan, about how his theological formation has informed my own, and how his ongoing interests clue me in on what I should be thinking about. His faithful witness to the gospel is a compass for me as I continue to navigate through this world.

Response to *Kingdom Come*

Jonathan R. Wilson

Around 11:00 p.m. on my seventieth birthday (August 10, 2021), Leah and her family—husband Jonathan, children Jaimichael (sixteen), Nora (eleven), and Nathan (seven)—arrived at our home in Nanaimo, BC. Soohwan and I had not seen them in person since May 2019. Since they had traveled under COVID-19 restrictions for almost twenty-two hours, we celebrated my birthday with a brunch the next morning. They gave me a card and some special chocolate bars (Trader Joe's!), then told me that I had one more present coming: some of my friends would be on Zoom at noon to wish me a happy birthday.

So I shaved and changed out of my pandemic pajamas into some appropriate clothes. As Soohwan and I were in my study waiting for the Zoom link and password, I was guessing which four to five friends would be wishing me happy birthday. When Leah finally gave us the password, Zoom opened to two windows with more than forty-five screens.

I was overwhelmed; I still am.

There were friends from 1976 to the present, representing six continents: students, teachers, church members, colleagues in mission, ministry, and life. Friends all.

Then they told me there was one more part of the surprise. Nora brought me a black spiral-bound "book" like the course readers I used to put together. I thought, "How nice. They collected a bunch of reflections from my friends and put them in spiral binding."

I was overwhelmed. I still am.

Then they showed me a book cover. A book? No. I never imagined a collection of "essays" in my honor. My life's path simply did not lead to such a thing. I listened intently and gratefully for the next hour as friends recalled our times together. And at another level I was still thinking, "A book? Really?"

I was overwhelmed. I still am.

But what overwhelms me is the grace—the sheer undeserved gift—of God: the faith that trusts in the Way of Jesus; family and friends on the Way; good work; comfort in sorrow and confusion and sin. As David Ford taught me, the gift of God is the most overwhelming reality of life.[1]

In Honor of Jonathan R. Wilson

I am indeed "honored" by the reflections in this book. In "the academy," which has provided most of the income during my life (for which I am grateful), a collection of essays honoring a senior scholar would be called a Festschrift. Although I now qualify for senior discounts, I am not a "senior scholar" in my field. So what honors me in this book are the friendships that are represented. The reflections in this book gather not around my scholarship but around my friendships.

I am honored by the friends I have been given. And who have given pieces of their lives to me and continue to do so. As I said at the online gathering, anything I've given to others I've received. That's how the life God has given us works: receiving and giving (not taking and keeping).

The friends who gathered online and contributed to this book represent six continents (where's that Adélie penguin I befriended?), the years of my life from my first year at Regent College to the present, and many circumstances where they are following Jesus. This variety honors and fits my pilgrimage as entrepreneur, business manager, chaplain, pastor, professor, and mission consultant—all part of my desire to follow God's particular call on my life.

Reflections

The word "reflections" rather than "essays" (the usual term for a collection honoring someone in the academy), is delightful and exactly right.

---

1. David F. Ford, *The Shape of Living: Spiritual Directions for Everyday Life* (1997; reprint, Grand Rapids: Baker, 2004).

"Reflections" embraces a range of genres and points to the intention in this collection and in my own writing to point toward something, to bear witness, to say, "See, there's something life-giving going on, there's good news." These reflections are in part our attempts to make sense of things in the light of the reality of God's rule. Yes, they are reflections *on* that reality, but even more they seek to be reflections *of* that reality. The aim is not to draw attention to oneself but to the reality of the redemption of creation by the One God: Father, Son, and Holy Spirit.

The work of art that Joy Banks has contributed and her artist's statement capture this with remarkable depth. The disciples on the road to Emmaus lament—things are not as they should be. They reflect—perhaps there is another reality, they certainly thought the new had come in Jesus. They invite—the kingdom of God does not coerce, it invites, so these disciples "reflect the kingdom." They celebrate—their eyes are opened and they see Jesus, the *risen* Jesus, present with them. (Another time, there is much to contemplate in his immediate disappearance.) The work of these disciples, then, is to bear witness along with others.

This collection of reflections continues the journey to Emmaus with lamentation, reflection, invitation, and celebration. What ties this collection together and ties it to Cleopas and his companion (his wife?) is the desire to "reflect" the kingdom come in Jesus Christ so others may see and believe and live.

Kingdom Come

For most of my life, I have been in passionate pursuit of the reality of the kingdom of God. It began sometime in 1974 after a talk by Robert Bryan, a Free Will Baptist missionary who with his wife Judy went to Côte d'Ivoire when my father was director of foreign missions for the National Association of FWB. Robert and I were musing over the possibility of "Christian culture" and I asked if the kingdom of God could be the name for Christian culture."

"Maybe so," Robert replied.

Since that time I've been seeking to understand, see, and grow in the life of the kingdom, because that's where the Holy Spirit gives life in Messiah Jesus. Many friends (in person and in books) and experiences have guided me along my journey into the kingdom of God. Chief among those guides is Julian Hartt, the subject of my dissertation. Hartt's work is dense and difficult. I had tried twice before to enter his theology through his books. The third time, for my dissertation, I began to be grasped by his vision. For all his complexity and density, the passion that propels his work is the kingdom of God. In our correspondence he continually pointed me to the kingdom of God. In a letter dated October 8, 1998, he wrote: "What I would really like to hear from you is how you are setting up the christological venture, for I have little doubt that the Kingdom of God ought to be the heart and mind of it. If Mark is right it was the controlling passion of Jesus Christ, from first to last, and beyond." And in a handwritten note of July 18, 2002, he concluded with this benediction: "May God be with you as you devote yourself to the proclamation of the Kingdom of the beloved Son, our Lord Jesus Christ."

As I devoted myself to the "proclamation" of the kingdom, I was grasped by the *reality*, or, as I write in some places, the *actuality* of the kingdom. The kingdom of God is not a dream or an illusion or a human projection or an ideology. Nor is it merely a proposition or a piece on the gameboard of exegetes, theologians, historians, missiologists, or culture critics. The kingdom of God is real. To leave the ways that lead to death and enter this Way that is life, we need the gifts and abilities of all God's people scattered among us by the Holy Spirit in order to open our eyes to see, our ears to hear, our hearts to desire, our bodies to be given as holy sacrifices.

This book of reflections, in its rich diversity, may help us see, hear, desire the kingdom of "the beloved Son, our Lord Jesus Christ," and lay down our lives knowing that through his resurrection we will rise to New Creation, the unveiling of the fullness of the kingdom. I hasten to add that I am still learning what it means to lay down my life for the kingdom and not for an ideology, a needy person, a great cause, or any other penultimate good that turns me aside from the actuality of the kingdom. I am also still in the school of discipleship as I seek with others under the guidance of the Holy Spirit to discern what the actuality of kingdom reveals to me 1) about ideologies, all of which take life instead of giving life; 2) about meeting the needs of persons and communities in alignment with the life given by the One God: Father, Son, and Holy Spirit; 3) how the kingdom is the correction, purgation, and fulfillment of the desires and dreams of all great causes.

To be grasped by the life of the kingdom of God, we require all the resources that God has given God's people. Since the kingdom is actual, we must not reduce it to a system, a definition, a set of propositions.

Instead, we need oral, visual, written, and "performed" language to engage whole persons in friendships and make them agents of the kingdom in a world and age that is in rebellion against this kingdom. Each of the contributions to this book gather around that one mission, that one passion: to be grasped by the life of Jesus Christ through the Holy Spirit, which is the reality of the kingdom.

I am still overwhelmed by this gift and more, by the givers, the friends who honor me in our common calling. "Kingdom come" is proclamation and prayer. As proclamation, it declares through word and deed the present reality of the kingdom. As prayer, it cries out for the full unveiling of the kingdom to the glory of God and all creation. When that prayer is fully answered, injustice and oppression, sorrow and suffering, death itself, will be everlastingly overwhelmed as God's grace gives birth to New Creation.

Selected Bibliography of Jonathan R. Wilson's Writing

Books

God's Good World: Reclaiming the Doctrine of Creation. Grand Rapids: Baker Academic, 2013.

God So Loved the World: A Christology for Disciples. Grand Rapids: Baker Academic, 2001.

Gospel Virtues: Practicing Faith, Hope, and Love in Uncertain Times. Eugene, OR: Wipf & Stock, 2004.

Grace upon Grace: Essays in Honor of Thomas A. Langford. Co-editor with Robert K. Johnston and L. Gregory Jones. Nashville: Abingdon, 1999.

The Julian Hartt Library. 8 vols. Eugene, OR: Wipf & Stock, 2005–7. Series foreword by Jonathan R. Wilson.
    I. *Toward a Theology of Evangelism*. Volume foreword by Stanley Hauerwas.
    II. *Being Known and Being Revealed*. Volume foreword by Walter J. Lowe.
    III. *The Lost Image of Man*. Volume foreword by John D. Sykes Jr.
    IV. *Theology and the Church in the University*. Volume foreword by Stanley Hauerwas.
    V. *A Christian Critique of American Culture: An Essay in Practical Theology*. Volume foreword by David H. Kelsey.
    VI. *The Restless Quest*. Volume foreword by Jonathan R. Wilson.
    VII. *Theological Method and Imagination*. Volume foreword by Ray L. Hart.
    VIII. *What We Make of the World: Memoirs of Julian Hartt*. Volume foreword by Jonathan R. Wilson.

Langford, Thomas A. *Reflections on Grace*. Edited and introduced by Philip A. Rolnick and Jonathan R. Wilson, with a foreword by William H. Willimon. Eugene, OR: Cascade, 2007.

Living Faithfully in a Fragmented World: From "After Virtue" to a New Monasticism. 1st ed., Atlanta: Trinity, 1998; 2nd ed., Eugene, OR: Cascade, 2010.

A Primer for Christian Doctrine. Grand Rapids: Eerdmans, 2005.

Theology as Cultural Critique: The Achievement of Julian Hartt. Macon, GA: Mercer University Press, 1997.

Why Church Matters: Worship, Ministry, and Mission in Practice. Grand Rapids: Brazos, 2007.

Journal Articles and Book Chapters

"The Aesthetics of the Kingdom: Apocalypsis, Eschatos, and Vision for Mission." In *Revisioning, Renewing, Rediscovering the Triune Center: Essays in Honor of Stanley J. Grenz*, edited by Derek Tidball et al., 157–74. Eugene, OR: Cascade, 2014.
"Beloved Community as Missional Witness." In *Christian Witness in Cascadian Soil: Coworkers with God in the Land of Hiking, Hipsters, and Hand-Crafted Lattes*, edited by Ross A. Lockhart, 169–80. Eugene, OR: Cascade, 2021.
"Biblical Realism in the Work of John Howard Yoder." *Perspectives in Religious Studies* 40 (2013) 109–21.
"Biblical Wisdom, Spiritual Formation, and the Virtues." In *The Way of Wisdom: Essays in Honor of Bruce K. Waltke*, edited by J. I. Packer and Sven K. Soderlund, 297–307. Grand Rapids: Zondervan, 2000.
"By the Logic of the Gospel: Proposal for a Theology of Culture." *Modern Theology* 10 (1994) 401–14.
"Can Narrative Christology Be Orthodox?" *International Journal of Systematic Theology* 8 (2006) 371–81.
"Canon and Theology: What Is at Stake?" In *Exploring the Origins of the Bible*, edited by Craig A. Evans and Emanuel Tov, 241–53. Grand Rapids: Baker Academic, 2008.
"Character Ethics and the New Testament: Moral Dimensions of Scripture." *Bulletin for Biblical Research* 19 (2009) 304–5.
"Character Ethics and the Old Testament: Moral Dimensions of Scripture." *Bulletin for Biblical Research* 19 (2009) 283–84.
"Clarifying Vision, Empowering Witness." In *What Does It Mean to be Saved?*, edited by John G. Stackhouse Jr., 185–94. Grand Rapids: Baker, 2002.
"Contextualized Faith: Douglas John Hall's Theological Project." *Modern Theology* 15 (1999) 85–92.
"Do Pietists Need a Doctrine of Creation? God's World in the Baptist Tradition and Stanley J. Grenz." *Pacific Journal of Theological Research* 6 (2010) 65–78.
"Evangelicals and the Environment: A Theological Concern." *Christian Scholar's Review* 28 (1998) 298–307.
"From Theology of Culture to Theological Ethics: The Hartt-Hauerwas Connection." *Journal of Religious Ethics* 23 (1995) 149–64.
"The Gospel as Revelation in Julian N. Hartt." *Journal of Religion* 72 (1992) 549–59.
"Grace Incarnate: Jesus Christ." In *Grace upon Grace: Essays in Honor of Thomas A. Langford*, edited by Robert K. Johnston et al., 141–52. Nashville: Abingdon, 1999.
"Introduction." In *School(s) for Conversion: 12 Marks of the New Monasticism*, edited by Rutba House, 1–9. Eugene, OR: Cascade, 2005.
"Living Faithfully in a Fragmented World: Four Lessons for the Church from MacIntyre's *After Virtue*." *CRUX* 26 (1990) 38–42.
"Old Testament Narrative and Christian Ethics." In *The Bible in World Christian Perspective: Studies in Honor of Carl Edwin Armerding*, edited by David Baker and Ward Gasque, 165–74. Vancouver, BC: Regent College Publishing, 2009.
"The Pastor as Language Teacher." *CRUX* 31 (1995) 15–22.
"The Peace of Creation: Recovering a Theological Balance." *CRUX* 40 (2004) 1–7.
"The Place of 'Professional Development' in the Mission of Christian Higher Education." *Faculty Dialogue* 25 (1996) n.p.

"Practicing Church: Evangelical Ecclesiologies at the End of Modernity." In *Community of the Word: Toward an Evangelical Theology*, edited by Mark Husbands and Daniel J. Treier, 59–75. Downers Grove, IL: InterVarsity, 2005.

"Reality?" In *The Interface of Science, Theology, and Religion: Essays in Honor of Alister E. McGrath*, edited by Dennis Ngien, 118–36. Eugene, OR: Pickwick, 2019.

"Revising Macintosh by Hartt: On the Possibilities of Empirical Theology." *Perspectives in Religious Studies* 20 (1993) 43–55.

"The Role of the Natural Sciences in an Ecclesially Based University." In *Conflicting Allegiances*, edited by Michael Budde and John Wright, 128–39. Grand Rapids: Brazos, 2004.

"The Scrolls and Christian Theology." In *Christian Beginnings and the Dead Sea Scrolls*, edited by John J. Collins and Craig A. Evans, 121–28. Grand Rapids: Baker Academic, 2006.

"Simpletons, Fools, and Mockers." *Christian Reflection: A Series in Faith and Ethics* (2002) 24–30.

"Spiritual Formation, Biblical Wisdom, and the Virtues." In *Spiritual Formation: An Evangelical Perspective*, edited by Richard A. Averbeck, n.p. Grand Rapids: Eerdmans, forthcoming.

"Stanley J. Grenz: Generous Faith and Faithful Engagement." *Modern Theology* 23 (2007) 113–21.

"Theology and the Kingdom." In *From Biblical Criticism to Biblical Faith*, edited by William H. Brackney and Craig A. Evans, 282–93. Macon, GA: Mercer University Press, 2007.

"Theology and the Old Testament." In *Guide to Old Testament Exegesis*, edited by Craig C. Broyles, 245–64. Grand Rapids: Baker, 2001.

"Toward a New Evangelical Paradigm of Biblical Authority." In *The Nature of Confession: Postliberals and Evangelicals in Conversation*, edited by Dennis Okholm and Timothy Phillips, 151–61. Downers Grove, IL: InterVarsity, 1996.

"Toward a Trinitarian Rule of Worship." *CRUX* 29.2 (1993) 35–39.

"Whose Purpose? Whose Drive? Thinking Teleologically about Purpose Drivenness." *Reformation and Revival Journal* 14 (2005) 55–65.

"World Right-Side Up: Acts and the Mission of God's People." In *Serving God's Community: Studies in Honor of W. Ward Gasque*, edited by Susan S. Phillips and Soo-Inn Tan, 337–59. Vancouver, BC: Regent College Publishing, 2014.

Book Reviews

The Actuality of the Atonement, by Colin E. Gunton. *Crux* 27 (1991) 48.

After Baptism: Shaping the Christian Life, by John P. Burgess. *Journal of the Society of Christian Ethics* 27 (2007) 327–29.

Aspects of Christian Integrity, by Alan P. F. Sell, and *Sex in the Parish*, by Karen Lebacqz and Ronald G. Barton. *Ashland Theological Journal* 25 (1993) 170–71, 178–80.

Bodying Forth: Aesthetic Liturgy, by Patrick W. Collins. *Horizons* 21 (1994) 209.

Can These Dry Bones Live? An Introduction to Christian Theology, by Frances M. Young. *Pro Ecclesia* 4 (1995) 248–50.

Christ Plays in Ten Thousand Places: A Conversation in Spiritual Theology, by Eugene H. Peterson. *Pro Ecclesia* 16 (2007) 114–16.

Selected Bibliography of Jonathan R. Wilson's Writing

Christian Ethics in Secular Worlds, by Robin Gill. *Modern Theology* 10 (1994) 125–27.

Creation Set Free: Spirit as Liberator of Nature, by Sigurd Bergman. *Studies in Religion/Sciences Religieuses* 36 (2007) 595–96.

Creation Set Free: Spirit as Liberator of Nature, by Sigurd Bergman. *Studies in Religion/Sciences Religieuses* (forthcoming).

Creation, by David Fergusson. *Journal of Reformed Theology* 10 (2016) 270–71.

The Cross in Our Context: Jesus and the Suffering World, by Douglas John Hall. *Studies in Religion/Sciences Religieuses* 34 (2005) 134–35.

Discipleship between Creation and Redemption, by Philip LeMasters; *Beyond Sectarianism*, by Philip D. Kenneson; and *Another City* by Barry A. Harvey. *Perspectives in Religious Studies* 27 (2000) 223–26.

Divine Freedom and the Doctrine of the Immanent Trinity: In Dialogue with Karl Barth and Contemporary Theology, by Paul D. Molnar. *Pro Ecclesia* 13 (2004) 108–9.

The Doctrine of Creation: A Constructive Kuyperian Approach, by Bruce Riley Ashford and Craig G. Bartholomew. Perspectives on Science and Christian Faith (forthcoming).

Faith, Theology and Imagination, by John McIntyre. *Modern Theology* 7 (1991) 294–96.

Freedom for Obedience, by Donald Bloesch. *Perspectives in Religious Studies* 16 (1989) 82–84.

God Crucified, by Richard Bauckham, and *Christ the Center*, by George A. F. Knight. *Pro Ecclesia* 11 (2002) 105–8.

God in History, by Peter C. Hodgson. *Christian Scholar's Review* 20 (1991) 427–29.

God, the Mind's Desire, by Paul Janz. *Studies in Religion/Sciences Religieuses* 34 (2005) 589–90.

The Hermeneutics of Charity: Interpretation, Selfhood, and Postmodern Faith, edited by James K. A. Smith and Henry Isaac Venema. *Studies in Religion/Sciences Religieuses* 35 (2006) 613–14.

Imago Trinitatis: Toward a Relational Understanding of Becoming Human, by Mark S. Medley; *The Trinity*, by Roger E. Olson and Christopher A. Hall; *The Recovery of Doctrine in the Contemporary Church: An Essay in Philosophical Ecclesiology*, by Richard Heyduck; and *Jesus the Savior: The Meaning of Jesus Christ for Christian Faith*, by William C. Placher. *Perspectives in Religious Studies* 31 (2004) 242–47.

Justice, and Only Justice, by Naim Stifan Ateek, and *Freedom and Discipleship: Liberation Theology in an Anabaptist Perspective*, edited by Daniel S. Schipani. *Perspectives in Religious Studies* 18 (1991) 86–88.

Kant's Philosophy of Religion Reconsidered, edited by Philip J. Rossi and Michael Wreen. *Christian Scholar's Review* 23 (1994) 458–59.

Life on the Vine, by Philip D. Kenneson; *Communion Shapes Character*, by Eleanor Kreider; and *The Story of Discipleship*, by Elizabeth Barnes. *Perspectives in Religious Studies* 28 (2001) 131–34.

Rationality, Humility, and Spirituality in Christian Life, by Dennis Hiebert. *Didaskalia* (forthcoming).

Reason Informed by Faith, by Richard M. Gula, and *Critical Voices in American Catholic Thought* by John J. Mitchell. *Perspectives in Religious Studies* 20 (1993) 210–12.

The Religious Imagination, edited by James Mackey. *Modern Theology* 6 (1989) 116–18.

A Scientific Theology 1: Nature, by Alister E. McGrath. *Journal of the American Academy of Religion* 71 (2003) 955–58.

A Scientific Theology 2: Reality, by Alister E. McGrath. *Christian Scholar's Review* 33 (2004) 282–85.
A Scientific Theology 3: Theory, by Alister E. McGrath. *Christian Scholar's Review* 33 (2004) 417–19.
A Theology of the Built Environment, by Timothy J. Gorringe. *Christian Scholar's Review* 33 (2004) 608–9.
There Shall Be No Poor among You: Poverty in the Bible, by Leslie Hoppe. *Bulletin of Biblical Research* 16 (2006) 149–50.
Traces of Understanding: A Profile of Heidegger's and Ricoeur's Hermeneutics, by Patrick Bourgeois and Frank Schalow. *Journal of the American Academy of Religion* 60 (1992) 770–71.
Virtues and Practices in the Christian Tradition: Christian Ethics after MacIntyre, edited by Nancey Murphy et al. *Christian Scholar's Review* 28 (1999) 505.

List of Contributors

A. K. M. Adam is a tutor in New Testament and Greek at Oriel College, Oxford University.

Margaret B. Adam is visiting tutor of Christian ethics at St Stephen's House, Oxford University.

Joy Banks is the pastor of Grandview Calvary Baptist Church in East Vancouver, British Columbia.

John Berkman is professor of moral theology at Regis College, the University of Toronto.

Anthony Brown is the senior minister of First Baptist Church, Vancouver.

Jason Byassee is the Butler Chair in Homiletics and Biblical Interpretation at the Vancouver School of Theology.

Tim Dickau is an associate with the Center for Missional Leadership.

Rob Filgate is pastor of Mount Zion Church in Cardigan, Wales (UK).

Jeffrey P. Greenman is president and professor of theology and ethics at Regent College.

Chris Hall is the president of renovare, an international spiritual formation movement.

Peter Harris is co-founder and president emeritus of A Rocha, an international conservation ministry.

Jennifer Harvey is the associate provost of campus equity and inclusion at Drake University.

W. Ross Hastings is the Sangwoo Youtong Chee Professor of Theology at Regent College.

List of Contributors

Stanley Hauerwas is the Gilbert T. Rowe Professor Emeritus of Theological Ethics at Duke Divinity School.

Matthew W. Humphrey is an educator with A Rocha Canada.

Reinhard Hütter is the ordinary professor of fundamental and dogmatic theology at the Catholic University of America.

Willie James Jennings is associate professor of systematic theology and Africana studies at Yale University.

Christopher Johnston is pastor of Billtown Baptist Church in the Annapolis Valley of Nova Scotia.

L. Gregory Jones is president of Belmont University and dean emeritus of Duke Divinity School.

Philip D. Kenneson is associate dean of the School of Bible and Ministry and professor of theology and philosophy at Milligan University.

Jeremy Kidwell is senior lecturer in theological ethics at the University of Birmingham (UK).

Scott Kohler is lead pastor of Bedford Baptist Church in Bedford, Nova Scotia.

Ross Lockhart is dean of St. Andrew's Hall and professor of mission studies at Vancouver School of Theology.

Chandra Mallampalli is the Fletcher Jones Foundation Chair of the Social Sciences and professor of history at Westmont College.

Marilyn McEntyre is a celebrated independent author and speaker.

Gato Munyamasoko is peace and reconciliation specialist with Canadian Baptist Ministries in the Democratic Republic of Congo.

Jonas Kambale Musamba is an evangelist with the Baptist Church in Central Africa.

Soohwan Park is an adviser of Christian leaders in the local and global NGO sector. Soohwan and Jonathan have a home of hospitality and prayer in Nanaimo, British Columbia.

Mike Pears is the director of the International Baptist Theological Study Centre, Amsterdam.

Susan S. Phillips is a sociologist and spiritual director on the faculty of New College Berkeley and is on the Core Doctoral Faculty of the Graduate Theological Union.

List of Contributors

Jim Purves is mission and ministry advisor to the Baptist Union of Scotland and adjunct research supervisor for doctoral students with the International Baptist Theological Study Centre in Amsterdam.

Anna Robbins is president of Acadia Divinity College and dean of theology at Acadia University, where she also directs the Andrew D. MacRae Centre for Theology and Culture.

Philip A. Rolnick is professor of theology at the University of St. Thomas, Minnesota, and director of the Science and Theology Network (STN).

Axel Schoeber is a retired pastor and professor of church history.

Andrew Shepherd is lecturer in theology and public issues in the Theology Programme, University of Otago/Mātai Whakapono Karaitiana, Te Whare Wānanga o Otāgo in Aotearoa/New Zealand.

Craig A. Smith teaches New Testament at Simpson University and Tozer Seminary in Redding, California.

Terry Smith is the executive director of Canadian Baptist Ministries.

Mike Swalm is pastor of Abundant Life Church in Calgary, Alberta, and adjunct professor of theology and ethics at Rocky Mountain College.

Isaac Villegas is pastor of Chapel Hill Mennonite Fellowship and president of the North Carolina Council of Churches.

Loren Wilkinson is professor emeritus of interdisciplinary studies and philosophy at Regent College.

Reggie L. Williams is professor of Christian ethics at McCormick Theological Seminary.

Jonathan Wilson-Hartgrove directs the School for Conversion in Durham, North Carolina.

Leah Wilson-Hartgrove is coordinator of Restorative Justice Durham in Durham, North Carolina.

H. Daniel Zacharias is a Cree-Anishinaabe and Austrian man originally from Treaty 1 territory (Winnipeg), and currently lives with his wife and four children in Wolfville, Nova Scotia, located in the unceded territory of the Mi'kmaw people. He serves as associate professor of New Testament Studies at Acadia Divinity College and as adjunct professor with NAIITS: An Indigenous Learning Community.

www.ingramcontent.com/pod-product-compliance
Lightning Source LLC
Chambersburg PA
CBHW020606300426
44113CB00007B/530